ANNUAL EDITIONS

Psychology
Thirty-Fifth Edition

05/06

EDITOR

Karen G. Duffy

SUNY at Geneseo (Emerita)

Karen G. Duffy holds a doctorate in psychology from Michigan State University, and she is an emerita Distinguished Service Professor of State University of New York at Geneseo. Dr. Duffy continues to work on her books and research, and she is also involved in several community service projects both in the United States and Russia.

McGraw-Hill/Dushkin
2460 Kerper Blvd., Dubuque, IA 52001

Visit us on the Internet
http://www.dushkin.com

Credits

1. **The Science of Psychology**
   Unit photo—© Getty Images/Nick Koudis
2. **Biological Bases of Behavior**
   Unit photo—© Getty Images/Nick Koudis
3. **Perceptual Processes**
   Unit photo—© CORBIS/Royalty-Free
4. **Learning and Remembering**
   Unit photo—© 2004 by PhotoDisc, Inc.
5. **Cognitive Processes**
   Unit photo—© Getty Images/Doug Meneuz
6. **Emotion and Motivation**
   Unit photo—© Getty Images/PhotoLink/Rim Light
7. **Development**
   Unit photo—Courtesy of McGraw-Hill/Dushkin.
8. **Personality Processes**
   Unit photo—© Getty Images/David Buffington
9. **Social Processes**
   Unit photo—© © Getty Images/Donna Day
10. **Psychological Disorders**
    Unit photo—Courtesy of Cheryl Greenleaf.
11. **Psychological Treatments**
    Unit photo—© 2004 by PhotoDisc, Inc.

Copyright

Cataloging in Publication Data
Main entry under title: Annual Editions: Psychology. 2005/2006.
1. Psychology—Periodicals. I. Duffy, Karen G., *comp.* II. Title: Psychology.
ISBN 0–07–310206–7   658'.05   ISSN 0272–3794

Thirty-Fifth Edition

Cover image © Mel Curtis/Getty Images and Photos.com
Printed in the United States of America   1234567890QPDQPD987654   Printed on Recycled Paper

Editors/Advisory Board

Members of the Advisory Board are instrumental in the final selection of articles for each edition of ANNUAL EDITIONS. Their review of articles for content, level, currentness, and appropriateness provides critical direction to the editor and staff. We think that you will find their careful consideration well reflected in this volume.

Preface

In publishing ANNUAL EDITIONS we recognize the enormous role played by the magazines, newspapers, and journals of the public press in providing current, first-rate educational information in a broad spectrum of interest areas. Many of these articles are appropriate for students, researchers, and professionals seeking accurate, current material to help bridge the gap between principles and theories and the real world. These articles, however, become more useful for study when those of lasting value are carefully collected, organized, and reproduced in a low-cost format, which provides easy and permanent access when the material is needed. That is the role played by ANNUAL EDITIONS.

Ronnie's parents couldn't understand why he didn't want to be picked up and cuddled as did his older sister when she was a baby. As an infant, Ronnie did not respond to his parents' smiles, words, or attempts to amuse him. By the age of two, Ronnie's parents knew that he was not like other children. He spoke no English, was very temperamental, and often rocked himself for hours. Ronnie is autistic. His parents feel that some of Ronnie's behavior may be their fault. As young professionals, they both work long hours and leave both of their children with an older woman during the workweek. Ronnie's pediatrician assures his parents that their reasoning, while logical, does not hold merit, because the causes of autism are little understood and are likely to be biological rather than parental. What can we do about children like Ronnie? From where does autism come? Can autism be treated or reversed? Can autism be prevented?

Psychologists attempt to answer these and other complex questions with scientific methods. Researchers, using carefully planned research designs, try to discover the causes of complex human behavior—normal or not. The scientific results of psychological research typically are published in professional journals, and therefore may be difficult for the lay person to understand.

Annual Editions: Psychology 05/06 is designed to meet the needs of lay people and introductory level students who are curious about psychology. This Annual Edition provides a vast selection of readable and informative articles primarily from popular magazines and newspapers. These articles are typically written by journalists, but a few are written by psychologists with writing styles that are clear yet retain the excitement of the discovery of scientific knowledge.

The particular articles selected for this volume were chosen to be representative of the most current work in psychology. They were selected because they are accurate in their reporting and provide examples of the types of psychological research discussed in most introductory psychology classes. As in any science, some of the findings discussed in this collection are startling, while others confirm what we already know. Some articles invite speculation about social and personal issues; others encourage careful thought about potential misuse of research findings. You are expected to make the investment of effort and critical reasoning necessary to answer such questions and concerns.

I assume that you will find this collection of articles readable and useful. I suggest that you look at the organization of this book and compare it to the organization of your textbook and course syllabus. By examining the topic guide provided after the table of contents, you can identify those articles most appropriate for any particular unit of study in your course. Your instructor may provide some help in this effort or assign articles to supplement the text. As you read the articles, try to connect their contents with the principles you are learning from your text and classroom lectures. Some of the articles will help you better understand a specific area of research while others are designed to help you connect and integrate information from diverse research areas. Both of these strategies are important in learning about psychology or any other science; it is only through intensive investigation and subsequent integration of the findings from many studies that we are able to discover and apply new knowledge.

Please take time to provide me with some feedback to guide the annual revision of this anthology by completing and returning the article rating form in the back of the book. With your help, this collection will be even better next year. Thank you.

Karen Grover Duffy

Karen Grover Duffy
Editor

Contents

Preface   iv
Topic Guide   xiii
Selected World Wide Web Sites   xv

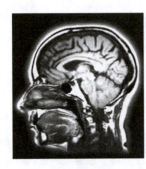

UNIT 1
The Science of Psychology

In this unit, three articles examine psychology as the science of behavior.

Unit Overview   xviii

1. **Why Study Psychology?**, *APS Observer,* February 2004
   Four well-known **psychologists** describe why they studied psychology and how
   they are currently using their training. Each psychologist works in a different but
   important **subfield of psychology**.   2

2. **Does Psychology Make a Significant Difference in Our Lives?**,
   Philip G. Zimbardo, *American Psychologist,* July/August 2004
   Noted psychologist Philip Zimbardo argues that **psychology** indeed does make
   a difference in our lives. Psychologists, however, need to continue to "give psychology away" to the public. Zimbardo highlights psychology's achievements in
   the fields of **testing, behavior change, therapy, life-span development, parenting, stress, the unconscious, work, and prejudice.** He also highlights areas
   where psychology can make a notable difference in the future, for example preventing the spread of **AIDS**.   5

3. **Causes and Correlations,** Massimo Pigliucci, *Skeptical Inquirer,*
   January/February 2003
   This article reminds the reader to **think critically about science.** Too many phenomena, such as ESP (extra-sensory perception), are explained post hoc. Few
   lay people understand the difference between **correlation** and **causation.** The
   author reviews these two concepts and also explains **control, experimentation,
   and statistical inference.**   18

The concepts in bold italics are developed in the article. For further expansion, please refer to the Topic Guide.

UNIT 2
Biological Bases of Behavior

Three unit selections discuss the biological bases of behavior. Topics include the nature-nurture controversy and the brain's control over the body.

Unit Overview 20

4. **What Makes You Who You Are,** Matt Ridley, *Time,* June 2, 2003
For decades, psychologists and biologists have tried to determine what plays a greater role in human behavior—*genes or the environment.* This controversy is known as *the nature-nurture controversy.* The newest theory suggests that both factors shape us and, surprisingly, that each affects the other. 23

5. **Genetic Influence on Human Psychological Traits,** Thomas J. Bouchard, Jr., *Current Directions in Psychological Science,* August 2004
A large body of evidence supports the conclusion that *individual differences* in many psychological characteristics, normal or not, are influenced by *genetic factors.* Bouchard reviews why the study of genetics is important to psychology and then provides estimates of the magnitude of genetic influence on various traits such as *intelligence, interests, mental health, personality, and social attitudes.* 28

6. **Neuroscience: Breaking Down Scientific Barriers to the Study of Brain and Mind,** Eric R. Kandel and Larry R. Squire, *Science,* November 10, 2000
An important aspect of the biological basis for behavior is *the nervous system.* In this article, Eric Kandel and Larry Squire first review the history of *neuroscience* and then detail the various ways that *psychology* and *neurological science* are related. 33

UNIT 3
Perceptual Processes

The impact of the senses on human perceptual processes is addressed in six unit articles.

Unit Overview 44

7. **Vision Seekers: Giving Eyesight to the Blind Raises Questions About How People See,** Bruce Bower, *Science News,* November 22, 2003
Individuals who are given the gift of *sight* later in life see and perceive the world around them differently from individuals who are sighted at birth. Such unfortunate events, however, offer scientists the opportunity to study *vision as a perceptual process.* 47

The concepts in bold italics are developed in the article. For further expansion, please refer to the Topic Guide.

8. **A Matter of Taste,** Mary Beckman, *Smithsonian,* August 2004
The author reviews the research of psychologist Linda Bartoshuk who studies *taste*. Bartoshuk has found that there are differences in how well people can taste food. She has discovered "*supertasters*", individuals who have many taste buds (papillae on their tongues) and whose taste experiences are intense. For super- tasters, everyday foods can be delightful or repugnant. Bartoshuk also discovered that *taste sensitivity* can affect *health* via the foods people prefer. Many super- tasters, for example, find healthy vegetables too bitter.   50

9. **It's a Noisy, Noisy World Out There!,** Richard Carmen, *The Satur- day Evening Post,* March/April 2002
A clinical audiologist bemoans the ubiquitous assault of *noise* on our ears. About one-third of all *hearing loss* is the result of this cacophony. What we can do to *avoid hearing loss* is also covered in this article.   52

10. **Pain and Its Mysteries,** Marni Jackson, *Maclean's,* May 27, 2002
Pain is something we could all live without. In fact, some people do live without it—they have *congenital analgesia.* Pain—how and why it is experienced and how to reduce it—is being studied by scientists.   55

11. **Night Life,** Jill Neimark, *Psychology Today,* July/August 1998
Many Americans say that they cannot *sleep* or that they suffer from *insomnia*. The author delves into the field of *sleep problems* and finds that there are *psy- chological as well as physical problems* that lead to sleep deprivation and insomnia.   58

12. **Brains in Dreamland,** Bruce Bower, *Science News,* August 11, 2001
One hundred years have passed since Sigmund *Freud's work on the interpre- tation of dreams,* and scientists still cannot agree on their function. Bruce Bower reviews seminal theories on the subject as well as some of the *neurology* involved in these nightly theatrics.   61

UNIT 4
Learning and Remembering

Two selections in this section examine scientific principles of learning and remem- bering, explaining how forgetting occurs, and exploring the basis of implicit learning.

Unit Overview   64

13. **The Seven Sins of Memory: How the Mind Forgets and Remembers,** Daniel Schacter, *Psychology Today,* May/June 2001
Daniel Schacter explains why so much routine *forgetting* occurs. He discusses such processes as *transience, absentmindedness, blocking, misattribution, suggestibility, bias,* and *persistence.* He even delves into biological factors such as *Alzheimer's disease* and points out the paradox that memory's vices may also be its virtues.   66

The concepts in bold italics are developed in the article. For further expansion, please refer to the Topic Guide.

14. **Memories of Things Unseen,** Elizabeth F. Loftus, *Current Directions in Psychological Science,* August 2004

Memory researcher Elizabeth Loftus reveals new findings about the malleability of *memory*. Specifically, it is possible to change memory for events and in addition possible to *plant entirely false memories* of implausible or impossible events. Her findings are especially important given the fact that DNA evidence is not freeing individuals formerly convicted on faulty *eyewitness testimony*.   **70**

UNIT 5
Cognitive Processes

Two unit articles examine how social skills, common sense, and intelligence affect human cognitive processes.

Unit Overview   **74**

15. **The Power of Babble,** Mary Duenwald, *Discover,* December 2003

How babies begin to create their *first sounds* (babbles) intrigues researchers wanting to examine how *language contributes to consciousness* and how babies discriminate mere *sounds from actual words*. *Brain imaging* and other sophisticated techniques are used in this exciting research.   **77**

16. **The Mind's Self-Portrait: An Illusion of Conscious Will,** Phillip Ciske, *APS Observer,* August 2003

Psychologist Dan Wegner says that the *mind* cannot possibly know itself in all its richness. That's where psychologists enter. Wegner has developed *a theory about how we perceive causation*. For example, we often perceive we have more control over events than we actually do.   **79**

UNIT 6
Emotion and Motivation

In this unit, four articles discuss the influence of mental states, motivation, and emotion on the mental and physical health of the individual.

Unit Overview   **82**

17. **Fundamental Feelings,** Antonio Damasio, *Nature,* October 25, 2001

Antonio Damasio states that the scientific study of *emotions* is advancing. At present, one of the important issues is the discovery of the *relationship of the nervous system to bodily emotional responses*.   **85**

18. **The Value of Positive Emotions,** Barbara L. Fredrickson, *American Scientist,* July/August 2003

Positive psychology has taken root in mainstream psychology. Psychologists are being urged to study human *resilience* and *well-being* instead of typical and mostly negative human elements of past interest. The author of this article examines the history of the study of negativity and illuminates the reader about what positive psychology has to offer by way of science.   **87**

The concepts in bold italics are developed in the article. For further expansion, please refer to the Topic Guide.

19. **Can You Interview for Integrity?,** William C. Byham, *Across the Board,* March/April 2004

Some companies might want to utilize the polygraph to screen prospective employees in the belief that liars will register **guilt or other emotions** on the test. This article maintains that **integrity** as well as other personal characteristics can be detected by good **interview questions**.   **93**

20. **The Power of Goal-Setting,** Memory Nguwi, *Financial Gazette,* November 14, 2003

Setting goals is one way to ensure that we stay **motivated**. There are, however, productive and unproductive methods for goal-setting as well as better and worse means for achieving goals. This succinct article provides tips for readers about which methods are best.   **98**

UNIT 7
Development

Six articles in this section consider the importance of experience, discipline, familial support, and biological and psychological aging during the normal human development process.

Unit Overview   **100**

21. **The Biology of Aging,** Geoffrey Cowley, *Newsweek,* Special Issue, Fall/Winter 2001

Despite the title's implication that this article pertains only to the elderly, Geoffrey Cowley's comprehensive commentary provides an overview of the important **developmental and maturational sequences** that humans follow as they mature. While primary attention is given mostly to **biological aspects,** there is coverage of the **psychological aspects** of maturation as well.   **102**

22. **Inside the Womb,** J. Madeleine Nash, *Time,* November 11, 2002

This extensive article discusses **prenatal development,** or development before birth. The potential threats to the **fetus**—either **physiological or environmental**—are also reviewed.   **105**

23. **Heading Off Disruptive Behavior,** Hill M. Walker, Elizabeth Ramsey, and Frank M. Gresham, *American Educator,* Winter 2003/2004

American children are becoming more **disruptive and defiant** at home and at school. The authors identify reasons for **antisocial behavior** and what **schools and families** can do to intervene. The authors also discuss how and why **prevention** is the best approach.   **109**

24. **The Future of Adolescence: Lengthening Ladders to Adulthood,** Reed Larson, *The Futurist,* November/December 2002

Adolescence is the threshold to **adulthood.** Are today's adolescents prepared to become adults? The Study Group on Adolescence in the 21st Century says "yes." In fact, many adolescents rise to the challenge despite **increased risks** and **greater demands** on them compared to past generations.   **120**

The concepts in bold italics are developed in the article. For further expansion, please refer to the Topic Guide.

25. **The Methuselah Report,** Wayne Curtis, *AARP Bulletin,* July/August 2004

Scientists are finding ways to help us *live longer*. But is such a goal desirable? The important questions are, "Will we extend the number of days we live or actually extend the usefulness of our lives?" Author Wayne Curtis replies that the answer is complex; when we live longer, our *patterns of housing, work, interpersonal relationships, and other factors must also change*.　　**124**

26. **Start the Conversation,** *AARP Modern Maturity,* September/October 2000

Death is stigmatized in American society to the point that most people don't talk about it. This article is designed to motivate people to assess their *attitudes toward death,* to plan for the future, and to increase understanding of this issue when they or others near them are dying.　　**127**

UNIT 8
Personality Processes

A few of the processes by which personalities are developed are discussed in this section's three selections. Topics include psychoanalysis, the influence of media violence, and the secrets of happiness.

Unit Overview　　**134**

27. **Psychology Discovers Happiness. I'm OK, You're OK,** Gregg Easterbrook, *The New Republic,* March 5, 2001

Many *theories of personality* incorporate some aspect of *human misery as being normal.* Not so for the *humanists* who exalt *human worth* and *positive growth.* Some contemporary psychologists have now begun to examine positive aspects of the human experience in what has come to be known as *"positive psychology."* Author Gregg Easterbrook examines this new trend in psychology.　　**136**

28. **Companies Seeking "Right" Candidates Increasingly Turn to Personality Tests,** Damon Cline, *Knight-Ridder/Tribune Business News,* March 9, 2004

Personality is a slippery and abstract concept. Psychologists, for example, offer myriad definitions of personality. Despite this and despite the criticism of certain *personality tests,* businesses are increasingly turning to *standardized personality tests* for personnel selection. The pros and cons of this strategy are described in this essay.　　**141**

29. **Guns, Lies, and Video,** Karen Wright, *Discover,* April 2003

Psychologists have long been concerned about *televised violence*. A spate of new, high-violence *video games* has spawned little research on their effects. Studies are just now being conducted to determine what the effects of such games are—increased heart rate or worse yet increased *aggression* among other consequences.　　**144**

The concepts in bold italics are developed in the article. For further expansion, please refer to the Topic Guide.

UNIT 9
Social Processes

Two unit selections discuss how interpersonal interactions, irrational fears, and sexuality issues can affect an individual's social development.

Unit Overview 146

30. **Are You Looking at Me? Eye Gaze and Person Perception,** C. Neil Macrae et al., *Psychological Science,* September 2002
Gaze plays an important role in *interpersonal interactions.* Using the results of their research, the authors claim that gaze influences our *social memories* and our *social categorization* of others. 149

31. **Got Time for Friends?,** Andy Steiner, *Utne,* September/October 2001
Busy lives mean that adults often neglect *friendships,* which are psychologically important and valuable for many reasons. *Adult* friendships differ from *children's.* 155

UNIT 10
Psychological Disorders

In this unit, five articles examine several psychological disorders. Topics include severe anxiety, the impact of depression on a person's well-being, post-traumatic stress disorder, and schizophrenia.

Unit Overview 158

32. **How We Get Labeled,** John Cloud, *Time,* January 20, 2003
Mental health experts utilize a book mysterious to the public, *The Diagnostic and Statistical Manual of Mental Disorders* or the DSM. This account of how the book is used and the problems and issues it creates are highlighted in this article. 160

33. **The Power of Mood,** Michael D. Lemonick, *Time,* January 20, 2003
Symptoms of *depression* and its treatment and prognosis are central themes of this report. Today myriad treatments exist for this all-too-common disorder that the article suggests is physiologically or *brain* based. 163

34. **The Science of Anxiety,** Christine Gorman, *Time,* June 10, 2002
Anxiety in its intense form is a condition that plagues many individuals. Our *brains* are wired for fear, which helps us survive. However, the brain sometimes short-circuits. When this happens, the individual often suffers from an *anxiety disorder*—from *panic attacks* to *obsessive-compulsive disorder.* The many faces and causes of anxiety disorders are reviewed in this article. 167

35. **Post-Traumatic Stress Disorder,** *Harvard Health Letter,* November 2001
Post-traumatic stress disorder (PTSD) became a more important issue after the terrorist attacks in America. PTSD has specific causes and symptoms. *Who is at risk* and *how PTSD can be treated* are revealed in this article. 174

36. **Deconstructing Schizophrenia,** Constance Holden, *Science,* January 17, 2003
Studies on *heredity* and on new *medications* for *schizophrenia* are shedding light on this baffling disorder. Some psychologists now believe that schizophrenia is *a cognitive processing disorder* rather than solely a mental disorder. Brain images of people with schizophrenia elucidate some of the main points. 176

The concepts in bold italics are developed in the article. For further expansion, please refer to the Topic Guide.

UNIT 11
Psychological Treatments

Four selections in this unit discuss a few psychological treatments, including empirically supported psychotherapy, Internet-based interventions, and self-care.

Unit Overview   **180**

37. **Psychotherapies: Can We Tell the Difference?,** *Harvard Mental Health Letter,* October 2002
While **psychotherapists** often differentiate their brand of therapy from other forms, do studies demonstrate that one form of therapy actually does differ from another? Using therapists' descriptions of their own **therapy technique** and the **theory** from which it was derived, transcripts of therapists' and clients' sessions were assessed. Few actual differences among the various forms of therapy were found.   **182**

38. **Can Freud Get His Job Back?,** Lev Grossman, *Time,* January 20, 2003
In the age of pills and **managed care**, **classic psychoanalysis** appears outmoded. By comparing it to the new therapies, especially **cognitive therapy** that is briefer and more problem-oriented, Grossman lays out the future of psychoanalysis and other psychotherapies.   **183**

39. **Treating Anxiety,** Sarah Glazer, *CQ Researcher,* February 8, 2002
Anxiety disorders are rather pervasive in American society. The article presents information on how to identify anxiety disorders in **adults and children**, some of the available **treatments**, and a chronology of the study of anxiety disorders.   **187**

40. **Computer- and Internet-Based Psychotherapy Interventions,** C. Barr Taylor and Kristine H. Luce, *Current Directions in Psychological Science,* February 2003
The **Internet** offers great promise as an alternative to **face-to-face testing, diagnosis, and therapy.** One of the main problems, however, is that there is little actual **science** demonstrating that the Internet is a safe and effective place for people to find the psychological assistance they need.   **198**

Test Your Knowledge Form   **203**
Article Rating Form   **205**

The concepts in bold italics are developed in the article. For further expansion, please refer to the Topic Guide.

Topic Guide

This topic guide suggests how the selections in this book relate to the subjects covered in your course. You may want to use the topics listed on these pages to search the Web more easily.

On the following pages a number of Web sites have been gathered specifically for this book. They are arranged to reflect the units of this *Annual Edition.* You can link to these sites by going to the DUSHKIN ONLINE support site at *http://www.dushkin.com/online/*.

ALL THE ARTICLES THAT RELATE TO EACH TOPIC ARE LISTED BELOW THE BOLD-FACED TERM.

Adolescents
24. The Future of Adolescence: Lengthening Ladders to Adulthood

Aggression
29. Guns, Lies, and Video

Aging
21. The Biology of Aging

Anxiety
34. The Science of Anxiety
39. Treating Anxiety

Assessment
19. Can You Interview for Integrity?
28. Companies Seeking "Right" Candidates Increasingly Turn to Personality Tests
32. How We Get Labeled

Biological issues
4. What Makes You Who You Are
6. Neuroscience: Breaking Down Scientific Barriers to the Study of Brain and Mind
21. The Biology of Aging

Brain
6. Neuroscience: Breaking Down Scientific Barriers to the Study of Brain and Mind
7. Vision Seekers: Giving Eyesight to the Blind Raises Questions About How People See
15. The Power of Babble
17. Fundamental Feelings
34. The Science of Anxiety
36. Deconstructing Schizophrenia

Children
15. The Power of Babble
23. Heading Off Disruptive Behavior

Cognition
16. The Mind's Self-Portrait: An Illusion of Conscious Will
36. Deconstructing Schizophrenia

Cognitive therapy
38. Can Freud Get His Job Back?

Computers
40. Computer- and Internet-Based Psychotherapy Interventions

Criticisms of psychology
18. The Value of Positive Emotions

Death
26. Start the Conversation

Depression
33. The Power of Mood

Development
15. The Power of Babble
22. Inside the Womb

Dreams
11. Night Life

Drugs-drug treatment
33. The Power of Mood
39. Treating Anxiety

Emotions
17. Fundamental Feelings
18. The Value of Positive Emotions

Environment
4. What Makes You Who You Are
22. Inside the Womb

Fear
39. Treating Anxiety

Fetus
22. Inside the Womb

Freud
38. Can Freud Get His Job Back?

Gaze
30. Are You Looking at Me? Eye Gaze and Person Perception

Genes-genetics
4. What Makes You Who You Are

Goals
20. The Power of Goal-Setting

Happiness
18. The Value of Positive Emotions

History of psychology
18. The Value of Positive Emotions

Interpersonal relationships
30. Are You Looking at Me? Eye Gaze and Person Perception

Mental disorder
32. How We Get Labeled
33. The Power of Mood
35. Post-Traumatic Stress Disorder
36. Deconstructing Schizophrenia

39. Treating Anxiety

Mind
15. The Power of Babble
16. The Mind's Self-Portrait: An Illusion of Conscious Will

Motivation
20. The Power of Goal-Setting

Nature-nurture
4. What Makes You Who You Are
15. The Power of Babble

Nervous system
6. Neuroscience: Breaking Down Scientific Barriers to the Study of Brain and Mind
15. The Power of Babble
17. Fundamental Feelings

Neuroscience
6. Neuroscience: Breaking Down Scientific Barriers to the Study of Brain and Mind
7. Vision Seekers: Giving Eyesight to the Blind Raises Questions About How People See
15. The Power of Babble
17. Fundamental Feelings

Pain
10. Pain and Its Mysteries

Perception
7. Vision Seekers: Giving Eyesight to the Blind Raises Questions About How People See
15. The Power of Babble
16. The Mind's Self-Portrait: An Illusion of Conscious Will
30. Are You Looking at Me? Eye Gaze and Person Perception

Personality-personality tests
27. Psychology Discovers Happiness. I'm OK, You're OK
28. Companies Seeking "Right" Candidates Increasingly Turn to Personality Tests

Positive psychology
18. The Value of Positive Emotions
27. Psychology Discovers Happiness. I'm OK, You're OK

Post-traumatic stress disorder (PTSD)
35. Post-Traumatic Stress Disorder

Psychology
1. Why Study Psychology?

Psychopharmacology
33. The Power of Mood
39. Treating Anxiety

Psychotherapy
33. The Power of Mood
37. Psychotherapies: Can We Tell the Difference?
38. Can Freud Get His Job Back?
39. Treating Anxiety
40. Computer- and Internet-Based Psychotherapy Interventions

Punishment
23. Heading Off Disruptive Behavior

Research issues
3. Causes and Correlations
15. The Power of Babble

Schizophrenia
36. Deconstructing Schizophrenia

Scientific methods
3. Causes and Correlations

Sensation
7. Vision Seekers: Giving Eyesight to the Blind Raises Questions About How People See
15. The Power of Babble

Sleep
11. Night Life

Social behaviors
16. The Mind's Self-Portrait: An Illusion of Conscious Will
23. Heading Off Disruptive Behavior
30. Are You Looking at Me? Eye Gaze and Person Perception

Technology
15. The Power of Babble
29. Guns, Lies, and Video
40. Computer- and Internet-Based Psychotherapy Interventions

Terrorism
35. Post-Traumatic Stress Disorder

Theories
16. The Mind's Self-Portrait: An Illusion of Conscious Will
37. Psychotherapies: Can We Tell the Difference?

World Wide Web Sites

The following World Wide Web sites have been carefully researched and selected to support the articles found in this reader. The easiest way to access these selected sites is to go to our DUSHKIN ONLINE support site at *http://www.dushkin.com/online/*.

AE: Psychology 05/06

The following sites were available at the time of publication. Visit our Web site—we update DUSHKIN ONLINE regularly to reflect any changes.

General Sources

APA Resources for the Public
http://www.apa.org/psychnet/

Use the site map or search engine to access *APA Monitor,* the American Psychological Association newspaper, APA books on a wide range of topics, PsychINFO, an electronic database of abstracts on scholarly journals, and the HelpCenter.

Health Information Resources
http://www.health.gov/nhic/Pubs/tollfree.htm

Here is a long list of toll-free numbers that provide health-related information. None offer diagnosis and treatment, but some do offer recorded information; others provide personalized counseling, referrals, and/or written materials.

Mental Help Net
http://mentalhelp.net

This comprehensive guide to mental health online features more than 6,300 individual resources. Information on mental disorders and professional resources in psychology, psychiatry, and social work is presented.

Psychology: Online Resource Central
http://www.psych-central.com

Thousands of psychology resources are currently indexed at this site. Psychology disciplines, conditions and disorders, and self-development are among the most useful.

School Psychology Resources Online
http://www.schoolpsychology.net

Numerous sites on special conditions, disorders, and disabilities, as well as other data ranging from assessment/evaluation to research, are available on this resource page for psychologists, parents, and educators.

Social Psychology Network
http://www.socialpsychology.org

The social Psychology Network is the most comprehensive source of social psychology information on the Internet, including resources, programs, and research.

UNIT 1: The Science of Psychology

Abraham A. Brill Library
http://plaza.interport.net/nypsan/service.html

Containing data on over 40,000 books, periodicals, and reprints in psychoanalysis and related fields, the Abraham A. Brill Library has holdings that span the literature of psychoanalysis from its beginning to the present day.

American Psychological Society (APS)
http://www.psychologicalscience.org/about/links.html

The APS is dedicated to advancing the best of scientific psychology in research, application, and the improvement of human conditions. Links to teaching, research, and graduate studies resources are available.

Psychological Research on the Net
http://psych.hanover.edu/Research/exponnet.html

This Net site provides psychologically related experiments. Biological psychology/neuropsychology, clinical psychology, cognition, developmental psychology, emotions, health psychology, personality, sensation/perception, and social psychology are some of the areas covered.

UNIT 2: Biological Bases of Behavior

Division of Hereditary Diseases and Family Studies, Indiana University School of Medicine
http://www.iupui.edu/~medgen/division/hereditary/hereditary_diseases.html

The Department of Medical and Molecular Genetics is primarily concerned with determining the genetic basis of disease. It consists of a multifaceted program with a variety of interdisciplinary projects. The areas of twin studies and linkage analysis are also explored.

Institute for Behavioral Genetics
http://ibgwww.colorado.edu/index.html

Dedicated to conducting and facilitating research on the genetic and environmental bases of individual differences in behavior, this organized research unit at the University of Colorado leads to Genetic Sites, Statistical Sites, and the Biology Meta Index, as well as to search engines.

Serendip
http://serendip.brynmawr.edu/serendip/

Serendip, which is organized into five subject areas (brain and behavior, complex systems, genes and behavior, science and culture, and science education), contains interactive exhibits, articles, links to other resources, and a forum area.

UNIT 3: Perceptual Processes

Five Senses Home Page
http://www.sedl.org/scimath/pasopartners/senses/welcome.html

This elementary lesson examines the five senses and gives a list of references that may be useful.

Psychology Tutorials and Demonstrations
http://psych.hanover.edu/Krantz/tutor.html

Interactive tutorials and simulations, primarily in the area of sensation and perception, are available here.

UNIT 4: Learning and Remembering

Mind Tools
http://www.psychwww.com/mtsite/

Useful information on stress management can be found at this Web site.

www.dushkin.com/online/

The Opportunity of Adolescence
http://www.winternet.com/~webpage/adolescencepaper.html

According to this paper, adolescence is the turning point, after which the future is redirected and confirmed. The opportunities and problems of this period are presented with quotations from Erik Erikson, Jean Piaget, and others.

Project Zero
http://pzweb.harvard.edu

The Harvard Project Zero has investigated the development of learning processes in children and adults for 30 years. Today, Project Zero's mission is to understand and enhance learning, thinking, and creativity in the arts and other disciplines for individuals and institutions.

UNIT 5: Cognitive Processes

American Association for Artificial Intelligence (AAAI)
http://www.aaai.org/AITopics/index.html

This AAAI site provides a good starting point to learn about artificial intelligence (AI)--what artificial intelligence is and what AI scientists do.

Chess: Kasparov v. Deep Blue: The Rematch
http://www.chess.ibm.com/home/html/b.html

Clips from the chess rematch between Garry Kasparov and IBM's supercomputer, Deep Blue, are presented here along with commentaries on chess, computers, artificial intelligence, and what it all means.

UNIT 6: Emotion and Motivation

Emotional Intelligence Discovery
http://www.cwrl.utexas.edu/~bump/Hu305/3/3/3/

This site has been set up by students to talk about and expand on Daniel Goleman's book, *Emotional Intelligence*. There are links to many other EI sites.

John Suler's Teaching Clinical Psychology Site
http://www.rider.edu/users/suler/tcp.html

This page contains Internet resources for clinical and abnormal psychology, behavioral medicine, and mental health.

Nature vs. Nurture: Gergen Dialogue with Winifred Gallagher
http://www.pbs.org/newshour/gergen/gallagher_5-14.html

Experience modifies temperament, according to this TV interview. The author of *I.D.: How Heredity and Experience Make You Who You Are* explains a current theory about temperament.

UNIT 7: Development

American Association for Child and Adolescent Psychiatry
http://www.aacap.org

This site is designed to aid in the understanding and treatment of the developmental, behavioral, and mental disorders that could affect children and adolescents. There is a specific link just for families about common childhood problems that may or may not require professional intervention.

Behavioral Genetics
http://www.ornl.gov/hgmis/elsi/behavior.html

This government backed Web site includes helpful information on behavioral genetics.

UNIT 8: Personality Processes

The Personality Project
http://personality-project.org/personality.html

This Personality Project (by William Revelle) is meant to guide those interested in personality theory and research to the current personality research literature.

UNIT 9: Social Processes

National Clearinghouse for Alcohol and Drug Information
http://www.health.org

Information on drug and alcohol facts that might relate to adolescence and the issues of peer pressure and youth culture is presented here. Resources, referrals, research and statistics, databases, and related Net links are available.

Nonverbal Behavior and Nonverbal Communication
http://www3.usal.es/~nonverbal/

This Web site has a detailed listing of nonverbal behavior and nonverbal communication sites, including the work of historical and current researchers.

UNIT 10: Psychological Disorders

American Association of Suicidology
http://www.suicidology.org

The American Association of Suicidology is a nonprofit organization dedicated to the understanding and prevention of suicide. This site is designed as a resource to anyone concerned about suicide.

Anxiety Disorders
http://www.adaa.org/mediaroom/index.cfm

Anxiety Disorders Association of America (ADAA) reviews anxiety disorders in children, adolescents, and adults here. A detailed glossary is available.

Ask NOAH About: Mental Health
http://www.noah-health.org/english//illness/mentalhealth/mental.html

Information about child and adolescent family problems, mental conditions and disorders, suicide prevention, and much more is available here.

Mental Health Net Disorders and Treatments
http://www.mentalhelp.net/

Presented on this site are hotlinks to psychological disorders pages, which include anxiety, panic, phobic disorders, schizophrenia, and violent/self-destructive behaviors.

Mental Health Net: Eating Disorder Resources
http://www.mentalhelp.net/poc/center_index.php/id/46

This mental health Net site provides a complete list of Web references on eating disorders, including anorexia, bulimia, and obesity.

National Women's Health Resource Center (NWHRC)
http://www.healthywomen.org

NWHRC's site contains links to resources related to women's substance abuse and mental illnesses.

UNIT 11: Psychological Treatments

The C.G. Jung Page
http://www.cgjungpage.org

Dedicated to the work of Carl Jung, this is a comprehensive resource, with links to Jungian psychology, news and opinions, reference materials, graduate programs, dreams, multilingual sites, and related Jungian themes.

www.dushkin.com/online/

Knowledge Exchange Network (KEN)
http://www.mentalhealth.org

Information about mental health (prevention, treatment, and rehabilitation services) is available via toll-free telephone services, an electronic bulletin board, and publications.

NetPsychology
http://netpsych.com/index.htm

This site explores the uses of the Internet to deliver mental health services. This is a basic cybertherapy resource site.

Sigmund Freud and the Freud Archives
http://plaza.interport.net/nypsan/freudarc.html

Internet resources related to Sigmund Freud, which include a collection of libraries, museums, and biographical materials, as well as the Brill Library archives, can be found here.

We highly recommend that you review our Web site for expanded information and our other product lines. We are continually updating and adding links to our Web site in order to offer you the most usable and useful information that will support and expand the value of your Annual Editions. You can reach us at: *http://www.dushkin.com/annualeditions/*.

UNIT 1
The Science of Psychology

Unit Selections

1. **Why Study Psychology?**, APS Observer
2. **Does Psychology Make a Significant Difference in Our Lives?**, Philip G. Zimbardo
3. **Causes and Correlations**, Massimo Pigliucci

Key Points to Consider

- Which area of psychology (e.g. biological psychology, social psychology, human development, etc.) do you think is the most valuable and why? Many people are aware of clinical psychology by virtue of having watched films and television where psychotherapists are depicted. Is this the most valuable area of the discipline? About which other areas of psychology do you think the public is informed? What other areas ought the public to be informed? Why? How has psychology improved your life? What do you hope to learn about psychology in your class? Why?

- How do you think psychology relates well to other scientific disciplines, such as sociology, biology, and human medicine? Are there non-science disciplines to which psychology might be related, for example, philosophy and mathematics? How so?

- How and why should psychologists "give psychology away"? Do you think the general public has stereotypes or misconceptions about psychology and psychologists? Does the general public have enough knowledge of relevant issues, research, and data analysis to understand the intricacies of scientific findings?

- Why is research important to psychology? What kinds of information can be gleaned from psychological research? What types of research methods do psychologists utilize? Why do psychologists employ a variety of research methods?

- What is a correlation? Does correlation prove causation? How should a correlation be interpreted? Why are correlational methods used in psychology? What other methods do psychologists utilize? Why? What is the difference between experimentation and correlation? What does a psychologist mean by the word "control"? Why does a psychologist make a statistical inference or use inferential statistics?

- Do you think editors of psychological journals should publish results "as is" or should they exclude certain types of research or results from their journals? For example, would a study showing no differences between men and women be as a valuable as one that does demonstrate sex differences? If you excluded a study, what factors would make you as an editor exclude it?

 **Links: www.dushkin.com/online/**
These sites are annotated in the World Wide Web pages.

Abraham A. Brill Library
   http://plaza.interport.net/nypsan/service.html
American Psychological Society (APS)
   http://www.psychologicalscience.org/about/links.html
Psychological Research on the Net
   http://psych.hanover.edu/Research/exponnet.html

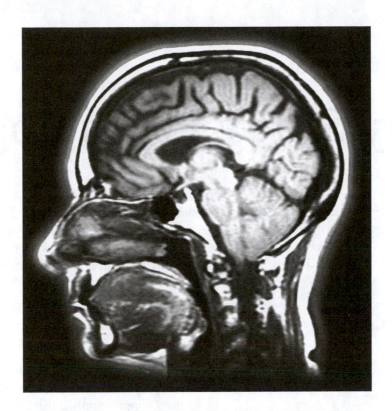

Little did Wilhelm Wundt realize his monumental contribution to science when, in 1879 in Germany, he opened the first psychological laboratory to examine consciousness. Wundt would barely recognize modern psychology compared to the way he practiced it.

Contemporary psychology is defined *as the science or study of individual mental activity and behavior.* This definition reflects the two parent disciplines from which psychology emerged: philosophy and biology. Compared to its parents, psychology is very much a new discipline. Some aspects of modern psychology are particularly biological, such as neuroscience, perception, psychophysics, and behavioral genetics. Other aspects are more philosophical such as the study of personality, while other areas within psychology approximate sociology, as does social psychology.

Today's psychologists work in a variety of settings. Many psychologists are academics, teaching and researching psychology on university campuses. Others work in applied settings such as hospitals, mental health clinics, industry, and schools. Most psychologists also specialize in psychology after graduate training. Industrial psychologists specialize in human performance in organizational settings while clinical psychologists are concerned about the assessment, diagnosis, and treatment of individuals with a variety of mental disorders. Each specialty typically requires a graduate education and sometimes requires a license to practice.

There are some psychologists who think that psychology is still in its adolescence and that the field seems to be experiencing growing pains. Since its establishment, the field has expanded to many different areas. As mentioned above, some areas are very applied. Other areas appear to emphasize theory and research. The growing pains have resulted in conflict over what the agenda of the first national psychological association, the American Psychological Association, should be. Because academics perceived this association as mainly serving practitioners, academics and researchers established their own competing association, the American Psychological Society. Despite its varied nature and growing pains, psychology remains a viable and exciting field. The first unit of the book is designed to introduce you to the study and history of psychology.

An excellent question and article begin this anthology. The first article addresses "Why Study Psychology?" Four renowned psychologists from various areas of the discipline reveal why they became psychologists and how they currently use their knowledge of the field.

The second article also addresses another cogent question, "Does Psychology Make A Significant Difference In Our Lives?" Noted psychologist Philip Zimbardo answers the question with a resounding affirmative. He suggests that we should "give away" psychology so that the general public knows more about important issues such as how to prevent AIDS and how to be better parents.

The third article, "Causes and Correlations," differentiates cause from correlation—an important point in psychology. The author also introduces other important concepts such as control of variables and the experimental method.

Why Study Psychology?

Why did psychology's leading researchers take that first course? Was it the compelling advice of a master? Perhaps a sudden epiphany? There's a story behind every good psychologist. A cross-section of psychologists were asked to share their stories and illuminate the heart of this career-making decision.

EVIDENTLY ENOUGH

Elizabeth Loftus,
University of California, Irvine
PhD, 1970

DAD HAD TO RAISE three kids alone after Mom died, so he was pretty busy. He worked all day, came home for dinner, and often just wanted to spend the evening in his room reading. But I found a way to get him to talk to me —I asked him for help with my math homework. He had been an award-winning math whiz as a kid, and math became the one thing we could talk about. With the benefit of Dad's "tutoring," I too would win mathematics awards. Since I seemed to be good at mathematics, my life plan was to become a high school math teacher.

But things changed. I was a math major at the University of California, Los Angeles, but of course I needed some electives. I took introductory psychology from Allen Parducci and got hooked. Nearly every elective course I took thereafter was in the field of psychology, and when it was all said and done I had enough credits for a double major. As luck—or perhaps wisdom—would have it, I chose to continue graduate work in psychology. I heard about a field called "mathematical psychology" and it sounded perfect for me. Stanford University was known to excel in that field, and that's where I wanted to go for graduate school.

During my third year at Stanford, I developed what was to become a consuming interest in long-term memory. I learned how to use the methods of experimental psychology to investigate human memory. But I also learned an important truth about science more generally. Science is not just a giant bowl of facts to remember, but rather a way of thinking. It's a process that is based on a fundamental insight, namely, that an idea may seem to be true, but this has nothing to do with whether it actually is true. In order to distinguish true ideas from false ones we must test them. My undergraduate and graduate education prepared me well to test ideas, often by experiments, and I happily applied this knowledge to the study of human memory. Discovering some fundamental facts about the malleability of memory has been pretty exciting.

Science is not just a giant bowl of facts to remember, but rather a way of thinking.

Years later, when I gave a commencement address to graduating college seniors, I told the graduates about these experiences. I talked about an important gift that the study of psychology gives to people. It is the gift of knowing how to ask the right questions about any claim that someone might try to fob off on you. Ask them: "What is the evidence?" for that claim, but don't stop there. Get more specific: What kind of study was done? What was the dependent variable? Was there a control group? What kinds of statistical tests were used to analyze the data? Has the study been replicated?

We need ask: "What *exactly* is the evidence?" because some evidence is so flimsy that it's not really evidence at all. I thank my professors, the authors of my textbooks, and my fellow students for helping me appreciate this gift, and of course my father for leading me, somewhat fortuitously, in its direction.

Three Strikes You're In

Jeffrey S. Katz,
Auburn University
PhD, 1998

IN LOOKING BACK on why I became an experimental psychologist, my first thought was, 'Why not?' What could be more important than understanding how the underlying mechanisms of the mind might work? Certainly, the problem was not going to be solved any time in the near future. I thought the complexities of how we think and behave and how that might differ from other species had to be as challenging as any problem that faces scientists in biology, chemistry, or physics.

That makes a nice story, but I'm not confident I was that savvy in my thinking 15 years ago. For the academic, there is one clear global career decision: to become an academic, with smaller, critical, perhaps serendipitous points along the way. Here are two events that started me on the path and a third that kept me on it.

> *During one class the professor was in the middle of a horrible lecture and I thought, "I could teach this at least as well, if not better.*

The first was discovering the information processing view. My first choice for an undergraduate major was computer science. During my sophomore year, I was enrolled in an experimental psychology class. At the same time, I was losing my passion for learning different data structures, search algorithms, and computer languages. When I learned that psychologists were using flowcharts to describe how memory worked, I saw the obvious connection between what I was learning in computer science and how that could be applied to human information processes.

The second event took place during my junior year, in another class. I had developed into one of those students who asked too many questions. During one class the professor was in the middle of a horrible lecture and I thought, "I could teach this at least as well, if not *better*." I was certainly naive and likely a little arrogant at the time, but, as I'll be the first to admit, I was probably right.

The third event occurred during a dinner conversation right around the time I had finished my master's thesis. A colleague of my graduate advisor had presented a colloquium earlier in the day, and I was invited to dinner with him that night. I'm sure I played every part of the wide-eyed graduate student that evening. The conversation turned to career decisions and, in particular, my ability to find an academic position. I was working in the field of animal learning and cognition and was fully aware of the scarcity of a tenure-track position in this area. I described these predicted difficulties to my dinner partner, and the advice I got in response was straightforward, and it went something like this: "Everyone who deserves a job gets one." The debatable veracity of this statement is of secondary importance to its service as a major motivating force in my career path.

Portrait of the Psychologist

Ben R. Slugoski,
James Cook University
Australia,
DPhil, 1985

IF MY DEVELOPMENTAL psychology colleagues are right, I began formulating conceptions of human psychological states and processes at about the age of three. Institutional recognition for my efforts came much later of course, with a DPhil in social psychology from Oxford University in 1985. In between, it was largely a matter of learning to put practice into theory.

In fact, it was only toward the end of my third year of undergraduate studies at Simon Fraser University that I committed to psychology as an administrative category. I had been double-majoring in psychology and English, and the latter was winning hands down in telling me anything of value about "human nature" and the "human condition." During those obsessively reflexive 70s at "Berkeley north," philosophy and English were king and queen, and from the top floor of 'academic quadrangle'—floating amongst the clouds seemingly tethered to Burnaby mountain—we English majors could spit on just about any other department in the university. Psychology, by contrast buried deep in the bowels of 'Classroom Complex' on the campus's periphery, often bore the brunt of our collective disdain; Laçan and Derrida were at home in English, unknown—or at least unmentioned—in Psychology; and who could argue that Skinner's *Beyond Freedom and Dignity* held a candle to Dostoevsky's *Notes from the Underground* in laying bare the central existential dilemma.

My decision to undertake Honors in psychology rather than English was driven only in small part by the expectation of having to feed a family down the road. First, I was something of an oddity among my peers in either discipline in finding an almost perverse pleasure in the counterpoint between the rhetorical and positivist approaches to understanding human nature. Or perhaps it was just because I got easily bored, and there was no antidote to a few hours deconstructing Coleridge or Blake like working out the expected mean squares for a tricky experimental design (a rakish sex-life not otherwise being in the cards!).

Far more important for choosing psychology was that I found all my beacons there. Erudite though my English professor's were, they were only vessels for conveying the brilliance of the 'Greats' and as such were never particularly good models for an aspiring player. What ultimately determined my allegiance to psychology was the brilliance personified in my psychology lecturers, of whom three in particular made an enormous impact: the late Kenneth Burstein, old school rat-runner, unabashed liberal, and the person whom you would least want as a relationship counsellor; Raymond Koopman, statistician and methodologist extraordinaire; and my recently retired, analytically-trained mentor through a Masters degree, James E. Marcia. A more diverse range of characters and backgrounds can hardly be imagined, and I can only trace their classroom influence on me to some uncanny ability to jar my presuppositions and enable me to recognize a 'good idea' when, if one came along. It is probably worthy of note in these days of multimedia, dot point-driven instruction that my beacons were invariably Socratic minimalists for whom the take-home message was quite subsidiary to the intellectual journey (seemingly) constructed *in situ*. Thus, I recall Burstein leading us from eye-blink conditioning with rabbits to human divorce statistics via a little sociobiology, Koopman had the class reinvent the correlation coefficient, and Marcia ... well, Marcia had us ruminating about the conditions and consequences of sleeping with ones' clients. Jarring a basic pedagogic assumption, Marcia also distributed his multiple-choice questions in advance of the exams, which I considered to be a very good idea. They certainly didn't do *that* in English!

So my choice was clear: first Honors and then a MA under Marcia investigating (in a supreme act of intellectualization) the 'Cognitive and social-interactional characteristics of ego identity statuses in college males.' I subsequently was able to reconnect my psychological studies with my abiding interest in language, and my reading on the plane delivering me to Oxford was John Austin's seminal *How to do things with words*. Ordinary language philosophy—Oxford philosophy—was to provide the machinery with which I have since been probing the interaction of linguistic and a variety of social cognitive variables and processes such as attribution, cognitive biases, and in one fit of post-modern nostalgia even Marcia's identity statuses. So I was able to reconect with my literary roots after all.

Shifting Winds

Michela Gallagher,
Johns Hopkins University
PhD, 1977

WHEN I WAS A STUDENT during the 60s at The Slade (the art school at University College, London), my tutor often referred to my paintings as 'cerebral,' not a favorable commentary in an era of late abstract expressionism. Little over a decade later I shifted from my life long love of art to a career in physiological psychology. For me the two had much in common; they elicited a fascination with the most compelling questions in nature about the human mind and required a good deal of time spent on matters technical in attempting to arrive at some approximate answers. I was able to balance my cerebral tendency with the practice of methods to formulate work that was part intentional, part unpredictable.

Of course a great teacher was influential in changing my path. Bruce Kapp, then a young assistant professor at University of Vermont, provided my introduction to physiological psychology. Bruce was an inspired and passionate teacher. At heart, his teaching was intimately tied to his deep interest in the work of science. By his example, I could hardly become interested in a topic without wanting to dig right in and study it, and I soon became his first PhD student. So I caught the bug from Bruce and have lived very happily with it since.

I could hardly become interested in a topic without wanting to dig right in and study it.

Making career decisions in the 60s was not at all what it is today, or so it seems to me. As I decided to go to graduate school and worked on my dissertation research, I gave little thought to work life down the road. Graduate training back then also gave little attention to professional development. Sometimes I wonder, as my own students cast a far-reaching eye on their careers, how a more realistic understanding of being a mature scientist would have affected my decision on a career, or tempered my experience as a wide-eyed child in those early days of training.

Does Psychology Make a Significant Difference in Our Lives?

Philip G. Zimbardo
Stanford University

The intellectual tension between the virtues of basic versus applied research that characterized an earlier era of psychology is being replaced by an appreciation of creative applications of all research essential to improving the quality of human life. Psychologists are positioned to "give psychology away" to all those who can benefit from our wisdom. Psychologists were not there 35 years ago when American Psychological Association (APA) President George Miller first encouraged us to share our knowledge with the public. The author argues that psychology is indeed making a significant difference in people's lives; this article provides a sampling of evidence demonstrating how and why psychology matters, both in pervasive ways and specific applications. Readers are referred to a newly developed APA Web site that documents current operational uses of psychological research, theory, and methodology (its creation has been the author's primary presidential initiative): www.psychologymatters.org.

Does psychology matter? Does what we do, and have done for a hundred years or more, really make a significant difference in the lives of individuals or in the functioning of communities and nations? Can we demonstrate that our theories, our research, our professional practice, our methodologies, our way of thinking about mind, brain, and behavior make life better in any measurable way? Has what we have to show for our discipline been applied in the real world beyond academia and practitioners' offices to improve health, education, welfare, safety, organizational effectiveness, and more?

Such questions, and finding their answers, have always been my major personal and professional concern. First, as an introductory psychology teacher for nearly six decades, I have always worked to prove relevance as well as essence of psychology to my students. Next, as an author of the now classic basic text, *Psychology and Life* (Ruch & Zimbardo, 1971), which claimed to wed psychology to life applications, I constantly sought to put more psychology in our lives and more life in our psychology (Gerrig & Zimbardo, 2004; Zimbardo, 1992). To reach an even broader student audience, I have coauthored *Core Concepts in Psychology* (Zimbardo, Weber, & Johnson, 2002) that strives to bring the excitement of scientific and applied psychology to students in state and community colleges.

In order to further expand the audience for what is best in psychology, I accepted an invitation to help create, be scientific advisor for, and narrator of the 26-program PBS TV series, *Discovering Psychology* (1990/2001). For this general public audience, we have provided answers—as viewable instances—to

their "so what?" questions. This award-winning series is shown both nationally and internationally (in at least 10 nations) and has been the foundation for the most popular telecourse among all the Annenberg CPB Foundation's many academic programs (see www.learner.org). Finally, as the 2002 president of the American Psychological Association, my major initiative became developing a compendium of exemplars of how psychology has made a significant difference in our lives. This Web-based summary of "psychology in applied action" has been designed as a continually modifiable and updateable repository of demonstrable evidence of psychological knowledge in meaningful applications. In a later section of this article, the compendium will be described more fully and some of its examples highlighted.

I was fortunate in my graduate training at Yale University (1954-1960) to be inspired by three exceptional mentors, each of whom modeled a different aspect of the relevance and applicability of basic psychology to vital issues facing individuals and our society. Carl Hovland developed the Yale Communication and Attitude Change Program after coming out of his military assignment in World War II of analyzing the effectiveness of propaganda and training programs (Hovland, Lumsdaine, & Sheffield, 1949). He went on to transform what was at that time a complex, global, and vague study of communication and persuasion into identifiable processes, discrete variables, and integrative hypotheses that made possible both experimental research and applications (Hovland, Janis, & Kelley, 1953). Neal Miller always straddled the fence between basic and applied research, despite being known for his classic experimental and theoretical formulations of motivation and reward in learning and conditioning. His World War II experience of training pilots to overcome fears so that they could return to combat was an applied precursor of his later role in developing biofeedback through his laboratory investigations of conditioning autonomic nervous system responses (N. E. Miller, 1978, 1985, 1992). The last of my Yale mentors, Seymour Sarason, moved out from his research program on test anxiety in children into the community as one of the founders of Community Psychology (Sarason, 1974). It was a daring move at that time in a field that honored only the scientific study of *individual* behavior.

Psychology of the 50s was also a field that honored basic research well above applied research, which was typically accorded second-class status, if not denigrated by the "experimentalists," a popular brand name in that era. Psychology at many major universities aspired to be "soft physics," as in the heady days of our Germanic forebears, Wundt, Fechner, Ebbinghaus, Titchner, and others (see Green, Shore, & Teo, 2001). Anything applied was seen at best as crude social engineering by tinkerers, not real thinkers. Moreover, behaviorism was still rampant, with animal models that stripped away from learning what nonsense syllable memory researchers had deleted from memory—merely the context, the content, the human meaning, and the culture of behavior. The most prominent psychologist from the 50s through the 80s, B.F. Skinner, was an anomaly in this regard. Half of him remained a Watsonian radical behaviorist who refused to admit the existence of either motivation or cognition into his psychology (Skinner, 1938, 1966, 1974). Meanwhile, the other Skinner side applied operant conditioning principles to train pigeons for military duties and outlined a behaviorist Utopia in *Walden Two* (Skinner, 1948).

Giving Psychology Away: The Call for Societal Accountability

And then along came George Miller whose American Psychological Association (APA) presidential address in 1969 stunned the psychological establishment because one of its own first-born sons committed the heresy of exhorting them to go public, get real, get down, give it up, and be relevant. Well, that is the way I think I heard it back then when George Miller (1969) told his audience that it was time to begin "to give psychology away to the public." It was time to stop talking only to other psychologists. It was time to stop writing only for professional journals hidden away in library stacks. It was time to go beyond the endless quest for experimental rigor in the perfectly designed study to test a theoretically derived hypothesis. Maybe it was time to begin finding answers to the kinds of questions your mother asked about why people acted the way they did. Perhaps it was acceptable to start considering how best to translate what we knew into a language that most ordinary citizens could understand and even come to appreciate.

I for one applauded George Miller's stirring call to action for all these reasons. It was heady for me because I believed that

coming from such a distinguished serious theorist and researcher—not some do-gooder, liberal communitarian whom the establishment could readily dismiss—his message would have a big impact in our field Sadly, the banner raised by Miller's inspirational speech, did not fly very high over most psychology departments for many years to come. Why not? I think for four reasons: Excessive modesty about *what* psychology really had of value to offer the public, ignorance about *who* was "the public," cluelessness about *how* to go about the mission of giving psychology away, and lack of sufficient concern about *why* psychology needed to be accountable to the public.

How shall we counterargue against such reasoning? First, scanning the breadth and depth of our field makes apparent that there is no need for such professional modesty. Rather, the time has come to be overtly proud of our past and current accomplishments, as I will try to demonstrate here. We have much to be proud of in our heritage and in our current accomplishments. Second, the public starts with our students, our clients, and our patients and extends to our funding agencies, national and local politicians, all nonpsychologists, and the media. And it also means your mother whose "bubba psychology" sometimes needs reality checks based on solid evidence we have gathered. Third, it is essential to recognize that the media are the gatekeepers between the best, relevant psychology we want to give away and that elusive public we hope will value what we have to offer. We need to learn how best to utilize the different kinds of media that are most appropriate for delivering specific messages to particular target audiences that we want to reach. Psychologists need to learn how to write effective brief press releases, timely op-ed newspaper essays, interesting articles for popular magazines, valuable trade books based on empirical evidence, and how best to give radio, TV, and print interviews. Simple awareness of media needs makes evident, for example, that TV requires visual images, therefore, we should be able to provide video records of research, our interventions, or other aspects of the research or therapeutic process that will form a story's core.

"Media smarts" also means realizing that to reach adolescents with a helpful message (that is empirically validated), a brief public service announcement on MTV or an article in a teen magazine will have a broader impact than detailed journal articles or even popular books on the subject.[1] Thus, it becomes essential to our mission of making the public wiser consumers of psychological knowledge to learn how to communicate effectively to the media and to work with the media.

Finally, we can challenge the fourth consideration regarding societal accountability with the awareness that taxpayers fund much of our research as well as some of the education of our graduate students. It is imperative that we convey the sense to the citizens of our states and nation that we are responsive to society's needs and, further, that we feel responsible for finding solutions to some of its problems (Zimbardo, 1975). It has become standard operating procedure for most granting agencies now to require a statement about the potential societal value of any proposed research. That does not mean that all research must be applied to dealing with current social or individual problems because there is considerable evidence that research that originally seemed esoterically "basic" has in time found valuable applications (see Swazey, 1974). It does mean that although some of our colleagues begin with a focus on a problem in an applied domain, the others who start with an eye on theory testing or understanding some basic phenomena should feel obligated to stretch their imaginations by considering potential applications of their knowledge. I believe we have much worthy applicable psychology, basic research, theory, and methodology that is awaiting creative transformations to become valuable applied psychology.

The Profound and Pervasive Impact of Past Psychological Knowledge

Before I outline some recent, specific instances of how psychological research, theory, and methodology have been applied in various settings, I will first highlight some of the fundamental contributions psychology has already made in our lives. Many of them have become so pervasive and their impact so unobtrusively profound that they are taken for granted. They have come to be incorporated into the way we think about certain domains, have influenced our attitudes and values, and so changed the way individuals and agencies behave that they now seem like the natural, obvious way the world should be run. Psychology often gets little or no credit for these contributions—when we should be deservedly proud of them.

Psychological Testing and Assessment

One of psychology's major achievements has been the development and the extensive reliance on objective, quantifiable means of assessing human talents, abilities, strengths, and weaknesses. In the 100 years since Alfred Binet first measured intellectual performance, systematic assessment has replaced the subjective, often biased judgments of teachers, employers, clinicians, and others in positions of authority by objective, valid, reliable, quantifiable, and normed tests (Binet, 1911; Binet & Simon, 1915). It is hard to imagine a test-free world. Modern testing stretches from assessments of intelligence, achievement, personality, and pathology to domains of vocational and values assessment, personnel selection, and more. Vocational interest measures are the backbone of guidance counseling and career advising. The largest single application of classified testing in the world is the Armed Services Vocational Aptitude Battery that is given to as many as 2 million enlisted personnel annually. Personnel selection testing has over 90 years of validity research and proven utility.

We are more familiar with the SAT and GRE standardized testing, currently being revised in response to various critiques, but they are still the yardstick for admission to many colleges and universities (Sternberg, 2000). Workplace job skills assessment and training involves huge numbers of workers and managers in many countries around the world (DuBois, 1970). Little wonder, then, that such pervasive use of assessments has spawned a multibillion dollar industry. (Because I am serving here in this article in the capacity as cheerleader for our disci-

pline, I will not raise questions about the political misuse or overuse of testing nor indeed be critical of some of the other contributions that follow; see Cronbach, 1975.)

Positive Reinforcement

The earlier emphasis in schools and in child rearing on punishment for errors and inappropriate behavior has been gradually displaced by a fundamentally divergent focus on the utility of positive reinforcement for correct, appropriate responding (Straus & Kantor, 1994). Punishing the "undesirable person" has been replaced by punishing only "undesirable behavioral acts." Time-outs for negative behavior have proven remarkably effective as a behavior-modification strategy (Wolfe, Risley, & Mees, 1965). It has become so effective that it has become a favorite technique for managing child behavior by parents in the United States. "Half the parents and teachers in the United States use this nonviolent practice and call it 'time-out,' which makes it a social intervention unmatched in modern psychology," according to the American Academy of Pediatrics' (1998) publication.

Animal training has benefited enormously from procedures of shaping complex behavioral repertoires and the use of conditioned reinforcers (such as clickers' soundings paired with food rewards). An unexpected value of such training, as reported by animal caregivers, is that they enhance the mental health of many animal species through the stimulation provided by learning new behaviors (*San Francisco Chronicle*, 2003). Skinner and his behaviorist colleagues deserve the credit for this transformation in how we think about and go about changing behavior by means of response-contingent reinforcement. Their contributions have moved out of animal laboratories into schools, sports, clinics, and hospitals (see Axelrod & Apsche, 1983; Druckman & Bjork, 1991; Kazdin, 1994; Skinner, 1974).

Psychological Therapies

The mission of our psychological practitioners of relieving the suffering of those with various forms of mental illness by means of appropriately delivered types of psychological therapy has proven successful. Since Freud's (1896/1923, 1900/1965) early cases documenting the efficacy of "talk therapy" for neurotic disorders, psychotherapy has taken many forms. Cognitive behavior modification, systematic desensitization, and exposure therapies have proven especially effective in treating phobias, anxiety disorders, and panic attacks, thanks to the application of Pavlovian principles of classical conditioning (Pavlov, 1897/1902, 1897/1927), first developed by Joseph Wolpe (1958). Even clinical depression is best treated with a combination of psychotherapy and medication, and psychotherapy has been shown to be as effective as the drugs alone (Hollon, Thase, & Markowitz, 2002). At a more general level, psychology has helped to demystify "madness," to bring humanity into the treatment of those with emotional and behavioral disorders, and to give people hope that such disorders can be changed (Beck, 1976). Our practitioners and clinical theorists have also developed a range of treatments designed especially for couples, families, groups, for those in rehabilitation from drugs or physical disabilities, as well as for many specific types of problems such as, addictions, divorce, or shyness.

Self-Directed Change

The shelves of most bookstores in the United States are now as likely to be filled with "self-help" books as they are with cooking and dieting books. Although many of them can be dismissed as bad forms of "pop psych" that offer guidance and salvation without any solid empirical footing to back their claims, others provide a valuable service to the general public. At best, they empower people to engage in self-directed change processes for optimal personal adjustment (see Maas, 1998; Myers, 1993; Zimbardo, 1977). In part, their success comes from providing wise advice and counsel based on a combination of extensive expert experience and relevant research packaged in narratives that ordinary people find personally meaningful.

Dynamic Development Across the Life Span

Earlier conceptions of children as small adults, as property, and later as valuable property were changed in part by the theories and research of developmental psychologists (see McCoy, 1988; Pappas, 1983). In recent times, the emerging status of "the child as person" has afforded children legal rights, due process, and self-determination, along with the recognition that they should be regarded as competent persons worthy of considerable freedom (Horowitz, 1984). Psychology has been a human service profession whose knowledge base has been translated into support for a positive ideology of children (Hart, 1991). The human organism is continually changing, ever modifying itself to engage its environments more effectively, from birth through old age. This fundamental conception has made evident that babies need stimulation of many kinds for optimal development, just as do their grandparents. There is now widespread psychological recognition that infants do experience pain; learning often depends on critical age-related developmental periods; nature and nurture typically interact in synergistic ways to influence our intelligence and many attributes; mental growth follows orderly progressions, as does language acquisition and production; and that the elderly do not lose their mental agility and competence if they continue to exercise their cognitive skills throughout life (see Baltes & Staudinger 2000; Bee, 1994; Erikson, 1963; Piaget, 1954; Pinker, 1994; Plomin & McClearn, 1993; Scarr, 1998). These are but a few of the fundamental contributions of psychology to the way our society now thinks about human development over the course of a lifetime because of decades of research by our developmentalist colleagues.

Parenting

Advice by psychologists on best parental practices has varied in quality and value over time. However, there now seems to be agreement that children need to develop secure attachments to parents or caregivers and that the most beneficial parenting style for generating an effective child-parent bond is authoritative. Authoritative parents make age-appropriate demands on children while being responsive to their needs, autonomy, and freedom (see Baumrind, 1973; Collins, Maccoby, Steinberg, Hetherington, & Bornstein, 2000; Darling & Steinberg, 1993; Maccoby, 1980, 1992, 2000).

Psychological Stress

Is there any day in our modern lives that stress does not seem to be omnipresent? We are stressed by time pressures on us, by our jobs (Maslach, 1982), by our marriages, by our friends or by our lack of them. Back when I was a graduate student, stress was such a novel concept that it was surprising when our professor Irving Janis (1958) wrote one of the first books on the subject of psychological stress. The concept of psychological stress was virtually unrecognized in medical care in the 50s and 60s. Psychosomatic disorders baffled physicians who never recognized stress as a causal factor in illness and disease. Since then, psychological research and theorizing has helped to move the notion of stress to the center of the bio-psychosocial health model that is revolutionizing medical treatments (Ader & Cohen, 1993; Cohen & Herbert, 1996). Psychologists have shown that our appraisals of stress and our lifestyle habits have a major impact on many of the major causes of illness and death (see Lazarus, 1993; Lazarus & Folkman, 1984). We have made commonplace the ideas of coping with stress, reducing lifestyle risk factors, and building social support networks to enable people to live healthier and longer lives (see Coe, 1999; Cohen & Syme, 1985; Taylor & Clark, 1986).

Unconscious Motivation

Psychology brought into the public mind, as did dramatists such as William Albee, Arthur Miller, and Tennessee Williams, that what we think and do is not always based on conscious decisions. Rather, human behavior may be triggered by unconscious motivations of which we have no awareness. Another nod of thanks goes out to the wisdom of Sigmund Freud and of Carl Jung (1936/1959) for helping to illuminate this previously hidden side of human nature. In a similar vein, slips of the tongue and pen are now generally interpreted as potentially meaningful symptoms of suppressed intentions. It is relatively common in many levels of U.S. society for people to believe that accidents may not be accidental but motivated, that dreams might convey important messages, and also that we use various defense mechanisms, such as projection, to protect fragile egos from awareness of negative information.

Prejudice and Discrimination

Racial prejudice motivates a range of emotions and behaviors among both those targeted and those who are its agents of hatred. Discrimination is the overt behavioral sequeala of prejudiced beliefs. It enforces inequalities and injustices based on categorical assignments to presumed racial groups. Stereotypes embody a biased conception of the attributes people presumably possess or lack. The 1954 decision by the Supreme Court of the United States (*Brown v. Board of Education of Topeka, KS*) that formally desegregated public schools was based on some critical social psychological research. The body of empirical research by Kenneth and Mamie Clark (1939a, 1939b, 1940, 1950) effectively demonstrated for the Court that the segregated educational conditions of that era had a negative impact on the sense of self-worth of Negro (the then-preferred term) school children. The Court, and the thoughtful public since then, accepted the psychological premise that segregated education, which separates the races, can never be really equal for those being stigmatized by that system of discrimination. Imposed segregation not only is the consequence of prejudice, it contributes further to maintaining and intensifying prejudice, negative stereotypes, and discrimination. In the classic analysis of the psychology of prejudice by Gordon Allport (1954), the importance of equal status contact between the races was advanced as a dynamic hypothesis that has since been widely validated in a host of different contexts (Pettigrew, 1997).

Humanizing Factory Work

Dehumanizing factory assembly lines in which workers were forced to do the same repetitive, mindless task, as if they were robots, initially gave Detroit automakers a production advantage. However, Japanese automakers replaced such routinized assembly lines with harmonious, small work teams operating under conditions of participatory management and in-group democratic principles. The remarkable success of the Japanese automakers in overtaking their American counterparts in a relatively short time is due in part to their adaptation of the principles of group dynamics developed by Kurt Lewin, his colleagues and students at the Massachusetts Institute of Technology, and the University of Michigan (Lewin, 1947a, 1947b, 1948). Paradoxically, U.S. auto manufacturers are now incorporating this Japanese work model into their factories, decades after they should have done so. This is one way in which psychological theory can be credited with a humanizing impact on industrial work. But psychologists working in the industrial/organizational framework have done even more to help businesses appreciate and promote the importance of goal setting, worker-job fit, job satisfaction, and personnel selection and training.

Political Polling

It is hard to imagine elections without systematic polling of various segments of the electorate using sampling techniques as predictors of election outcomes. Polling for many other purposes by Gallup, Roper, and other opinion polling agencies has become big business. Readers might be surprised to learn that psychologist Hadley Cantril (1991) pioneered in conducting research into the methodology of polling in the 1940s. Throughout World War II, Cantril provided President Roosevelt with valuable information on American public opinion. He also established the Office of Public Opinion Research, which became a central archive for polling data.

How and Why Psychology Matters in Our Lives

I am proud to be a psychologist. As the 2002 APA president, one of my goals was to spread that pride far and wide among my colleagues as well as among all students of psychology. For starters, we can all be proud of the many contributions we have made collectively to enrich the way people think about the human condition, a bit of which was outlined above. I am also proud of the fact that our scientific approach to understanding the behavior of individuals has guided some policy and improved some operating procedures in our society. We have always been one of the most vigilant and outspoken proponents of the use of the scientific method for bringing reliable evidence to bear on a range of issues (Campbell, 1969). Given any intervention or new policy, psychologists insist on raising the question, "but does it really work?" and utilizing evaluative methodologies and meta-analyses to help make that decision. Psychologists have modeled the approach to reducing errors in advancing behavior-based conclusions through random assignment, double-blind tests, and sensitivity to the many biases present in uncontrolled observations and research procedures. Many of us have also been leaders in advancing a variety of innovations in education through our awareness of principles of attention, learning, memory, individual differences, and classroom dynamics. In addition, I am proud of our discipline's dedication to relieving all forms of human suffering through effective therapeutic interventions along with promoting prevention strategies and appropriate environmental change. As psychologists, we should also be pleased by discovering that our theories, research, and methodologies are serving to influence individual and societal actions, as will be shown next.

Psychologymatters.org

The scaffolding for such pride in psychology might best be manifest in a newly developed compendium, which shows society what we have done and are doing to improve the quality of life. I wanted to have available in one easily accessible and indexed source a listing of the research and theories that have been translated into practice. Such a resource would indicate how each item is being applied in various settings, such as schools, clinics, hospitals, businesses, community services, and legal and governmental agencies. It would establish the fact that psychology makes a significant difference in our lives by means of these concrete exemplars of its relevant applications. Ideally, this compendium would indicate how psychological contributions have saved lives, reduced or prevented suffering, saved money, made money, enhanced educational goals, improved security and safety, promoted justice and fairness, made organizations operate more effectively, and more. By designing this compendium as a Web-based open file, it can be continually updated, modified, and expanded as promising research meets the criterion of acceptability as having made a practically significant difference.

This effort to devise a compendium began with the help of APA's Science Directorate, by issuing a call for submissions to many e-mail lists serving APA members and through requests in APA's *Monitor on Psychology* and on the www.apa.org Web site. The initial set of items was vetted independently by Len Mitnick (formerly of the National Institute of Mental Health) and me. A "blue-ribbon" task force of journal editors, textbook authors, and senior scientists was formed to further vet these final items, help revise them, and then to work at expanding our base.[2]

Because this compendium offers the opportunity to portray an attractive, intelligent face of psychology to the public, final drafts have been edited or rewritten by science writers in APA's Public Communication's office, ably directed by Rhea Farberman. Ideally, the submissions appear in a jargon-free, readable style appealing to the nonpsychologist public, as well as to our professional colleagues. In addition to having the individual items categorized into many general topical domains, readily searchable by key words or phrases, we have expanded the value of this site by adding an extensive glossary of psychological terms, a historical timeline of major psychological events and contributors, and basic information on "how to be a wiser consumer of research." We will include other extensions as appropriate based on feedback from colleagues and the public we are serving.

The criteria for inclusion are that each submission be presented (a) in sufficient detail to allow an independent assessment; (b) with evidence of significant statistical effects obtained within the study; (c) with reported application or extension of the submitted research, methodology, or theory in some specific domain of relevance; and (d) with evidence of where and how it has made a significant difference, such as citation of a new law, policy, standardized procedure, or operating system that was based on the submitted item. Items with *promise* of such applicability in the future (because they were too new to have been subject to any evaluation of outcome effectiveness) are being held in a "wait-and-check-back-later" file. I should mention in passing that many submitted items described research that was interesting, including some classic studies, but they have never met the test of societal applicability.

I welcome the feedback of *American Psychologist* readers on this first phase of our efforts, while also issuing a cordial invitation to add your voice to this compendium with additional worthy submissions. The reach of these initial efforts will hopefully be extended by having this compendium serve as a model to the psychological associations of countries around the world, adding to psychology's global relevance.

Please visit us at www.psychologymatters.org. But please wait a moment before booting up your computer, until you finish reading the next section of this article, which highlights a sampling of what you will find there.

Highlights of Psychology's Real World Relevance

I want to conclude with a dozen or so examples taken from our compendium that illustrate a range of its different topics and domains of applicability. This presentation will end with one extended instance of what I consider a model collaboration of theory, research, media applicability, and global dissemination of psychological knowledge conveyed in a unique format—soap operas! It is the ingenious application of the theory of social modeling by Albert Bandura (1965, 1977) in the design of scenarios

used in soap operas to encourage literacy, birth control, the education of woman, environmental sustainability, and more.

Human Factors

Traffic safety has been improved by researchers in the area of human factors and ergonomics through a better understanding of visual perception. We now know that changing the standard color of red emergency trucks to a lime-green color reduces accidents because that greenish hue is better perceived in dim light. Similarly, changing traffic sign fonts to increase their recognition at night is another safety improvement resulting from psychological research by Allen (1970), Solomon and King (1985), and Garvey, Pietrucha, and Meeker (1997).

Scott Geller's (2001, 2003) research program applies Skinnerian behavior analysis to increase safe behaviors, reduce at-risk behaviors, and prevent unintentional injuries at work and on the road. Such unintentional injury is the leading cause of death to people ages 44 years and under. The behavior-based safety (BBS) approach for increasing safety identifies critical behaviors that are targeted for change, establishes baselines, applies change interventions, and evaluates workers' change away from specific risky behaviors to more beneficial directions. This approach has been applied in thousands of organizations with great success, such as in having people wear seat belts and in occupational safety programs. The rate of reported injuries after five years of implementation of this behavioral approach decreased by as much as an average 72% across a number of organizations (for a summary of the evidence for the extent of injury reduction, see the report by Beth Sulzer-Azaroff & John Austin, 2000). One indicator of the social significance of applying behavior analysis is apparent in the *Clinical Practice Guidelines* of New York States' (1999) Department of Health, Early Intervention Program: "It is recommended that principles of applied behavior analysis (ABA) and behavior intervention strategies be included as important elements in any intervention program for young children with autism" (p. 13).

Navigational aids for the blind and visually impaired people have been developed by psychologists Roberta Klatsky and Jack Loomis, working with geographer Reginald Golledge (Loomis, Klatsky, & Golledge, 2001) over several decades. They utilize principles of spatial cognition along with those of space and auditory perception to guide locomotion. Their new technology is now in development funded by the National Institute for Disability and Rehabilitation Research.

Criminal Justice

Cognitive and social psychologists have shown that eyewitness testimony is surprisingly unreliable. Their research reveals the ease with which recall of criminal events is biased by external influences in interrogations and police line-ups. The seminal work of Beth Loftus (1975, 1979, 1992) and Gary Wells (Wells & Olson, 2003), among others, has been recognized by the U.S. Attorney General's office in drawing up national guidelines for the collection of accurate and unbiased eyewitness identification (see Malpass & Devine, 1981; Stebley, 1997).

The Stanford Prison Experiment has become a classic demonstration of the power of social situational forces to negatively impact the behavior of normal, healthy participants who began to act in pathological or evil ways in a matter of a few days (Zimbardo, Haney, Banks, & Jaffe, 1973). It added a new awareness of institutional power to the authority power of Stanley Milgram's (1974) blind obedience studies (see Blass, 1999; Zimbardo, Maslach, & Haney, 1999). The lessons of this research have gone well beyond the classroom. In part as a consequence of my testimony before a Senate judiciary committee on crime and prisons (Zimbardo, 1974), its committee chair, Senator Birch Bayh, prepared a new law for federal prisons requiring juveniles in pretrial detention to be housed separately from adult inmates (to prevent their being abused). Our participants were juveniles in the pretrial detention facility of the Stanford jail. A video documentary of the study, "Quiet Rage: The Stanford Prison Experiment," has been used extensively by many agencies within the civilian and military criminal justice system as well as in shelters for abused women. I recently discovered that it is even used to educate role-playing military interrogators in the Navy SEAR (survival, evasion, and resistance) program about the dangers of abusing their power against others role-playing pretend spies and terrorists (Annapolis Naval College psychology staff, personal communication, September 18, 2003). The Web site for the Stanford Prison Experiment gets more than 500 visitors daily and has had more than 13 million unique page views in the past four years (www.prisonexp.org). Those surprising figures should be telling us that we must focus more effort on utilizing the power of the Web as a major new medium for disseminating psychology's messages directly to a worldwide audience.

Education

Among the many examples of psychology at work in the field of education, two of my favorites naturally have a social psychological twist. Elliot Aronson and his research team in Austin, Texas, dealt with the negative consequences of desegregated schools by creating "jigsaw classrooms." Prejudice against minority children was rampant, those children were not performing well, and elementary school classes were marked by high degrees of tension. But when all students were taught to share a set of materials in small learning teams where each child has one set of information indispensable to the rest of the team, and on which tests and grades depend, remarkable things happened. All kids started to listen to the other kids, especially minority kids who they used to ignore or disparage, because such attention and cooperation is essential to getting a good grade. Not only did the self-esteem of the minority children escalate, but so did their academic performance, as prejudice and discrimination went down. The techniques of the jigsaw classroom are inexpensive for teachers to learn and to operationalize, so it is no wonder that Aronson's simple concept is now being incorporated into the curricula of hundreds of schools in many states, with similarly impressive results (Aronson, 1990; Aronson, Blaney, Stephan, Sikes, & Snapp, 1978; Aronson & Gonzalez, 1988; Aronson & Patnoe, 1997).

Teaching young children interpersonal cognitive problem solving skills, known as ICPS, reduces physical and verbal aggression, increases coping with frustrations, and promotes positive peer relationships. This research program developed by Myrna Shure and George Spivak (1982) over the past several decades is a major violence prevention approach being applied in schools and family agencies in programs called "Raising a Thinking Child" and by the U.S. Department of Education's "I Can Problem Solve" program.

Health

Environmental health is threatened by a host of toxic substances, such as lead, mercury, solvents, and pesticides. Experimental psychologists, behavioral analysts, and psychometricians have helped create the field of behavioral toxicology that recognizes the nervous system as the target for many toxins, with defects in behavior and mental processes as the symptomatic consequences. Pioneering work by psychologist Bernard Weiss (1992, 1999) and others has had a significant impact on writing behavioral tests into federal legislation, thereby better regulating the use of a wide range of neurotoxins in our environment. That research documents the vulnerability of children's developing brains to chemicals in the environment.

Among the many negative consequences of America's involvement in the Vietnam War was the explosion of the phenomenon of posttraumatic stress disorder (PTSD). Many veterans were experiencing this debilitating disorder that was uncovered during their psychotherapy treatments. The more we discovered about this delayed, persistent, intense stress reaction to violence and trauma, the more we realized that veterans of earlier wars had also experienced PTSD, but it was unlabeled. That was also the case with many civilian victims of trauma, among them rape victims and those who had experienced child abuse. PTSD has become a well-recognized and publicly acknowledged phenomenon today because it was one of the mental health consequences of the monumental trauma from the terrorist attacks on September 11, 2001, in New York City and Washington, DC. Credit for the early recognition, identification, measurement, and treatment of PTSD goes to the programs of research funded by the Veteran's Administration, which was pioneered by the research team of clinical psychologist Terry Keane (Keane, Malloy, & Fairbank, 1984; Weathers, Keane, & Davidson, 2001).

The Magic of Touch

One of the consequences of a host of amazing medical advances is saving the lives of many premature infants who would have died even just a decade ago. With modern intensive care, preemies weighing only a few pounds now survive, but the essential hospital costs are staggering, up to $10,000 a day for weeks or months! One simple solution for sending them home sooner depends on accelerating their growth by means of touch therapy. Psychologist Field extended earlier research she had done with biologist Saul Shanberg (Field, 1998; Field & Schanberg, 1990; Field et al., 1986) on massaging infant rat pups that were motherless. Just as the infant rats rapidly grew in response to that vigorous touch, so did the human preemies. Massaging them several times a day for only 15 minutes was sufficient to stimulate growth hormones. On average, such massaged infants are able to go home six days sooner than comparison preemies treated in the conventional way. Given 470,000 premature infants are born each year in the United States alone, it is evident that billions of dollars in health care costs could be saved if this simple, inexpensive treatment was made standard procedure in more hospital intensive care units (see also Meltz, 2000).

To establish the societal value of any intervention designed to save lives or enhance health and well-being, one must systematically evaluate its cost-effectiveness. That means establishing a ratio of the benefits compared with various cost estimates of putting the intervention into operation and sustaining it over time. Such a ratio was developed for dollar costs per year of life saved and applied to more than 500 life-saving interventions (Tengs et al., 1995). Across all of these interventions, the median cost was $42,000 per year of life saved. Although some programs save more resources than they cost, others cost millions of dollars for each year of life they save and thus become of questionable social value. Using this standard measure, we discover that new neonatal intensive care for low-birth-weight infants (preemies) costs a whooping $270,000 for each year of their lives saved. By that yardstick, the inexpensive touch therapy intervention would dramatically reduce that cost-effectiveness ratio.

The puzzling issue then is why such a simple procedure is not now standard operating procedure in every such intensive care unit in the nation or the world? One goal of our compendium development team is also to investigate why some potentially useful interventions have not been applied in the venues where they could make a significant difference. For instance, social psychologists have shown convincingly that elderly patients in a home for the aged who were given a sense of control and responsibility over even minor events became healthier and lived significantly longer than comparison patients (Langer & Rodin, 1976; Rodin & Langer, 1977). Amazingly, this simple, powerful intervention has not ever been utilized—even in the institution where the research was conducted.

Undoing Dyslexia via Video Games

Treatment for dyslexia by speech therapists and counselors is a slow, long, expensive, and frustrating experience for professionals, parents, and children. Cognitive neuroscientist, Paula Tallal, is using new functional magnetic resonance imaging techniques to identify the source of reading dyslexia in brain regions that do not adequately process fast appearing sound-sight phonemic combinations. She then worked with a computer-programming agency to develop special video games that systematically shape these children's ever-faster responses to various sights and sounds in the games. With this new technology, children treat themselves in an atmosphere of entertainment and adventure, rely only on intrinsic motivation of game playing, get personalized feedback, and need minimal supervision by highly skilled professionals.

The special computerized video game is called "Fast For-Word." It provides intensive, highly individualized adaptive training across a large number of cognitive, linguistic, and reading skills that are vital for academic success. By adapting trial by trial to each child's performance, progress in aural and written language skills of children with dyslexia is reduced to but a few weeks from what had been typically years of intervention efforts. Approximately 375,000 individuals have completed such training across 2,200 public schools nationwide, and over 2,000 private practice professionals use Fast ForWord programs in their clinics (for more information, visit www.scientificlearning.com and www.brainconnection.com).

This sensitive application of psychological knowledge and new methods blended with high technology has resulted in enhanced quality of life for these children as well as their families and teachers, not to mention much money and resources saved (see Holly Fitch & Tallal, 2003; Tallal & Benasich, 2002; Tallal, Galaburda, Llinas, & Von Euler, 1993).

An Idealized Example of Psychology Applied Globally

The use of intrinsically interesting media, such as video games and Tele-Health dynamic systems, enables adults as well as children to play central roles in individualized health-management programs. The power of the media also has been extended to television as a far-reaching medium to convey vital persuasive messages about behavior changes that are essential to cope with many of the social, economic, political, and health problems facing individuals around the globe. Can psychology contribute to effectively dealing with the population explosion in many countries, increase the status and education of women, and minimize or prevent AIDS? A tall order, for sure. However, it is now happening through a remarkable collaboration of a wise TV producer, a brilliant psychologist, and an international agency that distributes their unusual messages worldwide (Bandura, 2002; Smith, 2002).

Promoting Family Planning

The explosion in population around the world is one of our most urgent global problems. Ecologically sustainable development and growth is being challenged by a variety of entwined phenomena, such as high fertility rates in many countries coupled with suboptimal birth rates in others, dramatically increased longevity in some nations along with the spread of deadly communicable diseases in others. One means of population control in overpopulated countries involves women and men actively engaged in their own family planning. However, the question is how to do so effectively and efficiently because most previous efforts have met with minimal success?

A TV producer in Mexico, Miguel Sabido, created soap operas that were serialized daily dramas, with prosocial messages about practicing family planning and also others that promote literacy and education of women. Woven into the narrative of his commercial dramas were elements taken from Albert Bandura's sociocognitive theory of the importance of social models in shaping desired behaviors (Bandura, 1965, 1977, 1986). In many Spanish-speaking countries, most family members watch soap operas fervently each day as their plots unfold over many weeks or months. Viewers identify with attractive, desirable models and dis-identify with those whose actions seem repulsive or create unwanted problems for the "good" guys. In some scenarios, there are also actors who represent "transitional models," starting off engaging in high-risk or undesirable behaviors but then changing in socially appropriate directions. After some programs, there is informational or community support for the cause being projected, by celebrities, government officials, or members of the clergy. This secondary influence path for behavior change adds the key element of making connections to the viewers' personal social networks and community settings in addition to the direct path from the media message to desired changes in target behaviors.

Does it really work? After watching the Mexican programs promoting family planning, many women enrolled in family planning clinics. The 32% increase of woman starting to use this service was similar to the increase in contraceptive users. This was true even though there was never an explicit message about contraception for family planning (in deference to the negative position on this birth control issue by the Catholic Church). Another key result was that the greater the level of media exposure to these family-oriented TV soap operas, the greater was the percentage of women using contraceptives and also discussing family planning with spouses "many times" (Bandura, 2002).

Preventing the Spread of AIDS

These dramas were shown in one region of Tanzania, Africa, and their effects compared with a control region where TV viewers were not exposed to the dramas (later on they got to see the same soap operas). One of the many prosocial effects was an increase in new family planning adopters following the viewing of these dramatic serials compared with no change in the control region. Seventeen segments were included in dramas in Tanzania to prevent the spread of the AIDS virus, a special problem among truck drivers who have unprotected sex with hundreds of prostitutes working at truck stop hubs. Actors portrayed positive models who adopt safe sex practices or negative ones who do not—and then they die of AIDS! Condom distribution soared following viewing this series, whereas it remained low in the control, no soap opera region. Along with this critical change in behavior were also reports of reduced number of sexual partners, more talk about HIV infection, and changed beliefs in personal risk of HIV infection from unprotected sex. Such attitudinal and behavioral changes are vital to slowing the spread of AIDS, which is estimated to make orphans of up to 25 million children worldwide in the next half dozen years (Naik, 2002; The Straits Times, 2002).

Female Literacy

Education of women is one of the most powerful prophylaxes for limiting population growth, so these soap opera programs in many countries show stories that endorse women continuing with their education as one way of liberating young women from male and matriarchal dominance. In one village in India, there was an immediate 30% increase in women going to school after the airing of these soap operas.

A Potent Blending of Talents, Wisdom, and Resources for Social Good

So here we have the unique case of a wise person in the media borrowing ideas from a psychologist and then extending the scope of influence by pairing up with a nonprofit agency, Population Communications International (PCI) to disseminate these dramas worldwide. PCI's "mission is to work creatively with the media and other organizations to motivate individuals and communities to make choices that influence population trends encouraging development and environmental protection" (PCI, 2002). PCI's efforts at social diffusion span more than 17 countries worldwide with radio and TV serial dramas, comic books, and videos for classroom use. Finally, there is a fourth essential component: systematic evaluation of outcomes by an independent organization of all of these entertainment-educational change programs (see www.population.org).

It is evident that these serial dramatizations use the power of narrative story telling over an extended time, which the public views voluntarily, to motivate specific behavior change in directions guided by the information conveyed in the drama, which in turn has its origins in sound psychological theory and research. What also becomes evident is that when psychologists want to give psychology away to the public, we need to collaborate with those who understand best *how* to reach the public, namely those intimately involved with the mass media. They are our gatekeepers to the audiences we want to reach and influence. We have to find ways of inviting and intriguing media with the utility of psychological knowledge for crafting entertaining stories that can make a significant difference in the quality of lives of individuals and society.

Accentuating Psychology's Positive Messages

The collaboration between psychologist Albert Bandura, media master Miguel Sabido, and the resourcefulness of the PCI agency is an ideal model for us to emulate and extend in spreading more of our positive messages. Among those new messages are the two exciting directions that psychology can be expected to take in the next decade. The emergence of Martin Seligman's (2002) revolutionary "Positive Psychology" enterprise is creating a new vital force for recognizing and enriching the talents, strengths, and virtues of even ordinary people (see Diener, 2000; Myers, 2002; Snyder & Lopez, 2002). It is shifting attention away from deficits, disabilities, and disorders toward a focus on what is special about human nature like our resilience in the face of trauma, our joys, our sense of wonder and curiosity, and our capacity for goodness and love.

The fertile field of "behavioral economics" integrates psychology with economics and neuroscience to understand the economically irrational human element in judgments under uncertainty (see Kahneman & Tversky, 1979; Simon, 1955;

Tversky & Kahneman, 1974, 1986). We can anticipate that Daniel Kahneman's winning the 2003 Nobel Prize in economics has made him a role model for the next generation of professional psychologists to emulate and to enter this exciting domain of relevant inquiry.

In conclusion, I repeat the questions that got me to this point and the simple answer that I now feel is justified—and I hope readers of this article agree with its positive bias.

Does psychology matter? Can psychological research, theory, methods, and practice make a significant difference in the lives of individuals, communities, and nations? Do we psychologists have a legacy of which we can be proud? Can we do more and better research that has significant applicable effects in the real world? Are we ready now "to give psychology away to the public" in useful, accessible ways? And finally, can we learn how better to collaborate with the media, with technology experts, with community leaders, and with other medical and behavioral scientists for psychology to make an even more significant difference in the coming decade?

My final answer is simply YES, YES indeed! May the positive forces of psychology be with you, and with our society.

Editor's note. Philip G. Zimbardo was president of APA in 2002. This article is based on his presidential address, delivered in Toronto, Canada, at APA's 111th Annual Convention on August 9, 2003. Award addresses and other archival materials, including presidential addresses, are peer reviewed but have a higher chance of publication than do unsolicited submissions. Presidential addresses are expected to be expressions of the authors' reflections on the field and on their terms as president. Both this address and that of Robert J. Sternberg, the 2003 APA president, were presented at this convention to catch up on the year lag that had developed in the last decade of giving presidential addresses.

Author's note. Correspondence concerning this article should be addressed to Philip G. Zimbardo, Department of Psychology, Stanford University Building 430, Mail Code 380, Stanford, CA 94305. E-mail: zim@stanford.edu

NOTES

1. Recognizing the importance of bringing psychology's understanding that violence is a learned behavior to the public, APA has joined with the National Association for the Education of Young Children and the Advertising Council to create a national multimedia public service advertising campaign designed to remind adults of the role they play in teaching children to use or avoid violence and then empower these adults to model and teach the right lessons. The campaign, first launched in 2000, has reached over 50 million households. At the community level, the campaign includes collaborations with local groups in a train-the-trainer model to bring early childhood violence prevention awareness and know-how to parents, teachers, and other caregivers.

2. The task force selected to identify and evaluate the research, theory, and methodology in psychology that qualified for inclusion in the Psychology Matters compendium has been ably cochaired by David Myers and Robert Bjork. Other members have included Alan Boneau. Gordon Bower, Nancy Eisenberg, Sam Glucksberg, Philip Kendall, Kevin Murphy, Scott Pious, Peter Salovey, Alana Conner-Snibbe, Beth Sulzer-Azaroff, Chris Wickens, and Alice Young. They have been assisted by the addition of Brett Pelham and David Partenheimer. Rhea Farberman and her staff in APA's Office of Public Communications have played a vital role in the development and continuing evolution of this project. The staff of the Science Directorate aided in the early development of the survey that was circulated to initiate electronic input of candidate items from APA constituent groups.

REFERENCES

Ader, R., & Cohen, N. (1993). Psychoneuroimmunology: Conditioning and stress. *Annual Review of Psychology, 44,* 53–85.

Alien, M. J. (1970). *Vision and highway safety.* Philadelphia: Chilton.

Allport, G. (1954). *The nature of prejudice.* Reading, MA: Addison-Wesley.

American Academy of Pediatrics, Committee on Psychosocial Aspect of Child and Family Health. (1998). Guidance for effective discipline. *Pediatrics, 101,* 723–728.

Aronson, E. (1990). Applying social psychology to desegregation and energy conservation. *Personality and Social Psychology Bulletin, 16,* 118–132.

Aronson, E., Blaney, N., Stephan, C., Sikes, J.. & Snapp, M. (1978). *The jigsaw classroom.* Beverly Hills, CA: Sage.

Aronson, E., & Gonzalez, A. (1988). Desegregation jigsaw, and the Mexican-American experience. In P. A. Katz & D. Taylor (Eds.), *Eliminating racism: Profiles in controversy* (pp. 301–314). New York: Plenum Press.

Aronson, E., & Patnoe, S. (1997). *The jigsaw classroom: Building cooperation in the classroom* (2nd ed.). New York: Addison Wesley Longman.

Axelrod, S., & Apsche, H. (1983). *Effects of punishment on human behavior.* New York: Academic Press.

Baltes, P. B., & Staudinger, U. M. (2000). Wisdom: A metaheuristic (pragmatic) to orchestrate mind and virtue toward excellence. *American Psychologist, 55,* 122–136.

Bandura, A. (1965). Influence of models' reinforcement contingencies on the acquisition of imitated responses. *Journal of Personality and Social Psychology. 1,* 589–595.

Bandura, A. (1977). *Social learning theory.* Englewood Cliffs, NJ: Prentice Hall.

Bandura, A. (1986). *Social foundations of thought and action: A social cognitive theory.* Englewood Cliffs, NJ: Prentice Hall.

Bandura, A. (2002). Environmental sustainability by sociocognitive deceleration of population growth. In P. Schmuck & W. Schultz (Eds.), *The psychology of sustainable development* (pp. 209–238). Dordrecht, the Netherlands: Kluwer.

Baumrind, D. (1973). The development of instrumental competence through socialization. In A. Pick (Ed.), *Minnesota Symposium on Child Development* (Vol. 6, pp. 3–46). Minneapolis: University of Minnesota Press.

Beck, A. T. (1976). *Cognitive therapy and emotional disorders.* New York: International Universities Press.

Bee, H. (1994). *Lifespan development.* New York: HarperCollins.

Binet, A. (1911). *Les idé es modernes sur les enfants* [Modern ideas about children]. Paris: Flammarion.

Binet, A., & Simon. T. (1915). *A method of measuring the development of intelligence of young children.* Chicago: Chicago Medical Books.

Blass, T. (Ed.). (1999). *Obedience to authority: Current perspectives on the Milgram Paradigm* (pp. 193–237). Mahwah, NJ: Erlbaum.

Campbell. D. T. (1969). Reforms as experiments. *American Psychologist, 24,* 409–429.

Cantril, A. H. (1991). *The opinion connection: Polling, politics, and the press.* Washington, DC: CQ Press.

Clark, K. B., & Clark, M. K. (1939a). The development of consciousness of self and the emergence of racial identification in negro preschool children. *Journal of Social Psychology, 10,* 591–599.

Clark, K. B., & Clark, M. K. (1939b). Segregation as a factor in the racial identification of negro preschool children: A preliminary report. *Journal of Experimental Education, 8,* 161–163.

Clark, K. B., & Clark, M. K. (1940). Skin color as a factor in racial identification of negro preschool children. *The Journal of Social Psychology, II,* 159–169.

Clark, K. B., & Clark, M. K. (1950). Emotional factors in racial identification and preference in negro children. *Journal of Negro Education, 19,* 341–350.

Coe, C. L. (1999). Psychosocial factors and psychoneuroimmunology within a lifespan perspective. In D. P. Keating & C. Hertzman (Eds.), *Developmental health and the wealth of nations: Social, biological, and educational dynamics* (pp. 201–219). New York: Guilford Press.

Cohen, S., & Herbert, T. B. (1996). Health psychology: Psychological factors and physical disease from the perspective of human psychoneuroimmunology. *Annual Review of Psychology, 47,* 113—142.

Cohen, S., & Syme, S. L. (Eds.). (1985). *Social support and health.* Orlando. FL: Academic Press.

Collins, W. A., Maccoby, E. E., Steinberg, L., Hetherington, E. M., & Bornstein, M. H. (2000). Contemporary research on parenting: The case for nature and nurture. *American Psychologist, 55,* 218–232.

Cronbach, L. J. (1975). Five decades of public controversy over mental testing. *American Psychologist, 30,* 1–14.

Darling, N., & Steinberg, L. (1993). Parenting style as context: An integrative model. *Psychological Bulletin, 113,* 487–496.

Diener, E. (2000). Subjective well-being: The science of happiness and a proposal for a national index. *American Psychologist, 55,* 34–43.

Discovering psychology [Television series]. (1990; updated 2001). Boston: WGBH, with the American Psychological Association. (Funded and distributed by the Annenberg CPB Foundation, Washington, DC)

Druckman. D., & Bjork, R. A. (1991). *In the mind's eye: Enhancing human performance.* Washington, DC: National Academy Press.

DuBois, P. H. (1970). *A history of psychological testing.* Boston: Allyn & Bacon.

Erikson, E. H. (1963). *Childhood and society* (2nd ed.). New York: Norton.

Field, T. (1998). Massage therapy effects. *American Psychologist, 53,* 1270–1281.

Field, T., & Schanberg, S. M. (1990). Massage alters growth and catecholamine production in preterm newborns. In N. Gunzenhauser (Ed.), *Advances in touch* (pp. 96–104). Skillman, NJ: Johnson & Johnson.

Field, T., Schanberg, S. M., Scafidi, F., Bauer, C. R., Vega-Lahr, N., Garcia, R., et al. (1986). Tactile/kinesthetic stimulation effects on preform neonates. *Pediatrics, 77,* 654–658.

Freud, S. (1923). *Introductory lectures on psycho-analysis* (J. Riviera, Trans.). London: Allen & Unwin. (Original work published 1896)

Freud, S. (1965). *The interpretation of dreams.* New York: Avon. (Original work published 1900)

Garvey, P. M., Pietrucha, M. T., & Meeker, D. (1997). Effects of font and capitalization on legibility of guide signs. *Transportation Research Record No. 1605,* 73–79.

Geller, E. S. (2001). *The psychology of safety handbook.* Boca Raton, FL: CRC Press.

Geller, E. S. (2003). Behavior-based safety in industry: Realizing the large-scale potential of behavior analysis to promote human welfare. *Applied & Preventive Psychology, 10,* 87–105.

Gerrig, R., & Zimbardo, P. G. (2004). *Psychology and life* (17th ed.). Boston: Allyn & Bacon.

Green, C. D., Shore, M., & Teo, T. (2001). *The transformation of psychology: Influences of 19th century philosophy, technology, and natural science.* Washington, DC: American Psychological Association.

Hart, S. N. (1991). From property to person status: Historical perspective on children's rights. *American Psychologist, 46,* 53–59.

Hollon, S. D., Thase, M. E., & Markowitz, J. C. (2002). Treatment and prevention of depression. *Psychological Science in the Public Interest, 3,* 39–77.

Holly Fitch, R., & Tallal, P. (2003). Neural mechanisms of language-based learning impairments: Insights from human populations and animal models. *Behavior and Cognitive Neuroscience Reviews, 2,* 155–178.

Horowitz, R. M. (1984). Children's rights: A look backward and a glance ahead. In R. M. Horowitz & J. B. Lazar (Eds.), *Legal rights of children* (pp. 1–9). New York: McGraw-Hill.

Hovland, C. I., Janis, I. L., & Kelley, H. H. (1953). *Communication and persuasion.* New Haven, CT: Yale University Press.

Hovland, C. I., Lumsdaine, A. A., & Sheffield, F. D. (1949). *Experiments on mass communication.* Princeton, NJ: Princeton University Press.

Janis, I. L. (1958). *Psychological stress: Psychoanalytical and behavioral studies of surgical patients.* New York: Wiley.

Jung, C. G. (1959). The concept of the collective unconscious. In *The archetypes and the collective unconscious, collected works* (Vol. 9, Part 1, pp. 54–74). Princeton, NJ: Princeton University Press. (Original work published 1936)

Kahneman, D.. & Tversky, A. (1979). Prospect theory: An analysis of decision under risk. *Econometrica, 47,* 263–291.

Kazdin, A. E. (1994). *Behavior modification in applied settings* (5th ed.). Pacific Grove, CA: Brooks/Cole.

Keane, T. M., Malloy, P. F., & Fairbank, J. A. (1984). Empirical development of an MMPI subscale for the assessment of PTSD. *Journal of Consulting and Clinical Psychology, 52,* 138–140.

Langer, E. F., & Rodin, J. (1976). The effects of choice and enhanced personal responsibility for the aged: A field experiment in an institutionalized setting. *Journal of Personality and Social Psychology, 34,* 191–198.

Lazarus, R. S. (1993). From psychological stress to the emotions: A history of changing outlooks. *Annual Review of Psychology, 44,* 1–21.

Lazarus, R. S., & Folkman, S. (1984). *Stress, appraisal, and coping.* New York: Springer.

Lewin, K. (1947a). Frontiers in group dynamics: Concept, method and reality in social science; social equilibria and social change. *Human Relations, 1,* 5–41.

Lewin, K. (1947b). Frontiers in group dynamics: II. Channels of group life; social planning and action research. *Human Relations, 1,* 143–153.

Lewin, K. (1948). *Resolving social conflicts.* New York: Harper.

Loftus, E. F. (1975). Leading questions and the eyewitness report. *Cognitive Psychology, 7,* 560–572.

Loftus, E. F. (1979). Eyewitness testimony. Cambridge, MA: Harvard University Press. Loftus, E. F. (1992). When a lie becomes memory's truth: Memory distortion after exposure to misinformation. *Current Directions in Psychological Science, 1,* 121–123.

Loomis, J. M., Klatsky, R. L., & Golledge, R. G. (2001). Navigating without vision: Basic and applied research. *Optometry and Vision Science, 78,* 282–289.

Maas, J. (1998). *Power sleep: The revolutionary program that prepares your mind for peak performance.* New York: Villard.

Maccoby, E. E. (1980). *Social development: Psychological growth and the parent-child relationship.* San Diego, CA: Harcourt Brace Jovanovich.

Maccoby, E. E. (1992). The role of parents in the socialization of children: An historical overview. *Developmental Psychology, 28,* 1006–1017.

Maccoby, E. E. (2000). Parenting and its effects on children: On reading and misreading behavior genetics. *Annual Review of Psychology, 51,* 1–27.

Malpass, R. S., & Devine, P. G. (1981). Eyewitness identification: Lineup instructions and the absence of the offender. *Journal of Applied Psychology, 66*, 482–489.

Maslach, C. (1982). *Burnout: The cost of caring.* Englewood Cliffs, NJ: Prentice Hall.

McCoy, E. (1988). Childhood through the ages. In K. Finsterbush (Ed.), *Sociology 88/89* (pp. 44–47). Guilford, CT: Duskin.

Meltz, B. F. (2000, November 2). Do you touch your baby enough? *Boston Globe*, p. H1.

Milgram, S. (1974). *Obedience to authority.* New York: Harper & Row.

Miller, G. (1969). Psychology as a means of promoting human welfare. *American Psychologist, 24*, 1063–1075.

Miller, N. E. (1978). Biofeedback and visceral learning. *Annual Review of Psychology, 29*, 373–404.

Miller, N. E. (1985). The value of behavioral research on animals. *American Psychologist, 40*, 423–440.

Miller, N. E. (1992). Introducing and teaching much-needed understanding of the scientific process. *American Psychologist, 47*, 848–850.

Myers, D. G. (1993). *The pursuit of happiness.* New York: Avon.

Myers, D. G. (2002). *Intuition: Its powers and perils.* New Haven, CT: Yale University Press.

Naik, G. (2002, July 5). Uganda AIDS study suggests education stems spread of HIV. *Wall Street Journal*, p. A14.

New York State. (1999). *Clinical practice guidelines.* New York: Department of Health, Early Intervention Program, Autism.

Pappas. A. M. (1983). Introduction. In A. M. Pappas (Ed.), *Law and the status of the child* (pp. xxvii–lv). New York: United Nations Institute for Training and Research.

Pavlov, I. P. (1902). *The work of the digestive glands* (W. H. Thompson, Trans.) London: Griffin. (Original work published in 1897)

Pavlov, I. P. (1927). *Conditioned reflexes* (G. V. Anrep, Trans.). London: Oxford University Press. (Original work published 1897)

Pettigrew, T. F. (1997). Generalized intergroup contact effects on prejudice. *Personality and Social Psychology Bulletin, 23*, 173–185.

Piaget, J. (1954). *The construction of reality in the child.* New York: Basic Books.

Pinker, S. (1994). *The language instinct: How the mind creates language.* New York: Morrow.

Plomin, R., & McClearn, G. E. (1993). *Nature, nurture, and psychology.* Washington, DC: American Psychological Association.

Population Communications International. (2002). *15th anniversary: Keeping pace with change.* New York: Author.

Rodin, J., & Langer, E. F. (1977). Long-term effects of a control-relevant intervention with the institutionalized aged. *Journal of Personality and Social Psychology. 35*, 897–902.

Ruch, F. L., & Zimbardo, P. G. (1971). *Psychology and life* (8th ed.). Glenview, IL: Scott, Foresman.

Sarason, S. B. (1974). *The psychological sense of community: Prospects for a community psychology.* Oxford, England: Jossey-Bass.

Scarr, S. (1998). American child care today. *American Psychologist, 53*, 95–108.

Seligman, M. (2002). *Authentic happiness: Using the new positive psychology to realize your potential for lasting fulfillment.* New York: Free Press.

Shure, M. B., & Spivak, G. (1982). Interpersonal problem solving in children: A cognitive approach to prevention. *American Journal of Community Psychology, 10*, 341–356.

Simon, H. (1955). A behavioral model of rational choice. *Quarterly Journal of Economics, 69*, 99–118.

Skinner, B. F. (1938). *The behavior of organisms: An experimental analysis.* New York: Appleton-Century.

Skinner, B. F. (1948). *Walden two.* New York: Macmillan.

Skinner, B. F. (1966). What is the experimental analysis of behavior? *Journal of the Experimental Analysis of Behavior, 9*, 213–218.

Skinner, B, F. (1974). *About behaviorism.* New York: Knopf.

Smith, D. (2002). The theory heard "round the world." *Monitor on Psychology, 33*, 30–32.

Snyder, C. R., & Lopez, S. J. (2002). *Handbook of positive psychology.* New York: Oxford University Press.

Solomon, S. S., & King, J. G. (1985). Influence of color on fire vehicle accidents. *Journal of Safety Research, 26*, 47.

Stebley, N. M. (1997). Social influence in eyewitness recall: A meta-analytic review of line-up instruction effects. *Law and Human Behavior, 21*, 283–298.

Sternberg, R. J. (Ed.). (2000). *Handbook of intelligence.* Cambridge, England: Cambridge University Press.

The Straits Times. (2002, July 12). *The HIV orphan mega-crises.* Hong Kong: 14th International AIDS Conference.

Straus, M. A., & Kantor, G. K. (1994). Corporal punishment of adolescents by parents: A risk factor in the epidemiology of depression, suicide, alcohol abuse, child abuse, and wife beating. *Adolescence, 29*, 543–561.

Sulzer-Azaroff, B., & Austin, J. (2000, July). Does BBS work? Behavior-based safety and injury reduction: A survey of the evidence. *Professional Safety*, 19–24.

Swazey, J. P. (1974). *Chlorpromazine in psychiatry: A study of therapeutic innovation.* Cambridge, MA: MIT Press.

Tallal, P., & Benasich, A. A. (2002). Developmental language learning impairments. *Development and Psychopathology, 14*, 559–579.

Tallal, P., Galaburda, A. M., Llinas, R. R., & Von Euler, C. (Eds.). (1993). *Temporal information processing in the nervous system: Special reference to dyslexia and dysphasia* (Vol. 682). New York: New York Academy of Sciences

Taylor, S. E., & Clark, L. F. (1986). Does information improve adjustments to noxious events? In M. J. Saks & L. Saxe (Eds.), *Advances in applied social psychology* (Vol. 3, pp. 1–28). Hillsdale, NJ: Erlbaum.

Tengs, T, O., Adams, M. E., Pliskin, J. S., Safan, D. G., Siegel, J. E., Weinstein, M. C., & Graham, J. D, (1995). Five-hundred life-saving interventions and their cost effectiveness. *Risk Analysis, 15*, 369–390.

Tversky, A., & Kahneman, D. (1974). Judgment under uncertainty: Heuristics and biases. *Science, 185*, 1124–1131.

Tversky, A., & Kahneman, D. (1986). The framing of decisions and the psychology of choice. *Science, 211*, 453–458.

Weathers, F. W., Keane, T. M., & Davidson, J. R. T. (2001). Clinicians' administered PTSD scale: A review of the first ten years of research. *Depression & Anxiety, 13*, 132–156.

Weiss, B. (1992). Behavioral toxicology: A new agenda for assessing the risks of environmental pollution. In J. Grabowski & G. VandenBos (Eds.), *Psychopharmacology: Basic mechanisms and applied interventions. Master lectures in psychology* (pp. 167–207). Washington, DC: American Psychological Association.

Weiss, B. (1999, May). *The vulnerability of the developing brain to chemicals in the environment.* Paper presented at the New York Academy of Medicine conference on Environmental Toxins and Neurological Disorders, New York.

Wells, G. L., & Olson, E. A. (2003). Eyewitness testimony. *Annual Review of Psychology, 54*, 277–295.

Wolfe, M. M., Risely, T. R., & Mees, H. L. (1965). Application of operant conditioning procedures to behavior problems of an autistic child. *Research and Therapy, 1*, 302–312.

Wolpe, J. (1958). *Psychotherapy by reciprocal inhibition.* Stanford, CA: Stanford University Press.

Zimbardo, P. G. (1974). *The detention and jailing of juveniles* (pp. 141–161) [Hearings before U. S. Senate Committee to Investigate Juvenile Delinquency, September 10, 11, 17, 1973], Washington, DC: U.S. Government Printing Office.

Zimbardo, P. G. (1975). On transforming experimental research into advocacy for social change. In M. Deulsch & H. Hornstein (Eds.), *Applying social psychology: Implications for research, practice and training* (pp. 33–66). Hillsdale, NJ: Erlbaum.

Zimbardo, P. G. (1977). *Shyness: What it is, what to do about it.* Reading, MA: Addison-Wesley.

Zimbardo, P. G. (1992). *Psychology and life* (13th ed.). New York: HarperCollins.

Zimbardo, P. G., Haney, C., Banks, W. C., & Jaffe, D. (1973, April 8). The mind is a formidable jailer: A Pirandellian prison. *The New York Times Magazine,* Section 6, pp. 38–46.

Zimbardo, P. G., Maslach, C., & Haney, C. (1999). Reflections on the Stanford prison experiment: Genesis, transformations, consequences. In T. Blass (Ed.), *Obedience to authority: Current perspectives on the Milgram Paradigm* (pp. 193–237). Mahwah, NJ: Erlbaum.

Zimbardo, P. G., Weber, A. L., & Johnson, R. L. (2002). *Psychology: Core concepts* (4th ed.). Boston, MA: Allyn & Bacon.

THINKING ABOUT SCIENCE

Causes and Correlations

MASSIMO PIGLIUCCI

One of the most common fallacies committed by believers in the paranormal is what in philosophy is known by the Latin name of *post hoc, ergo propter hoc*, which loosely translates to "after this, therefore because of this." Surely you have heard some version of it: "I dreamed of my brother the other night, and the following morning he called me, though he rarely does." The implication here is that there is some causal connection between the dream and the phone call, that one happened because of the other. We all know what is wrong with this argument: a correlation between two events does not constitute good enough evidence of a causal connection between them. In the case of the dream as precognition, we probably dream of our relatives often enough, and most often the dream is not followed by their call; yet, because of an innate tendency of the human brain to remember hits and forget misses, we pay attention to the exceptions and charge them with special meaning.

But the good skeptic could go further and ask herself what exactly we mean by causation to begin with. If a correlation is not the hallmark of a causal relationship, what is? The modern study of causation started with the Italian physicist Galileo Galilei, who viewed causes as a set of necessary and sufficient conditions for a given effect. According to Galileo, the dream can be considered a cause of

the call only if every time the subject dreams of his brother, the following morning the brother actually does call. The problem with this idea is that it is too restrictive: many phenomena have multiple causes, a subset of which may be sufficient to generate the effect. The brother could call for other reasons than the dream, notwithstanding a true causal connection between dreaming and calling. Or, the dream may be causing the brother to have the impulse to call, but he can't do it because he is at a vacation spot where there are no phones in sight (as hard as this may seem to believe).

Scottish skeptic philosopher David Hume made the next important contribution to our understanding of causality, one that many philosophers (and a few scientists) are still grappling with. Hume argued that we never actually have any evidence that causal connections are real, we only have perceptions of the likely association between what we call a cause and an effect. Here Hume was being a good empiricist, something that a skeptic ought to appreciate. For him, talk of "causes" sounded as strange as talking of action at a distance, which in pre-Newtonian times was an exercise for mystics, not scientists. So Hume decided to settle on a very pragmatic concept of causality. He suggested that we are justified in talking about causes and effects if three conditions hold: 1) the first event (say, the dream) precedes the second one

(say, your brother's call); 2) the two events are contiguous in time, i.e., your brother called the morning after the dream, not a month or a year later; 3) there is a constant conjunction between the two events, i.e., every time you dream of your brother, he will call. As the reader will have noticed, however, the latter clause is very similar to Galileo's idea of necessary and sufficient condition, and will not actually help the scientist in real situations.

John Stuart Mill, well known as a utilitarian, proposed a concept of causation that is at the basis of much modern experimental science and, hence, of skeptical investigations. Mill argued that causality simply cannot be demonstrated without experimentation. Essentially, Mill said that in order to establish a causal connection between two phenomena, we have to be able to do experiments that allow us to manipulate the conditions so that only one factor at a time is allowed to change. A series of these experiments will eventually pinpoint the cause(s) of certain effects.

While Mill's idea has been of fundamental importance for modern science, the problem with it is that it imposes on the investigators logistic requirements that are often too restrictive. What if it is not possible to control all variables but one during an inquiry? Carefully controlled manipulative experiments are possible only in certain fields and under very taxing conditions. Should we then give up the concept of causality for the much larger number of instances in which such manipulations are not possible, unethical, or simply too expensive? That would be problematic because, for example, we could nor conclude that smoking causes cancer. It is simply not possible to do the right experiment, especially with human beings: there are too many variables, nor to mention deep ethical issues.

What then? One of the most modern conceptions of causality is the so-called probabilistic one. According to probabilistic causality we can reasonably infer that, say, cancer is caused by smoking if the probability of getting cancer is measurably higher when the subjects smoke than when they don't. Other factors here are taken into consideration statistically, not necessarily by experimental manipulation. That is, one carries out the investigation taking care of sampling individuals with different socio-economic backgrounds, diets, exercise habits, and genetic constitution. If, when these other variables are kept in check statistically, we still detect an increase in the likelihood of getting cancer in the smokers compared to the nonsmokers, we are justified in tentatively accepting a causal connection.

Notice, however, that while the probabilistic account of causality is indeed very powerful in practice, conceptually it brings us back toward Hume: the only reason we are talking about causality is because we perceive a series of regularities, not because we know that actual causes are at play. So, in science as in skeptical investigations, we might have to admit that the most we can get is a certain probability of being right. Definitive truth is a chimera that does not belong to science after all.

Further Reading

David Hume (1739–1740). *A Treatise of Human Nature.*

Author **Massimo Pigliucci** is an associate professor in the Departments of Botany and Ecology & Evolutionary Biology at the University of Tennessee at Knoxville and author of the new book *Denying Evolution: Creationism, Scientism, and the Nature of Science* (Sinauer 2002). His earlier SKEPTICAL INQUIRER articles include "Hypothesis Testing and the Nature of Skeptical Investigations" (November/ December 2002), "Design Yes, Intelligent No" (September/October 2001), and "Where Do We Come From? A Humbling Look at the Biology of Life's Origins" (September/October 1999). His Web site is www.rationallyspeaking.org

From *Skeptical Inquirer*, January/February 2003, pp. 15-16. © 2003 by Skeptical Inquirer, www.csicop.org. Reprinted by permission.

UNIT 2
Biological Bases of Behavior

Unit Selections

4. **What Makes You Who You Are**, Matt Ridley
5. **Genetic Influence on Human Psychological Traits**, Thomas J. Bouchard, Jr.
6. **Neuroscience: Breaking Down Scientific Barriers to the Study of Brain and Mind**, Eric R. Kandel and Larry R. Squire

Key Points to Consider

• What do you think contributes most to our psychological make-up and behaviors: the influence of the environment, the expression of genes, evolution, or the functioning of the nervous system? Do you believe that some combination of these factors accounts for psychological characteristics and behaviors? Are all of these studied the same way, for example, under a microscope or with imaging technology? How are these contributors to behavior studied?

• What is genetic research? Why do genetic research? How much of human behavior is influenced by genes? Do you agree that evolution or genetics account for most of our "humanness"? Can you give some examples of the influence of genes on human behavior?

• How could brain imaging research help experts in psychology and medicine predict and treat various disorders? Do you think such information could be or has been misused? How? When? Why? What environmental factors affect genetic expression? Or do they?

• Why do psychologists study the human brain? Do you know the names and functions of the brain? Of other parts of the nervous system? What parts of the brain control various aspects of our behavior? That is, how does the brain influence human behavior and psychological characteristics? If an individual experiences brain damage, can other parts of the brain take over functions controlled by the damaged area?

• What is neuroscience? How are psychology and neuroscience related? Are there some realms of psychology that are not related to neuroscience? If yes, which ones? Are there areas of neuroscience that are not related to psychology?

 **Links: www.dushkin.com/online/**
These sites are annotated in the World Wide Web pages.

Division of Hereditary Diseases and Family Studies, Indiana University School of Medicine
http://www.iupui.edu/~medgen/division/hereditary/hereditary_diseases.html
Institute for Behavioral Genetics
http://ibgwww.colorado.edu/index.html
Serendip
http://serendip.brynmawr.edu/serendip/

As a child, Angelina vowed she did not want to turn out like either of her parents. Angelina's mother was very passive and acquiescent about her father's drinking. When Dad was drunk, Mom always called his boss to report that Dad was "sick" and then acted as if there was nothing wrong at home. Angelina's childhood was a nightmare. Her father's behavior was erratic and unpredictable. If he drank just a little bit, most often he was happy. If he drank a lot, which was usually the case, he frequently but not always became belligerent.

Despite vowing not to become her father, as an adult Angelina found herself in the alcohol rehabilitation unit of a large hospital. Angelina's employer could no longer tolerate her on-the-job mistakes or her unexplained absences from work. Angelina's supervisor therefore referred her to the clinic for help. As Angelina pondered her fate, she wondered whether her genes preordained her to follow in her father's inebriated footsteps or whether the stress of her childhood had brought her to this point in her life. After all, being the child of an alcoholic is not easy.

Just as Angelina is, psychologists also are concerned with discovering the causes of human behavior. Once the cause is known, treatments for problematic behaviors can be developed. In fact, certain behaviors might even be prevented when the cause is known. But for Angelina, prevention was too late.

One of the paths to understanding humans is to understand the biological underpinnings of their behavior. Genes and chromosomes, the body's chemistry (as found in hormones, neurotransmitters, and enzymes), and the nervous system comprised of the brain, spinal cord, nerve cells, and other parts are all implicated in human behavior. All represent the biological aspects of behavior and ought, therefore, to be worthy of study by psychologists.

Physiological psychologists and psychobiologists are often the ones who examine the role of biology in behavior. The neuroscientist is especially interested in brain functioning; the psychopharmacologist is interested in the effects of various pharmacological agents or psychoactive drugs on behavior.

These psychologists often utilize one of three techniques to understand the biology-behavior connection. Animal studies involving manipulation, stimulation, or destruction of certain parts of the brain offer one method of study. There is also a second available technique that includes the examination of unfortunate individuals whose brains are malfunctioning at birth or damaged later by accidents or disease. We can also use animal models to understand genetics; with animal models we can control reproduction as well as manipulate and develop various strains of animals if necessary. Some individuals consider research with animals to be inhumane; such tactics with humans would be considered extremely unethical. However, by studying an individual's behavior in comparison to both natural and adoptive parents or by studying identical twins reared together or apart we can begin to understand the role of genetics versus environment in human behavior.

The articles in this unit are designed to familiarize you with the knowledge psychologists have gleaned by using these and other techniques to study physiological processes and other underlying mechanisms in human behavior. Each article should interest you and make you more curious about the role of biology in human actions.

In the first article in this important unit, Matt Ridley reviews the nagging nature-nurture controversy—the debate about whether environment or heredity plays a larger role in shaping us. Ridley introduces a rather new element into this issue, the fact that both are similarly important because each affects the other.

The second article, entitled "Genetic Influence on Human Psychological Traits," written by Thomas Bouchard is also about the nature-nurture dispute, but he falls heavily on the side of nurture. He explains what genetics is, why it is important, and how much it impacts various psychological characteristics, such as intelligence and mental health.

The final article in this section discusses the nervous system. Kandel and Squire claim that as time progresses psychology and neuroscience are becoming more and more important to one another. The authors cite some of the various ways that neuroscience is informing psychological science and vice versa.

WHAT MAKES YOU WHO YOU ARE

Which is stronger—nature or nurture?
The latest science says genes and your
experience interact for your whole life

By MATT RIDLEY

THE PERENNIAL DEBATE ABOUT NATURE AND NURTURE—
which is the more potent shaper of the human essence?—
is perennially rekindled. It flared up again in the London
Observer of Feb. 11, 2001. REVEALED: THE SECRET OF HU-
MAN BEHAVIOR, read the banner headline. ENVIRONMENT,
NOT GENES, KEY TO OUR ACTS. The source of the story was
Craig Venter, the self-made man of genes who had built a
private company to read the full sequence of the human
genome in competition with an international consortium
funded by taxes and charities. That sequence—a string of
3 billion letters, composed in a four-letter alphabet, containing the complete recipe for building and running a
human body—was to be published the very next day (the
competition ended in an arranged tie). The first analysis
of it had revealed that there were just 30,000 genes in it,
not the 100,000 that many had been estimating until a few
months before.

Details had already been circulated to journalists under embargo. But Venter, by speaking to a reporter at a
biotechnology conference in France on Feb. 9, had effectively broken the embargo. Not for the first time in the increasingly bitter rivalry over the genome project, Venter's
version of the story would hit the headlines before his ri-
vals'. "We simply do not have enough genes for this idea
of biological determinism to be right," Venter told the *Observer*. "The wonderful diversity of the human species is
not hard-wired in our genetic code. Our environments
are critical."

In truth, the number of human genes changed nothing.
Venter's remarks concealed two whopping nonsequiturs:
that fewer genes implied more environmental influences
and that 30,000 genes were too few to explain human nature, whereas 100,000 would have been enough. As one
scientist put it to me a few weeks later, just 33 genes, each
coming in two varieties (on or off), would be enough to
make every human being in the world unique. There are
more than 10 billion combinations that could come from
flipping a coin 33 times, so 30,000 does not seem such a
small number after all. Besides, if fewer genes meant
more free will, fruit flies would be freer than we are, bacteria freer still and viruses the John Stuart Mill of biology.

Fortunately, there was no need to reassure the population with such sophisticated calculations. People did not
weep at the humiliating news that our genome has only
about twice as many genes as a worm's. Nothing had
been hung on the number 100,000, which was just a bad
guess.

But the human genome project—and the decades of research that preceded it—did force a much more nuanced
understanding of how genes work. In the early days, scientists detailed how genes encode the various proteins
that make up the cells in our bodies. Their more sophisti-

cated and ultimately more satisfying discovery—that gene expression can be modified by experience—has been gradually emerging since the 1980s. Only now is it dawning on scientists what a big and general idea it implies: that learning itself consists of nothing more than switching genes on and off. The more we lift the lid on the genome, the more vulnerable to experience genes appear to be.

This is not some namby-pamby, middle-of-the-road compromise. This is a new understanding of the fundamental building blocks of life based on the discovery that genes are not immutable things handed down from our parents like Moses' stone tablets but are active participants in our lives, designed to take their cues from everything that happens to us from the moment of our conception.

Early Puberty
Girls raised in FATHERLESS HOUSE-HOLDS experience puberty earlier. Apparently the change in timing is the reaction of a STILL MYSTERIOUS set of genes to their ENVIRONMENT. Scientists don't know how many SETS OF GENES act this way

For the time being, this new awareness has taken its strongest hold among scientists, changing how they think about everything from the way bodies develop in the womb to how new species emerge to the inevitability of homosexuality in some people. (More on all this later.) But eventually, as the general population becomes more attuned to this interdependent view, changes may well occur in areas as diverse as education, medicine, law and religion. Dieters may learn precisely which combination of fats, carbohydrates and proteins has the greatest effect on their individual waistlines. Theologians may develop a whole new theory of free will based on the observation that learning expands our capacity to choose our own path. As was true of Copernicus's observation 500 years ago that the earth orbits the sun, there is no telling how far the repercussions of this new scientific paradigm may extend.

To appreciate what has happened, you will have to abandon cherished notions and open your mind. You will have to enter a world in which your genes are not puppet masters pulling the strings of your behavior but puppets at the mercy of your behavior, in which instinct is not the opposite of learning, environmental influences are often less reversible than genetic ones, and nature is designed for nurture.

Fear of snakes, for instance, is the most common human phobia, and it makes good evolutionary sense for it to be instinctive. Learning to fear snakes the hard way would be dangerous. Yet experiments with monkeys reveal that their fear of snakes (and probably ours) must still be acquired by watching another individual react with fear to a snake. It turns out that it is easy to teach monkeys to fear snakes but very difficult to teach them to fear flowers. What we inherit is not a fear of snakes but a predisposition to learn a fear of snakes—a nature for a certain kind of nurture.

Before we dive into some of the other scientific discoveries that have so thoroughly transformed the debate, it helps to understand how deeply entrenched in our intellectual history the false dichotomy of nature vs. nurture became. Whether human nature is born or made is an ancient conundrum discussed by Plato and Aristotle. Empiricist philosophers such as John Locke and David Hume argued that the human mind was formed by experience; nativists like Jean-Jacques Rousseau and Immanuel Kant held that there was such a thing as immutable human nature.

It was Charles Darwin's eccentric mathematician cousin Francis Galton who in 1874 ignited the nature-nurture controversy in its present form and coined the very phrase (borrowing the alliteration from Shakespeare, who had lifted it from an Elizabethan schoolmaster named Richard Mulcaster). Galton asserted that human personalities were born, not made by experience. At the same time, the philosopher William James argued that human beings have more instincts than animals, not fewer.

In the first decades of the 20th century, nature held sway over nurture in most fields. In the wake of World War I, however, three men recaptured the social sciences for nurture: John B. Watson, who set out to show how the conditioned reflex, discovered by Ivan Pavlov, could explain human learning; Sigmund Freud, who sought to explain the influence of parents and early experiences on young minds; and Franz Boas, who argued that the origin of ethnic differences lay with history, experience and circumstance, not physiology and psychology.

Homosexuality
GAY MEN are more likely to have OLDER BROTHERS than either gay women or heterosexual men. It may be that a FIRST MALE FETUS triggers an immune reaction in the mother, ALTERING THE EXPRESSION of key gender genes

Galton's insistence on innate explanations of human abilities had led him to espouse eugenics, a term he coined. Eugenics was enthusiastically adopted by the Nazis to justify their campaign of mass murder against the disabled and the Jews. Tainted by this association, the idea of innate behavior was in full retreat for most of the middle years of the century. In 1958, however, two men began the counterattack on behalf of nature. Noam Chomsky, in his review of a book by the behaviorist B.F. Skinner, argued that it was impossible to learn human language by trial and error alone; human beings must come already equipped with an innate grammatical skill. Harry Harlow did a simple experiment that showed that a baby monkey prefers a soft, cloth model of a mother to a hard, wire-frame mother, even if the wire-frame mother provides it with all its milk; some preferences are innate.

Fast-forward to the 1980s and one of the most stunning surprises to greet scientists when they first opened up animal genomes: fly geneticists found a small group of genes called the hox genes that seemed to set out the body plan of the fly during its early development—telling it roughly where to put the head, legs, wings and so on. But then colleagues studying mice found the same hox genes, in the same order, doing the same job in Mickey's world—telling the mouse where to put its various parts. And when scientists looked in our genome, they found hox genes there too.

Hox genes, like all genes, are switched on and off in different parts of the body at different times. In this way, genes can have subtly different effects, depending on where, when and how they are switched on. The switches that control this process—stretches of DNA upstream of genes—are known as promoters.

Small changes in the promoter can have profound effects on the expression of a hox gene. For example, mice have short necks and long bodies; chickens have long necks and short bodies. If you count the vertebrae in the necks and thoraxes of mice and chickens, you will find that a mouse has seven neck and 13 thoracic vertebrae, a chicken 14 and seven, respectively. The source of this difference lies in the promoter attached to HoxC8, a hox gene that helps shape the thorax of the body. The promoter is a 200-letter paragraph of DNA, and in the two species it differs by just a handful of letters. The effect is to alter the expression of the HoxC8 gene in the development of the chicken embryo. This means the chicken makes thoracic vertebrae in a different part of the body than the mouse. In the python, HoxC8 is expressed right from the head and goes on being expressed for most of the body. So pythons are one long thorax; they have ribs all down the body.

Divorce
If a **FRATERNAL TWIN** gets divorced, there's a **30% CHANCE** that his or her twin will get divorced as well. If the twins are **IDENTICAL**, however, one sibling's divorce **BOOSTS THE ODDS** to 45% that the other will split

To make grand changes in the body plan of animals, there is no need to invent new genes, just as there's no need to invent new words to write an original novel (unless your name is Joyce). All you need do is switch the same ones on and off in different patterns. Suddenly, here is a mechanism for creating large and small evolutionary changes from small genetic differences. Merely by adjusting the sequence of a promoter or adding a new one, you could alter the expression of a gene.

In one sense, this is a bit depressing. It means that until scientists know how to find gene promoters in the vast text of the genome, they will not learn how the recipe for a chimpanzee differs from that for a person. But in another sense, it is also uplifting, for it reminds us more forcefully than ever of a simple truth that is all too often forgotten: bodies are not made, they grow. The genome is not a blueprint for constructing a body. It is a recipe for baking a body. You could say the chicken embryo is marinated for a shorter time in the HoxC8 sauce than the mouse embryo is. Likewise, the development of a certain human behavior takes a certain time and occurs in a certain order, just as the cooking of a perfect souffle requires not just the right ingredients but also the right amount of cooking and the right order of events.

How does this new view of genes alter our understanding of human nature? Take a look at four examples.

LANGUAGE Human beings differ from chimpanzees in having complex, grammatical language. But language does not spring fully formed from the brain; it must be learned from other language-speaking human beings. This capacity to learn is written into the human brain by genes that open and close a critical window during which learning takes place. One of those genes, FoxP2, has recently been discovered on human chromosome 7 by Anthony Monaco and his colleagues at the Wellcome Trust Centre for Human Genetics in Oxford. Just having the FoxP2 gene, though, is not enough. If a child is not exposed to a lot of spoken language during the critical learning period, he or she will always struggle with speech.

Crime Families

GENES may influence the way people respond to a "crimogenic" ENVIRONMENT. How else to explain why the BIOLOGICAL children of criminal parents are more likely than their ADOPTED children to break the LAW?

LOVE Some species of rodents, such as the prairie vole, form long pair bonds with their mates, as human beings do. Others, such as the montane vole, have only transitory liaisons, as do chimpanzees. The difference, according to Tom Insel and Larry Young at Emory University in Atlanta, lies in the promoter upstream of the oxytocin- and vasopressin-receptor genes. The insertion of an extra chunk of DNA text, usually about 460 letters long, into the promoter makes the animal more likely to bond with its mate. The extra text does not create love, but perhaps it creates the possibility of falling in love after the right experience.

ANTISOCIAL BEHAVIOR It has often been suggested that childhood maltreatment can create an antisocial adult. New research by Terrie Moffitt of London's Kings College on a group of 442 New Zealand men who have been followed since birth suggests that this is true only for a genetic minority. Again, the difference lies in a promoter that alters the activity of a gene. Those with high-active monoamine oxidase A genes were virtually immune to the effects of mistreatment. Those with low-active genes were much more antisocial if maltreated, yet—if anything—slightly less antisocial if not maltreated. The low-active, mistreated men were responsible for four times their share of rapes, robberies and assaults. In other words, maltreatment is not enough; you must also have the low-active gene. And it is not enough to have the low-active gene; you must also be maltreated.

HOMOSEXUALITY Ray Blanchard at the University of Toronto has found that gay men are more likely than either lesbians or heterosexual men to have older brothers (but not older sisters). He has since confirmed this observation in 14 samples from many places. Something about occupying a womb that has held other boys occasionally results in reduced birth weight, a larger placenta and a greater probability of homosexuality. That something, Blanchard suspects, is an immune reaction in the mother, primed by the first male fetus, that grows stronger with each male pregnancy. Perhaps the immune response affects the expression of key genes during brain development in a way that boosts a boy's attraction to his own sex. Such an explanation would not hold true for all gay men, but it might provide important clues into the origins of both homosexuality and heterosexuality.

TO BE SURE, EARLIER SCIENTIFIC DISCOVERIES HAD HINTED AT the importance of this kind of interplay between heredity and environment. The most striking example is Pavlovian conditioning. When Pavlov announced his famous experiment a century ago this year, he had apparently discovered how the brain could be changed to acquire new knowledge of the world—in the case of his dogs, knowledge that a bell foretold the arrival of food. But now we know how the brain changes: by the real-time expression of 17 genes, known as the CREB genes. They must be switched on and off to alter connections among nerve cells in the brain and thus lay down a new long-term memory. These genes are at the mercy of our behavior, not the other way around. Memory is in the genes in the sense that it uses genes, not in the sense that you inherit memories.

In this new view, genes allow the human mind to learn, remember, imitate, imprint language, absorb culture and express instincts. Genes are not puppet masters or blueprints, nor are they just the carriers of heredity. They are active during life; they switch one another on and off; they respond to the environment. They may direct the construction of the body and brain in the womb, but then almost at once, in response to experience, they set about dismantling and rebuilding what they have made. They are both the cause and the consequence of our actions.

Will this new vision of genes enable us to leave the nature-nurture argument behind, or are we doomed to reinvent it in every generation? Unlike what happened in previous eras, science is explaining in great detail precisely how genes and their environment—be it the womb, the classroom or pop culture—interact. So perhaps the pendulum swings of a now demonstrably false dichotomy may cease.

It may be in our nature, however, to seek simple, linear, cause-and-effect stories and not think in terms of circular causation, in which effects become their own causes. Perhaps the idea of nature via nurture, like the ideas of quantum mechanics and relativity, is just too counterintuitive for human minds. The urge to see ourselves in terms of nature versus nurture, like our instinctual ability to fear snakes, may be encoded in our genes.

ANCIENT QUARREL

How much of who we are is learned or innate is an argument with a fruitful but fractious pedigree

Nature We may be destined to be bald, mourn our dead, seek mates, fear the dark	**Nurture** But we can also learn to love tea, hate polkas, invent alphabets and tell lies
IMMANUEL KANT His philosophy sought a native morality in the mind	**JOHN LOCKE** Considered the mind of an infant to be a tabula rasa, or blank slate
FRANCIS GALTON Math geek saw mental and physical traits as innate	**IVAN PAVLOV** Trained dogs to salivate at the sound of the dinner bell
KONRAD LORENZ Studied patterns of instinctive behavior in animals	**SIGMUND FREUD** Felt we are formed by mothers, fathers, sex, jokes and dreams
NOAM CHOMSKY Argued that human beings are born with a capacity for grammar	**FRANZ BOAS** Believed chance and environs are key to cultural variation

Matt Ridley is an Oxford-trained zoologist and science writer whose latest book is Nature via Nurture *(HarperCollins)*

Genetic Influence on Human Psychological Traits

A Survey

Thomas J. Bouchard, Jr.

There is now a large body of evidence that supports the conclusion that individual differences in most, if not all, reliably measured psychological traits, normal and abnormal, are substantively influenced by genetic factors. This fact has important implications for research and theory building in psychology, as evidence of genetic influence unleashes a cascade of questions regarding the sources of variance in such traits. A brief list of those questions is provided, and representative findings regarding genetic and environmental influences are presented for the domains of personality, intelligence, psychological interests, psychiatric illnesses, and social attitudes. These findings are consistent with those reported for the traits of other species and for many human physical traits, suggesting that they may represent a general biological phenomenon.

Among knowledgeable researchers, discussions regarding genetic influences on psychological traits are not about whether there is genetic influence, but rather about how much influence there is, and how genes work to shape the mind. As Rutter (2002) noted, "Any dispassionate reading of the evidence leads to the inescapable conclusion that genetic factors play a substantial role in the origins of individual differences with respect to all psychological traits, both normal and abnormal" (p. 2). Put concisely, all psychological traits are heritable. Heritability (h^2) is a descriptive statistic that indexes the degree of population variation in a trait that is due to genetic differences. The complement of heritability ($1 - h^2$) indexes variation contributed by the environment (plus error of measurement) to population variation in the trait. Studies of human twins and adoptees, often called behavior genetic studies, allow us to estimate the heritability of various traits. The name behavior genetic studies is an unfortunate misnomer, however, as such studies are neutral regarding both environmental and genetic influences. That they repeatedly and reliably reveal significant heritability for psychological traits is an empirical fact and

one not unique to humans. Lynch and Walsh (1998) pointed out that genetic influence on most traits, as indexed by estimates of heritability, is found for all species and observed that "the interesting questions remaining are, How does the magnitude of h^2" differ among characters and species and why?" (p. 175).

WHY STUDY GENETIC INFLUENCES ON HUMAN BEHAVIORAL TRAITS?

A simple answer to the question of why scientists study genetic influences on human behavior is that they want a better understanding of how things work, that is, better theories. Not too many years ago, Meehl (1978) argued that "most so-called 'theories' in the soft areas of psychology (clinical, counseling, social, personality, community, and school psychology) are scientifically unimpressive and technologically worthless" (p. 806). He listed 20 fundamental difficulties faced by researchers in the social sciences. Two are relevant to the current discussion: heritability and nuisance variables. The two are closely related. Nuisance variables are variables assumed to be causes of group or individual differences irrelevant to the theory of an investigator. Investigators seldom provide a full theoretical rationale in support of their choice of nuisance variables to control. As Meehl pointed out, removing the influence of parental socioeconomic status (SES; i.e., treating it as a nuisance variable) on children's IQ, when studying the causes of individual differences in IQ, makes the assumption that parental SES is exclusively a source of environmental variance, as opposed to being confounded with genetic influence. Meehl argued that this example "is perhaps the most dramatic one but other less emotion-laden examples can be found on all sides in the behavioral sciences" (p. 810). His point was that knowledge of how genetic factors influence any given measure (e.g., SES) or trait (e.g., IQ) will allow scientists to develop more scientifically impressive and worthwhile theories about the sources of individual differences in psychological traits.

Evidence of genetic influence on a psychological trait raises a series of new questions regarding the sources of population variance for that trait. All the questions addressed in quantitative genetics (Lynch & Walsh, 1998) and genetic epidemiology (Khoury, 1998) become relevant. What kind of gene action is involved? Is it a simple additive influence, with the effects of genes simply adding up so that more genes cause greater expression of the trait, or is the mode of action more complex? Are the effects of genes for a particular trait more pronounced in men or women? Are there interactions between genes and the environment? For example, it has been known for a long time that stressful life events lead to depression in some people but not others. There is now evidence for an interaction. Individuals who carry a specific genetic variant are more susceptible to depression when exposed to stressful life events than individuals who do not carry the genetic variant (Caspi et al., 2003). Are there gene-environment correlations? That is, do individuals with certain genetic constitutions seek out specific environments? People who score high on measures of sensation seeking certainly, on average, tend to find themselves in more dangerous environments than people who score low for this trait. McGue and I have provided an extended list of such questions (Bouchard & McGue, 2003).

ESTIMATES OF THE MAGNITUDE OF GENETIC INFLUENCE ON PSYCHOLOGICAL TRAITS

Table 1 reports typical behavior genetic findings drawn from studies of broad and relatively representative samples from affluent Western societies. In most, but not all, of these studies, estimates of genetic and environmental influences were obtained from studies of twins. Because the studies probably undersampled people who live in the most deprived segment of Western societies, the findings should not be considered as generalizable to such populations. (Documentation for most of the findings can be found in Bouchard & McGue, 2003.)

Personality

Psychologists have developed two major schemes for organizing specific personality traits into a higher-order structure, the Big Five and the Big Three. As Table 1 shows, the findings using the two schemes are much the same. Genetic influence is in the range of 40 to 50%, and heritability is approximately the same for different traits. There is evidence of nonadditive genetic variance. That is, genes for personality, in addition to simply adding or subtracting from the expression of a trait, work in a more complex manner, the expression of a relevant gene depending to some extent on the gene with which it is paired on a chromosome or on genes located on other chromosomes. Research has yielded little evidence for significant shared environmental influence, that is, similarity due to having trait-relevant environmental influences in common. Some large studies have investigated whether the genes that influence personality traits differ in the two sexes (sex limitation). The answer is no. However, sometimes there are sex differences in heritability.

Mental Ability

Early in life, shared environmental factors are the dominant influence on IQ, but gradually genetic influence increases, with the effects of shared environment dropping to near zero (see the twin studies in Table 1). Although not reported here, adoption studies of (a) unrelated individuals reared together and (b) adoptive parents and their adopted offspring have reported similar results—increasing genetic influence on IQ with age and decreasing shared environmental influence. Results from two twin studies of IQ in old age (over 75) are reported in Table 1. Both studies found a substantial level of genetic influence and little shared environmental influence. The results do, however, suggest some decline in heritability when compared with results for earlier ages. There is no evidence for sex differences in heritability for IQ at any age.

Psychological Interests

Heritabilities for psychological interests, also called vocational or occupational interests, are also reported in Table 1. These heritabilities were estimated using data gathered in a single large study that made use of a variety of samples (twins, siblings, parents and their children, etc.) gathered over many years. All respondents completed one form or another of a standard vocational interest questionnaire. There is little variation in heritability for the six scales, with an average of .36. As with personality traits, there is evidence for nonadditive genetic influence. Unlike personality, psychological interests show evidence for shared environmental influence, although this influence is modest, about 10% for each trait.

Psychiatric Illnesses

Schizophrenia is the most extensively studied psychiatric illness, and the findings consistently suggest a very high

TABLE 1
Estimates of Broad Heritability and Shared Environmental Influence and Indications of Nonadditive Genetic Effects and Sex Differences in Heritability for Representative Psychological Traits

Trait	Heritability	Nonadditive genetic effect	Shared environmental effect	Sex differences in heritabililiy
Personality (adult samples)				
Big Five				
Extraversion	.54	Yes	No	Perhaps
Agreeableness (aggression)	.42	Yes	No	Probably not
Conscientiousness	.49	Yes	No	Probably not
Neuroticism	.48	Yes	No	No
Openness	.57	Yes	No	Probably not
Big Three				
Positive emotionality	.50	Yes	No	No
Negative emotionality	.44	Yes	No	No
Constraint	.52	Yes	No	No
Intelligence				
By age in Dutch cross-sectional twin data				
Age 5	.22	No	.54	No
Age 7	.40	No	.29	No
Age 10	.54	No	.26	No
Age 12	.85	No	No	No
Age 16	.62	No	No	No
Age 18	.82	No	No	No
Age 26	.88	No	No	No
Age 50	.85	No	No	No
In old age (> 75 years old)	.54-.62	Not tested	No	No
Psychological interests				
Realistic	.36	Yes	.12	NA
Investigative	.36	Yes	.10	NA
Artistic	.39	Yes	.12	NA
Social	.37	Yes	.08	NA
Enterprising	.31	Yes	.11	NA
Conventional	.38	Yes	.11	NA
Psychiatric illnesses (liability estimates)				
Schizophrenia	.80	No	No	No
Major depression	.37	No	No	Mixed findings
Panic disorder	.30-.40	No	No	No
Generalized anxiety disorder	.30	No	Small female only	No
Phobias	.20-.40	No	No	No
Alcoholism	.50-.60	No	Yes	Mixed findings
Antisocial behavior				
Children	.46	No	.20	No
Adolescents	.43	No	.16	No
Adults	.41	No	.09	No
Social attitudes				
Conservatism				
Under age 20 years	.00	NR	Yes	NR
Over age 20 years	.45-.65	Yes	Yes in females	Yes
Right-wing authoritarianism (adults)	.50-.64	No	.00-.16	NA
Religiousness				
16-year-olds	.11-.22	No	.45-.60	Yes
Adults	.30-.45	No	.20-.40	Not clear
Specific religion	Near zero	NR	NA	NR

Note. NA = not available: NR = not relevant.

degree of genetic influence (heritability of about .80), mostly additive genetic influence, with no shared environmental influence. There do not appear to be gender differences in the heritability of schizophrenia. Major depression is less heritable (about .40) than schizophrenia. Men and women share most, but not all, genetic influences for depression. Panic disorder, generalized anxiety disorder, and phobias are moderately heritable, and the effect is largely additive, with few if any sex differences. The heritability of alcoholism is in the range of .50 to .60. mostly because of additive genetic effects. Findings regarding the possibility of sex differences in the heritability of alcoholism are mixed.

Antisocial behavior has long been thought to be more heritable in adulthood than childhood. The results of a recent analysis do not support that conclusion. The genetic influence is additive and in the range of .41 to .46. Shared environmental influences decrease from childhood to adulthood, but do not entirely disappear in adulthood. There are no sex differences in heritability.

Social Attitudes

Twin studies reveal only environmental influence on conservatism up to age 19; only after this age do genetic influences manifest themselves. A large study (30,000 adults, including twins and most of their first-degree relatives) yielded heritabilities of .65 for males and .45 for females. Some of the genetic influence on conservatism is nonadditive. Recent work with twins reared apart has independently replicated these heritability findings. Conservatism correlates highly, about .72, with right-wing authoritarianism, and that trait is also moderately heritable.

Religiousness is only slightly heritable in 16-year-olds (.11 for girls and .22 for boys in a large Finnish twin study) and strongly influenced by shared environment (.60 in girls and .45 in boys). Religiousness is moderately heritable in adults (.30 to .45) and also shows some shared environmental influence. Good data on sex differences in heritability of religiousness in adults are not available. Membership in a specific religious denomination is largely due to environmental factors.

A Note on Multivariate Genetic Analysis

In this review, I have addressed only the behavior genetic analysis of traits taken one at a time (univariate analysis). It is important to recognize that it is possible to carry out complex genetic analyses of the correlations among traits and compute genetic correlations. These correlations tell us the degree to which genetic effects on one score (trait measure) are correlated with genetic effects on a second score, at one or at many points in time. The genetic correlation between two traits can be quite high regardless of whether the heritability of either trait is high or low, or whether the correlation between the traits is high or low. Consider the well-known positive correlation between tests of mental ability, the evidentiary base for the general

intelligence factor. This value is typically about .30. The genetic correlation between such tests is, however, much higher, typically closer to .80. Co-occurrence of two disorders, a common finding in psychiatric research, is often due to common genes. The genetic correlation between anxiety and depression, for example, is estimated to be very high. Multivariate genetic analysis of behavioral traits is a very active domain of research.

CONCLUDING REMARKS

One unspoken assumption among early behavior geneticists, an assumption that was shared by most for many years, was that some psychological traits were likely to be significantly influenced by genetic factors, whereas others were likely to be primarily influenced by shared environmental influences. Most behavior geneticists assumed that social attitudes, for example, were influenced entirely by shared environmental influences, and so social attitudes remained largely unstudied until relatively recently. The evidence now shows how wrong these assumptions were. Nearly every reliably measured psychological phenotype (normal and abnormal) is significantly influenced by genetic factors. Heritabilities also differ far less from trait to trait than anyone initially imagined. Shared environmental influences are often, but not always, of less importance than genetic factors, and often decrease to near zero after adolescence. Genetic influence on psychological traits is ubiquitous, and psychological researchers must incorporate this fact into their research programs else their theories will be "scientifically unimpressive and technologically worthless," to quote Meehl again.

At a fundamental level, a scientifically impressive theory must describe the specific molecular mechanism that explicates how genes transact with the environment to produce behavior. The rudiments of such theories are in place. Circadian behavior in humans is under genetic influence (Hur, Bouchard, & Lykken, 1998), and some of the molecular mechanisms in mammals are now being revealed (Lowrey & Takahashi, 2000). Riclley (2003) and Marcus (2004) have provided additional examples of molecular mechanisms that help shape behavior. Nevertheless, the examples are few, the details are sparse, and major mysteries remain. For example, many behavioral traits are influenced by nonadditive genetic processes. These processes remain a puzzle for geneticists and evolutionists, as well as psychologists, because simple additive effects are thought to be the norm (Wolf, Brodie, & Wade, 2000). We also do not understand why most psychological traits are moderately heritable, rather than, as some psychologists expected, variable in heritability, with some traits being highly heritable and others being largely under the influence of the environment. It seems reasonable to suspect that moderate heritability may be a general biological phenomenon rather than one specific to human psychological traits, as the profile of genetic and environmental influences on psychological traits is not that different from the profile of these influences on similarly complex physical traits (Boomsma, Busjahn, & Peltonen, 2002) and similar findings apply to most organisms.

Recommended Reading

Bouchard, T.J., Jr., & McGue. M. (2003). (See References)

Carey, G. (2003). *Human genetics for the social sciences.* Thousand Oaks, CA: Sage.

Plomin, R., DeFries, J.C.. Craig, I.W., & McGuffin, P. (Eds.). (2003). *Behavioral genetics in the post genomic era.* Washington, DC: American Psychological Association.

Rutter, M., Pickels, A., Murray, R., & Eaves, L.J. (2001). Testing hypotheses on specific environmental causal effects on behavior. *Psychological bulletin, 127,* 291-324.

Note

1. See Evans (2004, Fig. 1) for a recent commission of this error.

REFERENCES

Boomsma, D.I., Busjahn, A., & Peltonen, L. (2002). Classical twin studies and beyond. *Nature Reviews: Genetics, 3,* 872–882.

Bouchard, T.J., Jr., & McGue, M. (2003). Genetic and environmental influences on human psychological differences. *Journal of Neurobiology, 54,* 4–45.

Caspi, A., Sugden, K., Moffitt, T.E., Taylor. A., Craig, I.W., Harrington, H., McClay, J., Mill, J., Martin, J., Braiwaite. A., & Poulton, R. (2003). Influence of life stress on depression: Moderation by a polymorphism in the 5-HTT gene. *Science, 301,* 386–389.

Evans, G.W. (2004). The environment of childhood poverty. *American Psychologist, 59,* 77–92.

Hur, Y.-M., Bouchard, T.J., Jr., & Lykken. D.T. (1998). Genetic and environmental influence on morningness-eveningness. *Personality and Individual Differences, 25,* 917–925.

Khoury, M.J. (1998). Genetic epidemiology. In K.J. Rothman & S. Greenland (Eds.), *Modem epidemiology* (pp. 609–622). Philadelphia: Lippincott-Raven.

Lowrey, P.L., & Takahashi, J.S. (2000). Genetics of the mammalian circadian system: Photic entrainment, circadian pacemaker mechanisms, and postranslational regulation. *Annual Review of Genetics, 34,* 533–562.

Lynch, M., & Walsh, B. (1998). *Genetics and analysis of quantitative traits.* Sunderland. MA: Sinauer.

Marcus, G. (2004). *The birth of the mind: How a tiny number of genes creates the complexities of human thought.* New York: Basic Books.

Meehl, P.E. (1978). Theoretical risks and tabular asterisks: Sir Karl, Sir Ronald, and the slow progress of soft psychology. *Journal of Consulting and Clinical Psychology, 46,* 806–834.

Ridley, M. (2003). *Nature via nurture: Genes, experience and what makes us human.* New York: HarperCollins.

Rutter, M. (2002). Nature, nurture, and development: From evangelism through science toward policy and practice. *Child Development, 73,* 1–21.

Wolf, J.B., Brodie. E.D.I., & Wade. M.J. (Eds.), (2000). *Epistasis and the evolutionary process.* New York: Oxford University Press.

From *Current Directions in Psychological Science,* Vol. 13, No. 4, August 2004, pp. 148-151. Copyright © 2004 by Blackwell Publishers, Ltd. Reprinted by permission.

Neuroscience: Breaking Down Scientific Barriers to the Study of Brain and Mind

Eric R. Kandel and Larry R. Squire

During the latter part of the 20th century, the study of the brain moved from a peripheral position within both the biological and psychological sciences to become an interdisciplinary field called neuroscience that now occupies a central position within each discipline. This realignment occurred because the biological study of the brain became incorporated into a common framework with cell and molecular biology on the one side and with psychology on the other. Within this new framework, the scope of neuroscience ranges from genes to cognition, from molecules to mind.

What led to the gradual incorporation of neuroscience into the central core of biology and to its alignment with psychology? From the perspective of biology at the beginning of the 20th century, the task of neuroscience—to understand how the brain develops and then functions to perceive, think, move, and remember—seemed impossibly difficult. In addition, an intellectual barrier separated neuroscience from biology, because the language of neuroscience was based more on neuroanatomy and electrophysiology than on the universal biological language of biochemistry. During the last 2 decades this barrier has been largely removed. A molecular neuroscience became established by focusing on simple systems where anatomy and physiology were tractable. As a result, neuroscience helped delineate a general plan for neural cell function in which the cells of the nervous system are understood to be governed by variations on universal biological themes.

From the perspective of psychology, a neural approach to mental processes seemed too reductionistic to do justice to the complexity of cognition. Substantial progress was required to demonstrate that some of these reduc-tionist goals were achievable within a psychologically meaningful framework. The work of Vernon Mountcastle, David Hubel, Torsten Wiesel, and Brenda Milner in the 1950s and 1960s, and the advent of brain imaging in the 1980s, showed what could be achieved for sensory processing, perception, and memory. As a result of these advances, the view gradually developed that only by exploring the brain could psychologists fully satisfy their interest in the cognitive processes that intervene between stimulus and response.

Here, we consider several developments that have been particularly important for the maturation of neuroscience and for the restructuring of its relationship to biology and psychology.

The Emergence of a Cellular and Molecular Neuroscience

The modern cellular science of the nervous system was founded on two important advances: the neuron doctrine and the ionic hypothesis. The neuron doctrine was established by the brilliant Spanish anatomist Santiago Ramón y Cajal[1], who showed that the brain is composed of discrete cells, called neurons, and that these likely serve as elementary signaling units. Cajal also advanced the principle of connection specificity, the central tenet of which is that neurons form highly specific connections with one another and that these connections are invariant and defining for each species. Finally, Cajal developed the principle of dynamic polarization, according to which information flows in only one direction within a neuron, usually from the dendrites (the neuron's input component) down the axon shaft to the axon terminals (the output component). Although exceptions to this principle have emerged, it has proved extremely influential, because it tied structure to function and provided guidelines for constructing circuits from the images provided in histological sections of the brain.

Cajal and his contemporary Charles Sherrington[2] further proposed that neurons contact one another only at specialized points called synapses, the sites where one neuron's processes contact and communicate with another neuron. We now know that at most synapses, there is a gap of 20 nm—the synaptic cleft—between the pre- and postsynaptic cell. In the 1930s, Otto Loewi, Henry Dale, and Wilhelm Feldberg established (at peripheral neuromuscular and autonomic synapses) that the signal that bridges the synaptic cleft is usually a small chemical, or neurotransmitter, which is released from the presynaptic terminal, diffuses across the gap, and binds to receptors on the postsynaptic target cell. Depending on the specific receptor, the postsynaptic cell can either be excited or inhibited. It took some time to establish that chemical transmission also occurs in the central nervous system, but by the 1950s the idea had become widely accepted.

Even early in the 20th century, it was already understood that nerve cells have an electrical potential, the resting membrane potential, across their membrane, and that signaling along the axon is conveyed by a propagated electrical signal, the action potential, which was thought to nullify the resting potential. In 1937 Alan Hodgkin discovered that the action potential gives rise to local current flow on its advancing edge and that this current depolarizes the adjacent region of the axonal membrane sufficiently to trigger a traveling wave of depolarization. In 1939 Hodgkin and Andrew Huxley made the surprising discovery that the action potential more than nullifies the resting potential—it reverses it. Then, in the late 1940s, Hodgkin, Huxley, and Bernard Katz explained the resting potential and the action potential in terms of the movement of specific ions—potassium (K^+), sodium (Na^+), and chloride (Cl^-)—through pores (ion channels) in the axonal membrane. This ionic hypothesis unified a large body of descriptive data and offered the first realistic promise that the nervous system could be understood in terms of physicochemical principles common to all of cell biology[3].

The next breakthrough came when Katz, Paul Fatt, and John Eccles showed that ion channels are also fundamental to signal transmission across the synapse. However, rather than being gated by voltage like the Na^+ and K^+ channels critical for action potentials, excitatory synaptic ion channels are gated chemically by ligands such as the transmitter acetylcholine. During the 1960s and 1970s, neuroscientists identified many amino acids, peptides, and other small molecules as chemical transmitters, including acetylcholine, glutamate, GABA, glycine, serotonin, dopamine, and norepinephrine. On the order of 100 chemical transmitters have been discovered to date. In the 1970s, some synapses were found to release a peptide cotransmitter that can modify the action of the classic, small-molecule transmitters. The discovery of chemical neurotransmission was followed by the remarkable discovery that transmission between neurons is sometimes electrical[4]. Electrical synapses have smaller synaptic clefts, which are bridged by gap junctions and allow current to flow between neurons.

In the late 1960s information began to become available about the biophysical and biochemical structure of ionic pores and the biophysical basis for their selectivity and gating—how they open and close. For example, transmitter binding sites and their ion channels were found to be embodied within different domains of multimeric proteins. Ion channel selectivity was found to depend on physical-chemical interaction between the channel and the ion, and channel gating was found to result from conformational changes within the channel[5].

The study of ion channels changed radically with the development of the patch-clamp method in 1976 by Erwin Neher and Bert Sakmann[6], which enabled measurement of the current flowing through a single ion channel. This powerful advance set the stage for the analysis of channels at the molecular level and for the analysis of functional and conformational change in a single membrane protein. When applied to non-neuronal cells, the method also revealed that all cells—even bacteria—express remarkably similar ion channels. Thus, neuronal signaling proved to be a special case of a signaling capability inherent in most cells.

The development of patch clamping coincided with the advent of molecular cloning, and these two methods brought neuroscientists new ideas based on the first reports of the amino acid sequences of ligand- and voltage-gated channels. One of the key insights to emerge from molecular cloning was that amino acid sequences contain clues about how receptor proteins and voltage-gated ion channel proteins are arranged across the cell membrane. The sequence data also often pointed to unexpected structural relationships (homologies) among proteins. These insights, in turn, revealed similarities between molecules found in quite different neuronal and non-neuronal contexts, suggesting that they may serve similar biological functions.

By the early 1980s, it became clear that synaptic actions were not always mediated directly by ion channels. Besides ionotropic receptors, in which ligand binding directly gates an ion channel, a second class of receptors, the metabotropic receptors, was discovered. Here the binding of the ligand initiates intracellular metabolic events and leads only indirectly, by way of "second messengers," to the gating of ion channels[7].

The cloning of metabotropic receptors revealed that many of them have seven membrane-spanning regions and are homologous to bacterial rhodopsin as well as to the photoreceptor pigment of organisms ranging from fruit flies to humans. Further, the recent cloning of receptors for the sense of smell[8] revealed that at least 1000 metabotropic receptors are expressed in the mammalian olfactory epithelium and that similar receptors are present in flies and worms. Thus, it was instantly understood that the class of receptors used for phototransduction, the initial step in visual perception, is also used for smell and aspects of taste, and that these receptors share key features with many other brain receptors that work through second-messenger signaling. These discoveries demonstrated the evolutionary conservation of receptors and emphasized the wisdom of studying a wide variety of experimental systems—vertebrates, invertebrates, even single-celled organisms—to identify broad biological principles.

The seven transmembrane-spanning receptors activate ion channels indirectly through coupling proteins (G proteins). Some G proteins have been found to activate ion channels directly. However, the majority of G proteins activate membrane enzymes that alter the level of second messengers, such as cAMP, cGMP, or inositol triphosphate, which initiate complex intracellular events leading to the activation of protein kinases and phosphatases and then to the modulation of channel perm-eability, receptor sensitivity, and transmitter release. Neuroscientists now appreciate that many of these synaptic actions are mediated intracellularly by protein phosphorylation or dephosphorylation[9]. Nerve cells use such covalent modifications to control protein activity reversibly and thereby to regulate function. Phosphorylation is also critical in other cells for the action of hormones and growth factors, and for many other processes.

Directly controlled synaptic actions are fast, lasting milliseconds, but second-messenger actions last seconds to minutes. An even slower synaptic action, lasting days or more, has been found to be important for long-term memory. In this case, protein kinases activated by second messengers translocate to the nucleus, where they phosphorylate transcription factors that alter gene expression, initiate growth of neuronal processes, and increase synaptic strength.

Ionotropic and metabotropic receptors have helped to explain the postsynaptic side of synaptic transmission. In the 1950s and 1960s, Katz and his colleagues turned to the presynaptic terminals and discovered that chemical transmitters, such as acetylcholine, are released not as single molecules but as packets of about 5000 molecules called quanta[10]. Each quantum is packaged in a synaptic vesicle and released by exocytosis at sites called active zones. The key signal that triggers this sequence is the influx of Ca^{2+} with the action potential.

In recent years, many proteins involved in transmitter release have been identified[11]. Their functions range from targeting vesicles to active zones, tethering vesicles to the cell membrane, and fusing vesicles with the cell membrane so that their contents can be released by exocytosis. These molecular studies reflect another example of evolutionary conservation: The molecules used for vesicle fusion and exocytosis at nerve terminals are variants of those used for vesicle fusion and exocytosis in all cells.

A Mechanistic View of Brain Development

The discoveries of molecular neuroscience have dramatically improved the understanding of how the brain develops its complexity. The modern molecular era of developmental neuroscience began when Rita Levi-Montalcini and Stanley Cohen isolated nerve growth factor (NGF), the first peptide growth factor to be identified in the nervous system[12]. They showed that injection of antibodies to NGF into newborn mice caused the death of neurons in sympathetic ganglia and also reduced the number of sensory ganglion cells. Thus, the survival of both sympathetic and sensory neurons depends on NGF. Indeed, many neurons depend for their survival on NGF or related molecules, which typically provide feedback signals to the neurons from their targets. Such signals are important for programmed cell death—apoptosis—a developmental strategy which has now proved to be of general importance, whereby many more cells are generated than eventually survive to become functional units with precise connectivity. In a major advance, genetic study of worms has revealed the *ced* genes and with them a universal cascade critical for apoptosis in which proteases—the caspases—are the final agents for cell death[13].

Cajal pointed out the extraordinary precision of neuronal connections. The first compelling insights into how neurons develop their precise connectivity came from Roger Sperry's studies of the visual system of frogs and salamanders beginning in the 1940s, which suggested that axon outgrowth is guided by molecular cues. Sperry's key finding was that when the nerves from the eye are cut, axons find their way back to their original targets. These seminal studies led Sperry in 1963 to formulate the chemoaffinity hypothesis[14], the idea that neurons form connections with their targets based on distinctive and matching molecular identities that they acquire early in development.

Stimulated by these early contributions, molecular biology has radically transformed the study of nervous system development from a descriptive to a mechanistic field. Three genetic systems, the worm *Caenorhabditis elegans*, the fruit fly *Drosophila melanogaster*, and the mouse, have been invaluable; some of the molecules for key developmental steps in the mouse were first characterized by genetic screens in worms and flies. In some cases, identical molecules were found to play an equivalent role throughout phylogeny. The result of this work is that neuroscientists have achieved in broad outline an understanding of the molecular basis of nervous system development[15]. A range of key molecules has been identified, including specific inducers, morphogens, and guidance molecules important for differentiation, process outgrowth, pathfinding, and synapse formation. For example, in the spinal cord, neurons achieve their identities and characteristic positions largely through two classes of inductive signaling molecules of the Hedgehog and bone morphogenic protein families. These two groups of molecules control neuronal differentiation in the ventral and dorsal halves of the spinal cord, respectively, and maintain this division of labor through most of the rostrocaudal length of the nervous system.

The process of neuronal pathfinding is mediated by both short-range and long-range cues. An axon's growth cone can encounter cell surface cues that either attract or repel it. For example, ephrins are membrane-bound, are distributed in graded fashion in many regions of the nervous system, and can repel growing axons. Other cues, such as the netrins and the semaphorins, are secreted in diffusible form and act as long-range chemoattractants or chemorepellents. Growth cones can also react to the same cues differently at different developmental phases, for example, when crossing the midline or when switching from pathfinding to synapse formation. Finally, a large number of molecules are involved in synapse formation itself. Some, such as neuregulin, erbB kinases, agrin, and MuSK, organize the assembly of the postsynaptic machinery, whereas others, such as the laminins, help to organize the presynaptic differentiation of the active zone.

These molecular signals direct differentiation, migration, process outgrowth, and synapse formation in the absence of neural activity. Neural activity is needed, however, to refine the connections further so as to forge the adult pattern of connectivity [16]. The neural activity may be generated spontaneously, especially early in development, but later depends importantly on sensory input. In this way, intrinsic activity or sensory and motor experience can help specify a precise set of functional connections.

The Impact of Neuroscience on Neurology and Psychiatry

Molecular neuroscience has also reaped substantial benefits for clinical medicine. To begin with, recent advances in the study of neural development have identified stem cells, both embryonic and adult, which offer promise in cell replacement therapy in Parkinson's disease, demyelinating diseases, and other conditions. Similarly, new insights into axon guidance molecules offer hope for nerve regeneration after spinal cord injury. Finally, because most neurological diseases are associated with cell death, the discovery in worms of a universal genetic program for cell death opens up approaches for cell rescue based on, for example, inhibition of the caspase proteases.

Next, consider the impact of molecular genetics. Huntington's disease is an autosomal dominant disease marked by progressive motor and cognitive impairment that ordinarily manifests itself in middle age. The major pathology is cell death in the basal ganglia. In 1993, the Huntington's Disease Collaborative Research Group isolated the gene responsible for the disease [17]. It is marked by an extended series of trinucleotide CAG (cytosine, ad-

enine, guanine) repeats, thereby placing Huntington's disease in a new class of neurological disorders—the trinucleotide repeat diseases—that now constitute the largest group of dominantly transmitted neurological diseases.

The molecular genetic analysis of more complex degenerative disorders has proceeded more slowly. Still, three genes associated with familial Alzheimer's disease—those that code for the amyloid precursor protein, presenilin 1, and presenilin 2—have been identified. Molecular genetic studies have also identified the first genes that modulate the severity and risk of a degenerative disease [18]. One allele (APO E4) is a significant risk factor for late-onset Alzheimer's disease. Conversely, the APO E2 allele may actually be protective. A second risk factor is α_2-macroglobulin. All the Alzheimer's-related genes so far identified participate in either generating or scavenging a protein (the amyloid peptide), which is toxic at elevated levels. Studies directed at this peptide may lead to ways to prevent the disease or halt its progression. Similarly, the discovery of ß-secretase and perhaps γ-secretase, the enzymes involved in the processing of ß amyloid, represent dramatic advances that may also lead to new treatments.

With psychiatric disorders, progress has been slower for two reasons. First, diseases such as schizophrenia, depression, obsessive compulsive disorders, anxiety states, and drug abuse tend to be complex, polygenic disorders that are significantly modulated by environmental factors. Second, in contrast to neurological disorders, little is known about the anatomical substrates of most psychiatric diseases. Given the difficulty of penetrating the deep biology of mental illness, it is nevertheless remarkable how much progress has been made during the past 3 decades [19]. Arvid Carlsson and Julius Axelrod carried out pioneering studies of biogenic amines, which laid the foundation for psychopharmacology, and Seymour Kety pioneered the genetic study of mental illness [20]. Currently, new approaches to many conditions, such as sleep disorders, eating disorders, and drug abuse, are emerging as the result of insights into the cellular and molecular machinery that regulates specific behaviors [21]. Moreover, improvements in diagnosis, the better delineation of genetic contributions to psychiatric illness (based on twin and adoption studies as well as studies of affected families), and the discovery of specific medications for treating schizophrenia, depression, and anxiety states have transformed psychiatry into a therapeutically effective medical specialty that is now closely aligned with neuroscience.

A New Alignment of Neuroscience and Psychological Science

The brain's computational power is conferred by interactions among billions of nerve cells, which are assembled into networks or circuits that carry out specific operations in support of behavior and cognition. Whereas the molecular machinery and electrical signaling properties of neurons are widely conserved across animal species, what distinguishes one species from another, with respect to their cognitive abilities, is the number of neurons and the details of their connectivity.

Beginning in the 19th century there was great interest in how these cognitive abilities might be localized in the brain. One view, first championed by Franz Joseph Gall, was that the brain is composed of specialized parts and that aspects of perception, emotion, and language can be localized to anatomically distinct neural systems. Another view, championed by Jean-Pierre-Marie Flourens, was that cognitive functions are global properties arising from the integrated activity of the entire brain. In a sense, the history of neuroscience can be seen as a gradual ascendancy of the localizationist view.

To a large extent, the emergence of the localizationist view was built on a century-old legacy of psychological science. When psychology emerged as an experimental science in the late 19th century, its founders, Gustav Fechner and Wilhelm Wundt, focused on psychophysics—the quantitative relationship between physical stimuli and subjective sensation. The success of this endeavor encouraged psychologists to study more complex behavior, which led to a rigorous, laboratory-based tradition termed behaviorism.

Led by John Watson and later by B. F. Skinner, behaviorists argued that psychology should be concerned only with observable stimuli and responses, not with unobservable processes that intervene between stimulus and response. This tradition yielded lawful principles of behavior and learning, but it proved limiting. In the 1960s, behaviorism gave way to a broader approach concerned with cognitive processes and internal representations. This new emphasis focused on precisely those aspects of mental life—from perception to action—that had long been of interest to neurologists and other students of the nervous system.

The first cellular studies of brain systems in the 1950s illustrated dramatically how much neuroscience derived from psychology and conversely how much psychology could, in turn, inform neuroscience. In using a cellular approach, neuroscientists relied on the rigorous experimental methods of psychophysics and behaviorism to explore how a sensory stimulus resulted in a neuronal response. In so doing, they found cellular support for localization of function: Different brain regions had different cellular response properties. Thus, it became possible in the study of behavior and cognition to move beyond description to an exploration of the mechanisms underlying the internal representation of the external world.

In the late 1950s and 1960s Mountcastle, Hubel, and Wiesel began using cellular approaches to analyze sensory processing in the cerebral cortex of cats and monkeys[22]. Their work provided the most fundamental advance in understanding the organization of the brain since the work of Cajal at the turn of the century. The cellular physiological techniques revealed that the brain both filters and transforms sensory information on its way to and within the cortex, and that these transformations are critical for perception. Sensory systems analyze, decompose, and then restructure raw sensory information according to built-in connections and rules.

Mountcastle found that single nerve cells in the primary somatic sensory cortex respond to specific kinds of touch: Some respond to superficial touch and others to deep pressure, but cells almost never respond to both. The different cell types are segregated in vertical columns, which comprise thousands of neurons and extend about 2 mm from the cortical surface to the white matter below it. Mountcastle proposed that each column serves as an integrating unit, or logical module, and that these columns are the basic mode of cortical organization.

Single-cell recording was pioneered by Edgar Adrian and applied to the visual system of invertebrates by H. Keffer Hartline and to the visual system of mammals by Stephen Kuffler, the mentor of Hubel and Wiesel. In recordings from the retina, Kuffler discovered that, rather than signaling absolute levels of light, neurons signal contrast between spots of light and dark. In the visual cortex, Hubel and Wiesel found that most cells no longer respond to spots of light. For example, in area V1 at the occipital pole of the cortex, neurons respond to specific visual features such as lines or bars in a particular orientation. Moreover, cells with similar orientation preferences were found to group together in vertical columns similar to those that Mountcastle had found in somatosensory cortex. Indeed, an independent system of vertical columns—the ocular dominance columns—was found to segregate information arriving from the two eyes. These results provided an entirely new view of the anatomical organization of the cerebral cortex.

Wiesel and Hubel also investigated the effects of early sensory deprivation on newborn animals. They found that visual deprivation in one eye profoundly alters the organization of ocular dominance columns [23]. Columns receiving input from the closed eye shrink, and those receiving input from the open eye expand. These studies led to the discovery that eye closure alters the pattern of synchronous activity in the two eyes and that this neural activity is essential for fine-tuning synaptic connections during visual system development [16].

In the extrastriate cortex beyond area V1, continuing electrophysiological and anatomical studies have identified more than 30 distinct areas important for vision [24]. Further, visual information was found to be analyzed by two parallel processing streams [25]. The dorsal stream, concerned with where objects are located in space and how to reach objects, extends from area V1 to the parietal cortex. The ventral stream extends from area V1 to the inferior temporal cortex and is concerned with analyzing the visual form and quality of objects. Thus, even the apparently simple task of perceiving an object in space engages a disparate collection of specialized neural areas that represent different aspects of the visual information—what the object is, where it is located, and how to reach for it.

A Neuroscience of Cognition

The initial studies of the visual system were performed in anaesthetized cats, an experimental preparation far removed from the behaving and thinking human beings that are the focus of interest for cognitive psychologists. A pivotal advance occurred in the late 1960s when single-neuron recordings were obtained from awake, behaving monkeys that had been trained to perform sensory or motor tasks [26]. With these methods, the response of neurons in the posterior parietal cortex to a visual stimulus was found to be enhanced when the animal moved its eyes to attend to the stimulus. This moved the neurophysiological study of single neurons beyond sensory processing and showed that reductionist approaches could be applied to higher order psychological processes such as selective attention.

It is possible to correlate neuronal firing with perception rather directly. Thus, building on earlier work by Mountcastle, a monkey's ability to discriminate motion was found to closely match the performance of individual neurons in area MT, a cortical area concerned with visual motion processing. Further, electrical microstimulation of small clusters of neurons in MT shifts the monkey's motion judgments toward the direction of motion that the stimulated neurons prefer [27]. Thus, activity in area MT appears sufficient for the perception of motion and for initiating perceptual decisions.

These findings, based on recordings from small neuronal populations, have illuminated important issues in perception and action. They illustrate how retinal signals are remapped from retinotopic space into other coordinate frames that can guide behavior; how attention can modulate neuronal activity; and how meaning and context influence neuronal activity, so that the same retinal stimulus can lead to different neuronal responses depending on how the stimulus is perceived [28]. This same kind of work (relating cellular activity directly to perception and action) is currently being applied to the so-called binding problem—how the multiple features of a stimulus object, which are represented by specialized and distributed neuronal groups, are synthesized into a signal that represents a single percept or action and to the fundamental question of what aspects of neuronal activity (e.g., firing rate or spike timing) constitute the neural codes of information processing [29].

Striking parallels to the organization and function of sensory cortices have been found in the cortical motor areas supporting voluntary movement. Thus, there are several cortical areas directed to the planning and execution of voluntary movement. Primary motor cortex has columnar organization, with neurons in each column governing movements of one or a few joints. Motor areas receive input from other cortical regions, and information moves through stages to the spinal cord, where the detailed circuitry that generates motor patterns is located [30].

Although studies of single cells have been enormously informative, the functioning brain consists of multiple brain systems and many neurons operating in concert. To monitor activity in large populations of neurons, multi-electrode arrays as well as cellular and whole-brain imaging techniques are now being used. These approaches are being supplemented by studying the effect of selective brain lesions on behavior and by molecular methods, such as the delivery of markers or other molecules to specific neurons by viral transfection, which promise fine-resolution tracing of anatomical connections, activity-dependent labeling of neurons, and ways to transiently inactivate specific components of neural circuits.

Invasive molecular manipulations of this kind cannot be applied to humans. However, functional neuroimaging by positron emission tomography (PET) or functional magnetic resonance imaging (fMRI) provides a way to monitor large neuronal populations in awake humans while they engage in cognitive tasks [31]. PET involves measuring regional blood flow using $H_2{}^{15}O$ and allows for repeated measurements on the same individual. fMRI is based on the fact that neural activity changes local oxygen levels in tissue and that oxygenated and deoxygenated hemoglobin have different magnetic properties. It is now possible to image the second-by-second time course of the brain's response to single stimuli or single events with a spatial resolution in the millimeter range. Recent success in obtaining fMRI images from awake monkeys, combined with single-cell recording, should extend the utility of functional neuroimaging by permitting parallel studies in humans and nonhuman primates.

One example of how parallel studies of humans and nonhuman primates have advanced the understanding of brain systems and cognition is in the study of memory. The neuroscience of memory came into focus in the 1950s when the noted amnesic patient H.M. was first described [32]. H.M. developed profound forgetfulness after sustaining a bilateral medial temporal lobe resection to relieve severe epilepsy. Yet he retained his intelligence, perceptual abilities, and personality. Brenda Milner's elegant studies of H.M. led to several important principles. First, acquiring new memories is a distinct cerebral function, separable from other perceptual and cognitive abilities. Second, because H.M. could retain a number or a visual image for a short time, the medial temporal lobes are not needed for immediate memory. Third, these structures are not the ultimate repository of memory, because H.M. retained his remote, childhood memories.

It subsequently became clear that only one kind of memory, declarative memory, is impaired in H.M. and other amnesic patients. Thus, memory is not a unitary faculty of the mind but is composed of multiple systems that have different logic and neuroanatomy [33]. The major dis-

A Timeline of Neuroscience

2nd Century A.D.
Galen of Pergamum identifies the brain as the organ of the mind.

17th Century
The brain becomes accepted as the substrate of mental life rather than its ventricles, as early writers had proposed.

1664
Thomas Willis publishes *Cerebri anatome*, with illustrations of the brain by Christopher Wren. It is the most comprehensive treatise on brain anatomy and function published up to that time.

1791
Luigi Galvani reveals the electric nature of nervous action by stimulating nerves and muscles of frog legs.

1808
Franz Joseph Gall proposes that specific brain regions control specific functions.

1852
Hermann von Helmholtz measures the speed of a nerve impulse in the frog.

1879
Wilhelm Wundt establishes the first laboratory of experimental psychology in Leipzig, Germany.

1891
Wilhelm von Waldeyer-Hartz introduces the term neuron.

1897
Charles Sherrington introduces the term synapse.

1898–1903
Edward Thorndike and Ivan Pavlov describe operant and classical conditioning, two fundamental types of learning.

1906
Santiago Ramón y Cajal summarizes compelling evidence for the neuron doctrine, that the nervous system is composed of discrete cells.

1906
Alois Alzheimer describes the pathology of the neurodegenerative disease that comes to bear his name.

1914
Henry Dale demonstrates the physiological action of acetylcholine, which is later identified as a neurotransmitter.

1929
In a famous program of lesion experiments in rats, Karl Lashley attempts to localize memory in the brain.

1929
Hans Berger uses human scalp electrodes to demonstrate electroencephalography.

1928–32
Edgar Adrian describes method for recording from single sensory and motor axons; H. Keffer Hartline applies this method to the recording of single-cell activity in the eye of the horseshoe crab.

1940s
Alan Hodgkin, Andrew Huxley, and Bernard Katz explain electrical activity of neurons by concentration gradients of ions and movement of ions through pores.

1946
Kenneth Cole develops the voltage-clamp technique to measure current flow across the cell membrane.

1949
Donald Hebb introduces a synaptic learning rule, which becomes known as the Hebb rule.

1930s to 1950s
The chemical nature of synaptic transmission is established by Otto Loewi, Henry Dale, Wilhelm Feldberg, Stephen Kuffler, and Bernard Katz at peripheral synapses and is extended to the spinal cord by John Eccles and others.

1930s to 1950s
Wilder Penfield and Theodore Rasmussen map the motor and sensory homunculus and illustrate localization of function in the human brain.

1950s
Karl von Frisch, Konrad Lorenz, and Nikolaas Tinbergen establish the science of ethology (animal behavior in natural contexts) and lay the foundation for neuroethology.

1955–60
Vernon Mountcastle, David Hubel, and Torsten Wiesel pioneer single-cell recording from mammalian sensory cortex; Nils-Ake Hillarp introduces fluorescent microscopic methods to study cellular distribution of biogenic amines.

1956
Rita Levi-Montalcini and Stanley Cohen isolate and purify nerve growth factor.

1957
Brenda Milner describes patient H.M. and discovers the importance of the medial temporal lobe for memory.

1958
Arvid Carlsson finds dopamine to be a transmitter in the brain and proposes that it has a role in extrapyramidal disorders such as Parkinson's disease.

(continued)

A Timeline of Neuroscience (continued)

1958

Simple invertebrate systems, including *Aplysia*, *Drosophila*, and *C. elegans*, are introduced to analyze elementary aspects of behavior and learning at the cellular and molecular level.

1962–63

Brain anatomy in rodents is found to be altered by experience; first evidence for role of protein synthesis in memory formation.

1963

Roger Sperry proposes a precise system of chemical matching between pre- and postsynaptic neuronal partners (the chemoaffinity hypothesis).

1966–69

Ed Evarts and Robert Wurtz develop methods for studying movement and perception with single-cell recordings from awake, behaving monkeys.

1970

Synaptic changes are related to learning and memory storage in *Aplysia*.

Mid-1970s

Paul Greengard shows that many neurotransmitters work by means of protein phosphorylation.

1973

Timothy Bliss and Terje Lomo discover long-term potentiation, a candidate synaptic mechanism for long-term mammalian memory.

1976

Erwin Neher and Bert Sakmann develop the patch-clamp technique for recording the activity of single ion channels.

Late 1970s

Neuroimaging by positron emission tomography is developed.

1980s

Experimental evidence becomes available for the divisibility of memory into multiple systems; an animal model of human amnesia is developed.

1986

H. Robert Horvitz discovers the *ced* genes, which are critical for programmed cell death.

1986

Patient R.B. establishes the importance of the hippocampus for human memory.

1990

Segi Ogawa and colleagues develop functional magnetic resonance imaging.

1990

Mario Capecchi and Oliver Smythies develop gene knockout technology, which is soon applied to neuroscience.

1991

Linda Buck and Richard Axel discover that the olfactory receptor family consists of over 1000 different genes. The anatomical components of the medial temporal lobe memory system are identified.

1993

The Huntington's Disease Collaborative Research Group identifies the gene responsible for Huntington's disease.

1990s

Neural development is transformed from a descriptive to a molecular discipline by Gerald Fischbach, Jack McMahan, Tom Jessell, and Corey Goodman; neuroimaging is applied to problems of human cognition, including perception, attention, and memory.

1990s

Reinhard Jahn, James Rothman, Richard Scheller, and Thomas Sudhof delineate molecules critical for exocytosis.

1998

First 3D structure of an ion channel is revealed by Rod MacKinnon.

---

tinction is between our capacity for conscious, declarative memory about facts and events and a collection of unconscious, nondeclarative memory abilities, such as skill and habit learning and simple forms of conditioning and sensitization. In these cases, experience modifies performance without requiring any conscious memory content or even the experience that memory is being used.

An animal model of human amnesia in the nonhuman primate was achieved in the early 1980s, leading ultimately to the identification of the medial temporal lobe structures that support declarative memory—the hippocampus and the adjacent entorhinal, perirhinal, and parahippocampal cortices [34]. The hippocampus has been an especially active target of study, in part because this was one of the structures damaged in patient H.M. and also because of the early discovery of hippocampal place cells, which signal the location of an animal in space [35]. This work led to the idea that, once learning occurs, the hippocampus and other medial temporal lobe structures permit the transition to long-term memory, perhaps by binding the separate cortical regions that together store memory for a whole event. Thus, long-term memory is thought to be stored in the same distributed set of cortical structures that perceive, process, and analyze what is to be remembered, and aggregate changes in large assemblies of cortical neurons are the substrate of long-term memory. The frontal lobes are also thought to influence what is selected for storage, the ability to hold information in mind for the short term, and the ability later on to retrieve it [36].

Whereas declarative memory is tied to a particular brain system, nondeclarative memory refers to a collection of learned abilities with different brain substrates. For example, many kinds of motor learning depend on the cerebellum, emotional learning and the modulation of memory strength by emotion depend on the amygdala, and habit learning depends on the basal ganglia [37]. These forms of nondeclarative memory, which provide for myriad unconscious ways of responding to the world, are evolutionarily ancient and observable in simple invertebrates such as *Aplysia* and *Drosophila*. By virtue of the unconscious status of these forms of memory, they create some of the mystery of human experience. For here arise the dispositions, habits, attitudes, and preferences that are inaccessible to conscious recollection, yet are shaped by past events, influence our behavior and our mental life, and are a fundamental part of who we are.

Bridging Cognitive Neuroscience and Molecular Biology in the Study of Memory Storage

The removal of scientific barriers at the two poles of the biological sciences—in the cell and molecular biology of nerve cells on the one hand, and in the biology of cognitive processes on the other—has raised the question: Can one anticipate an even broader unification, one that ranges from molecules to mind? A beginning of just such a synthesis may be apparent in the study of synaptic plasticity and memory storage.

For all of its diversity, one can view neuroscience as being concerned with two great themes—the brain's "hard wiring" and its capacity for plasticity. The former refers to how connections develop between cells, how cells function and communicate, and how an organism's inborn functions are organized—its sleep-wake cycles, hunger and thirst, and its ability to perceive the world. Thus, through evolution the nervous system has inherited many adaptations that are too important to be left to the vagaries of individual experience. In contrast, the capacity for plasticity refers to the fact that nervous systems can adapt or change as the result of the experiences that occur during an individual lifetime. Experience can modify the nervous system, and as a result organisms can learn and remember.

The precision of neural connections poses deep problems for the plasticity of behavior. How does one reconcile the precision and specificity of the brain's wiring with the known capability of humans and animals to acquire new knowledge? And how is knowledge, once acquired,

retained as long-term memory? A key insight about synaptic transmission is that the precise connections between neurons are not fixed but are modifiable by experience. Beginning in 1970, studies in invertebrates such as *Aplysia* showed that simple forms of learning—habituation, sensitization, and classical conditioning—result in functional and structural changes at synapses between the neurons that mediate the behavior being modified. These changes can persist for days or weeks and parallel the time course of the memory process[38]. These cell biological studies have been complemented by genetic studies in *Drosophila*. As a result, studies in *Aplysia* and *Drosophila* have identified a number of proteins important for memory [39].

In his now-famous book, *The Organization of Behavior,* Donald Hebb proposed in 1949 that the synaptic strength between two neurons should increase when the neurons exhibit coincident activity [40]. In 1973, a long-lasting synaptic plasticity of this kind was discovered in the hippocampus (a key structure for declarative memory) [41]. In response to a burst of high-frequency stimuli, the major synaptic pathways in the hippocampus undergo a long-term change, known as long-term potentiation or LTP. The advent in the 1990s of the ability to genetically modify mice made it possible to relate specific genes both to synaptic plasticity and to intact animal behavior, including memory. These techniques now allow one to delete specific genes in specific brain regions and also to turn genes on and off. Such genetic and pharmacological experiments in intact animals suggest that interference with LTP at a specific synapse—the Schaffer collateral-CA1 synapse—commonly impairs memory for space and objects. Conversely, enhancing LTP at the same synapse can enhance memory in these same declarative memory tasks. The findings emerging from these new methods [42] complement those in *Aplysia* and *Drosophila* and reinforce one of Cajal's most prescient ideas: Even though the anatomical connections between neurons develop according to a definite plan, their strength and effectiveness are not predetermined and can be altered by experience.

Combined behavioral and molecular genetic studies in *Drosophila*, *Aplysia*, and mouse suggest that, despite their different logic and neuroanatomy, declarative and nondeclarative forms of memory share some common cellular and molecular features. In both systems, memory storage depends on a short-term process lasting minutes and a long-term process lasting days or longer. Short-term memory involves covalent modifications of preexisting proteins, leading to the strengthening of preexisting synaptic connections. Long-term memory involves altered gene expression, protein synthesis, and the growth of new synaptic connections. In addition, a number of key signaling molecules involved in converting transient short-term plasticity to persistent long-term memory appear to be shared by both declarative and nondeclarative memory. A striking feature of neural plasticity is that long-term memory involves structural and functional change [38, 43]. This has been shown most directly in invertebrates and is likely to apply to vertebrates as well, including primates.

It had been widely believed that the sensory and motor cortices mature early in life and thereafter have a fixed organization and connectivity. However, it is now clear that these cortices can be reshaped by experience [44]. In one experiment, monkeys learned to discriminate between two vibrating stimuli applied to one finger. After several thousand trials, the cortical representation of the trained finger became more than twice as large as the corresponding areas for other fingers. Similarly, in a neuroimaging study of right-handed string musicians the cortical representations of the fingers of the left hand (whose fingers are manipulated individually and are engaged in skillful playing) were larger than in nonmusicians. Thus, improved finger skills even involve changes in how sensory cortex represents the fingers. Because all organisms experience a different sensory environment, each brain is modified differently. This gradual creation of unique brain architecture provides a biological basis for individuality.

Coda

Physicists and chemists have often distinguished their disciplines from the field of biology, emphasizing that biology was overly descriptive, atheoretical, and lacked the coherence of the physical sciences. This is no longer quite true. In the 20th century, biology matured and became a coherent discipline as a result of the substantial achievements of molecular biology. In the second half of the century, neuroscience emerged as a discipline that concerns itself with both biology and psychology and that is beginning to achieve a similar coherence. As a result, fascinating insights into the biology of cells, and remarkable principles of evolutionary conservation, are emerging from the study of nerve cells. Similarly, entirely new insights into the nature of mental processes (perception, memory, and cognition) are emerging from the study of neurons, circuits, and brain systems, and computational studies are providing models that can guide experimental work. Despite this remarkable progress, the neuroscience of higher cognitive processes is only beginning. For neuroscience to address the most challenging problems confronting the behavioral and biological sciences, we will need to continue to search for new molecular and cellular approaches and use them in conjunction with systems neuroscience and psychological science. In this way, we will best be able to relate molecular events and specific changes within neuronal circuits to mental processes such as perception, memory, thought, and possibly consciousness itself.

References and Notes

1. S. Ramón y Cajal, Nobel Lectures: Physiology or Medicine (1901–1921) (Elsevier, Amsterdam, 1967), pp. 220–253.

2. C. S. Sherrington, The Central Nervous System, vol. 3 of A Textbook of Physiology, M. Foster, Ed. (MacMillan, London, ed. 7, 1897).

3. A. L. Hodgkin and A. F. Huxley, Nature 144, 710 (1939); A. L. Hodgkin et al., J. Physiol. (Lond.) 116, 424 (1952); A. L. Hodgkin and A. F. Huxley, J. Physiol. (Lond.) 117, 500 (1952).

4. E. J. Furshpan and D. D. Potter, Nature 180, 342 (1957); M. V. L. Bennett, in Structure and Function of Synapses, G. D. Pappas and D. P. Purpura, Eds. (Raven Press, New York, 1972), pp. 221-256.

5. C. M. Armstrong and B. Hille, Neuron 20, 371 (1998); W. A. Catterall, Neuron, in press; B. Hille et al., Nature Medicine 5, 1105 (1999); D. A. Doyle et al., Science 280, 69 (1998); J. P. Changeux and S. J. Edelstein, Neuron 21, 959 (1998); A. Karlin, Harvey Lecture Series 85, 71 (1991).

6. E. Neher and B. Sakmann, Nature 260, 799 (1976).

7. R. J. Lefkowitz, Nat. Cell Biol. 2, E133-6 (2000).

8. L. Buck and R. Axel, Cell 65, 175 (1991).

9. E. J. Nestler and P. Greengard, Protein Phosphorylation in the Nervous System (Wiley, New York, 1984).

10. J. Del Castillo and B. Katz, J. Physiol. 124, 560 (1954); B. Katz, in The Xth Sherrington Lecture (Thomas, Springfield, IL, 1969).

11. T. Sudhof, Nature 375, 645 (1995); R. Scheller, Neuron 14, 893 (1995); J. A. McNew et al., Nature 407, 153 (2000).

12. S. Cohen and R. Levi-Montalcini, Proc. Natl. Acad. Sci. U.S.A. 42, 571 (1956); W. M. Cowan, Neuron 20, 413 (1998).

13. M. M. Metzstein et al., Trends Genet. 14, 410 (1998).

14. R. W. Sperry, Proc. Natl. Acad. Sci. U.S.A. 50, 703 (1963); R. W. Hunt and W. M. Cowan, in Brain, Circuits and Functions of Mind, C. B. Trevarthen, Ed. (Cambridge Univ. Press, Cambridge, 1990), pp. 19–74.

15. M. Tessier-Lavigne and C. S. Goodman, Science 274, 1123 (1996); T. M. Jessell, Nature Rev. Genet. 1, 20 (2000); T. M. Jessell and J. R. Sanes, Curr. Opin. Neurobiol., in press.

16. L. C. Katz and C. J. Shatz, Science 274, 1133 (1996).

17. Huntington's Disease Collaborative Research Group, Cell 72, 971 (1993); H. L. Paulson and K. H. Fischbeck, Annu. Rev. Neurosci. 19, 79 (1996).

18. D. M. Walsh et al., Biochemistry 39, 10831 (2000); W. J. Strittmatter and A. D. Roses, Annu. Rev. Neurosci. 19, 53 (1996); D. L. Price, Nature 399 (6738) (Suppl), A3–5 (1999).

19. S. E. Hyman, Arch. Gen. Psychiatr. 157, 88 (2000); D. Charney et al., Eds., Neurobiology of Mental Illness (Oxford, New York, 1999); S. H. Barnodes, Molecules and Mental Illness (Scientific American Library, New York, 1993); S. Snyder, Drugs and the Brain (Scientific American Library, New York, 1986).

20. A. Carlsson, Annu. Rev. Neurosci. 10, 19 (1987); J. Axelrod, Science 173, 598 (1971); S. S. Kety, Am. J. Psychiatr. 140, 720 (1983); N. A. Hillarp et al., Pharmacol. Rev. 18, 727 (1966).

21. T. S. Kilduff and C. Peyron, Trends Neurosci. 23, 359 (2000); K. L. Houseknecht et al., J. Anim. Sci. 76, 1405 (1998); G. F. Koob, Ann. N.Y. Acad. Sci. 909, 17 (2000); E. J. Nestler, Curr. Opin. Neurobiol. 7, 713 (1997).

22. V. B. Mountcastle, J. Neurophysiol. 20, 408 (1957); D. H. Hubel and T. N. Wiesel, J. Physiol. 148, 574 (1959); D. H. Hubel and T. N. Wiesel, Neuron 20, 401 (1998).

23. T. Wiesel and D. Hubel, J. Neurophysiol. 26, 1003 (1963).

24. D. Van Essen, in Cerebral Cortex, A. Peters and E. G. Jones, Eds. (Plenum Publishing Corp., New York, 1985), vol. 3, pp. 259-327; S. Zeki, Nature 274, 423 (1978); J. Kaas and P. Garraghty, Curr. Opin. Neurobiol. 4, 522 (1992).

25. L. Ungerleider and M. Mishkin, in The Analysis of Visual Behavior, D. J. Ingle et al., Eds. (MIT Press, Cambridge, MA,

1982), pp. 549–586; A. Milner and M. Goodale, The Visual Brain in Action (Oxford, New York, 1995).

26. R. H. Wurtz, J. Neurophysiol. 32, 727 (1969); E. V. Evarts, in Methods in Medical Research, R. F. Rushman, Ed. (Year Book, Chicago, 1966), pp. 241–250.

27. W. T. Newsome et al., Nature 341, 52 (1989); C. D. Salzman et al., Nature 346, 174 (1990).

28. R. A. Andersen et al., Annu. Rev. Neurosci. 20, 303 (1997); R. Desimone and J. Duncan, Annu. Rev. Neurosci. 18, 193 (1995); M. I. Posner and C. D. Gilbert, Proc. Natl. Acad. Sci. U.S.A. 96, 2585 (1999); T. D. Albright and G. R. Stoner, Proc. Natl. Acad. Sci. U.S.A. 92, 2433 (1995); C. D. Gilbert, Physiol. Rev. 78, 467 (1998); N. K. Logothetis, Philos. Trans. R. Soc. London, Ser. B 353, 1801 (1998).

29. For the binding problem, see Neuron 24 (1) (1999); for neural codes, see M. N. Shadlen and W. T. Newsome, Curr. Opin. Neurobiol. 4, 569 (1994); W. R. Softky, Curr. Opin. Neurobiol. 5, 239 (1995).

30. S. Grillner et al., Eds., Neurobiology of Vertebrate Locomotion, Wenner-Gren Center International Symposium Series, vol. 45 (Macmillan, London, 1986); A. P. Georgopoulos, Curr. Opin. Neurobiol. 10, 238 (2000).

31. L. Sokoloff et al., J. Neurochem. 28, 897 (1977); M. Reivich et al., Circ. Res. 44 127 (1979); M. I. Posner and M. E. Raichle, Images of Mind (Scientific American Library, New York, 1994); S. Ogawa et al., Proc. Natl. Acad. Sci. U.S.A. 87, 9868 (1990); B. R. Rosen et al., Proc. Natl. Acad. Sci. U.S.A. 95, 773 (1998).

32. W. B. Scoville and B. Milner, J. Neurol., Neurosurg., Psychiatr. 20, 11 (1957); B. Milner et al., Neuron 20, 445 (1998).

33. L. R. Squire, Psychol. Rev. 99, 195 (1992); D. L. Schacter and E. Tulving, Eds., Memory Systems (MIT Press, Cambridge, MA, 1994).

34. M. Mishkin, Philos. Trans. R. Soc. London, Ser. B 298, 85 (1982); L. R. Squire and S. Zola-Morgan, Science 253, 1380 (1991).

35. J. O'Keefe and J. Dostrovsky, Brain Res. 34, 171 (1971); H. Eichenbaum et al., Neuron 23, 209 (1999).

36. L. R. Squire and E. R. Kandel, Memory: From Mind to Molecules (Scientific American Library, New York, 1999); H. Eichenbaum, Nature Rev. Neurosci. 1, 1 (2000); P. Goldman-Rakic, Philos. Trans. R. Soc. London, Ser. B 351, 1445 (1996); R. Desimone, Proc. Natl. Acad. Sci. U.S.A. 93, 13494 (1996); S. Higuchi and Y. Miyashita, Proc. Natl. Acad. Sci. U.S.A. 93, 739 (1996).

37. R. F. Thompson and D. J. Krupa, Annu. Rev. Neurosci. 17, 519 (1994); J. LeDoux, The Emotional Brain (Simon & Schuster, New York, 1996); J. L. McGaugh, Science 287, 248 (2000); M. Mishkin et al., in Neurobiology of Learning and Memory, G. Lynch et al., Eds. (Guilford, New York, 1984),

pp. 65–77; D. L. Schacter and R. L. Buckner, Neuron 20, 185 (1998).

38. V. Castellucci et al., Science 167, 1745 (1970); M. Brunelli et al., Science 194, 1178 (1976); C. Bailey et al., Proc. Nat. Acad. Sci. U.S.A. 93, 13445 (1996).

39. S. Benzer, Sci. Am. 229, 24 (1973); W. G. Quinn and R. J. Greenspan, Annu. Rev. Neurosci. 7, 67 (1984); R. L. Davis, Physiol. Rev. 76, 299 (1996); J. Yin and T. Tully, Curr. Opin. Neurobiol. 6, 264 (1996).

40. D. O. Hebb, The Organization of Behavior: A Neuropsychological Theory (Wiley, New York, 1949).

41. T. V. P. Bliss and T. Lomo, J. Physiol. (Lond.) 232, 331 (1973).

42. M. Mayford et al., Science 274, 1678 (1996); J. Tsien et al., Cell 87, 1327 (1996); A. Silva et al., Annu. Rev. Neurosci. 21, 127 (1998); S. Martin et al., Annu. Rev. Neurosci. 23, 613 (2000); E. P. Huang and C. F. Stevens, Essays Biochem. 33, 165 (1998); R. C. Malenka and R. A. Nicoll, Science 285, 1870 (1999); H. Korn and D. Faber, CR Acad. Sci. III 321, 125 (1998).

43. W. T. Greenough and C. H. Bailey, Trends Neurosci. 11, 142 (1998).

44. D. V. Buonomano and M. M. Merzenich, Annu. Rev. Neurosci. 21, 149 (1998); C. Gilbert, Proc. Nat. Acad. Sci. U.S.A. 93 10546 (1996); T. Elbert et al., Science 270, 305 (1995).

The work of E.R.K. is supported by NIMH, the G. Harold and Leila Y. Mathers Foundation, the Lieber Center for Research on Schizophrenia, and the Howard Hughes Medical Institute. The work of L.R.S. is supported by the Medical Research Service of the Department of Veterans Affairs, NIMH, and the Metropolitan Life Foundation. We thank Thomas Jessell and Thomas Albright for their helpful comments on the manuscript.

Eric R. Kandel is University Professor, Columbia University, New York, and Senior Investigator at the Howard Hughes Medical Institute. He is a member of the National Academy of Sciences and the Institute of Medicine and a past president of the Society for Neuroscience. This past October, he was named a co-recipient of the Nobel Prize in physiology or medicine.

Larry R. Squire is Research Career Scientist at the Veterans Affairs San Diego Healthcare System and Professor of Psychiatry, Neurosciences, and Psychology, University of California, San Diego. He is a member of the National Academy of Sciences and the Institute of Medicine and a past president of the Society for Neuroscience.

UNIT 3
Perceptual Processes

Unit Selections

7. **Vision Seekers: Giving Eyesight to the Blind Raises Questions About How People See**, Bruce Bower
8. **A Matter of Taste**, Mary Beckman
9. **It's a Noisy, Noisy World Out There!**, Richard Carmen
10. **Pain and Its Mysteries**, Marni Jackson
11. **Night Life**, Jill Neimark
12. **Brains in Dreamland**, Bruce Bower

Key Points to Consider

- Why would psychologists be interested in studying sensations and perceptions? Can you differentiate the two terms? Isn't sensation the domain of biologists and physicians? Can you rank-order the senses, that is, place them in a hierarchy of importance? Can you justify your rankings?

- What role does the brain play in sensation and perception? Can you give specific information about the role of the brain for each sense? Are some senses "distant" senses and some "near" senses in terms of how we perceive a stimulus, despite whether the stimulus is physical or social? Can you think of other ways to categorize the various senses?

- Do you think vision is the most important human sense? Is it the dominant sense in all other animals? How is the brain involved in vision? How can scientists help blind people to see? If you were blind, would you want an implant to help you be sighted?

- Why is taste important? Do other organisms possess a sense of taste? What role does taste play in survival? How do sensation and perception interact to determine our food preferences?

- What is synesthesia? Can you describe the experiences a person with synesthesia has? From where does this strange process come? That is, what causes synesthesia?

- Why is it important to study pain? Why are psychologists interested in pain and pain management? How can pain be better managed?

- What are the various types of sleep? What are some of the problems sleep researchers encounter? What are some of the disorders that sleepers encounter? How can we help people with various disorders, for example insomnia?

 **Links: www.dushkin.com/online/**
These sites are annotated in the World Wide Web pages.

Five Senses Home Page
http://www.sedl.org/scimath/pasopartners/senses/welcome.html
Psychology Tutorials and Demonstrations
http://psych.hanover.edu/Krantz/tutor.html

Marina and her roommate have been friends since freshmen year. Because they share so much in common, they decided to become roommates in their sophomore year. They both want to travel abroad one day. Both date men from the same college, are education majors, and want to work with young children after graduation from college. Today they are at the local art museum. As they walk around the galleries, Marina is astonished at her roommate's taste in art. Whatever her roommate likes, Marina hates. The paintings and sculptures that Marina admires are the very ones to which her roommate turns up her nose. "How can their tastes in art be so different when they share so much in common?" Marina wonders.

What Marina and her roommate are experiencing is a difference in perception or the interpretation of the sensory stimulation provided by the artwork. Perception and its sister area of psychology, sensation, are the focus of this unit.

For many years, it was popular for psychologists to consider sensation and perception as two distinct processes. Sensation was defined in passive terms as the simple event of some stimulus energy (i.e. a sound wave) impinging on the body or on a specific sense organ that then reflexively transmitted appropriate information to the central nervous system. With regard to the concept of sensation, in the past both passivity and simple reflexes were stressed. Perception, on the other hand, was defined as an integrative and interpretive process that the higher centers of the brain supposedly accomplish based on sensory information and available memories for similar events.

The Gestalt psychologists, early German researchers, were convinced that perception was a higher order function compared to sensation. The Gestalt psychologists believed that the whole stimulus was more than the sum of its individual sensory parts; Gestalt psychologists believed this statement was made true by the process of perception.

For example, some of you listen to a song and hear the words, the loudness, and the harmony as well as the main melody. However, you do not really hear each of these units; what you hear is a whole song. If the song is pleasant to you, you may exclaim that you like the song and even buy the CD. If the song is raucous to you, you may perceive that you do not like it and hope it ends soon. However, even the songs you first hear and do not like may become liked after repeated exposure to those songs. Hence perception, according to these early Gestalt psychologists, was a more advanced and complicated process than sensation.

This dichotomy of sensation and perception is no longer widely accepted. The revolution came in the mid-1960s when a psychologist published a then-radical treatise in which he reasoned that perceptual processes included *all* sensory events that he believed were directed by an actively searching central nervous system. Also, this view provided that certain perceptual patterns, such as recognition of a piece of artwork, may be species-specific. That is, all humans, independent of learning history, should share some of the same perceptual repertoires. This unit on perceptual processes is designed to further your understanding of these complex and interesting processes.

The first article is entitled "Vision Seekers: Giving Eyesight to the Blind Raises Questions About How People See." Vision usually is the dominant sense in humans. Vision, however, is a complicated process that can be studied in both sighted and impaired individuals. The study of giving sight to previously blind people has scientists gleaning new information about how the eyes and the brain function together. How long an individual has been blind is crucial to the science of understanding vision as well as to whether treatment is effective.

Another article pertains to taste. Humans can often be particular about how things taste and what food they will eat. Their pickiness might have survival underpinnings or, on the other hand, might be learned. The author showcases work on super-tasters or individuals who have ultra-sensitive tastes buds. Supertasters may eat or refuse foods that affect their long-term health; thus, it is important to understand the sense of taste. This topic also provides good insight into how sensation and perception typically operate in tandem.

In the article by Marni Jackson, she describes how and why scientists are studying pain and what they have learned thus far. One important finding could lead to scientists knowing better how to control pain.

The final selection of this unit relates to an altered state of perception or altered state of consciousness (something outside of normal sensation and perception). This last article is about sleeping, something we all do but think about very little. By studying sleep, researchers are beginning to understand why we sleep and what causes certain sleep disorders. As scientists have discovered, some disorders are psychological while others are physiological.

VISION SEEKERS

Giving eyesight to the blind raises questions about how people see

BY BRUCE BOWER

One witheringly hot day last summer, a 10-year-old boy performed a few miracles at a hospital near Calcutta, India. For openers, he caught a balled-up piece of paper thrown to him. Then, he picked up paper clips and inserted them into a holder through a small opening. Looking determined, the boy proceeded to identify, drawings of an elephant and other animals. Finally, he greeted all of his physicians and nurses, referring to each by name.

Not impressed? These accomplishments sure looked miraculous to Pawan Sinha, a neuroscientist at the Massachusetts Institute of Technology (MIT) who was in Calcutta visiting the hospital. Sinha knew that the boy had had severe cataracts in both eyes since birth. He had grown up in a poor family; and the reason for his blindness went undiagnosed until he tripped and broke his leg at age 10. A physician treating the boy's leg instantly noticed the youngster's cataracts and arranged for free surgery.

Five weeks later, the boy—a newcomer to the world of sight—dazzled Sinha with visual feats. It's not yet clear whether a child deprived of sight for many years can learn to see the world with all the subtlety and skill of a person who grew up with normal vision, however. Researchers are just beginning to piece together how the brain responds to blindness early in life and then how it reacts to the sudden unleashing of vision, however years or even decades later.

What's evident, though, is that sight requires far more than simply opening one's eyes and letting reality in. Perception, whether through vision or any other sense, is an acquired taste. People learn to make visual sense of faces and other items of interest, often during infancy and early childhood but sometimes over much longer periods.

A person's view of the world feeds off his or her past experiences with three-dimensional space, the physical details of particular settings, and the predictable shapes and colors of various items, to name a few.

When the loss of sight deprives young eyes of visual experience, other faculties fill the void: Brain regions traditionally thought to handle only vision commit to duties ranging from touch processing to verbal memory.

Sinha now finds himself in a position to explore how kids' brains adapt to years of blindness and then respond to the onset of sight. He and his coworkers are tracking the progress of 20 children in India, ages 6 to 15, who grew up sightless before the surgical removal of their cataracts. "I'm amazed at how much these kids can do based on vision shortly after cataract surgery," the MIT scientist says. "No one knows if the visual modality will reclaim areas in their brains that it lost to other senses due to blindness."

FACE TIME It's particularly gratifying to observe the success of formerly blind children at recognizing the faces of their family members, physicians, and other familiar people, Sinha says. He estimates that cataract-induced blindness affects as many as 100,000 children in India.

The "fairly crummy" level of visual detail available to most of the Indian children after cataract surgery encourages them to concentrate on the geography of entire faces, while ignoring the nuances of eyes, mouths, noses, or hair, Sinha says. These children also often recognize even partial or faded pictures of familiar faces, indicating that the youngsters refer to a mental catalogue of whole faces, Sinha says.

Babies, whose vision is also blurry, may similarly perceive whole faces rather than specific facial features, he theorizes.

Yet such speculation runs smack into scientists' limited knowledge about the nature of face perception in formerly blind children, as well as in infants (*SN: 7/7/01, p. 10*).

At least some data on the subject come from studies of Canadians directed by psychologist Daphne Maurer of McGill University in Hamilton, Canada. Children subjected to cataract-induced blindness in only the left eye for the first 2 to 6 months of life lose an element crucial for discerning facial configurations, Maurer's team reports in the October *Nature Neuroscience*. As teenagers and young adults, these individuals find it difficult to detect differences in the spacing of eyes and other facial features from one person to another.

In contrast, people of the same age who had right-eye cataracts for 2 to 6 months after birth can discern the distance between facial features as well as people with no prior vision problems do.

Despite lacking this face-recognition skill, adults who had left-eye cataracts removed during infancy still manage to recognize their friends and family and don't report any problems in telling familiar faces apart.

Individual facial features evidently guide recognition. McGill psychologist Catherine J. Mondloch and her coworkers found that people deprived of left-eye vision as babies could accurately tell when the researchers had substituted different eyes or mouths on previously seen images of faces or had digitally thinned or fattened the faces.

The results, which so far derive from 10 volunteers born with left-eye cataracts and another 10 born with right-eye cataracts, implicate the brain's right side in expert face processing, Mondloch says. It is only during infancy that visual information entering the left eye goes mainly to the right hemisphere, while the right eye sends most of its visual input to the left hemisphere. Thus, the capacity to notice the spacing of facial features develops only if the right hemisphere receives visual stimulation during that brief period of time. Even then, according to other studies directed by Mondloch, this skill isn't fully developed until about age 18.

For instance, when asked to identify matches between pairs of faces with assorted head angles—posed so that the spacing of facial features appeared to vary—10-year-olds with no prior eye problems performed as poorly as adults with former left-eye cataracts did. Given normal visual development, face processing improves sharply between ages 16 and 18, Mondloch says.

She plans to conduct brain-scan and brain-wave studies of cataract patients to determine their neural responses to faces. The McGill researchers also want to see whether people who had left-eye cataracts removed can be trained to recognize faces solely on the basis of the spacing of eyes and mouths.

Sinha hopes to direct similar studies of Indian youngsters treated for cataracts. Those children will undoubtedly become visually adept in many ways, but they were blind far too long to become face-processing experts, Mondloch suspects. "It's already too late if you receive cataract surgery 2 months after birth," she says.

EYE REVIVAL Even if improvements in vision are marginal for those children surgically thrust into the sighted world after years of blindness, there's room for optimism regarding their adaptation to whatever sight they acquire.

"The kids I've studied show good emotional adjustment after cataract surgery," Sinha says. "It probably helps that adults don't have a lot of expectations about what these children should be able to do as sighted individuals."

Adults who regain their sight after being blind for all or most of their lives are often not so fortunate. Published reports of such cases, which date to 1,000 years ago, often describe an initial elation at being able to see, followed by emotional turmoil, depression, and even suicide.

In his hook *An Anthropologist On Mars* (1995, Knopf), neurologist Oliver Sacks of Albert Einstein College of Medicine in New York recounts the story of Virgil, a man who saw little until having cataract surgery at age 50. Sacks calls Virgil's behavior after cataract removal that of a "mentally blind" person—someone who sees but can't decipher what's out there.

Virgil's perceptual identity, his sense of himself was tied to experiences that had nothing to do with sight. He often felt torn between first looking at objects or touching them instead, as he had always done. When feeling visually overloaded, he would act as if he were still blind. Often confused, Virgil rapidly sank into depression. About 4 months after his surgery, he died of pneumonia.

Michael G. May has adapted much better to his recovered vision. A stem-cell transplant delivered sight to his right eye in 2001 when he was 43, after 40 years of blindness. Ione Fine of the University of Southern California in Los Angeles and her colleagues describe May's visual progress in the September *Nature Neuroscience*.

May regards the challenge of learning to see as an exciting new chapter in his life. It helps that he's an outgoing, optimistic person with a supportive spouse, according to Fine.

"Mike certainly sees the world differently than others do," she notes. Two years after his surgery May still has no intuitive grasp of depth perception. As people walk away from him, he perceives them in as literally shrinking in size and has to remind himself that they're farther away than they were before.

Objects and faces also puzzle May. He has difficulty identifying everyday items, distinguishing male from female faces, and recognizing emotional expressions on unfamiliar faces. May keeps track of people's faces by noting hair length, eyebrow shape, and other individual features.

May does track his own and others' movements with precision. He also distinguishes shaded areas from illuminated surfaces. With these capabilities, he's made a transition from being an expert blind skier who depended on verbal directions from a sighted guide, to being a competent sighted skier.

May's chipper outlook and visual accomplishments so far are inspiring, remarks psychologist Richard L. Gregory of the University of Bristol in England. Says Gregory: "It is possible to live happily with delayed sight and to gain from the new experiences."

BLIND BRAINS The transition from prolonged blindness to sudden sight doesn't demand just psychological resilience. It requires unprecedented accommodations from the brain.

Brain-imaging studies indicate that neural areas devoted to vision, which comprise as much as one-quarter of the brain in primates, take on entirely different responsibilities in blind individuals. For instance, vision-associated regions of the brain appear to facilitate the sensitivity of touch among those without sight. In 1996, researchers reported that the visual cortex at the back of the brain showed increased activity when blind people use the tips of their fingers to read Braille publications.

Moreover, psychological investigations suggest that blind people perform better than their sighted peers do on tests of verbal memory. Parts of the brain's visual system—including tissue that otherwise serves as an entry point for visual information from the eyes—become more active when blind participants recall previously studied words and generate verbs for a list of braille nouns, according to a report in the July *Nature Neuroscience.*

Blind volunteers with the strongest verbal memories displayed especially intense activity in these brain areas when they performed the word tasks. In sighted volunteers, these neural tissues remained calm during the same verbal tests, say neuroscientist Ehud Zohary of Hebrew University in Jerusalem and his colleagues. In sighted people, language-related brain areas far removed from the visual cortex handle verbal memory.

Studies such as Zohary's suggest that the brain undergoes a major reorganization in people who are blind from birth to adulthood, enabling tissue that would otherwise deal in vision to take on other sensory duties, as well as language and memory assignments.

If so, the brains of formerly blind children should yield scientific surprises. Sinha's 10-year-old cataract patient in India undoubtedly relishes the possibility of mustering a few neural revelations. In this boy's case, eyesight may spark insight. ■

A Matter of Taste

Are you a supertaster? Just stick out your tongue and say "yuck"

BY MARY BECKMAN

THERE'S GOOD TASTE, and according to scientists, there's supertaste. Blue food coloring is going to tell me where I lie on the continuum. Armed with a bottle of blue dye No. 1 and a Q-tip, I paint my tongue cobalt, swish some water in my mouth and spit into the bathroom sink. In the mirror I see a smattering of pink bumps—each hiding as many as 15 taste buds apiece—against the lurid blue background. Now I'm supposed to count how many of those bumps, called fungiform papillae, appear inside a circle a quarter-inch in diameter, but I don't need to do that. Obviously, I have fewer than the 30 that would qualify me as having an extraordinary palate. I am not a supertaster. Thank goodness.

Normally, people prize highly acute senses. We brag about twenty-twenty vision or the ability to eavesdrop on whispers from across the room. But taste is not so simple: supertaste may be too much of a good thing, causing those who have it to avoid bitter compounds and find some spicy foods too hot to handle. This unusual corner of perception science has been explored by Linda Bartoshuk of Yale University, who first stumbled upon supertasting about 15 years ago while studying saccharin. While most people found the sugar substitute sweet and palatable, others sensed a bitter aftertaste. She went on to test hundreds of volunteers with a host of chemicals found in food. About one in four, she discovered, qualified as supertasters, a name she coined.

To find what made them special, Bartoshuk zeroed in on the tongue's anatomy. She found that people have different numbers of fungiform papillae, with tongue topography ranging from, say, sparse cactus-pocked deserts to lush lawns. To qualify for supertasterdom, which is a genetically inherited trait, a person has to have wall-to-wall papillae on his or her tongue and also have an ability to readily taste PROP, a bitter synthetic compound also known as 6-*n*-propylthiouracil, which is used as a thyroid medication.

As it happens, Bartoshuk is a non-taster—she's among another one in four who can't detect PROP at all—and likes it that way. "I prefer the dumb, happy life I lead," she says. "'Super' connotes superiority, but supertaste often means sensory unpleasantness." In the course of her research she has relied on volunteers and colleagues to perceive what she cannot, such as the difference in creaminess between skim and 2 percent milk. "PROP tastes like quinine," says Laurie Lucchina, a supertaster who made this discovery about ten years ago when she worked with Bartoshuk. Another person in the lab, Valerie Duffy, now at the University of Connecticut, is a medium taster. Bartoshuk routinely tested "the junk food of the month," sent to the lab through a food subscription service, on the two women. "Once she brought in a cookie that she thought was very bland. But to me, it tasted just right," recalls Lucchina.

"Mother's milk reflects the culture into which babies are born."

Perhaps not surprisingly, supersensitive taste influences what people eat. Bartoshuk and other researchers found that supertasters tend to shun or restrict strong-flavored foods and drinks—coffee, frosted cake, greasy barbequed ribs, hoppy hand-crafted ales. Also, supertasters tend to crave neither fats nor sugars, which probably helps explain why researchers have found that supertasters also tend to be slimmer than people without the sensitivity. When it comes to rich desserts, Lucchina says, "I usually eat just a bite or two and then I'm done."

Taste sensitivity may also affect health. According to recent studies, supertasters have better cholesterol profiles than the norm, helping reduce their risk of heart disease. Yet supertasting may also have a downside. Some scientists have speculated that supertasters don't eat enough bitter vegetables, which are believed to protect against various types of cancer. And in a still-preliminary study of 250 men by Bartoshuk and co-workers, nontasters had fewer colon polyps, a risk factor for colon cancer, than did medium tasters or supertasters. To be sure, not everyone is convinced that supertasters put themselves in harm's way by skimping on vegetables. Adam Drewnowski, a nutrition scientist at the University of Washington, says a dollop of butter or maybe a splash of cheese sauce may be all a supertaster needs to find spinach or broccoli palatable. Still, the new data intrigue medical researchers, who don't usually consider taste an inherited factor in disease risk.

Of course, there's more to satisfaction than meets the tongue. Flavors are a combination of taste and odors, which float up through the back of our mouths to activate a suite of smell receptors in the nose. (Hold your nose while tasting a jellybean. You can tell it's sweet but not what flavor it is. Then unplug your nose. See?) Each smell tingles a different constellation of neurons in the brain, and with experience we learn what these different patterns mean—it's bacon sizzling in the kitchen, not liver. Nature may dictate whether or not we're supertasters, but it's nurture that shapes most of our food preferences.

And taste training starts earlier than one might think—during breast-feeding or even in the womb, according to biopsychologist Julie Mennella of the Monell Chemical Senses Center in Philadelphia. She asked pregnant women and breast-feeding mothers to drink carrot juice for three weeks. In both cases, when it came time to switch to solid food, babies of these mothers liked carrots better than babies whose mothers never drank the stuff. "These are the first ways they learn what foods are safe," Mennella says. "Mother's milk reflects the culture into which babies are born."

Learning can even trump innate good sense, according to a study Mennella reported this past April. She found that 7-month-old babies normally disliked bitter and sour flavors, and when given a bottle with a slightly bitter, sour formula, they pushed it away and wrinkled their angelic faces in disgust. But 7-month-olds who had been introduced to the bitter formula months earlier happily drank it again. In another study of babies who'd never been fed carrots, she found that those who'd been exposed to a variety of other vegetables clearly enjoyed carrots more than did babies who'd dined on a more monotonous diet. She suggests that early exposure to a diversity of flavors enables babies to trust new foods later in life. "Clearly experience is a factor in developing food habits," says Mennella. "But we don't know how that interacts with genetics."

Beyond genes and even learning lies a more ineffable aspect of taste: its emotional content. Certain foods can bring back unpleasant experiences; it may take only one rotten hot dog to put you off franks for life. Other tastes unlock happy memories. To an extent that researchers are still trying to understand, learning which foods are safe to eat while in the security of mother's arms may be the source of some of our most enduring desires. This learning process could be, Mennella says, "one of the foundations of how we define what is a comfort food."

MARY BECKMAN, a freelance writer in Idaho, specializes in the life sciences.

IT'S A NOISY, NOISY WORLD OUT THERE!

From the acoustic trauma of airbag deployment to the blast of personal stereos, we must stop turning a deaf ear to the daily menace of noise in our environment.

by Dr. Richard Carmen

The 80-decibel (dB) alarm clock (two feet from my head) shatters the silence at 6:45 a.m. and does bad things to nice dreams. Anything less noisy risks not waking me up.

Moments later, the electric shaver mows precariously near my ears at 85 dB. After the shower, it's time for the hair-blower endurance test of 112 dB. If decibels were converted to wind velocity, the hair dryer could self-propel. This new dryer—a "Turbo-Rocket Torque-357"—should require special handling and be reclassified as a leaf blower. On days when I'm short on time, I move it closer to my hair and therefore nearer to my ears. Not a good idea.

This racket signals my four-year-old daughter that my day has begun. She bolts into the bathroom shouting louder than the dryer, sometimes toting her toy megaphone to amplify her morning song, "Fe Fi Fo Fum!" (135 dB one foot away) If this cacophony were to occur outside, my neighbors could have me fined and, in some cities, even arrested!

By the time I make it to my quiet morning coffee, a short but heartfelt reprieve, the doorbell is intermittently emitting sounds that remind me of an Alfred Hitchcock movie. Each 115 dB buzz (just below my auditory discomfort but exceeding my annoyance level) reminds me I have to get rid of it.

It's my daughter's ride to school. She dashes out the door, and I'm right behind her. We're greeted with a blare of the horn. It feels like dual five-inch cannons against our foreheads. Reflexively, I raise my arms and drop her lunchbox. Ears slightly ringing, I accept the driver's wave of apology and hobble back to my tepid coffee. I would normally use the microwave to reheat it, but the "Ready" alarm is just more than I can handle this morning. And the day has just begun.

I escape momentarily into the TV room, when my wife walks in. "How can you stand it that loud?" she queries. "You better check your hearing, honey!" she adds as she leaves.

I follow her into the kitchen where a high-speed blender prepares her morning nutritional drink. Military assault weapons make less noise.

"How can you stand it that loud?" I shout, wondering if the noise does as much mixing as the blades.

"What?" she asks. At least I think that's what she says; it was the right lip movement. I don't answer her because she can't read lips, and besides, she's turned on the disposal (94 dB)—loud, but inconsequential, considering the blender. I blow her a kiss, and I'm off to work.

The slam of the door on my old truck, metal to metal, surely has acoustic peaks exceeding 120 dB. It hurts, but if I don't slam it, the door remains ajar. I've noticed ringing in that left ear lately.

On the highway, I wave to a physician friend riding his motorcycle without a helmet, and wonder if he knows that riding at 80 mph for just one hour puts him at risk for hearing loss.

And so it goes for families all across America.

Despite the Occupational Safety and Health Administration's (OSHA) decree stating that workers should not be exposed to more than 90 dB for an eight-hour period, these limits

How's Your Hearing?

The following questions can help you determine if you have a hearing loss and need to have your hearing evaluated.

❏ Do you have a problem hearing over the telephone?

❏ Do you hear better with one ear than the other when you are on the telephone?

❏ Do you have trouble following the conversation when two or more people are talking at the same time?

❏ Do people complain that you turn the TV volume up too high?

❏ Do you have to strain to understand conversation?

❏ Do you have trouble hearing in a noisy background?

❏ Do you have trouble hearing in restaurants?

❏ Do you have dizziness, pain, or ringing in your ears?

❏ Do you find yourself asking people to repeat themselves?

❏ Do family members or coworkers remark about your missing what has been said?

❏ Do many people you talk to seem to mumble (or not speak clearly)?

❏ Do you misunderstand what others are saying and respond inappropriately?

❏ Do you have trouble understanding the speech of women and children?

❏ Do people get annoyed because you misunderstand what they say?

If you answer yes to more than two of these questions, you should have your hearing tested by a licensed audiologist.

are exceeded every day throughout U.S. industry. I've been in paper mills and factories where hard hats and earplugs are required upon entry.

The workers' biggest complaint about hearing protection is that they can't hear one another or potentially lifesaving warnings, like backup signals of heavy equipment. With good ear protection, you're not supposed to hear well. The solution is to provide ear defenders that incorporate telecommunication ability, like the kind pit crews wear at auto races so coworkers can share essential information. Although this technology works, it's expensive. Nevertheless, corporations should realize that protection is in their best interest; the average annual cost of medical management for hearing loss is $56 billion.

Unfortunately, government-approved noise levels for an eight-hour day are not proven to be safe. Furthermore, for many of us, dangerously loud noise levels may not even end at work. And if you happen to work around certain chemicals (e.g., lacquer or varnish containing toluene) while exposed to high-level noise, you have a significantly increased risk for hearing loss.

Noise holds a certain "prestige" for some. "Manly" men who model themselves after the character Tim Allen played on his TV show are proud to show off their latest power mowers (105 dB), sandblasters (110 dB), power drills (115 dB), or chain saws that can V-cut right into the hardest knot of an oak tree (135 dB)!

Recreational "boy toys" (yes, and "girl toys," too) range from snowmobiles (110 dB) to rifles and guns (120 to 140 dB). Then there are those kids with boom boxes (better identified as "bomb boxes") in their cars. The average continuous output of these devices exceeds 120 dB; these kids' window-rattling "music" will surely come back to haunt them one day.

Because women aren't typically exposed to as much noise as men, they may think they're safe from noise hazards. Not so. That sweet bundle of joy sleeping peacefully in your arms is capable of hurling cries at 120-plus dB. The toys that accompany such bundles can put not only children but also caretakers at risk.

Every year, children's toys are removed from the market because of their intolerably dangerous noise levels. Some peaks reach 150 dB. Despite the watchful eye of OSHA,

Noise Levels

dBA*	NOISE SOURCE
190 ...	105mm howitzer
170 ...	deployed auto airbag
163 ...	bazooka at one foot
155 ...	assault rifles 13 feet from the muzzle
150 ...	child's toy mimicking an assault rifle
145 ...	U.S. Army Sergeant missile at 100 feet
140 ...	threshold of pain; military assault rifle; toy cap gun; siren at 100 feet
135 ...	U.S. Army tactical launcher at 400 feet; jet taking off; child's voice-amplified toy; amplified music
130 ...	miniature rifles; air-raid siren
125 ...	child's toy phone
120 ...	threshold of discomfort; auto horn; chain saw; jackhammer; snowmobile (driver's seat); child's musical instruments
110 ...	MRI (at head location in the isocenter); inboard motorboat; sandblaster; baby rattle; films in movie theaters
105 ...	power saw; helicopter
100 ...	subway train; tractor; farm equipment
95 ...	ride in a convertible car on freeway
90 ...	industrial noise
80 ...	live piano music
70 ...	dog bark
60 ...	vacuum cleaner
50 ...	conversation; some vowels in conversation
40 ...	soft music
30 ...	some high-frequency consonants
20 ...	dripping water
10 ...	soft whisper
5 ...	soft rustling leaves
0 ...	the best hearing threshold

* Sound pressure levels as measured on the A scale.

This table was compiled by the author from a variety of scientific sources.

some toys sneak through, even by brand-name companies we've come to trust.

A couple of years ago, one toy manufacturer's trendy slogan flashed through our industry like a thunderbolt: "Play It Loud." After much opposition from the hearing industry, this company backed down and eliminated the banner line. Yet, toy cellular telephones and walkie-talkies at clearly hazardous levels are still marketed to our children.

Although the polls say that women continue to shoulder the load when it comes to housework, heavy cleaning can be an equal-opportunity noise hazard. A manufacturer once put a quiet vacuum cleaner on the market, a product that was proven to be as effective as its competition. It died quietly in stores throughout the country. Consumers didn't believe it; noise is equated with power and effectiveness. We like it loud!

A front-row seat at a rock concert or in a bar with a live band can easily carry acoustic peaks exceeding 130 dB. This sound level can wreak the same results as excessive drinking: nausea and vomiting.

With the advent of CD-quality TVs, stereos, telephones, and the like, the tremendous enhancement in fidelity requires less volume. Improved signal-to-noise ratios produce less internal noise; however, we still demand louder volume levels. The problem is that we've grown accustomed to it, and the misperception that "louder is better" persists.

Current statistics suggest that about a third of all hearing loss is attributable to noise. From health club fitness classes, where bombardment

of music is maintained at 110 dB for 30 minutes or more, to movie theaters that exceed 130 dB (actually replicating the sound pressure level of a gun!), you as a willing participant are at risk. In a sure sign of progress, the associations for both these groups, The International Association of Fitness Professionals and the National Association of Theater Owners, are at long last recommending sound-level reductions, indicating that maybe "softer is better."

We all differ in our sensitivities. Some people have a more highly developed sense of smell, taste, vision, touch, or hearing. While there may be established norms, individual variability can be great. Some people with more acute hearing have an increased susceptibility to noise-induced hearing loss. Research data have shown that people with light-colored eyes (vs. dark eyes) run an increased risk of hearing loss when around high-level noise.

Furthermore, *The Lancet* (Jan. 2, 1999) reported on a French study among 1,208 men aged 18 to 24. They found that those who had regularly used personal stereo headsets for at least an hour daily and who also had a history of ear infections had significantly greater incidence of hearing loss.

Permanent, irreversible, instantaneous hearing loss occurs every day. Acoustic trauma is inflicted upon people in seemingly innocuous situations such as air-bag deployment, where sound-pressure levels can reach 170 dB. An estimated 30 million construction workers are at risk. Many airport workers are losing their hearing. And data now impli-

cate MRIs as a factor in hearing loss, a situation that can be solved by wearing earplugs during the test. Dentists and dental hygienists are at risk due to daily exposure to dental equipment such as blasters, drills, ultrasonic scalers, and so forth.

This is to name but a few of the culprits.

What are we doing to ourselves? While we don't have to buy products that emit toxic noise, sometimes we cannot escape, it, particularly when the noise is part of the work environment. Most of us can't just quit our jobs, but we can influence change.

Writing letters to manufacturers can make a difference. Professionals who use equipment with high noise levels (like dentists) must exert pressure on their suppliers. If we simply stopped purchasing their goods, manufacturers would respond accordingly. Nearly all products have noise reduction capability.

As parents, we must not support toy manufacturers that place our kids at risk. Stop buying their toys.

It has been said that one letter of complaint represents a hundred voices. Write one. When enough of us do, manufacturers will listen. Complain to theater managers and workout instructors. Noise will come down.

One person can make a difference. But in today's world, you may need to shout to be heard.

Richard Carmen, Au.D., FAAA, is a clinical audiologist and editor of the book *The Consumer Handbook on Hearing Loss & Hearing Aids: A Bridge to Healing*. His article appeared originally in *Hearing Health* magazine.

PAIN AND ITS MYSTERIES

Genetic and psychological factors help determine how well we withstand it

BY MARNI JACKSON

I was riding a bike in the Rockies, near Banff, when a bee flew into my mouth, and I felt a slim, unambiguous lance of pain, like a splinter of glass. Right away, I noticed, this sensation began to sprout a narrative. It wasn't just bad luck that the bee had stumbled into me; I saw the sting as punishment for biking "the wrong way"—distracted, churning along too fast, panting with open mouth. I had not been paying attention. Then pain had come along and rinsed the morning clear of small deceptions.

The next day, apart from having fabulous Angelina Jolie lips, I was back to normal. Unlike the chronic ache of arthritis or the lightning stab of trigeminal neuralgia, a bee sting is a wonderfully minor, finite form of pain. But the experience had nevertheless raised a swarm of questions about the mysterious nature of pain, and our relationship to it. For instance, why do we still talk about mental pain versus physical pain, when pain is always an emotional experience? How has it come about that something so universal remains so poorly understood, especially in an age of relentless self-scrutiny? And why hasn't anyone noticed the embarrassing fact that science is about to clone a human being, but it still can't cure the pain of a bad back?

The U.S. National Pain Foundation says more than four out of 10 American adults experience pain every day. The situation is likely much the same in Canada. North Americans consume four tons of ASA, a year, while chronic pain is on the rise. It's almost as if pain flourishes on our diet of analgesics. And it seems the more science learns how pain behaves (a quantum leap in the last 50 years), the less doctors want to do to treat it. To try to understand how we got ourselves in this pickle, I embarked on a four-year inquiry that zigzagged between art and science, doctor and patient. I talked to pain experts, and people who have learned to live with chronic pain. I tried to integrate the migrainish portrait of pain in Emily Dickinson's poetry or Virginia Woolf's novels with the latest MRI images of pain in the brain. I went back into the history of ideas about pain, where I encountered eccentric thinkers and unsung heroes, and forward into the genetic research into pain—where, once again, I ran into bees.

The inability to feel any pain at all is something that is inherited. Imagine: no hangovers, no sore pitching arm, no tremors in the dentist's chair. But congenital analgesia (as it's known) turns out to be both a nuisance and a life-threatening peril. Dr. Ron Melzack of McGill University and his British colleague, Dr. Patrick Wall—the two researchers whose "gate-control theory" revolutionized the way science now views pain—describe the consequences of a pain free life in their classic study, *The Challenge of Pain.* One girl with this condition suffered third-degree burns on her knees after climbing up on a hot radiator. And because there was no discomfort to let her know when she should shift her weight or posture, she eventually developed an inflammation in her joints and died at the age of 29.

Be glad it hurts when you stub your toe, because pain plays a vital role in our lives

Another woman with congenital analgesia felt nothing but a "funny, feathery feeling" when she delivered the first of her two children. But one of the best known examples of this rare inherited disorder was an American vaudeville performer in the 1920s, Edward H. Gibson, known as the Human Pincushion. His act involved sticking 50 to 60 pins into his body and then slowly removing them. It seems that for those born incapable of feeling pain, the career options are narrow, and life is short. Be glad it hurts when you stub your toe, because pain plays a vital, protective role in our lives.

Congenital analgesia is at the far end of a wide spectrum of inherited pain disorders. Genetic factors are involved in 39 to 55 per cent of migraines, 55 per cent of menstrual pain, and half of the back-pain population. Gender also has an influence, which will come as a surprise to no one. Men appear to suffer less pain, but require more pain relievers. There's no proof that women tolerate pain better than men, but they are three times more likely to suffer migraines, and six times more vulnerable to fibromyalgia. In a 1999 Gallup survey, 46 per cent of American women said they felt daily pain, compared to 37 per cent of men. And whether it's gene-related or stiletto-induced, one in four women also reported that their feet hurt.

"For a long time, people have accepted that there are wide variations in the way people respond to pain or to analgesics, but no one ever seriously considered attributing it to genetics, until now."

I was talking to Jeff Mogil, the first person in the world to put together training in psychology, genetics and pain. Mogil studied under psychologist and pain science pioneer John Liebeskind in California. After post-doctoral training in genetics, he joined the faculty at the University of Illinois in 1996. In 2001, Melzack lured him up to McGill University, where Mogil has succeeded him as the E. P. Taylor professor of pain research in psychology. This suggests that the pendulum is swinging back: science has moved away from seeing pain as a slippery psychological interpretation of something that only happens to the body, to approaching it as an experience that is at once neural, emotional and deeply rooted in our cells and genes.

"Pain genetics is where all the action is now, but it was a totally empty field when I moved into it," says Mogil, who is 35. "Nobody thought that pain had anything to do with genes. But then other people started working with knock-out mice, figuring out what happens when you remove this or that protein from a gene, and now knock-out mice are everywhere."

"Knock-out mice" always sounded to me like something you could order by the dozen at 3 a.m., from an infomercial. The sea monkeys of science. These mice are bred to lack a particular gene, and the protein it produces. "Then you look for what's wrong with the knock-out mouse when it doesn't have this or that protein any more," said Mogil. "It's the hottest technique in biology right now, and in pain research, too." It used to be that scientists didn't concern themselves with whatever strain of mouse they used in their studies, he added. But with knock-out mice "they discovered that the genetic background of the mouse was affecting their outcomes. It turned out that I was the only person paying attention to this sort of information."

When it comes to pain, he found, there is no such thing as a "universal rat." Pain sensitivity varies widely from strain to strain of rats and mice. Mogil also discovered that some mice are born either "doubly unlucky"—both over-sensitive to pain and under-responsive to analgesics—or vice versa, the lucky ones who feel less pain and require less painkiller.

"What the study of knock-out mice means for humans," Mogil said, "is that it helps explain individual sensitivities to pain and to drugs, as well as the fact that while most people will recover from an injury, some five per cent won't. They'll go on to develop chronic pain. Obviously, the factors that determine this are both environmental and genetic, and it's very tricky to sort these out. But if we know that some people have a propensity to chronic pain, then we might be able to find ways to keep it from developing in the first place. And as we learn more about pharmacogenetics, we can target their treatment with more precision. It also means that people who complain more about pain aren't necessarily whiners—they may actually feel more than other people. If humans really are like mice, then roughly half of that variability in pain response is due to their inherited genes."

Mogil has also studied the variety of ways people respond to painkillers. Indeed, the world seems to be divided into "responders" and "non-responders," since morphine is only successful with about 65 per cent of the population. This explains why pain doctors have to fiddle with a variety of pain medications before they get it right. Among Caucasians, about seven to 10 per cent are known as "poor metabolizers" who won't respond to codeine. They end up getting all the side effects, but none of the pain relief.

I asked Mogil whether this news would encourage more magic-bullet thinking—the notion that we can simply zero in on these "pain genes," knock them out, and throw away the Tylenol.

Genes don't work like that, he replied. "Just as there is no pain centre, there is no single pain gene that controls it. But it doesn't look like there's a hundred of them either. We're looking for a particular type of gene that exists in different forms that can be inherited—and of those genes, there are five to 10, maybe 20 tops."

But people are so eager to blame their genes for everything now, I said. Doesn't this new focus on the genetic aspect downplay the way cultural, political and social forces shape our perception of pain?

"But that's the thing about pain—the cortical stuff is really, really important," he said. Mogil automatically translates the word "culture" as "cortical activity," but I got his drift. He was referring to the emotions, ideas and attitudes that are the result of our memory, learning, and experience. And in Melzack and Wall's gate-control theory of pain, it is the "cortical stuff" that descends to the spinal cord, amplifying or muting the pain signals coming in from the periphery of the body. In other words sensory data travels up; "culture" moves down. And for both Mogil and Melzack, "everything is equally biological."

Melding neuroscience and psychology, Mogil (like Melzack before him) seems to be describing culture not as something "out there" but embodied in the way the brain shapes our experience of pain. It's interesting, I said to Mogil, that he and Melzack are both psychologists, sometimes seen as low men on the totem pole when the hard-science boys get together.

"Pain *is* psychological," Mogil emphasized. "There's all this neural activity going on, but it can always be trumped by culture, attitudes and behaviour. Being a psychologist lets me do work with a high level of variability in my tests. Most scientists don't want to see variability in their results. They're looking for consistency. But I get happy when I see messy data."

Then the bee came back into the picture. It turns out that pain researchers will sometimes use bee venom to induce what Ron Melzack calls a "good, classic pain, the type we can learn a lot from." Although bee venom has a long list of active ingredients, the main toxin is a peptide called melittin. This can produce chemicals known as cytokines that play an important role in painkilling.

(Tests on beekeepers who have been stung repeatedly have revealed elevated levels of cytokines.) In fact, bee venom has been popular in treating the pain of arthritis for centuries, especially in Europe. Now it's also being touted as helpful therapy for autoimmune conditions like multiple sclerosis, and a protective agent against X-irridiation in cancer patients. The alternative-network literature for BVT (bee venom therapy) is vast, and that's only one aspect of apitherapy, which uses everything from bee pollen, royal jelly and honey to the wax and venom to treat an array of disorders.

So my original suspicion that a bee sting is a complicated thing was not entirely off-base. It turns out that everything involved in the orchestration of the event we call pain—the swelling, inflammation, redness, heat and stinging sensation—may, under different, controlled circumstances, also offer pain relief. In other words, better pain treatment may not lie in our efforts to suppress it or surgically excise it, but in a deeper understanding of how the body can use aspects of the pain process to promote healing and recovery. The answer to pain may lie inside pain itself.

As science looks beyond the role of pain as symptom, its hidden narrative will continue to unfold. If Jeff Mogil is right, 50 years from now we will look at pain quite differently. Tylenol tablets will seem as quaint to us as sarsaparilla tonic. Instead, we'll take our ID bracelet to the local pharmacologist to order some bespoke analgesics, tailored to gender and genotype. Some of us may rise at 4 a.m. to meditate, and feel the struggle against pain lighten. We'll carry geno-cards that list our inherited predispositions: photosensitivity, osteoporosis and poor response to codeine.

Addiction might be redefined not as a character flaw but as "biochemical deficit management." Medical schools will actually teach doctors about the way pain behaves, and how to treat it. Our emotional habits will become an accepted factor of good health, and we'll know whether we're at risk for depression or rheumatoid arthritis in the same way we know that we're Scottish, or hazel-eyed. How we live with this new information, of course, will still be our choice. But we will understand that pain is sometimes history, in the body.

Adapted from Pain: The Fifth Vital Sign *by Marni Jackson. Copyright 2002 Marni Jackson. Reproduced by permission of the publisher, Random House Canada.*

Night life

by Jill Neimark

Dreams are our built-in entertainment as well as a porthole to the inner workings of our minds. New findings show they are a form of creative insanity that the brain uses for everything from mood regulation to learning, to memory—maybe even messages from beyond.

Ten years ago, in New Mexico, I had a startling dream. I'd made an appointment by phone to see an acupuncturist, and the night before my visit, I dreamed about him. "Listen," my dream-self said, "I'm still adjusting to the altitude here and need an unusually gentle treatment, or I'll get sick."

When I walked into his office the next day, he was exactly the man of my dream, down to each fine detail of his wavy brown hair and boyish face. I told him so, and he replied that he believed in precognition. He gave me a gentle treatment.

That dream was a small anomaly, but one that ripped opened my perspective: if in a dream I could know what someone looked like before I actually met him, then the dreaming mind is capable of spectacular range. That is the only precognitive dream I've ever had, but, like most of us, I've found my dreams to be deep and shallow, beautiful, nutty, mysterious, chaotic, and sometimes meaningful enough to trigger big life decisions.

From the Australian aborigines, who believe that the dreaming and waking worlds are equally real, to Freud, who felt dreams were a braid of repressed wishes; from Jung, who saw dreams as stories dipped in our collective unconscious, to Nobel-prize-winning scientist Francis Crick, who has suggested dreams are just the brain's way of forgetting, a sloughing-off of each day's meaningless events; from the cognitive neuroscientists who have discovered that dreams and REM sleep are linked to our ability to learn and remember, to those who believe dreaming is the meaningless and random sputtering of nerve cells, dreams are the sphinx-like riddle we keep trying to solve.

Robert Stickgold, Ph.D., a Harvard neuroscientist, has his own fascinating description: "The mind becomes clinically insane while dreaming." Stickgold says we're so comfortable with dreaming "that we don't realize how strange it is to lie in bed hallucinating patently impossible things without ever noticing that these things might be impossible."

"You're delusional and hyper-emotional and you might even suddenly wonder, 'Is this a dream?' but nine times out of ten you'll decide it's definitely real." Even stranger, Stickgold observes, is the fact that "for every person in the world, the same brain that works one way during the day shifts into a completely different mode at night."

According to Stickgold, dreams are proof that "the mechanism for producing insanity is present in all of us." The only questions are: "How do we throw that switch every night?" and "Why do we bother to do it at all?" He and others are now beginning to sketch out some intriguing answers.

Do we dream to forget? Or to remember? The answer seems to lie in new findings on REM sleep and its unique biological function. First, however, let's shatter a myth. Dreams and rapid-eye-movement (REM) sleep are not one and the same. We dream throughout the night, while in deep sleep—the sleep marked by slow EEG waves, during which the body repairs itself, releasing growth hormone. REM sleep, in contrast, is a violently "awake" sleep; the muscles are at rest but the brain and nervous system are highly active.

The brain cycles through REM sleep about four to six times a night, each time marked by irregular breathing, increased heart rate and brain temperature, general physiological arousal, and, in men, erections. Arousal is such that ulcer sufferers secrete twenty times more stomach acid in REM than in non-REM sleep.

The first REM cycle follows ninety minutes of slow-wave deep sleep and lasts about ten minutes. REM cycles lengthen through the night and the dreams in them get more bizarre and detailed, like wacky movies. REM dreams tend to be uniformly more emotional and memorable than non-REM ones. One of the most interesting aspects of REM sleep is that, for its duration, we are paralyzed from the neck down, and our threshold for sensory input is raised, so that external stimuli rarely reach and wake us. The brain is soaked in acetylcholine, which seems to stimulate nerve cells while it strips muscles of tone and tension. At the same time, serotonin levels plummet, changes are swift and global. It's as if during these cycles we are functioning with a different brain entirely.

Because we are literally paralyzed while we dream, we do not act out our nightly hallucinations. Otherwise, we might gesticulate, twitch, and actually stand up and play out our dreams. It's interesting that our eye muscles do not become paralyzed, and researchers have speculated that nature did not bother to develop a mechanism to paralyze our eye muscles simply because eye movement is a kind of gratuitous detail—it doesn't have much impact on the dreamer. Whatever fine reason, REM has been a boon to dream researchers, since it's a clear indication that we've slipped into that particular phase of sleep.

As the biology of dreams is being pieced together, the theories of Freud have begun to seem more improbable. Dreams are likely not the eruptions of the repressed primal self, disguised in clever puzzles that only your psychiatrist can decipher at $180 an hour. The first blow to this theory was dealt in 1977, when Harvard's J. Allan Hobson, Ph.D., proposed that dreams are a kind of narrative structure we impose on the random firing of neurons in the brainstem. The neocortex, our meaning-maker, creates stories out of this neuronal chaos—just as it does of waking life.

Those stories may indeed be clues to our inner selves. But when brains are dreaming, researchers find that the frontal lobes, which integrate information, are shut down, and the brain is driven by its emotional centers. Just last year, researchers Allen R. Braun, M.D., the National Institutes of Health, and Thomas J. Balkin, M.D., of the Walter Reed Army Institute, scanned the brain in both slow-wave and REM sleep and found that during the latter, the visual cortex and frontal lobes were both shut down. That deals yet another blow to Freud: if dream content were being monitored, with unconscious wishes being actively repressed and disguised, the frontal lobes would have to be active.

What is the purpose of the neural chaos of dreaming? Scientists are still puzzling that out. In 1983, Nobelist Francis Crick, of the Salk Institute in La Jolla, suggested that the brain was actually "reverse learning," that REM sleep allows the neurons to spew out each day's spurious and extra stimuli, cleansing the brain. "We dream to forget," Crick wrote, to enormous outcry. In 1986, he revised the hypothesis, noting that perhaps we dream to reduce fantasy and obsession—that dreams are a way of forgetting material that might otherwise needlessly intrude on everyday life.

"Then, in 1994, two researchers showed that our ability to learn seems dependent on REM sleep. Scientists Avi Karni and Dov Sagi, at Israel's Weitzman Institute, found that if someone is trained in a task and allowed a normal night's sleep, they will show improvement the next day. But if sleep is interrupted in each REM cycle, they show no improvement at all.

And the particular cycle of REM that gets interrupted is crucial. It's REM sleep in the last quarter of the night that counts. Bob Stickgold trained 57 individuals in a task and then tested them 3, 6, 9, or 12 hours later the same day, or overnight after an interval of 13, 16, or 22 hours. The task involved visual discrimination: a subject looks for diagonal lines against a background of horizontal lines.

The time interval had no influence on performance; the amount of sleep did. "If they had less than six hours of sleep, they did not improve," says Stickgold.

One might simply conclude that people need a lot of sleep in order to learn. The truth seems to be: they need certain cycles of sleep, and when awakened before their last REM cycle, the brain is unable to consolidate the memory of the task. But Stickgold and his colleagues found that more than REM cycles were at stake.

"A student of mine did another experiment and found that the amount of slow-wave sleep in the first two hours of the night is highly correlated with the amount of learning as well." How might the two sleep cycles—REM and deep slow—work together? There may be a two-step process of memory enhancement. "We know that levels of acetylcholine are high in REM sleep and low in slow-wave sleep. Perhaps as you cycle from one to the other, you're passing information back and between different parts of the brain. Its as if the brain is holding a conversation with itself and identifying exactly what it needs to know."

Stickgold thinks REM sleep may have yet another purpose: to actually alter intrusive experiences and memories from the day. "I was putting my son, who is ten, to bed after a day of skiing together. We were lying there with our eyes closed and I said, 'I feel I'm back on the ski slope. He said. 'Really? I'm on the ski lift.'" There's a tendency to have an intrusive replay of novel experiences when you go to sleep, says Stickgold, especially ones that involve the vestibular system of the brain, which plays a role in balance. "If I fall asleep, go through one REM cycle, and wake two hours later, the feeling is gone. I can't reproduce it. Something has happened to that memory in those two hours."

Stickgold is looking at this effect in people who play the computer game Tetris, which requires rotating small blocks that float down the screen. "More than one person has told me that the day they first got hooked on the game, they went to bed, closed their eyes, and could see these blocks floating. It's gone the next day. Something in your brain in that first two hours has taken a memory that at sleep onset is incredibly intrusive and altered it so that it no longer behaves that way."

Rosalind Cartwright, Ph.D., the doyenne of dream research, has also found that sleep softens intrusive experience, especially depressing feeling moods. Director of the sleep disorders service and head of psychology at Chicago's Rush Presbyterian-St. Luke's Medical Center, she has evidence that dreams help regulate and stabilize mood, defusing negative feelings.

By observing sixty normal and seventy clinically depressed adults, Cartwright found that among those who had a mildly unpleasant day or experience, dreams were negative at the beginning of the night and became pleasant by the end. Among the clinically depressed, dreams were bland at the beginning and negative by night's end. "Normal individuals wake up in a better mood after a depressing day," she says. "Depressed individuals wake up feeling worse."

Cartwright adds a coda. "I'll tell you the kicker: a few of the depressed people showed the opposite pattern. Their dreams got more positive across the night. And those were the ones who got over their depression. You could predict it from a single night of dreaming."

Dreams, Cartwright believes, are our "internal therapist"; they offer an emotional information processing system. When that therapist isn't functioning—if, for example, you suffer from post-traumatic stress disorder manifested by recurrent nightmares—you may actually be able to lend it some help. Recently, researchers in Canada have found that consciously changing your dream in any direction while awake may stop the recurrence.

Tony Zadra, Ph.D., of the Dream and Nightmare Laboratory at the University of Montreal, studied six cases of recurrent nightmares—"and all got better," he says. The technique? While awake, the dreamers were taken on a guided visualization into the nightmare, and, at an emotional moment in the dream, were asked to visualize a simple task, such as looking at their hands. Then they were asked to respond differently—say, confront an aggressor or otherwise create a positive outcome.

After rehearsing the new ending while awake, the dreamers go to sleep as usual. And then an interesting thing happens: "Some people actually remember to look at their hands at the right moment, and then become aware that they are dreaming and that they can consciously carry out their dream differently. Others don't remember to look at their hands, but they dream the new dream they created while awake."

Either way, the nightmares stop. Says Zadra: "Some studies show that you can change absolutely anything in the nightmare, rehearse that change, and the nightmare will get better." It's the change that counts—it dismantles the dream and pries loose its hold on the dreamer.

It seems that dreams are many-purposed. They invite us into the truly interesting frontier of the mind. That may be why Stickgold says, "I love dreaming. And I love dreams."

Brains in Dreamland

Scientists hope to raise the neural curtain on sleep's virtual theater

By BRUCE BOWER

After his father's death in 1896, Viennese neurologist Sigmund Freud made a momentous career change. He decided to study the mind instead of the brain. Freud began by probing his own mind. Intrigued by his conflicted feelings toward his late father, the scientist analyzed his own dreams, slips of the tongue, childhood memories, and episodes of forgetfulness.

Freud's efforts culminated in the 1900 publication of *The Interpretation of Dreams*. In that book, he depicted dreams as symbolic stories in which sleepers' unconscious sexual and aggressive desires play out in disguised forms.

Later in his life, Freud acknowledged that dreams don't always gratify wishes. For instance, he noted that some dreams represent attempts to master a past traumatic experience. Yet the father of psychoanalysis always held that dreams contain both surface events and subterranean themes of great personal importance. For that reason, he wrote, "the interpretation of dreams is the royal road to a knowledge of the unconscious activities of the mind."

Freud's theory of how dreams work has had a huge cultural impact over the past century, even as it attracted intense criticism. Now, brain scientists—members of the discipline that Freud left behind—have stepped to the forefront of this passionate dream dispute.

One prominent group of scientists asserts that Freud profoundly misunderstood dreams. In their view, the act of dreaming yields a guileless collage of strange but heartfelt images that carry no hidden meanings.

These scientists say that dreaming occurs when a primitive structure called the brain stem stirs up strong emotions, espe-cially anxiety, elation, and anger. At the same time, neural gateways to the external world shut down, as do centers of memory and rational thought. The brain then creates bizarre, internal visions that strongly resonate for the dreamer.

An opposing view corresponds in many ways to Freud's ideas. Its supporters portray dreams as products of a complex frontal-brain system that seeks out objects of intense interest or desire. When provoked during sleep, this brain system depicts deep-seated goals in veiled ways so as not to rouse the dreamer.

A third group of investigators regards the brain data as intriguing but inconclusive. Dreams may serve any of a variety of functions, they argue. Depending on the society, these uses include simulating potential threats, grappling with personal and community problems, sparking artistic creativity, and diagnosing and healing physical illnesses.

"It is striking that 100 years after Freud [published *The Interpretation of Dreams*], there is absolutely no agreement as to the nature of, function of, or brain mechanism underlying dreaming," says neuroscientist Robert Stickgold of Harvard Medical School in Boston.

A broad consensus exists on one point, though. If neuroscientists hope to understand the vexing relationship of brain and mind, they need to get a handle on dreams.

Freud's royal road to the unconscious looks like a scientific dead-end to psychiatrist J. Allan Hobson. Neuroscientific evidence indicates that the sleeping brain churns out dreams as an afterthought to its other duties, argue Hobson, Stickgold, and Edward F. Pace-Schott, also of Harvard Medical School.

"Unconscious wishes play little or no part in dream instigation, dream emotion is uncensored and undisguised, sleep is not protected by dreaming, and dream interpretation has no scientific status," Hobson says.

Hobson's assault on Freudian dream theory began more than a decade ago. At that time, he proposed that dreams result from random bursts of activity in a brain stem area that regulates breathing and other basic bodily functions. These brain stem blasts zip to the frontal brain during periods of rapid eye movement (REM) sleep, when the entire brain becomes nearly as active as when a person is awake.

Dreams most often occur during REM sleep. A slumbering individual enters REM sleep about every 90 minutes.

Hobson's group published a revision of this theory in the December 2000 BEHAVIORAL AND BRAIN SCIENCES. Their new approach grants that dreams harbor emotional significance, but not in the way Freud posited.

Brain imaging and sleep-laboratory data clearly delineate among wakefulness, REM sleep, and non-REM sleep, the Harvard scientists note.

Three essential processes during REM sleep make it the prime time for dreaming, they say. First, brain stem activity surges and sets off responses in emotional and visual parts of the brain. Second, brain regions that handle sensations from the outside world, control movement, and carry out logical analysis shut down. Third, brain stem cells pump out acetylcholine, a chemical messenger that jacks up activity in emotional centers.

At the same time, two neurotransmitters essential for waking activity—noradrenaline and serotonin—take a snooze.

The result, in Hobson's view: a vivid hallucination, informed by strong emotions, that takes bizarre twists and turns. REM sleep's biological makeup fosters the mistaken belief that one is awake while dreaming, saps the ability to reflect on the weirdness of dreams as they occur, and makes it difficult to recall dreams after waking up.

REM sleep conducts far more important business than dreaming, Hobson argues. Its central functions may include supporting brain development, regulating body temperature, fortifying the immune system, and fostering memories of recently learned information. The last possibility evokes heated scientific debate (SN: 7/22/00, p. 55).

Hobson's theoretical focus on brain stems and REMs doesn't do dreams justice, argues neuropsychologist Mark Solms of St. Bartholomew's and Royal London (England) School of Medicine.

"Dreaming is generated under the direction of a highly motivated, wishful state of mind," Solms holds. "I won't be at all surprised if we find that Freud's understanding of [dream] mechanisms was basically on the right track."

To dream, the brain—both in and out of REM sleep—stimulates a frontal-lobe system that orchestrates motivation and the pursuit of goals and cravings, the British scientist proposes. A neurotransmitter called dopamine ferries messages in the brain's motivation system.

The crux of Solms' argument rests on studies of brain-damaged patients. In rare instances where people incur injuries only to their brain stem, dreaming continues despite severe disruptions of REM sleep. In contrast, people who suffer damage to frontal-brain regions involved in motivation report that they no longer dream but still have nightly REM sleep. These individuals also become apathetic and lose much of their initiative, imagination, and ability to plan. This group includes several hundred mental patients who decades ago, as a therapy, had some of their frontal-brain nerve fibers surgically cut.

Additional support for Solms' view comes from brain-imaging studies indicating that frontal areas involved in motivation, emotion, and memory exhibit elevated activity during REM sleep.

Various forms of cerebral activation can trigger the motivation system and lead to dreaming, Solms suggests. This explains why vivid dreams occur shortly after falling asleep and in the morning, not just in the depths of REM sleep, he says.

Brain data can't yet confirm or disprove Freud's idea that dreams play a symbolic game of hide-and-seek with unconscious desires, Solms adds.

For now, something of a standoff exists between the dreaming-brain theories of Hobson and Solms.

Hobson and his coworkers welcome the possibility, raised by neuroscientist Tore A. Nielsen of the University of Montreal, that crucial elements of REM sleep operate in non-REM states as well. For instance, as people fall asleep they display slow eye movements and electrical activity in the brain and muscles that may constitute a kind of "covert REM activity," Nielsen says.

If the REM state in one form or another saturates much of sleep, then the brain stem and related emotional centers create dreams throughout the night, Hobson asserts.

Solms regards "covert REM" as a hazy concept. REM sleep consists of diverse physiological changes in the brain and body. This sleep stage can't be equated with a few of its biological components that may appear at other times during the night, he contends.

Haziness also afflicts attempts to decipher dreams with recordings of brain activity, remarks neuroscientist Allen Braun of the National Institutes of Health in Bethesda, Md. These images of neural tissue show where the brain is stirring during specific sleep stages, Braun says, but not how those areas operate or whether they play a direct role in dreaming.

Brain-imaging reports generally support Solms' theory that dreams derive from a frontal-brain motivation system, Braun notes (SN: 1/17/98, p. 44). However, a frontal-brain area considered pivotal for self-monitoring and abstract thought naps throughout sleep. Braun considers this finding to clash with the Freudian notion of dreams as hotbeds of disguised meaning.

Freud's emphasis on wish fulfillment in dreams needs revision too, according to neuroscientist Antti Revonsuo of the University of Turku in Finland. Dreaming instead enables people to simulate threatening events so that they can rehearse ways to either deal with or avoid them, Revonsuo theorizes.

Threatening incidents of various kinds and degrees frequently appear in the dream reports of adults and children around the world, the Finnish scientist says. They also show up in descriptions of recurrent dreams, nightmares, and post-traumatic dreams.

Hunter-gatherer populations, such as the Mehinaku Indians in Brazil, report many dreams about threatening events, he adds. Mehinaku men's dreams range from fending off an attacking jaguar to dealing with an angry wife.

Revensuo's theory faces threats of its own, though. Evidence from contemporary hunter-gatherers indicates that dreaming functions in a variety of ways, argues psychologist Harry T. Hunt of Brock University in St. Catharines, Ontario. Members of these groups generally view dreams as real events in which a person's soul carries out activities while the person sleeps.

Hunter-gatherers' dreams sometimes depict encounters with supernatural beings who provide guidance in pressing community matters, aid in healing physical illnesses, or give information about the future, Hunt says. Individuals who are adept at manipulating their own conscious states may engage in lucid dreaming, in which the dreamer reasons clearly, remembers the conditions of waking life, and acts according to a predetermined plan.

Dreaming represents a basic orienting response of the brain to novel information, ideas, and situations, Hunt proposes. It occurs at varying intensities in different conscious states, including REM sleep, bouts of reverie or daydreaming, and episodes of spirit possession that individuals in some cultures enter while awake (SN: 2/17/01, p. 104).

Scientists, musicians, inventors, artists, and writers often use dreaming of one kind or another to solve problems and spark creativity, Hunt notes.

Whatever purposes dreaming serves, Hobson's group and many other researchers underestimate the extent to which the brain tunes in to the external world during sleep, says neuroscientist Chiara M. Portas of University College London. Several studies indicate that sensory areas of the brain respond to relevant sounds and other sensations during REM and non-REM sleep.

No conclusive results support any theory of dreaming or sleep, in her view.

Ironically, dreams are attracting growing scientific interest as they fade into the background of modern life. Artificial lighting and society's focus on daytime achievements have fueled this trend (SN: 9/25/99, p. 205).

Sleep now typically occurs in single chunks of 7 hours or less. Yet as recently as 200 years ago in Europe, people slept in two nightly phases of 4 to 5 hours each. Shortly after midnight, individuals awoke for 1 to 2 hours and frequently reflected on their dreams or talked about them with others.

Well before Freud's time, Europeans prized dreams for their personal insights, and particularly for what they revealed about a dreamer's relationship with God, says historian A. Roger Ekirch of Virginia Polytechnic Institute and State University in Blacksburg.

Organizing sleep into two segments encouraged people to remember dreams and to use them as paths to self-discovery, Ekirch contended in the April AMERICAN HISTORICAL REVIEW.

Dreams have lost their allure even for the psychoanalytic theorists and clinicians who are the heirs to Freud's ideas, remarks Paul Lippmann of the William Alanson White Psychoanalytic Institute in Stockbridge, Mass. These days, psychoanalysts show far more interest in dissecting the emotional nature of their dealings with patients than in eliciting and interpreting dreams, according to Lippmann, himself a psychoanalytic clinician.

Like Ekirch, Lippmann suspects that modern culture has eroded interest in dreaming. "The American Dream has little room for the nighttime variety," he said in the Fall 2000 PSYCHOANALYTIC PSYCHOLOGY.

Yet many neuroscientists seem determined to swim against that cultural tide. Even the researchers who see little psychological significance in sleep's visions want to explain how and why the brain produces them.

They can dream, can't they?

Reprinted by permission via the Copyright Clearance Center from *Science News,* August 11, 2001, pp. 90-92, copyright 2001 by Science Service. Inc.

UNIT 4
Learning and Remembering

Unit Selections

13. **The Seven Sins of Memory: How the Mind Forgets and Remembers**, Daniel Schacter
14. **Memories of Things Unseen**, Elizabeth F. Loftus

Key Points to Consider

- What is learning? What is memory? How are the two linked? Are they necessarily always linked to each other? Why is memory so bad sometimes? How can we improve memory and learning?

- What is implicit learning? Can you give some examples of information or behaviors that you learned implicitly this week? How does implicit learning differ from intentional learning? Which do you think is more important—implicit learning or intentional learning?

- Why is memory important? What is forgetting? Why do psychologists want to know about the various mechanisms that underlie learning and remembering? To what use can we put this information? Why do we forget? Why is memory important to eyewitnesses? Are eyewitnesses accurate? If not, under what circumstances are they less correct? What methods could you use to improve memory? What types of memory lapses are normal? What memory mistakes signal problems such as Alzheimer's?

- How do you define intelligence? How do scientists define intelligence? Can you think of people whom you would call "bright" by standards other than the traditional definitions of intelligence? Is the concept of intelligence unitary or are there subcomponents of intelligence? Why is the concept of intelligence so criticized?

- What are some of the myths Americans hold about intelligence? Are these myths true? Why use science to investigate these myths if they seem so commonsensical? What does science say about intelligence and our commonly held beliefs?

 **Links: www.dushkin.com/online/**
These sites are annotated in the World Wide Web pages.

Mind Tools
http://www.psychwww.com/mtsite/

The Opportunity of Adolescence
http://www.winternet.com/~webpage/adolescencepaper.html

Project Zero
http://pzweb.harvard.edu

Do you remember your first week of classes at college? There were so many new buildings and so many people's names to remember. And you had to recall accurately where all your classes were as well as your professors' names. Just remembering your class schedule was problematic enough. For those of you who lived in residence halls, the difficulties multiplied. You had to remember where your residence was, recall the names of individuals living on your floor, and learn how to navigate from your room to other places on campus, such as the dining halls and library. Then came examination time. Did you ever think you would survive college exams? The material, in terms of difficulty level and amount, was perhaps more than you thought you could manage.

What a stressful time you experienced when you first came to campus! Much of what created the stress was the strain on your learning and memory systems, two complicated processes unto themselves. Indeed, most of you survived just fine and with your memories, learning strategies, and mental health intact.

Two of the processes you depended on when you first came to college are the processes of learning and memorizing, some of the oldest psychological processes studied by psychologists. Today, with their sophisticated experimental techniques, psychologists have distinguished several types of memory processes and have discovered what makes learning more complete so that subsequent memory is more accurate. We also have discovered that humans aren't the only organisms capable of these processes. All types of animals can learn, even if the organism is as simple as an earthworm or amoebae.

Psychologists know, too, that rote learning and practice are not the only forms of learning. For instance, at this point in time in your introductory psychology class, you might be studying op-

erant and classical conditioning, two very simple but nonetheless important forms of learning of which both humans and simple organisms are capable. Both types of conditioning can occur without our awareness or active participation in them. The articles in this unit examine the processes of learning and remembering (or its reciprocal, forgetting) in some detail.

That which might underpin learning and memory abilities is intelligence. With regard to intelligence, one persistent problem has been the difficulty of defining just what intelligence is. David Wechsler, author of several of the most popular intelligence tests in current clinical use, defines intelligence as the global capacity of the individual to act purposefully, to think rationally, and to deal effectively with the environment. Other psychologists have proposed more complex definitions.

The definitional problem arises when we try to develop tests that validly and reliably measure such abstract, intangible concepts. A valid test is one that measures what it purports to measure. A reliable test yields the same score for the same individual over and over again. Because defining and assessing intelligence has been so controversial and so difficult, historian Edward Boring once suggested that we define intelligence as whatever it is that an intelligence test measures!

In "Memories of Things Unseen," Elizabeth Loftus, a respected researcher of eye witness reports and memory, reviews findings about the pliability of memory. Certain questions (e.g. leading questions) from law enforcement professionals can actually alter an eyewitness's memory. The results of Loftus's research lead us to wonder how many people have been falsely convicted of a crime.

The Seven Sins of Memory:

How the Mind Forgets and Remembers

Memory's errors are as fascinating as they are important

By Daniel Schacter, Ph.D.

In Yasunari Kawabata's unsettling short story, "Yumiura," a novelist receives an unexpected visit from a woman who says she knew him 30 years earlier. They met when he visited the town of Yumiura during a harbor festival, the woman explains. But the novelist cannot remember her. Plagued recently by other troublesome memory lapses, he sees this latest incident as a further sign of mental decline. His discomfort turns to alarm when the woman offers more revelations about what happened on a day when he visited her room. "You asked me to marry you," she recalls wistfully. The novelist reels while contemplating the magnitude of what he had forgotten. The woman explains that she had never forgotten their time together and felt continually burdened by her memories of him.

After she finally leaves, the shaken novelist searches maps for the town of Yumiura with the hope of triggering recall of the place and the reasons why he had gone there. But no maps or books list a town called Yumiura. The novelist then realizes that he could not have been in the part of the country the woman described at the time she remembered. Her detailed, heart-felt and convincing memories were entirely false.

Kawabata's story dramatically illustrates different ways in which memory can get us into trouble. Sometimes we forget the past and at other times we distort it; some disturbing memories haunt us for years. Yet we also rely on memory to perform an astonishing variety of tasks in our everyday lives. Recalling conversations with friends or recollecting family vacations; remembering appointments and errands we need to run; calling up words that allow us to speak and understand others; remembering foods we like and dislike; acquiring the knowledge needed for a new job—all depend, in one way or another, on memory. Memory plays such a pervasive role in our daily lives that we often take it for granted until an incident of forgetting or distortion demands our attention.

Memory's errors have long fascinated scientists, and during the past decade they have come to occupy a prom-

inent place in our society. Forgotten encounters, misplaced eyeglasses and failures to recall the names of familiar faces are becoming common occurrences for many adults who are busily trying to juggle the demands of work and family, and cope with the bewildering array of new communications technologies. How many passwords and "PINs" do you have to remember just to manage your affairs on the Internet, not to mention your voice mail at the office or on your cell phone?

In addition to dealing with the frustration of memory failures in daily life, the awful specter of Alzheimer's disease looms large on the horizon. As the general public becomes ever more aware of its horrors through such high-profile cases as Ronald Reagan's battle with the disorder, the prospects of a life dominated by catastrophic forgetting further increase our preoccupations with memory.

Although the magnitude of the woman's memory distortion in Yumiura seems to stretch the bounds of credulity, it has been equaled and even exceeded in everyday life. Consider the story of Binjimin Wikomirski, whose 1996 Holocaust memoir, *Fragments,* won worldwide acclaim for portraying life in a concentration camp from the perspective of a child. Wilkomirski presented readers with raw, vivid recollections of the unspeakable terrors he witnessed as a young boy. Even more remarkable, Wilkomirski had spent much of his adult life unaware of these traumatic childhood memories, only becoming aware of them in therapy. Because his story and memories inspired countless others, Wilkomirski became a sought-after international figure and a hero to Holocaust survivors.

The story began to unravel, however, in late August 1998, when Daniel Ganzfried, a Swiss journalist and himself the son of a Holocaust survivor, published a stunning article in a Zurich newspaper. Ganzfried revealed that Wilkomirski is actually Bruno Dossekker, a Swiss native born in 1941 to a young woman named Yvone Berthe Grosjean, who later gave him up for adoption to an orphanage. His foster parents, the Dossekkers, found him there. Young Bruno spent all of the war years in the safe confines of his native Switzerland. Whatever the basis for his traumatic "memories" of Nazi horrors, they did not come from childhood experiences in a concentration camp. Is Dossekker/Wilkomirski simply a liar? Probably not: he still strongly believes his recollections are real.

Memory's errors are as fascinating as they are important. They can be divided into seven fundamental transgressions or "sins," which I call transience, absentmindedness, blocking, misattribution, suggestibility, bias and persistence. Just like the ancient seven deadly sins—pride, anger, envy, greed, gluttony, lust and sloth—the memory sins occur frequently in everyday life and can have serious consequences for all of us.

Transience, absentmindedness and blocking are sins of omission: we fail to bring to mind a desired fact, event or idea. Transience refers to a weakening or loss of memory over time. It is a basic feature of memory, and the culprit in many memory problems. Absentmindedness involves a breakdown at the interface between attention and memory. Absentminded memory errors—misplacing your keys or eyeglasses, or forgetting a lunch appointment—typically occur because we are preoccupied with distracting issues or concerns, and don't focus attention on what we need to remember.

The third sin, blocking, entails a thwarted search for information we may be desperately trying to retrieve. We've all had the experience of failing to produce a name to a familiar face. This frustrating experience happens even though we are attending carefully to the task at hand, and even though the desired name has not faded from our minds—as we become acutely aware when we unexpectedly retrieve the blocked name hours or days later.

The next four sins of misattribution, suggestibility, bias and persistence are all sins of commission: some form of memory is present, but it is either incorrect or unwanted. The sin of misattribution involves assigning a memory to the wrong source: mistaking fantasy for reality, or incorrectly remembering that a friend told you a bit of trivia that you actually read about in a newspaper. Misattribution is far more common than most people realize, and has potentially profound implications in legal settings. The related sin of suggestibility refers to memories that are implanted as a result of leading questions, comments or suggestions when a person is trying to call up a past experience. Like misattribution, suggestibility is especially relevant to—and sometimes can wreak havoc within—the legal system.

The sin of bias reflects the powerful influences of our current knowledge and beliefs on how we remember our pasts. We often edit or entirely rewrite our previous experiences—unknowingly and unconsciously—in light of what we now know or believe. The result can be a skewed rendering of a specific incident, or even of an extended period in our lives, that says more about how we feel now than about what happened then.

The seventh sin—persistence—entails repeated recall of disturbing information or events that we would prefer to banish from our minds altogether: remembering what we cannot forget, even though we wish that we could. Everyone is familiar with persistence to some degree: Recall the last time you suddenly awoke at 3 a.m., unable to keep out of your mind a painful blunder on the job or a disappointing result on an important exam. In more extreme cases of serious depression or traumatic experience, persistence can be disabling and even life-threatening.

"Two regions of the brain showed greater activity when people made abstract/concrete judgments about words they later remembered compared with those they later forgot."

New discoveries, some based on recent breakthroughs in neuroscience that allow us to see the brain in action as it learns and remembers, are beginning to illuminate the basis of the seven sins. These studies allow us to see in a new light what's going on inside our heads during the frustrating incidents of memory failure or error that can have a significant impact on our everyday lives. But to understand the seven sins more deeply, we also need to ask why our memory systems have come to exhibit these bothersome and sometimes dangerous properties: Do the seven sins represent mistakes made by Mother Nature during the course of evolution? Is memory flawed in a way that has placed our species at unnecessary risk? I don't think so. To the contrary, I contend that each of the seven sins is a byproduct of otherwise desirable and adaptive features of the human mind. Let's consider two of the most common memory sins: transience and absentmindedness.

TRANSIENCE

On October 3, 1995 the most sensational criminal trial of our time reached a stunning conclusion: a jury acquitted O. J. Simpson of murder. Word of the verdict spread quickly, nearly everyone reacted with either outrage or jubilation, and many people could talk about little else for days and weeks afterward. The Simpson verdict seemed like just the sort of momentous event that most of us would always remember vividly: how we reacted to it, and where we were when we heard the news.

Now, can you recall how you found out that Simpson had been acquitted? Chances are that you don't remember, or that what you remember is wrong. Several days after the verdict, a group of California undergraduates provided researchers with detailed accounts of how they learned about the jury's decision. When the researchers probed students' memories again 15 months later, only half recalled accurately how they found out about the decision. When asked again nearly three years after the verdict, less than 30% of students' recollections were accurate; nearly half were dotted with major errors.

The culprit in this incident is the sin of transience: forgetting that occurs with the passage of time. Research has shown that minutes, hours or days after an experience, memory preserves a relatively detailed record, allowing us to reproduce the past with reasonable if not perfect accuracy. But with the passing of time, the particulars fade and opportunities multiply for interference—generated by later, similar experiences—to blur our recollections.

Consider the following question: If I measure activity in your brain while you are learning a list of words, can I tell from this activity which words you will later remember having studied, and which words you will later forget? In other words, do measurements of brain activity at the moment when a perception is being transformed into a memory allow scientists to predict future remembering and forgetting of that particular event? If so, exactly which regions allow us to do the predicting?

In 1997, our group at the imaging center of Massachusetts General Hospital came up with an experiment to answer the question. Holding still in this cacophonous tunnel [the magnetic resonance imaging or MRI scanner], participants in our experiment saw several hundred words, one every few seconds, flashed to them from a computer by specially arranged mirrors. To make sure that they paid attention to every word, we asked our volunteers to indicate whether each word refers to something abstract, such as "thought," or concrete, such as "garden." Twenty minutes after the scan, we showed subjects the words they had seen in the scanner, intermixed with an equal number of words they hadn't seen, and asked them to indicate which ones they did and did not remember seeing in the scanner. We knew, based on preliminary work, that people would remember some words and forget others. Could we tell from the strength of the signal when participants were making abstract/concrete judgments which words they would later remember and which ones they would later forget?

We could. Two regions of the brain showed greater activity when people made abstract/concrete judgments about words they later remembered compared with those they later forgot. One was in the inner part of the temporal lobe, a part of the brain that, when damaged, can result in severe memory loss. The other region whose activity predicted subsequent memory was located further forward, in the lower left part of the vast territory known as the frontal lobes.

This finding was not entirely unexpected, because previous neuroimaging studies indicated that the lower left part of the frontal lobe works especially hard when people elaborate on incoming information by associating it to what they already know.

These results were exciting because there is something fascinating, almost science fiction-like, about peering into a person's brain in the present and foretelling what she will likely remember and forget in the future. But beyond an exercise in scientific fortune-telling, these studies managed to trace some of the roots of transience to the split-second encoding operations that take place during the birth of a memory. What happens in frontal and temporal regions during those critical moments determines, at least in part, whether an experience will be remembered for a lifetime, or drop off into the oblivion of the forgotten.

ABSENTMINDEDNESS

On a brutally cold day in February 1999, 17 people gathered in the 19th floor office of a Manhattan skyscraper to compete for a title known to few others outside that room: National Memory Champion. The winner of the U.S. competition would go on to challenge for the world memory championship several months later in London.

The participants were asked to memorize thousands of numbers and words, pages of faces and names, lengthy poems and decks of cards. The victor in this battle of mnemonic virtuosos, a 27-year-old administrative assistant named Tatiana Cooley, relied on classic encoding techniques: generating visual images, stories and associations that link incoming information to what she already knows. Given her proven ability to commit vast amounts of information to memory, one might also expect that Cooley's everyday life would be free from the kinds of memory problems that plague others. Yet this memory champion considers herself dangerously forgetful. "I'm incredibly absentminded," Cooley told a reporter. Fearful that she will forget to carry out everyday tasks, Cooley depends on to-do lists and notes scribbled on sticky pads. "I live by Post-its," she admitted ruefully.

The image of a National Memory Champion dependent on Post-its in her everyday life has a paradoxical, even surreal quality: Why does someone with a capacity for prodigious recall need to write down anything at all? Can't Tatiana Cooley call on the same memory abilities and strategies that she uses to memorize hundreds of words or thousands of numbers to help remember that she needs to pick up a jug of milk at the store? Apparently not: The gulf that separates Cooley's championship memory performance from her forgetful everyday life illustrates the distinction between transience and absentmindedness.

The kinds of everyday memory failures that Cooley seeks to remedy with Post-it notes—errands to run, appointments to keep and the like—have little to do with transience. These kinds of memory failures instead reflect the sin of absentmindedness: lapses of attention that result in failing to remember information that was either never encoded property (if at all) or is available in memory but is overlooked at the time we need to retrieve it.

To appreciate the distinction between transience and absentmindedness, consider the following three examples:

A man tees up a golf ball and hits it straight down the fairway. After waiting a few moments for his partner to hit, the man tees up his ball again, having forgotten that he hit the first drive.

A man puts his glasses down on the edge of a couch. Several minutes later, he realizes he can't find the glasses, and spends a half-hour searching his home before locating them.

"Memory's errors have long fascinated scientists, and during the past decade they have come to occupy a prominent place in our society."

A man temporarily places a violin on the top of his car. Forgetting that he has done so, he drives off with the violin still perched on the roof.

Superficially, all three examples appear to reflect a similar type of rapid forgetting. To the contrary, it is likely that each occurred for very different reasons.

The first incident took place back in the early 1980s, when I played golf with a patient who had been taking part in memory research conducted in my laboratory. The patient was in the early stage of Alzheimer's disease, and he had severe difficulties remembering recent events. Immediately after hitting his tee shot, the patient was excited because he had knocked it straight down the middle; he realized he would now have an easy approach shot to the green. In other words, he had encoded this event in a relatively elaborate manner that would ordinarily yield excellent memory. But when he started teeing up again and I asked him about his first shot, he expressed no recollection of it whatsoever. This patient was victimized by transience: he was incapable of retaining the information he had encoded, and no amount of cueing or prodding could bring it forth.

In the second incident, involving misplaced glasses, entirely different processes are at work. Sad to say, this example comes from my own experience—and happens more often than I would care to admit. Without attending to what I was doing, I placed my glasses in a spot where I usually do not put them. Because I hadn't fully encoded

this action to begin with—my mind was preoccupied with a scientific article I had been reading—I was at a loss when I realized that my glasses were missing. When I finally found them on the couch, I had no particular recollection of having put them there. But unlike the golfing Alzheimer's patient, transience was not the culprit: I never adequately encoded the information about where I put my glasses and so had no chance to retrieve it later.

The third example, featuring the misplaced violin, turned into far more than just a momentary frustration. In August 1967, David Margetts played second violin in the Roth String Quartet at UCLA. He had been entrusted with the care of a vintage Stradivarius that was owned by the department of music. After Margetts put the violin on his car's roof and drove off without removing it, UCLA made massive efforts to recover the instrument. Nonetheless, it went missing for 27 years before resurfacing in 1994 when the Stradivarius was brought in for repair and a dealer recognized the instrument. After a lengthy court battle, the violin was returned to UCLA in 1998.

There is, of course, no way to know exactly what Margetts was thinking about when he put the violin on his car's roof. Perhaps he was preoccupied with other things, just as I was when I misplaced my glasses. But because one probably does not set down a priceless Stradivarius without attending carefully to one's actions, I suspect that had Margetts been reminded before driving off, he would have remembered perfectly well where he had just placed the violin. In other words, Margetts was probably not sabotaged by transience, or even by failure to encode the event initially. Rather, forgetting in Margett's case was likely attributable to an absent-minded failure to notice the violin at the moment he needed to recall where he had put it. He missed a retrieval cue—the violin on the car's roof—which surely would have reminded him that he needed to remove the instrument.

Even though they often seem like our enemies, the seven sins are an integral part of the mind's heritage because they are so closely connected to features of memory that make it work well. The seven sins are not merely nuisances to minimize or avoid. They illuminate how memory draws on the past to inform the present, preserves elements of present experience for future reference, and allows us to revisit the past at will. Memory's vices are also its virtues, elements of a bridge across time that allows us to link the mind with the world.

Adapted from Daniel Schacter, Ph.D.'s *The Seven Sins of Memory: How the Mind Forgets and Remembers* (Houghton-Mifflin, 2001)

Daniel L. Schacter, Ph.D., is chairman of the psychology department at Harvard University and also author of "Searching for Memory" (HarperCollins, 1997).

Memories of Things Unseen

New findings reveal more about the malleability of memory. Not only is it possible to change details of memories for previously experienced events, but one can sometimes also plant entirely false memories into the minds of unsuspecting individuals, even if the events would be highly implausible or even impossible. False memories might differ statistically from true ones, in terms of certain characteristics such as confidence or vividness, but some false memories are held with a great degree of confidence and expressed with much emotion. Moreover, false memories can have consequences for later thoughts and behaviors, sometimes rather serious ones.

Elizabeth F. Loftus

Faulty memory has led to more than its share of heartbreak. The cases of individuals who have been released from prison after DNA evidence revealed their innocence make compelling examples. Larry Mayes of Indiana had the dubious distinction of being the 100th such person to be freed in the United States. He was convicted of raping a gas station cashier after the victim positively identified him in court. Apparently it did not matter that she had failed to identify him in two earlier lineups and did so in court only after she was hypnotized by the police. Mayes spent 21 years in prison for a crime he did not commit. Attorney Thomas Vanes had prosecuted Mayes, believing at the time that Mayes was guilty. But two decades later, after Vanes saw the result of old evidence being subjected to new DNA testing, he changed his mind. "He was right, and I was wrong," wrote Vanes (2003), in a newspaper op-ed piece arguing for the DNA testing of another individual who was awaiting execution for an ugly robbery-murder of an elderly couple. For Vanes, it was a "sobering lesson."

The DNA exonerations have taught all of us a sobering lesson, namely, that faulty memory is the major cause of wrongful convictions. Concerns about justice are but one reason why the study of memory is so important.

MEMORY DISTORTION: FROM CHANGING DETAILS TO PLANTING FALSE MEMORIES

Pick up any textbook in the field of memory or cognition, and you will invariably find mention of faulty memory. That has been true for decades. But lately, the study of memory distortion has been thriving. In the 1970s through 1990s, hundreds of studies showed the power of new information to contaminate memory reports. Stop signs became yield signs, hammers turned into screwdrivers, and broken glass got "added" to memories for accidents. The inaccuracies in memory caused by erroneous information provided after the event became known as the "misinformation effect."

In the mid 1990s, memory investigators went further. It was one thing to change a detail in memory for a previously experienced event, but quite another thing to plant an entirely false memory into the mind. Using fairly strong suggestions, investigators succeeded in getting people to incorrectly believe that when they were children, they had been lost in a shopping mall for an extended time, hospitalized overnight, or involved in an unfortunate accident at a family wedding (see Loftus, 1997). The "strong suggestion" involved enlisting the help of family members to construct scenarios describing true and false experiences and feeding these scenarios to the subjects as if they were all true. The method was later dubbed the "familial-informant false-narrative procedure" (Lindsay, Hagen, Read, Wade, & Garry, 2004), but it is easier to call it the "lost in the mall" procedure. After being fed suggestive information that ostensibly came from their relatives, a significant minority of subjects came to accept all or part of the suggestion and claimed it as their own experience.

Would people also fall sway to suggestion if the to-be-planted event was particularly horrible? The answer is yes, as revealed in one study that convinced one third of subjects that when they were children they had nearly drowned and had to be rescued by a lifeguard (Heaps & Nash, 2001). Another research group convinced about half of their subjects that they had had particularly awful experiences as children, such as being a victim of a vicious animal attack (Porter, Yuille, & Lehman, 1999).

The suggestion used in these lost-in-the-mall studies was strong. In the real world, some forms of suggestion that are used are far more subtle. Perhaps their persuasive powers would be weaker. Take *guided imagination,* a technique in which individuals are led to imagine that they have had experiences (like breaking a window) that they have previously denied. Even a minute's worth of such imagination can increase people's confidence that in the past they had an experience like the imagined one—a phenomenon called *imagination inflation*. (See Garry & Polaschek, 2000, for an excellent review.) Imagining another person engaged in an event can also increase your confidence that it happened to you. Finally, some individuals, such as those who tend to have lapses in memory and attention, are more susceptible to imagination inflation than others. The clinical implications are evident—many therapy techniques involve imagination-based interventions; their capacity for distorting autobiography (an unexpected side effect?) needs to be appreciated.

PLANTING FALSE MEMORIES OR EXTRACTING TRUE MEMORIES?

When people claim, after suggestion, that they were lost in a mall, or attacked by an animal, perhaps the suggestive manipulation has extracted true memories rather than planting false ones. This quite-legitimate challenge has been met with research efforts to plant memories of events that would be highly implausible or even impossible.

In one such study, subjects evaluated advertisements under a pretense. One of the ads was for Disneyland and featured Bugs Bunny by the magic castle. The text made reference to meeting Bugs—the perfect end to the perfect day. After evaluating this ad, or a control ad, subjects were asked about their own childhood experiences at Disneyland (Braun, Ellis, & Loftus, 2002). About 16% of those who had been exposed to the fake Bugs ad later said they had personally met Bugs Bunny at Disneyland. Later studies showed that with multiple exposures to fake Disney ads that mentioned Bugs Bunny, the percentages rose even higher. Many of those subjects who fell sway to the suggestion remembered the impossible encounter in quite a bit of detail (e.g., they hugged Bugs or touched his ear). Of course, this memory is impossible because Bugs Bunny is a Warner Bros. character and would not be found at a Disney theme park. But the study shows that suggestive methods are indeed capable of leading to false beliefs or memories.

Other efforts to plant impossible or implausible memories show just how far one can go in tampering with people's autobiographies. In one case, people were led to believe that they had witnessed a person being demonically possessed as a child (Mazzoni, Loftus, & Kirsch, 2001). In the most powerful of these studies, subjects read articles that described demonic possession and were designed to increase its plausibility. One article was a testimonial from a prominent individual describing his own childhood experience with witnessing a possession. Subjects also received false feedback about causes of certain fears; they were told that witnessing a possession probably led to their particular childhood fears. Finally, they answered questions about their own childhood experiences. Relative to control subjects, those who had received the suggestion were more confident that they had witnessed possession as a child.

In yet another study, subjects were led to remember an event that never occurs in the country in which they lived, namely, "having a nurse remove a skin sample from my little finger" before age 6 (Mazzoni & Memon, 2003, p. 187). The most powerful method of suggestion in this study involved having subjects imagine that they had had the experience.

Perhaps you are thinking that these events are not sufficiently implausible—that Bugs might not be at Disneyland but other rabbits are, that demonic possession may not have been witnessed but other bizarre behavior was. Such critiques have encouraged researchers to come up with new pseudoevents that are less susceptible to these charges. Some researchers have also tried to make the false event so specific that it is unlikely to have happened to large numbers of people. So, in another study, subjects were persuaded that they had gotten in trouble with a friend for putting Slime (a brightly colored gelatinous substance manufactured as a toy) in their teacher's desk when in the first or second grade (Lindsay et al., 2004). The pseudoevent was chosen to be distinctive and memorable, and neither entirely implausible nor likely actually to have occurred. What was surprising about the findings was the sheer number of people who were led to believe that they had "Slimed" their teacher. The most powerful method of suggestion in this study involved the combination of a narrative and a photo ostensibly provided by the subject's parents. The narrative for the pseudoevent was customized for each subject by inserting the subject's name and the teacher's name into it:

> I remember when Jane was in Grade 1, and like all kids back then, Jane had one of those revolting Slime toys that kids used to play with. I remember her telling me one day that she had taken the Slime to school and slid it into the teacher's desk before she arrived. Jane claimed it wasn't her idea and that her friend decided they should do it. I think the teacher, Mrs. Smollett, wasn't very happy and made Jane and her friend sit with their arms folded and legs crossed, facing a wall for the next half hour. (Lindsay et al., 2004, p. 150)

The photo provided was the subject's actual class photo for Grade 1 or 2.

Using a fairly strict criterion for classifying a response as a pseudomemory, Lindsay and his colleagues found that when subjects returned to the lab for a second interview, more than 65% of subjects had developed such memories. Moreover, when debriefed and told their memories were false, some individuals expressed great surprise, as revealed in their verbalizations: "You mean that didn't happen to me?" and "No way! I remember it! That is so weird!" (Lindsay et al., 2004, pp. 152-153).

So (almost certainly), false memories do get planted by suggestion. Some methods are more powerful than others, leading to very high rates of false-memory reports. In the Slime study, the suggestion included a suggestive narrative ostensibly provided by an authoritative figure, namely, the subject's parent. Moreover, the class photo may have added to the authoritativeness of the suggestive narrative and increased the subject's confidence that the Slime event happened. The photo may have further encouraged speculation about the details of the pseudoevent. So, for example, a subject looking at the photo might have mused over who the co-perpetrator might have been in the Slime prank and even picked out a likely candidate. Finally, these studies indicate that rather unlikely events can be planted in the mind, and they counter the criticism that the events planted in such studies revive true memories.

CHARACTERISTICS OF FALSE MEMORIES

Can we tell the difference between true memories and false ones? Many studies show that there are some statistical differences, that true memories are held with more confidence or seem more vivid than false ones. But other studies do not demonstrate such differences. In the Slime study, for example, subjects rated their memories on a number of scales, including scales indicating their confidence that the event actually took place and the extent to which they felt their memory experience resembled reliving the event. False memories were as compelling as true memories, at least on these dimensions.

Are false memories felt with as much emotion as true ones? One answer to this question comes from research on individuals who presumably have false memories of events not planted experimentally. In a study of people who have memories of abduction by space aliens (McNally et al., 2004), physiological measures (e.g., heart rate and electrical conductance of the skin) were taken while abductees listened to tape-recorded accounts of their reported alien encounters.

The abductees showed greater reactivity to their abduction scripts than to other scripts (positive and neutral). Moreover, this effect was more pronounced among the abductees than among control subjects who did not have abduction memories and listened to the same accounts. Assuming no one was actually abducted, these results suggest that false memories of abduction can produce very strong physiological responses. Thus, a memory report accompanied by strong emotion is not good evidence that the memory report reflects a genuine experience (see also McNally, 2003).

CONSEQUENCES OF FALSE MEMORIES

Changing beliefs or memories can influence what people think or do later. In one study, people who were led by a fake advertisement to believe that they met Bugs at Disneyland were later asked to say how associated various pairs of characters were in their minds (e.g., How associated are Mickey Mouse and Minnie Mouse? How associated are Bugs Bunny and Mickey Mouse?). Those who fell for the fake ad and believed that they had met Bugs later on claimed that Bugs Bunny was more highly related to various Disney characters than did people who were not exposed to the fake ad. This suggests that the thought processes of ad-exposed individuals can be influenced (see Loftus, 2003, for other examples).

There are also real-world examples showing how false memories can have repercussions. Recall the Heaven's Gate cult, a group whose members had been led to believe they were in telepathic contact with aliens. Apparently the cult members had taken out an insurance policy, to insure against being abducted, impregnated, or killed by aliens. The group paid $1,000 a year for this coverage. So clearly their (presumably false) beliefs had economic consequences (Siepel, 1997). Thirty-nine members of the cult participated in the ultimate act of consequence: They partook in a mass suicide in 1997, killing themselves under the belief that to do so would free their souls.

FINAL REMARKS

There is now ample evidence that people can be led to believe that they experienced things that never happened. In some instances, these beliefs are wrapped in a fair amount of sensory detail and give the impression of being genuine recollections. Some researchers have suggested that implausible or unlikely events will be hard to plant into the minds of adults or children, but in fact people can be led to believe in experiences that are highly unlikely to be true (e.g., witnessing demonic possession, being abducted by aliens, being hugged by Bugs Bunny at Disneyland). In one recent study of false memories in children, the children came up with elaborate stories for such unlikely events as helping a woman find her lost monkey and helping a person who injured her ankle after spilling Play-Doh (Scullin, Kanaya, & Ceci, 2002). These "rich" false memories can have repercussions down the line, affecting later thoughts and behaviors.

A half century ago, Frederic C. Bartlett, the psychologist from Cambridge, England, shared his important insights about memory. He posited that remembering is "imaginative reconstruction, or construction," and "it is thus hardly ever exact" (Bartlett, 1932, p. 213). His insights link up directly with contemporary research on memory distortion, although even he might have been surprised to find out just how inexact memory can be. He might have also relished the contemporary research, which has brought us quite a ways toward understanding what it is like for people when they experience "imaginative construction" in both experimental and real-world settings. Bartlett died in 1969, just missing the beginning of a vast effort to investigate the memory processes that he so intelligently foreshadowed, and that show unequivocally how humans are the authors or creators of their own memories. They can also be the authors or creators of someone else's memory.

Address correspondence to Elizabeth F. Loftus, 2393 Social Ecology II, University of California, Irvine, CA 92697-7085; e-mail: eloftus@uci.edu.

Recommended Reading

Lindsay, D.S., Hagen, L., Read, J.D., Wade, K.A., & Garry, M. (2004). (See References)
Loftus, E.F. (2002). Memory faults and fixes. *Issues in Science and Technology, 18,* 41-50.
Loftus, E.F. (2003). (See References)
McNally, R.J. (2003). (See References)

REFERENCES

Bartlett, F.C. (1932). *Remembering: A study in experimental and social psychology.* Cambridge, England: Cambridge University Press.
Braun, K.A., Ellis, R., & Loftus, E.F. (2002). Make my memory: How advertising can change our memories of the past. *Psychology and Marketing, 19,* 1-23.

Garry, M., & Polaschek, D.L.L. (2000). Imagination and memory. *Current Directions in Psychological Science, 9,* 6-10.

Heaps, C.M., & Nash, M. (2001). Comparing recollective experience in true and false autobiographical memories. *Journal of Experimental Psychology: Learning, Memory, and Cognition, 27,* 920-930.

Lindsay, D.S., Hagen, L., Read, J.D., Wade, K.A., & Garry, M. (2004). True photographs and false memories. *Psychological Science, 15,* 149-154.

Loftus, E.F. (1997). Creating false memories. *Scientific American, 277*(3), 70-75.

Loftus, E.F. (2003). Make-believe memories. *American Psychologist, 58,* 864-873.

Mazzoni, G., & Memon, A. (2003). Imagination can create false autobiographical memories. *Psychological Science, 14,* 186-188.

Mazzoni, G.A.L., Loftus, E.F., & Kirsch, I. (2001). Changing beliefs about implausible autobiographical events. *Journal of Experimental Psychology: Applied, 7,* 51-59.

McNally, R.J. (2003). *Remembering trauma.* Cambridge, MA: Harvard University Press.

McNally, R.J., Lasko, N.B., Clancy, S.A., Macklin, M.L., Pitman, R.K., & Orr, S.P. (2004). Psychophysiological responding during script-driven imagery in people reporting abduction by space aliens. *Psychological Science, 15,* 493-497.

Porter, S., Yuille, J.C., & Lehman, D.R. (1999). The nature of real, implanted, and fabricated memories for emotional childhood events: Implications for the recovered memory debate. *Law and Human Behavior, 23,* 517-537.

Scullin, M.H., Kanaya, T., & Ceci, S.J. (2002). Measurement of individual differences in children's suggestibility across situations. *Journal of Experimental Psychology: Applied, 8,* 233-246.

Siepel, T. (1997, March 31). Leader's health tied to deaths. *San Jose Mercury News.* Retrieved June 24, 2003, from http://www.sacred-texts.com/ufo/39dead16.htm

Vanes, T. (2003, July 28). Let DNA close door on doubt in murder cases. *Los Angeles Times,* p. B11.

UNIT 5
Cognitive Processes

Unit Selections

15. **The Power of Babble**, Mary Duenwald
16. **The Mind's Self-Portrait: An Illusion of Conscious Will**, Phillip Ciske

Key Points to Consider

- Why study cognition? Why study the development of cognitive abilities; why would this be of interest to psychologists? What role do you think culture plays in cognitive development? What aspects of culture most influence how we process incoming information about our world? Besides culture, can you think of other factors that influence our cognitive activity?

- Why study infant language development? Because babies are not yet fluent, just how do psychologists study language and cognition in infants? In what ways are children's language abilities different from adults'?

- What role does brain imaging play in such research? How far advanced is the science of understanding the inter-relationship between neurology and cognition? How does science help us understand the human mind?

- Are learning and thinking central to our concepts of being human and being separate from or better than other animals? How so? How can our mind trick us into thinking something other than what is really true? As for the issue of causation, what errors in judgments are we likely to make?

 **Links: www.dushkin.com/online/**
These sites are annotated in the World Wide Web pages.

American Association for Artificial Intelligence (AAAI)
http://www.aaai.org/AITopics/index.html

Chess: Kasparov v. Deep Blue: The Rematch
http://www.chess.ibm.com/home/html/b.html

As Rashad watches his four-month old, he is convinced that the baby possesses a degree of understanding of the world around her. In fact, Rashad is sure he has one of the smartest babies in the neighborhood. Although he is indeed a proud father, he keeps these thoughts to himself so as not to alienate his neighbors whom he perceives as having less intelligent babies.

Gustav lives in the same neighborhood as Rashad. However, Gustav doesn't have any children, but he does own two fox terriers. Despite Gustav's most concerted efforts, the dogs never come to him when he calls them. In fact, the dogs have been known to run in the opposite direction on occasion. Instead of being furious, Gustav accepts his dogs' disobedience because he is sure the dogs are just dumb beasts and don't know any better.

Both of these vignettes illustrate important and interesting ideas about cognition or thought processes. In the first vignette, Rashad ascribes cognitive abilities and high intelligence to his child; in fact, Rashad per-

haps ascribes too much cognitive ability to his four-month old. On the other hand, Gustav assumes that his dogs are incapable of thought, more specifically incapable of premeditated disobedience, and therefore forgives the dogs.

Few adults would deny the existence of their cognitive abilities. Some adults, in fact, think about thinking, something which psychologists call metacognition. Cognition is critical to our survival as adults. But are there differences in mentation in adults? And what about other organisms? Can young children—infants for example—think? If they can, do they think like adults? And what about animals; can they think and solve problems? These and other questions are related to cognitive psychology and cognitive science, showcased in this unit.

Cognitive psychology has grown faster than most other specialties in psychology in the past 40 years. Much of this has occurred in response to new computer technology as well as to the growth of psycholinguistics. Computer technology has prompted an interest in artificial intelligence, the mimicking of human intelligence by machines. Similarly the study of psycholinguistics has prompted the examination of the influence of language on thought and vice versa.

The first article in this unit offers the reader a look into the world of cognitive development. Author Mary Duenwald discusses how babies create their first sounds and how language contributes to consciousness and cognition. Imaging studies are lending new insight into how babies learn to discriminate certain words and their meaning.

A second article examines adult cognition. Interestingly, Freud said long ago that we can trick or fool ourselves into purposely forgetting what we want to forget. Today, modern psychologist Dan Wegner has found this indeed to be the case. Wegner's research demonstrates that exactly what we don't want to remember is what we do remember and that which we believe we have control over we really don't control.

The Power of Babble

Why neuroscientists scientists go gaga over infants' goo-goos

By Mary Duenwald

REBECCA LOOKS BIZARRE WITH BRAIN-IMAGING gizmos attached to her little bald head—like a baby who has crept into Dr. Frankenstein's lab. A white terry-cloth headband holds two plastic squares against either side of her skull. Each contains a set of black rods with a welter of wires. Rebecca seems oblivious to the headgear as she turns her head from side to side with a wet, toothless grin. She isn't yet five months old, but according to Laura-Ann Petitto, a cognitive neuroscientist at Dartmouth College, she is already using the parts of her brain involved in language. And the contraption on her head is designed to let Petitto watch her do it.

Known as near-infrared spectroscopy, this technology is designed to show which part of the brain governs a given behavior by measuring where the brain uses the most oxygen. Petitto is learning how to use the device, and in time she hopes to zero in on an area just above the left ear that may play a prominent role in language acquisition. "Language is the looming contributor to this thing we call consciousness, which is at the heart of reason, emotion—the individual," she says. "Think about what we're doing right now. I'm sending sound waves through the air. I'm not even touching you. Yet you have explosions of meaning in your head. By what mechanism

does our species accomplish this truly astounding feat?"

For a scientist trying to answer this question, babies are the ultimate black box. They can't explain a word of what's happening inside their small developing brains, yet that's where language—with all its complexities of grammar and vocabulary—is born. "You wouldn't expect babies to be better than adults at anything," says Jenny Saffran, director of the Infant Learning Laboratory at the University of Wisconsin at Madison, "but they are better at learning language."

Babbling—the stringing together of repetitive syllables, as in *da, da, da, da, da* or *ga, ga, ga, ga, ga*—is one of the earliest stages of language acquisition. Babbling allows babies to learn and practice sounds they will one day use to create language. And so scientists have listened to babies babble, and they have watched babies babble. And if this new spectroscopy lives up to its promise, they may soon be able to watch babies' brains operate as they babble.

Babbling is universal. No matter where babies are born or to which language they're exposed, they begin—between 5 and 10 months of age—to rhythmically repeat syllables. Coincidentally, they often accompany themselves with equally rhythmic movements of their hands

and feet. Petitto says they're especially fond of shaking their right hand, or a rattle, while they babble.

"People used to think that language grew from our capacity to produce and hear speech," Petitto says. "If that were true, then a child who is stripped of speech should learn language in a different way." In fact, she says, babies can even babble in sign language.

Brain scans show that Broca's area, located behind the left temple, helps us produce language and understand grammar while Wernicke's area, just above the left ear, helps receive language and decipher its meaning. It's still not clear when these language centers develop.

A few years ago, Petitto and her colleagues attached light-emitting diodes to the hands of babies learning to sign and others learning to speak. An electronic device recorded the trajectory, velocity, and frequency of the babies' hand movements. Both groups, Petitto found, made rhythmic hand gestures with a frequency of about 3 hertz—three complete movements a second. But the babies exposed to sign made a second kind of movement as well, this one with a frequency of 1 hertz, or roughly one second.

The timing is significant because it's almost equivalent to the length of one unit of spoken babble: *da, da, da, da, da.* To Petitto, this suggests that language grows from a part of the brain that can work with either sign or sound—one that is wired to register the bursts of aural or visual communication that are the building blocks of words. "A baby finds delicious, and is very powerfully attracted to, anything that has these rhythmic undulations," she says.

Encouraged by parents and others, babies gradually learn to identify which of the millions of sounds they hear are actually words. They learn, for example, that when they hear someone say "pretty baby," *pretty* is a word and *baby* is a word, but *ty-ba* is not a word.

Saffran has looked into how babies do this by exposing them to made-up words, such as *golabu* and *daropi*, and repeating them over and over. She has found that babies compute, unconsciously, the probabilities that certain sounds will be paired together. "It's statistical learning," she says. "They learn how often they hear *pre* before *ty* and *ba* before *by*." If the sounds come up together often enough, the babies hear them as distinct words.

Petitto has begun to home in on the part of the brain that controls babbling and the early development of language. In a study reported in *Science* a year ago, she and her colleagues videotaped the mouths of babbling babies. They found that the babies were opening the right sides

---

Five Stages of Baby Talk

1 PHONATION (0 to 2 months): Babies make their first sounds other than crying, often without opening their mouths. Example: a staccato *hmm, hmm*, timed with exhalations.

2 PRIMITIVE ARTICULATION (1 to 4 months): Babies use their tongue and jaw to form new sounds. Examples: *gleh, glechh.*

3 EXPANSION (3 to 8 months): Babies squeal, yell, or whisper, as if exploring the range of sounds, pitch, and amplitude the mouth can manage. Examples: shrieks, growls, Bronx cheers.

4 BABBLING (5 to 10 months): Babies begin to form their first syllables. Examples: *ba, ba, ba, ba* or *da, da, da, da, da.*

5 SOPHISTICATED BABBLING (9 to 18 months): Babies combine syllables such as *ba, da, ga*, mix in real words such as *dada* or *mama*, and string together meaningless sounds with the rhythm and pacing of a real sentence.

Source: D. Kimbrough Oller, University of Memphis

---

of their mouths wider than the left. Given that the left side of the brain controls the right side of the body, this suggests that babbling is mainly a left-brain activity.

Within the left brain, Petitto has her sights set on the planum temporale, a piece of the superior temporal gyrus, which is a chunk of brain about the size and shape of an index finger that curves over the top of the ear. The superior temporal gyrus is known to be part of the broad neural network that adults use in listening to and producing language. In studies of adults, Petitto has found that both hearing and deaf adults use the planum temporale—mainly on the left side—to process syllables, whether signing or speaking aloud.

The beauty of near-infrared spectroscopy is that it enables Petitto to see how babies' brains operate while they're awake and learning to talk. MRI scans don't work because the babies would have to lie perfectly still. Petitto's machine, made by Hitachi, uses weak infrared light from a laser diode, which shines through the skull and then about an inch farther into the brain. The amount of light reflected back from each region is determined by how much blood and oxygen the brain is using in that area. The more oxygen being used, the harder the brain is working.

As the machine probes Rebecca's brain, she sits on her mother's lap and the room goes quiet and dark. On a video screen, a young woman silently holds her right palm up flat like a traffic cop, then rhythmically rotates it—palm, back of the hand, palm, back of the hand—every second and a half.

Rebecca watches for less than a minute before starting to sigh, fidget, and kick her feet. But in that time a computer has recorded how her brain operates. The planum temporale "was clearly the part of the brain that was activated," Petitto says, and the same was true for the 10 babies who were examined before Rebecca. So far, she says, "the data are gorgeous."

Petitto wants to scan at least 100 babies before reaching any conclusions. Then she wants to use near-infrared spectroscopy on babies who are in the act of babbling. "I want to crack the code," she says.

The Mind's Self-Portrait: An Illusion of Conscious Will

BY PHILLIP CISKE

I look on my brain as a mass of hydraulically com-
pacted thoughts, a bale of ideas, and my head as a
smooth, shiny Aladdin's lamp.

Bohumil Hrabal,
Too Loud a Solitude

An artist's or writer's self-portrait can run the gamut from realistic likeness to abstract beyond recognition. When you ask someone what a self-portrait of the mind might look like, most people would probably assume it would be a picture of the brain. But when the mind tries to construct a self-portrait, the closest it gets is a caricature. This inability to achieve a complete understanding of itself underlies the mind's inferences about the relationship between thought and action. These were some of the points raised in this year's Bring the Family address, "The Mind's Self-Portrait," presented at the APS Annual Convention by Daniel Wegner of Harvard University.

"The mind can't know itself in all the richness that we psychologists hope to," Wegner said, citing several limitations of the mind's capacity to portray itself. These limitations include the fact that, as Julian Jaynes put it, "we cannot be conscious of what we are not conscious of," meaning that the mind's self-portrait inherently doesn't include the unconscious mind.

Wegner, an APS Fellow, has developed a multi-dimensional framework, which he calls the "theory of apparent mental causation," to explore ways in which people infer that their thought is related to a particular action. This framework includes the straightforward dimensions of normal voluntary action — the feeling that we're doing something and in fact we are actually doing it; and normal voluntary inaction — where we don't feel we're doing something and we're in fact not doing it.

According to Wegner, there are other dimensions in which our interpretation of the causal connections between thought and action (or inaction) are configured differently. One such dimension is the illusion of control, where we feel that we're doing or causing something but we're actually not doing or causing it.

To illustrate this illusion, Wegner told the story of an American couple living in Paris who were entertaining one evening in their apartment overlooking the Eiffel Tower. Knowing that the tower's lights went on exactly at 6 p.m., they opened the drapes shortly before illumination. With a clandestine countdown, the husband went over to the wall and flipped the lightswitch at just the right time, making it appear that he was lighting the tower. "Needless to say, the visitors were very impressed," Wegner said. "Of course, this was an illusion of control, a feeling of doing, not accompanied by actually doing."

The opposite dimension, which Wegner calls automatism, involves instances where there is no feeling of doing something, but yet we are doing something. Popular examples of this include some old-fashioned parlor games, Ouija boards, and dowsing, where things that seem to move by themselves are believed to be disconnected from our actions. Hypnosis is another example of an automatism, Wegner said.

"The person who is hypnotized feels like everything they're doing is happening to them, that it's not something they're doing themselves." There is a syndrome called "alien hand," experienced by people with brain damage, in which the individual's hand begins to act — for example, unbuttoning clothing — without their feeling of consciously willing the hand movement. The actions are apparently voluntary, they look like normal human actions, but the person doesn't have the experience of willing the action.

Wegner also talked about Wilder Penfield's famous experiments in the 1950s in which electrical stimulation of the cortical motor area during brain surgery produced smooth, coordinated movements, not simple reflexes, which appeared voluntary and purposeful.

"Asked what happened when the stimulation caused the patient's hand to move, the patient [who had been under local anesthesia only] said 'I didn't do that, you did that.' There was no feeling of action. So without a prior consistent thought of the action, even a seemingly voluntary action can feel unwilled."

TIMING IS EVERYTHING

Wegner said that causal inferences linking thought to action draw from the same principles underlying perceived causation for events in the world, and that these principles — priority, consistency, and exclusivity — apply to the experience of will.

Under the priority principle, the apparent cause has to occur at the right time before the effect, or you will not perceive causation. In the case of will, the thought must precede action at an appropriate interval in order for us to infer a causal relationship.

To test the priority principle for thought and action, Wegner and his colleagues developed an experiment, called "I Spy" after the children's game, in which a participant and a confederate sit at a computer with a little table on top of the computer mouse. Both put their fingers on the top of the table, and together move the mouse pointer around the screen to various objects. Every 30 seconds, music comes on, during which they are asked to stop on some object on the screen. When they stop on the object, both participant and confederate then complete a rating of who stopped on the object: did I consciously will this stop or did the other person do it to me?

In a first set of trials, the unforced trials, the confederate does nothing to influence the movement of the mouse pointer. Under these conditions, naming the object to stop on five to 10 seconds before the music comes on was found to have no influence on the participant's movement. In a second set of trials, the forced trials, the confederate is instructed to force the participant to stop on the named object. In these trials, Wegner found that it matters very much when the object is named. If it is named 30 seconds before the stop is forced, the participant doesn't feel that they intended to stop, while if the object is named one or five seconds before, they have more of a feeling that they intended to stop.

"If there's some delay, if things don't happen in terms of proper priority, the experience of will goes away for the action," Wegner said. "Keep in mind — in all of the forced trials, the person didn't actually do it. They developed a sense of consciously willing something simply by having the appropriate thought just before the action was forced."

To illustrate the principle of consistency, in which the thought has to be relevant to and compatible with the action, Wegner and his colleagues conducted experiments involving beliefs about voodoo. In this instance, the theory of apparent mental causation would suggest that if people have evil thoughts prior to doing something that is apparently evil, they'd come to believe that they willed a negative effect.

First, a research subject is given some background reading indicating that people who believe in the effectiveness of voodoo experience negative effects on their health if someone has put a curse on them. Then, a situation is staged where the participant is assigned the role of a witchdoctor who casts a curse on a seemingly unknowing victim, played by a research confederate. The participant is instructed to generate evil thoughts about the victim for one minute prior to sticking pins in a voodoo

doll. The "victim" subsequently reports experiencing health effects, such as a headache. Then the experimenters asked the participant if they believed they caused the victim's symptoms. Wegner found that the participants in the evil thoughts condition feel they were more likely to have caused this headache compared to the no-evil-thoughts participants.

"I think all of us have had the case where the thoughts were there, the event occurs, we somehow now feel the author of that event as a result of having had thoughts consistent with it," whether negative or positive, Wegner said. Similarly, "there could be a lot of times when we feel that we control things around us simply because we had thoughts that end up being consistent with the way things turn out."

Wegner described the "helping hands" experiment, drawing from the party game by that name, which involved another set of studies also aimed at testing the consistency principle. Standing, facing a mirror, the participant wears a smock covering his or her own arms, and watches as the experimenter's arms, which are substituted for their own, engage in a series of rapid gestures and movements. In some versions, the participant hears the instructions for movement being given to the experimenter, while in others they don't hear the instructions.

"After this is all over, we ask the participant 'how much control do you feel you had over the arms' motions?'" While people don't completely feel that they're controlling the arms, Wegner and his colleagues found that participants who hear the instructions end up feeling more control, "a kind of vicarious control over these arms," compared to people who don't hear the instructions.

"It's as though knowing, having thoughts consistent with the actions that appear to be occurring at the ends of your arms, makes you own those actions somehow," Wegner said.

A related "helping hands" experiment measures skin conductance levels. With the same basic scenario describe above, when the experimenter ended by using one hand to snap a rubber band on the other wrist, participants who previously heard consistent instructions about the hand movements showed an empathetic emotional response to the rubber band snap. "It's almost as though in feeling this control over the arms, there's a feeling of the arms becoming one's own, such that there's a responsiveness to things that are happening to them," said Wegner.

Wegner also has conducted experiments that provide evidence for the exclusivity principle.

"In light of the experiments we've seen," Wegner said, "it could be that conscious will is based on interpreting one's thought as causing one's action through principles of consistency, exclusivity, and priority."

"This would suggest," he continued, "that the experience of will comes and goes in accord with principles governing an interpretive mechanism, not in accord with any actual causal link between the thought and action. So the mind's self-portrait could be a rough sketch of how the mind works, a sketch that produces an illusion of conscious will."

"A lot of us have the feeling that conscious will is a uniquely human characteristic; it's something about our minds that makes us special. Some commentators have suggested it's like having a god inside one's self, an agent that does things, that allows you to create actions from whole thought. The perspective I'm suggesting tonight is that humans are, in fact, mechanisms of some kind," said Wegner.

"Every one of us feels that we consciously will our actions many times every day. Every time you think of moving a finger or moving whatever body part, and then it happens, you feel that you do it. So the experience of will is a very dramatic and constant part of the mind's self-portrait. But what's it there for? I'd suggest that this is the mind's compass. The mind may not understand exactly how it steers the boat, but it tells us where we're going. The experience of will allows us the kind of authorship emotion, a feeling that accompanies everything we do that allows us to realize what it is we've done on a moment-to-moment basis.

Artists usually use a mirror when creating their self-portrait. But for the mind, "objects in the mirror are more complicated than they appear," concluded Wegner.

UNIT 6
Emotion and Motivation

Unit Selections

17. **Fundamental Feelings**, Antonio Damasio
18. **The Value of Positive Emotions**, Barbara L. Fredrickson
19. **Can You Interview for Integrity?**, William C. Byham
20. **The Power of Goal-Setting**, Memory Nguwi

Key Points to Consider

- What is motivation? What is an emotion? How are the two related to each other? Do you think they always affect one another?

- Are humans the only creatures that experience emotions, both positive and negative? Why did you answer as you did? Is your answer and method scientifically sound or based on mere anecdote?

- From where do emotions originate—nature or nurture? Why did you give the answer you did? Are various emotions controlled by different factors? For example, does the brain control some emotions while the situation controls other emotions? What role does the nervous system play in emotionality?

- What are some positive emotions? What are some examples of negative emotions? Do you think there is an "appropriate" emotion for every situation? Why are some people unemotional and others very expressive? Why are psychologists switching their emphasis from negative emotions, such as fear, to positive emotions, such as joy?

- What is integrity? What is morality? How is guilt related to these two concepts? Why is detecting a job applicant's integrity so important? How can interviewers measure the truthfulness of a prospective employee? How can interviewers improve their interviews?

- Do you sometimes feel unmotivated or overwhelmed by too much to do? How can setting goals motive you? Do you know how to prioritize goals such that the most important ones are attended to first? What are some of the more productive methods for setting goals?

 **Links: www.dushkin.com/online/**
These sites are annotated in the World Wide Web pages.

Emotional Intelligence Discovery
http://www.cwrl.utexas.edu/~bump/Hu305/3/3/3/

John Suler's Teaching Clinical Psychology Site
http://www.rider.edu/users/suler/tcp.html

Nature vs. Nurture: Gergen Dialogue with Winifred Gallagher
http://www.pbs.org/newshour/gergen/gallagher_5-14.html

Jasmine's sister was a working mother and always reminded Jasmine about how exciting life on the road as a sales representative was. Jasmine stayed home because she loved her children, two-year old Min, four-year-old Chi'Ming, and newborn Yuan. On the day of the particular incident described below, Jasmine was having a difficult time with the children. The baby, Yuan, had been crying all day from colic. The other two children had been bickering over their toys. Jasmine, realizing that it was already 5:15 and her husband would be home any minute, frantically started preparing dinner. She wanted to fix a nice dinner so that she and her husband could eat after the children went to bed, then relax and enjoy each other.

This was not to be. Jasmine sat waiting for her no-show husband. When he finally walked in the door at 10:15, Jasmine was furious. His excuse that his boss had invited the whole office for

dinner didn't reduce Jasmine's ire. Jasmine reasoned that her husband could have called to say that he wouldn't be home for dinner; he could have taken five minutes to do that. He said he did but the phone was busy. Jasmine berated her husband. Her face was taut and red with rage. Her voice wavered as she escalated her decibel level. Suddenly, bursting into tears, she ran into the living room. Her husband retreated to the safety of their bedroom and the respite that a deep sleep would bring.

Exhausted and disappointed, Jasmine sat alone and pondered why she was so angry with her husband. Was she just tired? Was she frustrated by negotiating with young children all day and simply wanted another adult around once in a while? Was she secretly worried and jealous that her husband was seeing another woman and had lied about his whereabouts? Was she combative because her husband's and her sister's lives seemed so much fuller than her own life? Jasmine was unsure just how she felt and why she exploded in such rage at her husband, someone she loved dearly.

This story, while sad and gender stereotypical, is not necessarily unrealistic when it comes to emotions. There are times when we are moved to deep emotion. On other occasions when we expect waterfalls of tears, we find that our eyes are dry or simply a little misty. What are these strange things we call emotions? What motivates us to rage at someone we love? And why do Americans seem to autopsy our every mood?

These questions and others have inspired psychologists to study emotions and motivation. The above episode about Jasmine, besides introducing these topics to you, also illustrates why these two topics are usually interrelated in psychology. Some emotions are pleasant, so pleasant that we are motivated to keep them going. Pleasant emotions are exemplified by love, pride, and joy. Other emotions are terribly draining and oppressive—so negative that we hope they will be over as soon as possible. Negative emotions are exemplified by anger, grief, and jealousy. Emotions and motivation and their relationship to each other are the focus of this unit.

Four articles round out this unit. "Fundamental Feelings" is the first article and was written by noted scientist, Antonio Dam-asio. Damasio is famous for his studies linking emotions to the nervous system. In this brief article he introduces us to his research and his ideas regarding emotionality.

A companion article, "The Value of Positive Emotions," incorporates more food for thought about emotions. Positive psychology and therefore the study of the benefits of positive emotions is its topic. In the past, psychologists have mostly studied negative emotions such as sadness and anxiety. Positive psychologists are changing the emphasis to joy and optimism.

The next article examines a crucial problem in trying to decipher others' emotions. In particular, the article discusses why and how employers attempt to understand a job applicant's level of morality or integrity (i.e. they try to read a person's guilt level). Well-honed interview questions and special techniques assist in this endeavor.

The final selection in this unit examines a concept traditionally related to emotions—motivation. Various motives guide our behaviors and emotions, such as the need to stay safe, the need for food and water, and so on. In specific, one motive is that we want to maintain positive emotions (e.g. happiness) while short-circuiting negative emotions, such as sadness. Many of us have difficulty maintaining motivation. This last article discusses goal-setting and how to stay motivated.

Fundamental feelings

Antonio Damasio

The groundwork for the science of emotion was laid down most auspiciously over a century ago, but neuroscience has given the problem a resolute cold shoulder until recently. By the time that Charles Darwin had remarked on the continuity of emotional phenomena from non-human species to humans; William James had proposed an insightful mechanism for its production; Sigmund Freud had noted the central role of emotions in psychopathological states; and Charles Sherrington had begun the physiological investigation of the neural circuits involved in emotion, one might have expected neuroscience to be poised for an all-out attack on the problem. It is not usually appreciated that the probable cause of the neglect of the topic was the improper distinction between the concepts of emotion and feelings.

Some traits of feelings—their subjective nature, the fact that they are private, hidden from view, and often difficult to analyse—were projected onto emotions, so that they too were deemed subjective, private, hidden and elusive. Not surprisingly, neuroscientists were disinclined to give their best efforts to a problem that did not seem to be amenable to proper hypothesizing and measurement. Somewhat alarmingly, this conflation of the two concepts persists, as does the idea that the neurobiology of feelings is out of reach. A clarification is in order.

An emotion, be it happiness or sadness, embarrassment or pride, is a patterned collection of chemical and neural responses that is produced by the brain when it detects the presence of an emotionally competent stimulus—an object or situation, for example. The processing of the stimulus may be conscious but it need not be, as the responses are engendered automatically.

Emotional responses are a mode of reaction of brains that are prepared by evolution to respond to certain classes of objects and events with certain repertoires of action. Eventually, the brain associates other objects and events that occur in individual experience with those that are innately set to cause emotions, so that another set of emotionally competent stimuli arises.

The main target of the emotional responses is the body—the internal milieu, the viscera and the musculoskeletal system—but there are also targets within the brain itself, for example, monoaminergic nuclei in the brainstem tegmentum. The result of the body-targeting responses is the creation of an emotional state—involving adjustments in homeostatic balance—as well as the enactment of specific behaviours, such as freezing or fight-or-flight, and the production of particular facial expressions. The result of the brain-targeting responses is an alteration in the mode of brain operation during the emotional body adjustments, the consequence of which is, for example, a change in the attention accorded to stimuli.

Emotion

Emotion and feelings are closely related but separable phenomena; their elucidation, at long last, is now proceeding in earnest.

Emotions allow organisms to cope successfully with objects and situations that are potentially dangerous or advantageous. They are just the most visible part of a huge edifice of undeliberated biological regulation that includes the homeostatic reactions that maintain metabolism; pain signalling; and drives such as hunger and thirst. Most emotional responses are directly observable either with the naked eye or with scientific probes such as psychophysiological and neurophysiological measurements and endocrine assays. Thus, emotions are not subjective, private, elusive or undefinable. Their neurobiology can be investigated objectively, not just in humans but in laboratory species, from *Drosophila* and *Aplysia* to rodents and non-human primates.

A working definition of feelings is a different matter. Feelings are the mental representation of the physiological changes that characterize emotions. Unlike emotions, which are scientifically public, feelings are indeed private, although no more subjective than any other aspect of the mind, for example my planning of this sentence, or the mental solving of a mathematical problem. Feelings are as amenable to scientific analysis as any other cognitive phenomenon, provided that appropriate methods are used. Moreover, because feelings are the direct consequences of emotions, the elucidation of emotional neurobiology opens the way to elucidating the neurobiology of feelings.

If emotions provide an immediate response to certain challenges and opportunities faced by an organism, the feeling of those emotions provides it with a mental alert. Feelings amplify the impact of a given situation, enhance learning, and increase the probability that comparable situations can be anticipated.

The neural systems that are involved in the production of emotions are being identified through studies of humans and other animals. Various structures, such as the amygdala and the ventromedial prefrontal cortices, trigger emotions by functioning as interfaces between the processing of emotionally competent stimuli and the execution of emotions. But the real executors of emotions are structures in the hypothalamus, in the basal forebrain (for example, the nucleus accumbens) and in the brainstem (for example, the nuclei in the periaqueductal grey). These are the structures that directly signal, chemically and neurally, to the body and brain targets at which alterations constitute an emotional state.

No less importantly, recent functional imaging studies reveal that body-sensing areas, such as the cortices in the insula, the second somatosensory region (S2) and the cingulate region of the brain, show a statistically significant pattern of activation or deactivation when normal individuals experience the emotions of sadness, happiness, fear and anger. Moreover, these patterns vary between different emotions. Those body-related patterns are tangible neural correlates of feelings, meaning that we know where to look further to unravel the remaining neurophysiological mysteries behind one of the most critical aspects of human experience.

FURTHER READING

Damasio, A. R. *The Feeling of What Happens: Body and Emotion in the Making of Consciousness* (Harcourt Brace, New York, 1999).

Davidson, R. J. & Irwin, W. *Trends Cogn. Neurosci.* **3**, 11–22 (1999).

Panksepp, J. *Affective Neuroscience: The Foundations of Human and Animal Emotions* (Oxford Univ. Press, New York, 1998).

Vuillemier, P., Driver, J., Armony, J. & Dolan, R. J. *Neuron* **30**, 829–841 (2000).

Antonio Damasio is in the Department of Neurology, University of Iowa College of Medicine, 200 Hawkins Drive, Iowa City, Iowa 52242, USA.

The Value of Positive Emotions

*The emerging science of positive psychology
is coming to understand why it's good to feel good*

Barbara L. Fredrickson

Back in the 1930s some young Catholic nuns were asked to write short, personal essays about their lives. They described edifying events in their childhood, the schools they attended, their religious experiences and the influences that led them to the convent. Although the essays may have been initially used to assess each nun's career path, the documents were eventually archived and largely forgotten. More than 60 years later the nuns' writings surfaced again when three psychologists at the University of Kentucky reviewed the essays as part of a larger study on aging and Alzheimer's disease. Deborah Danner, David Snowdon and Wallace Friesen read the nun's biographical sketches and scored them for positive emotional content, recording instances of happiness, interest, love and hope. What they found was remarkable: The nuns who expressed the most positive emotions lived up to 10 years longer than those who expressed the fewest. This gain in life expectancy is considerably larger than the gain achieved by those who quit smoking.

The nun study is not an isolated case. Several other scientists have found that people who feel good live longer. But why would this be so?

Some answers are emerging from the new field of positive psychology. This branch of psychological science surfaced about five years ago, as the brainchild of Martin E. P. Seligman, then president of the American Psychological Association (APA). Like many psychologists, Seligman had devoted much of his research career to studying mental illness. He coined the phrase *learned helplessness* to describe how hopelessness and other negative thoughts can spiral down into clinical depression.

At the start of his term as APA president, Seligman took stock of the field of psychology, noting its significant advances in curing ills. In 1947, none of the major mental illnesses were treatable, whereas today 16 are treatable by psychotherapy, psychopharmacology or both. Although psychology had become proficient at rescuing people from various mental illnesses, it had virtually no scientifically sound tools for helping people to reach their higher ground, to thrive and flourish. Seligman aimed to correct this imbalance when he called for a "positive psychology." With the help of psychologist Mihaly Csikszentmihalyi—who originated the concept of "flow" to describe peak motivational experiences—Seligman culled the field for scientists whose work might be described as investigating "that which makes life worth living."

This is how many research psychologists, myself included, were drawn to positive psychology. My own background is in the study of emotions. For more than a dozen years, I've been studying the positive emotions—joy, contentment, gratitude and love—to shed light on their evolved adaptive significance. Among scientists who study emotions, this is a rare specialty. Far more emotion researchers have devoted their careers to studying negative emotions, such as anger, anxiety and sadness. The study of optimism and positive emotions was seen by some as a frivolous pursuit. But the positive psychology movement is changing that. Many psychologists have now begun to explore the largely uncharted terrain of human strengths and the sources of happiness.

The new discoveries generated by positive psychology hold the promise of improving individual and collective functioning, psychological well-being and physical health. But to harness the power of positive psychology, we need to understand how and why "goodness" matters. Although the discovery that people who think positively and feel good actually live longer is remarkable, it raises more questions than it answers. Exactly how do positive thinking and pleasant feelings help people live longer? Do pleasant thoughts and feelings help people live better as well? And why are positive emotions a universal part of human nature? My research traces the possible pathways for the life-enhancing effects of positive emotions and attempts to understand why human beings evolved to experience them.

Why So Negative?

There are probably a number of reasons why the positive emotions received little attention in the past. There is, of course, the natural tendency to study something that afflicts the well-being of humanity—and the expression and experience of negative emotions are responsible for much of what ails this world. But it may also be that the positive emotions are a little harder to study. They are comparatively few and relatively undifferentiated—joy, amusement and serenity are not easily distinguished from one another. Anger, fear and sadness, on the other hand, are distinctly different experiences.

This lack of differentiation is evident in how we think about the emotions. Consider that scientific taxonomies of basic emotions typically identify one positive emotion for every three or four negative emotions and that this imbalance is also reflected in the relative numbers of emotion words in the English language.

Various physical components of emotional expression similarly reveal a lack of differentiation for the positive emotions. The negative emotions have specific facial configurations that imbue them with universally recognized signal value. We can readily identify angry, sad or fearful faces. In contrast, facial expressions for positive emotions have no unique signal value: All share the *Duchenne smile*—in which the corners of the lips are raised and the muscles are contracted around the eyes, which raises the cheeks. A sim-

ilar distinction is evident in the response of the autonomic nervous system to the expression of emotions. About 20 years ago, psychologists Paul Ekman and Wallace Friesen at the University of California, San Francisco, and Robert Levenson at Indiana University showed that anger, fear and sadness each elicit distinct responses in the autonomic nervous system. In contrast, the positive emotions appeared to have no distinguishable autonomic responses.

The study of positive emotions has also been hindered because scientists attempted to understand them with models that worked best for negative emotions. Central to many theories of emotion is that they are, by definition, associated with urges to act in particular ways. Anger creates the urge to attack, fear the urge to escape and disgust the urge to expectorate. Of course, no theorist argues that people invariably act out these urges; rather, people's ideas about possible courses of action narrow in on these specific urges. And these urges are not simply thoughts existing in the mind. They embody specific physiological changes that enable the actions called forth. In the case of fear, for example, a greater amount of blood flows to the large muscle groups to facilitate running.

The models that emphasize the role of these specific action tendencies typically cast the emotions as evolved adaptations. The negative emotions have an intuitively obvious adaptive value: In an instant, they narrow our thought-action repertoires to those that best promoted our ancestors' survival in life-threatening situations. In this view, negative emotions are efficient solutions to recurrent problems that our ancestors faced.

Positive emotions, on the other hand, aren't so easily explained. From this evolutionary perspective, joy, serenity and gratitude don't seem as useful as fear, anger or disgust. The bodily changes, urges to act and the facial expressions produced by positive emotions aren't as

specific or as obviously relevant to survival as those sparked by negative emotions. If positive emotions didn't promote our ancestors' survival in life-threatening situations, then what good were they? Did they have any adaptive value at all? Perhaps they merely signaled the absence of threats.

The Broaden-and-Build Theory

We gain some insight into the adaptive role of positive emotions if we abandon the framework used to understand the negative emotions. Instead of solving problems of immediate survival, positive emotions solve problems concerning personal growth and development. Experiencing a positive emotion leads to states of mind and to modes of behavior that indirectly prepare an individual for later hard times. In my broaden-and-build theory, I propose that the positive emotions broaden an individual's momentary mindset, and by doing so help to build enduring personal resources. We can test these ideas by exploring the ways that positive emotions change how people think and how they behave.

My students and I conducted experiments in which we induced certain emotions in people by having them watch short, emotionally evocative film clips. We elicited joy by showing a herd of playful penguins waddling and sliding on the ice, we elicited serenity with clips of peaceful nature scenes, we elicited fear with films of people at precarious heights, and we elicited sadness with scenes of deaths and funerals. We also used a neutral "control" film of an old computer screen saver that elicited no emotion at all.

We then assessed the participant's ability to think broadly. Using global-local visual processing tasks, we measured whether they saw the "big picture" or focused on smaller details (*Figure 1, left*). The participant's task is to judge which of two comparison figures is more similar to a "standard" figure. Neither choice is right or wrong, but one comparison figure

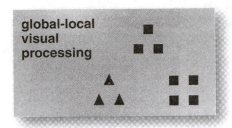 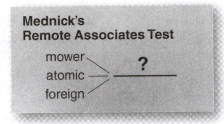

Figure 1. Psychological tests reveal that people tend to think broadly when they experience positive emotions. A global-local visual processing test *(left)* asks participants to judge which of two comparison figures *(bottom)* is most similar to a standard figure *(top)*. People experiencing positive emotions tend to choose the figure that resembles the standard configuration in global configuration *(the triangles)*. Similarly, people experiencing positive emotions score highly on tests of creativity such as Mednick's Remote Associates Test *(right)*, which asks people to think of a word that relates to each of three other words. (The answer is in the text on the previous page.) The positive emotions broaden people's mindsets, which allows them to solve problems like this more readily.

resembles the standard in global configuration, and the other in local, detailed elements. Using this and similar measures, we found that, compared to those in negative or neutral states, people who experience positive emotions (as assessed by self-report or electromyographic signals from the face) tend to choose the global configuration, suggesting a broadened pattern of thinking.

This tendency to promote a broader thought-action repertoire is linked to a variety of downstream effects of positive emotions on thinking. Two decades of experiments by Alice Isen of Cornell University and her colleagues have shown that people experiencing positive affect (feelings) think differently. One series of experiments tested creative thinking using such tests as Mednick's Remote Associates Test, which asks people to think of a word that relates to each of three other words. So, for example, given the words mower, atomic and foreign, the correct answer is power *(Figure 1, right)*. Although this test was originally designed to assess individual differences in the presumably stable trait of creativity, Isen and colleagues showed that people experiencing positive affect perform better on this test than people in neutral states.

In other experiments, Isen and colleagues tested the clinical reasoning of practicing physicians. They made some of the physicians feel good by giving them a small bag of candy, then asked all of them to think aloud while they solved a case of a patient with liver disease. Content analyses revealed that physicians who felt good were faster to integrate case information and less likely to become anchored on initial thoughts or come to premature closure in their diagnosis. In yet another experiment, Isen and colleagues showed that negotiators induced to feel good were more likely to discover integrative solutions in a complex bargaining task. Overall, 20 years of experiments by Isen and her colleagues show that when people feel good, their thinking becomes more creative, integrative, flexible and open to information.

Even though positive emotions and the broadened mindsets they create are themselves short-lived, they can have deep and enduring effects. By momentarily broadening attention and thinking, positive emotions can lead to the discovery of novel ideas, actions and social bonds. For example, joy and playfulness build a variety of resources. Consider children at play in the schoolyard or adults enjoying a game of basketball in the gym. Although their immediate motivations may be simply hedonistic—to enjoy the moment—they are at the same time building physical, intellectual, psychological and social resources. The physical activity leads to long-term improvements in health, the game-playing strategies develop problem-solving skills, and the camaraderie strengthens social bonds that may provide crucial support at some time in the future. Similar links between playfulness and later gains in physical, social and intellectual resources are also evident in nonhuman animals, such as monkeys, rats and squirrels. In human beings, other positive states of mind and positive actions work along similar lines: Savoring an experience solidifies life priorities; altruistic acts strengthen social ties and build skills for expressing love and care. These outcomes often endure long after the initial positive emotion has vanished.

My students and I recently tested these ideas by surveying a group of people to examine their resilience and optimism. The people were originally interviewed in the early months of 2001, and then again in the days after the September 11th terrorist attacks. We asked them to identify the emotions they were feeling, what they had learned from the attacks and how optimistic they were about the future. We learned that after September 11 nearly everyone felt sad, angry and somewhat afraid. And more than 70 percent were depressed. Yet the people who were originally identified as being resilient in the early part of 2001 felt positive emotions strongly as well. They were also half as likely to be depressed. Our statistical analyses showed that their tendency to feel more positive emotions buffered the resilient people against depression.

Gratitude was the most common positive emotion people felt after the

September 11th attacks. Feeling grateful was associated both with learning many good things from the crisis and with increased levels of optimism. Resilient people made statements such as, "I learned that most people in the world are inherently good." Put differently, feeling grateful broadened positive learning, which in turn built optimism, just as the broaden-and-build theory suggests.

My students and I have recently completed an experimental test of the building effect of positive emotions. Over the course of a month-long study of daily experiences, we induced one group of college students to feel more positive emotions by asking them to find the positive meaning and long-term benefit within their best, worst and seem-ingly ordinary experiences each day. At the end of the month, compared to others who did not make this daily effort to find positive meaning, those who did showed increases in psychological resilience.

So "feeling good" does far more than signal the absence of threats. It can transform people for the better, making them more optimistic, resilient and socially connected. Indeed, this insight might solve the evolutionary mystery of positive emotions: Simply by experiencing positive emotions, our ancestors would have naturally accrued more personal resources. And when later faced with threats to life or limb, these greater resources translated into greater odds of survival and greater odds of living long enough to reproduce.

The Undoing Hypothesis

We might also ask whether there are other immediate benefits to experiencing positive emotions, aside from the tautology that they make us "feel good." One effect relates to how people cope with their negative emotions. If negative emotions narrow people's mindsets and positive emotions broaden them, then perhaps positive emotions undo the lingering effects of negative emotions.

Such effects may extend to the physiological realm. The negative emotions have distinct physiological responses associated with them—autonomic activity (as mentioned earlier), including cardiovascular activity, which represents the body's preparation for specific action. A number of studies suggest that the

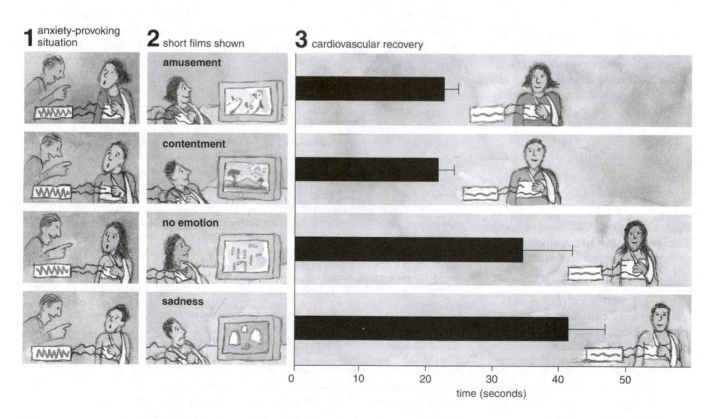

Figure 2. Undoing hypothesis suggests that positive emotions "undo" the lingering effects of negative emotions. This was examined by provoking anxiety in a group of participants by asking them to prepare a speech under time pressure. After learning that they did not have to deliver their speeches after all, the participants were shown one of four films, eliciting either amusement, contentment, no emotion or sadness. Measurements of the participants' heart rate, blood pressure and peripheral vasoconstriction revealed that feeling positive emotions leads to the quickest recovery to baseline measures obtained before they were placed in the anxiety-provoking situation. These undoing effects may partly explain the longevity of people who experience positive emotions more often.

cardiovascular activity associated with stress and negative emotions, especially if prolonged and recurrent, can promote or exacerbate heart disease. Experiments on non-human primates reveal that recurrent emotion-related cardiovascular activity also appears to injure the inner walls of arteries and initiate atherosclerosis. Because the positive emotions broaden people's thought-and-action repertoires, they may also loosen the hold that negative emotions gain on both mind and body, dismantle preparation for specific action and undo the physiological effects of negative emotions.

My colleagues and I tested this undoing hypothesis in a series of experiments. We began by inducing a negative emotion: We told participants that they had one minute to prepare a speech that would be videotaped and evaluated by their peers. The speech task induced the subjective feeling of anxiety as well as increases in heart rate, peripheral vasoconstriction and blood pressure. We then randomly assigned the participants to view one of four films: two films evoked mild positive emotions (amusement and contentment), a third served as a neutral control condition and a fourth elicited sadness.

We then measured the time elapsed from the beginning of the randomly assigned film until the cardiovascular reactions induced by the speech task returned to each participant's baseline levels. The results were consistent: Those individuals who watched the two positive-emotion films recovered to their baseline cardiovascular activity sooner than those who watched the neutral film. Those who watched the sad film showed the most delayed recovery (*Figure 2*). Positive emotions had a clear and consistent effect of undoing the cardiovascular repercussions of negative emotions.

At this point the cognitive and physiological mechanisms of the undoing effect are unknown. It may be that broadening one's cognitive perspective by feeling positive emotions

mediates the physiological undoing. Such ideas need further exploration.

Ending on a Positive Note

So how do the positive emotions promote longevity? Why did the happy nuns live so long? It seems that positive emotions do more than simply feel good in the present. The undoing effect suggests that positive emotions can reduce the physiological "damage" on the cardiovascular system sustained by feeling negative emotions. But some other research suggests that there's more to it than that. It appears that experiencing positive emotions increases the likelihood that one will feel good in the future.

My colleague Thomas Joiner and I sought to test whether positive affect and broadened thinking mutually enhance each other—so that experiencing one produces the other, which in turn encourages more of the first one, and so on in a mutually reinforcing ascent to greater well-being. We measured positive affect and broadened thinking strategies in 138 college students on two separate occasions, five weeks apart (times T1 and T2), with standard psychological tests. When we compared the students' responses on both occasions we found some very interesting results: Positive affect at T1 predicted increases in both positive affect and broadened thinking at T2; and broadened thinking at TI predicted increases in both positive affect and broadened thinking at T2. Further statistical analyses revealed that there was indeed a mutually reinforcing effect between positive affect and broadened thinking. These results suggest that people who regularly feel positive emotions are in some respects lifted on an "upward spiral" of continued growth and thriving.

But positive emotions don't just transform individuals. I've argued that they may also transform groups of people, within communities and organizations. Community transformation becomes possible because

each person's positive emotion can resound through others. Take helpful, compassionate acts as an example. Isen demonstrated that people who experience positive emotions become more helpful to others. Yet being helpful not only springs from positive emotions, it also produces positive emotions. People who give help, for instance, can feel proud of their good deeds and so experience continued good feelings. Plus, people who receive help can feel grateful, and those who merely witness good deeds can feel elevated. Each of these positive emotions—pride, gratitude and elevation—can in turn broaden people's mindsets and inspire further compassionate acts. So, by creating chains of events that carry positive meaning for others, positive emotions can trigger upward spirals that transform communities into more cohesive, moral and harmonious social organizations.

All of this suggests that we need to develop methods to experience more positive emotions more often. Although the use of humor, laughter and other direct attempts to stimulate positive emotions are occasionally suitable, they often seem poor choices, especially in trying times. Based on our recent experiment with college students, my advice would be to cultivate positive emotions indirectly by finding positive meaning within current circumstances. Positive meaning can be obtained by finding benefits within adversity, by infusing ordinary events with meaning and by effective problem solving. You can find benefits in a grim world, for instance, by focusing on the newfound strengths and resolve within yourself and others. You can infuse ordinary events with meaning by expressing appreciation, love and gratitude, even for simple things. And you can find positive meaning through problem solving by supporting compassionate acts toward people in need. So although the active ingredient within growth and resilience may be positive emotions, the leverage point for accessing these benefits is finding positive meaning.

So, what good is it to think about the good in the world? The mind can be a powerful ally. As John Milton told us, "The mind is its own place, and in itself can make a heaven of hell, a hell of heaven." The new science of positive psychology is beginning to unravel how such transformations can take place. Think about the good in the world, or otherwise find positive meaning, and you seed your own positive emotions. A focus on goodness cannot only change your life and your community, but perhaps also the world, and in time create a heaven on earth.

Acknowledgments
The author would like to thank the University of Michigan, the National institute of Mental Health (MH59615) and the John Templeton Foundation for supporting some of the research described in this article.

Bibliography

Aspinwall, L. G., and U. M. Staudinger. 2003. *A Psychology of Human Strengths: Fundamental Questions and Future Directions for a Positive Psychology.* Washington, D.C.: American Psychological Association.

Danner, D. D., D. A. Snowdon and W. V. Friesen. 2001. Positive emotions in early life and longevity: Findings from the nun study. *Journal of Personality and Social Psychology* 80:804–813.

Fredrickson, B. L. 1998. What good are positive emotions? *Review of General Psychology* 2:300–319.

Fredrickson, B. L. 2000. Cultivating positive emotions to optimize health and well-being. *Prevention and Treatment* 3.http://journals.apa.org/prevention/volume3/toc-mar07-00.html

Fredrickson, B. L. 2001. The role of positive emotions in positive psychology: The broaden-and-build theory of positive emotions. *American Psychologist* 56:218–226.

Fredrickson, B. L., and T. Joiner. 2002. Positive emotions trigger upward spirals toward emotional well-being. *Psychological Science* 13:172–175.

Fredrickson, B. L., and R. W. Levenson. 1998. Positive emotions speed recovery from the cardiovascular sequelae of negative emotions. *Cognition and Emotion* 12:191–220.

Fredrickson, B. L., M. M. Tugade, C. E. Waugh and G. Larkin. 2003. What good are positive emotions in crises?: A prospective study of resilience and emotions following the terrorist attacks on the United States on September 11th, 2001. *Journal of Personality and Social Psychology* 84:365–376.

Isen, A. M. 1987. Positive affect, cognitive processes and social behavior. *Advances in Experimental Social Psychology* 20:203–253.

Barbara L. Fredrickson is the director of the Positive Emotions and Psychophysiology Laboratory at the University of Michigan. In 2000 she won the Templeton Prize in Positive Psychology. Address: 3006 East Hall, 525 East University Avenue, University of Michigan, Ann Arbor, MI 48109–1109. Internet: blf@umich.edu

Can You Interview for Integrity?

Yes, and you don't need a lie detector to do it.

By William C. Byham

After a thorough search for a new employee, one candidate has risen to the top, and he has the look of a winner. Impeccable résumé. Extensive relevant experience. Great interpersonal skills. Plenty of energy and enthusiasm. Great new ideas he's eager to set in motion.

So you hire him. And it turns out to be one of the biggest mistakes you've ever made.

That glowing individual, so impressive sitting across the conference-room table, lies to clients and misrepresents your products. He can't satisfactorily explain the irregularities in his expense reports. He backstabs coworkers and takes credit for work he didn't do. You have to let him go. But in his wake the questions remain: How were we so misled and so wrong? Why couldn't we have seen what kind of person we were *really* hiring?

Scenarios like this one are all too familiar, perhaps painfully so. But in light of the numerous examples of illegal and unethical behavior that have garnered headlines in recent months and years, managers are more interested than ever in making sure that they hire people, for positions at all organizational levels, who are trustworthy and share the organization's ethical values.

But despite their interest in doing a better job of hiring for honesty and integrity, too many managers continue to believe that their hands are tied. This is a mistake: They *can* screen for integrity and ethical behavior when selecting new employees. It might be as simple as doing background checks and checking references-steps that many organizations had tended to skip in recent years but are resurrecting. Then there is the often-overlooked yet substantial information on ethical behavior that managers can obtain during the interviewing process—by having properly trained interviewers seek examples of how candidates have handled ethical situations in the past, and by having everyone who interviews a candidate share, cross-check, and evaluate the information.

"Doesn't Everyone Do It?"

Some people are understandably skeptical that dishonest and unethical individuals can be ferreted out simply by asking them questions about their past behavior. After all, won't a dishonest or unethical person just lie, anyway? Psychology suggests that the answer is no, they won't. People with low integrity tend to think that everybody else has the same degree or an even lower degree of integrity than they do; they readily admit to integrity lapses because they think that their behavior is normal and assume that the interviewer feels the same way.

I have seen this theory borne out many times in my own interviewing experiences and in those of others. On one occasion, I interviewed a prominent politician's administrative assistant who bragged about how she helped her boss pad his expense account. Another time, a candidate I interviewed for a sales position told me how he had obtained "gold status" on a major airline by taking needless flights—paid for out of his employer's travel budget.

Organizations must have leaders and associates who will share and live their ethical values.

The real key to effectively interviewing for integrity is seeking multiple examples of behaviors and asking probing follow-up questions that reveal the thinking behind the behaviors described. While integrity-focused questions need be only a small part of the total interview, any ethical issues that arise must be explored fully so that the examples can be accurately evaluated and the best hiring decision reached.

Timing Is Everything

It is important to incorporate integrity questions into an interview—and equally important to know when to ask those questions. Interviewers are wise to save sensitive ethical questions for late in the interview, after rapport has been developed. And, of course, as with all interview questions, once you have asked an ethical question, remember to listen and respond with empathy.

Empathy does not mean acceptance or agreement—it means understanding. You can be empathetic with a person who is telling you about an unethical behavior, without having to bend or sacrifice your own ethical standards, by reflecting the interviewee's feelings ("So you felt really good after the presentation," or "So you had second thoughts after the sales call"). And by showing empathy, you can keep the individual talking, providing other examples of behavior that will foster your understanding.

The recent bad behavior of high-profile executives has been nothing short of alarming. But it's an alarm that conscientious managers needed to hear—and to heed. Organizations must have leaders and associates who will share and live their ethical values, and extra care must be taken to ensure that these individuals are the ones who are brought into the organization—and promoted.

The Top 11

The first step in an interviewing process to screen for honesty and integrity is for interviewers to ask the right questions. These questions need to be geared toward gathering information on past behaviors that illustrate whether a candidate's own ethical values are compatible with those of the organization.

Following is a list of questions, any of which could be incorporated into an interview to elicit examples of a candidate's past ethical behavior and to reveal insights about the candidate's honesty and integrity. While I've included 11 questions, most interview situations will dictate using only two or three such questions to obtain examples of past ethical behavior.

I've also given examples of good and questionable answers that candidates might give to these questions. The "rightness" or the "wrongness" of the answers is up to the interviewer's judgment. As such, it's important to train interviewers to follow up answers with more questions to pin down behavior and the thinking behind the behavior, to ask for additional examples, and to have a systematic integration of data so that multiple interpretations of the answers can be obtained and discussed.

1. "We are often confronted with the dilemma of having to choose between what is right and what is best for the company. Give at least two examples of situations in which you faced this dilemma and how you handled them."

Good answer: Once, we discovered a technical defect in a product after it had been shipped and used by a cli-

ent. The client did not notice the defect. We debated whether to tell the client and admit we had made a stupid error, or just let things go because the client seemed to be using the product with no problem. We decided to tell the client and replace the product at no cost.

Questionable answer: We discovered that our sales clerks were making errors in charging for certain combinations of products and that the errors were almost always in favor of the company. In no way were the clerks encouraged or trained to make these errors. We also learned that, with training, the errors could be eliminated, but the training would be fairly expensive. I decided not to institute the training.

2. "How would you describe the ethics of your company? In which areas do you feel comfortable and uncomfortable with them? Why?"

Good answer: My company is extremely ethical, and I've never, ever run into a situation in which I disagreed with a decision made because of ethics. In fact, we bend over backward in the treatment of our customers—such as taking back out-of-date products and providing free service past warranty, whenever there is any question about our products and services.

Questionable answer: I'm not sure what the ethics of our company are. People seem to do what's necessary to get the job done.

3. "Give me an example of an ethical decision you have had to make on the job. What factors did you consider in reaching this decision?"

Good answer: We had a customer return a large shipment. While technically it was in the second quarter, it would have been very easy to move the revenue hit to the third quarter. Including it in the second quarter meant that we would not meet sales expectations. To me, it was a matter of borrowing from Peter to pay Paul, and we probably wouldn't meet our expectations the next quarter. Anyway, I felt that it was better to take the bad results when you were supposed to, rather than cook the books.

Questionable answer: I've never really had to make a tough decision regarding ethics.

4. "Have you ever observed someone stretching the rules at work? What did you do about it?"

Good answer: One of my fellow executives took a company car to use for a weekend vacation. I spoke to him, and he agreed that it was not right and that he would not do it again.

Questionable answer: Everybody stretches the rules sometimes.

5. "Have you ever had to bend the rules or exaggerate a little bit when trying to make a sale?"

Good answer: My experience is that when salespeople misrepresent products and services, customers buy less from them. Having credibility with customers brings in better long-term sales. For example, when I was selling servers, we had a proprietary server and operating system. The client asked me why my machine was really worth the higher cost. I listed the advantages and disad-

Why You Need to Read to Read Between the Lines

While interviews can uncover examples of a candidate's past unethical behavior or his lack of integrity, employers also are wise to closely scrutinize résumés. Studies find that 40 to 60 percent of résumés contain meaningful errors, such as dramatically inflated education, experience, or employment history.

These statistics and examples are hard to ignore, and demand that employers examine résumés with greater care.

Short of doing a background check before you interview an individual, there is little you can do about errors on résumés until you get into the interview. Then there are two things you *can* do.

First, look for holes, obvious or not, in the candidate's employment record and ask about those omissions.

Second, assign at least one interviewer to do a thorough review of the person's work or education record, asking questions like, "How did you get the job?" "What did you do?" "Why did you leave?" and, "How did you leave?" All dates should be verified. Often at this point an interviewee admits that perhaps the way that he presented information in the résumé is misleading: He didn't really graduate—he just attended courses; his title was sales manager but he didn't manage anybody. Often such education/job reviews are "assigned" to someone from HR and are done over the phone as part of a screening process. The interviewer covers the areas in a friendly way—"I just want to be sure that we're clear on everything so we can set you up for success if you come in for one-to-one interviews."

Sometimes dates don't line up for good reasons. For example, a candidate could show the date he received his master's degree well into the time that his résumé would indicate that he was living in another town and had a full-time job. The reason may well be that the university awards degrees only at certain times but the candidate finished his coursework for his master's degree months or even a year earlier. You should go over the dates with him and offer the chance to explain these discrepancies. Don't take action on a discrepancy without giving the candidate an opportunity to explain it.

Ultimately, recruiters and hiring managers must judge for themselves how important a particular résumé error is. But certainly the intentional deletion of critical information or inclusion of misinformation is a telling sign about what kind of person the candidate really is.

—W.C.B.

---

vantages, which indicated for him that the cheaper solution would work. I lost that sale but came back to win a much larger sale six months later.

Questionable answer: Sometimes when selling to a doctor, the doctor will state that he's heard that one of my products is effective against a certain disease. I listen and nod my head and say, "Interesting." I don't correct him even though I know that the drug is not recommended for that purpose. I'm not saying that it *does* work the way he thinks it does; I'm just not disagreeing with the doctor. You can't give advice to physicians.

6. "Have you ever been in a situation in which you had to make something seem better than it really was?"

Good answer: That's a big temptation in the high-tech field, particularly with new products. Often you know that there are errors in the program and that there are going to be some problems—what do you do? I try to be as honest as I can and give people realistic expectations.

Questionable answer: Our product has a very long sales cycle, and very often when we come out with a new release, it's not really done. It's "vaporware." We talk about it and sell it as if it were really done, with the expectation that by the time we make the sale and the client gets ready to have it installed, it *will* be ready. Most of the time we meet the client's deadlines, but we've had some really embarrassing situations when we didn't.

7. "Tell me about an instance when you've had to go against company guidelines or procedures in order to get something done."

Good answer: Like any manager, I move budget money around in order to get projects done with the resources that I have been allocated—for example, by reassigning people. That's what managers are expected to do. You can't precisely follow detailed budget allocations that are made six or nine months in advance.

Questionable answer: My wife works for one of our suppliers, and I actually buy things from her. This is technically in violation of company rules, but it doesn't hurt anything, and, frankly, it's the best product.

8. "We've all done things that we regretted. Can you give me an example that falls into this category for you? How would you handle it differently today?"

Good answer: When I first took over my job, I let seven people go without a whole lot of knowledge about their skills and contributions. Later I found that three of them were actually outstanding employees who should not have been let go. My jumping to conclusions hurt them and the company's operations. It took us several years to replace their knowledge of our equipment.

Questionable answer: I've never regretted anything about business. It's a game. I play the game to win.

9. "Have you ever had anyone who worked for you do or say something that was misleading to the company or to a client? How did you handle it?"

Good answer: I had a salesperson misrepresent a feature of one of our products in a presentation made to a client. I knew that the feature was important to the client. I asked the salesperson to meet again with the client to cor-

The Art of the Ego Boost

People don't want to look bad in an interview and will very naturally put their best foot forward. An effective interviewer makes the interviewee feel at ease in giving what potentially could be negative information about himself. The interviewer does this in three ways:

- Provide a rationale for talking about poor or unethical behavior prior to asking a question. For example, "Everyone in an organization breaks the rules sometime. Can you tell me about some times when you've broken the rules?"

With the opening phrase, the interviewer is giving an excuse to the interviewee up-front to offer an example of negative behavior.

- Help the interviewee maintain self-esteem when the interviewee has offered a behavior about which she is embarrassed or uncertain (e.g., the interviewee admits she got in trouble for overstating a product's functionality). The interviewer should help the individual rationalize the behavior disclosed by saying something like, "We all make mistakes sometimes, and at least they provide an opportunity for learning" or, "That's a common mistake made by new people in

sales." Such post-confession affirmation maintains self-esteem and keeps the individual talking and providing information that will help the evaluation of ethical behavior.

- Do not take notes on negative behaviors at the time the interviewee shares the information. If the interviewer begins to write on his notepad, it is doubtful that the candidate will continue to open up or give additional, meaningful examples. Rather, the interviewer should just remember the negative behavior and later on in the interview, when the subject is more positive, write down a few notes.

—W.C.B.

---

rect the misrepresentation, and I made a follow-up phone call to ensure that the discussion occurred.

Questionable answer: I was part of a sales presentation by one of my best salespeople to a very, very big client. In the presentation, the salesperson absolutely misrepresented one of our product's features. It was an important misrepresentation because a competitor for that business had that feature. I sat through the rest of the meeting thinking about what to do but decided that I just couldn't let the misunderstanding stand. So after we left the presentation, I asked him to call the client and clarify the situation. I think he did, but I'm not sure.

10. "There are two philosophies about regulations and policies. One is that they are to be followed to the letter; the other is that they are just guidelines. What is your opinion?"

Good answer: Regulations and policies are made for important reasons. A regulation seems to me to be stronger, and I feel that I follow all regulations, such as getting reports in at a certain time and accounting for expenses in a certain way. Policies are a little bit more indefinite. They express more of a guideline and a philosophy. There are circumstances when you fall into the "gray area" when applying a policy. When I have had questions, I've checked with my boss.

Questionable answer: In order to get things done, you can't be held back by old-fashioned policies of your organization. You have to know what's right and do the right thing. You have to have good ethics and make decisions based on those ethics. You may have to bend the rules sometimes.

11. "Have you ever felt guilty about receiving credit for work that was mostly completed by others? If so, how did you handle it?"

Good answer: I frequently encounter this situation. By nature of being the boss, I get the credit for many of the things that my people do. I try my best to redirect that credit to them. For example, I insist that everyone who works on a proposal has her name on that proposal. We have celebrations when we win a contract at which we particularly point out the contributions of various people.

Questionable answer: No, I've never felt guilty. The person at the top gets credit when things go well, and he gets the blame when things go poorly. It's the nature of the job.

Interviewers should gather multiple examples from each question by employing a simple follow-up query: "Can you give me another example?" This will tell the interviewer whether the dishonest or unethical behavior was a one-time event or if there is a pattern. Also, interviewees tend to be more truthful in later examples than they are in their first example, which may be more of a PR effort.

Finally, it is vitally important for the interviewer to pin down the circumstances of the behavior so that a fair evaluation can be made. Interviewers do this by seeking the situation or task in which the behavior occurred, the actions of the individual, and the results from that action. If an interviewer doesn't have all three of these elements, it's very easy to misinterpret the response.

A candidate might relate a story in which he had to "bend the rules" on what could be put on his expense account. At first blush, this might seem like a negative behavior, but when you fully understand the circumstances—for example, "There was an opportunity to obtain some critical competitive information" and the result "that a project launch was more successful"—a different interpretation might be appropriate.

For example, when I was working as an industrial/organizational psychologist at J.C. Penney, a professional acquaintance at Sears offered to share some information on his company's selection system for management trainees. He loved to eat and drink, so I took him out for a nice lunch with wine when I flew to Chicago to meet him. He gave me two suitcases of research reports that catapulted my work ahead. I didn't have to make the same mistakes that Sears had made. The meeting and lunch were certainly worth hundreds of thousands of dollars to J.C. Penney. However, my company had a very low expense cap for taking people to lunch and refused to reimburse any alcoholic beverages. With my boss's knowledge and approval, I covered the difference elsewhere on the expense form.

Once you have uncovered examples of questionable behavior, be sure to accurately report the candidate's response to the others who have interviewed the same candidate when you meet to compare notes and arrive at a hiring decision. By obtaining multiple perspectives, you can better understand the examples' importance and check your standards before arriving at a final decision. This sharing and open discussion is a crucial step, as ethical behavior is best evaluated by a consensus decision among several knowledgeable managers.

Yes, you can interview for honesty and integrity. What's more, it's critically important that you do.

William C. Byham is president and CEO of Development Dimensions International Inc., an HR organization based in Pittsburgh. His last article was "Bench Strength" in February 2000.

The Power of Goal Setting

by Memory Nguwi

SETTING goals is one of the most effective ways to getting things done. However, like strategy, if not properly done, setting goals will remain symbolic: vague statements of intent but very light on specifics.

Setting goals can focus people's energy by defining what needs to be done and by setting reasonable time limits in which to do it. When done effectively, goal setting can bring out the best in people.

It is, however, unfortunate that so many people become mere spectators of life, resigned to experience success vicariously through others' accomplishments. They can see success for others, but they can't imagine it for themselves.

People need to be aware that success is an internal matter. For you to succeed as an individual, you need to believe in the validity of your own dreams and goals.

We all know that we are not born with equal physical and mental abilities. Many of us will have to overcome the many challenges that we have inherited from our early family environment. We, however, have an equal opportunity to feel the excitement in life and motivation in believing that we deserve the very best in life.

We can all attain the best, but we must make an internal commitment to believe it and achieve it.

Believing as an individual that you can achieve your dreams and goals is the first step in successful goal accomplishment. Positive belief in the form of a goal is the key to success in life. Negative belief, on the other hand, can permanently prevent us from ever gaining access to success in life.

Generally, looking at successful people you would find that they have clearly defined goals and action plans. You can see they have a specific sense of direction and that direction is based upon their own desires and not those assigned to them by family or friends.

Besides this characteristic, successful people make their plans work by exerting effort, energy and whatever time it takes to reach their goals. Most of us are limited in what we can achieve in life because we think in terms of the normal working hours as the only time when we can achieve our goals.

Peak performers don't put any time limits on their commitment to success. Most of their finest accomplishments are achieved while others are resting. Successful people persevere despite all the odds against them.

While many of us are able to come up with clear goals, we normally fall short when it comes to taking the required action to ensure that we achieve our dreams. Both in professional and personal lives, many people fall short on action and take half-hearted approaches to goal achievement. Successful people are adaptable and flexible. They welcome change and the opportunities that always come with it. Individuals and organisational cultures that can adapt rapidly to change will survive and thrive.

It's very critical to be alert for new opportunities as one progresses along their chosen path. Open yourself to new ideas. There is no other choice. The acceptable alternative can be summed by an old Chinese definition of insanity: "Doing what you have always done, in exactly the same way, and expect a different outcome."

The reason why people do not pursue their goals and dreams to fruition is the amount of risk involved. As you pursue your goals, bear it in mind that it helps to make sensible risk a key ingredient of your achievements.

Those who want to avoid risk and seek a secure environment, success is simply a matter of avoiding failure. There is only one risk that people need to avoid at all costs: that's the risk of doing nothing. Procrastination is a form of trying to live risk-free. It's based on fear of failure.

Organisations and individuals cannot afford to take this route where success is a matter of avoiding failure.

Just as companies must "reinvent" themselves to meet new challenges, so must each individual. Most people want to succeed, but they lack two important ingredients: persistence and patience. They are often likened to a farmer who keeps digging up seeds to see how they are doing, never giving them an opportunity to take root. It's important to be willing to wait longer for your goals to bear fruit. Impatience is only a good quality if it helps sharpen your focus on what you need in order to succeed. Most people are almost constantly looking back in anger at events of their lives and when they are not looking back in anger, they are looking ahead in fear. The result is frustration and fatigue. It is important to note that you cannot control all the variables that are brought to bear on your life. But you can always control your responses and your expectations.

When setting your goals, avoid goals that depend primarily on others or luck to be accomplished. However, you still need to take into account the help you will need from others for you to succeed. You need ongoing contact with people who have experience or who have access to resources and contacts that you don't have.

Make sure sizeable goals you have set for yourself include all steps necessary to achieve them. Also check if your goals are consistent with the person you want to be. Do what is consistent with your values, your beliefs, your personality and what you enjoy. It's self-defeating to set goals for yourselves in areas where you have limited abilities or experience.

While it's important to have well-defined goals, it's equally important to keep your goals manageable. Always break them down into sub-goals that are easier to reach and easier to adjust. People need to remember that the results you achieve will be in direct proportion to the effort you apply. In organisations, goals are being set everyday but nothing is being done. Because we unconsciously convince ourselves that the future holds confusion and is unpredictable, we seek a sense of security by maintaining the status quo.

The best strategy for success includes a firm belief in your ability to control every aspect of your destiny. It's important to always make a realistic assessment of your abilities and the difficulties you will encounter in order to *achieve* your goals.

Memory Nguwi is the Group Human Resources Manager for Rapid Financial Holdings Limited.

UNIT 7
Development

Unit Selections

21. **The Biology of Aging**, Geoffrey Cowley
22. **Inside the Womb**, J. Madeleine Nash
23. **Heading Off Disruptive Behavior**, Hill M. Walker, Elizabeth Ramsey, and Frank M. Gresham
24. **The Future of Adolescence: Lengthening Ladders to Adulthood**, Reed Larson
25. **The Methuselah Report**, Wayne Curtis
26. **Start the Conversation**, AARP Modern Maturity

Key Points to Consider

- What are the various milestones or developmental landmarks that signal stages in human development? What purpose do various developmental events serve? Can you give examples of some of these events?

- Why is embryonic and fetal life so important? How do the experiences of the fetus affect the child after it is born? What factors deter the fetus from achieving its full potential? What advice would you give a pregnant woman to help her understand how important prenatal life is?

- Do parents matter or do you think that genes mostly dictate child development? Do you think that both nature and nurture affect development? Is it important for both parents to be present during their child's formative years? Do you think fathers and mothers differ in their interactions with their children? How so?

- What kinds of disruptive and negative behaviors typify American children? Why are children of today more disruptive than in the past? What can families and schools do when children are disruptive? Is there any way to prevent such behaviors? Do you feel that prevention is better than after-the-fact behavior management?

- What is adolescence? How are today's teens different from teens in the past, for example from their parents' generation? What societal factors influence teens today? If you had to rank these factors, which would you choose as most influential and which as least significant? Do you think teens actively search for identity? Do you think today's teens look forward to adulthood? What can parents do to help guide their teens toward a healthy identity and positive adulthood?

- What demographic trends among America's aged population are we witnessing? Why are these changes occurring? What consequences do these changes foretell?

- Why is death a stigmatized topic in America? Do you think people should discuss it more often and more openly? Do you think they ever will? How can we make dying easier for the dying person and for those close to the dying person? What in general can Americans do to help those with terminal illnesses?

 **Links: www.dushkin.com/online/**
These sites are annotated in the World Wide Web pages.

American Association for Child and Adolescent Psychiatry
http://www.aacap.org
Behavioral Genetics
http://www.ornl.gov/hgmis/elsi/behavior.html

The Garcias and the Szubas are parents of newborns. Both sets of parents wander down to the hospital's neonatal nursery where pediatric nurses care for both babies—José Garcia and Kimberly Szuba—when the babies are not in their mothers' rooms. Kimberly is alert, active, and often crying and squirming when her parents watch her. On the other hand, José is quiet, often asleep, and less attentive to external stimuli when his parents monitor him in the nursery.

Why are these babies so different? Are the differences gender related? Will these differences disappear as the children develop or will the differences become exaggerated? What does the future hold for each child? Will Kimberly excel at sports and José excel at English? Can Kimberly overcome her parents' poverty and succeed in a professional career? Will José become a doctor like his mother or a pharmacist as is his father? Will both of these children escape childhood disease, abuse, and the other misfortunes sometimes visited upon American children?

Developmental psychologists are concerned with all of the Kimberlys and Josés of our world. Developmental psychologists study age-related changes in language, motoric and social skills, cognition, and physical health. Developmental psychologists are interested in the common skills shared by all children as well as the differences between children and the events that create these differences.

In general, developmental psychologists are concerned with the forces that guide and direct development. Some developmental theorists argue that the forces that shape a child are found in the environment in such factors as social class, quality of available stimulation, parenting style, and so on. Other theorists insist that genetics and related physiological factors such as hormones underlie the development of humans. A third set of psychologists, in fact many psychologists, believe that some combination or interaction of all these factors, physiology and environment or nature and nurture, are responsible for development.

In this unit, we are going to look at issues of development in a chronological fashion. In the first article, "The Biology of Aging," an overview of human development is given. Psychologists and others have identified fundamental stages through which humans pass as they mature.

The very first stage is fetal development, crucial to the physical and psychological growth of the child after it is born. Various environmental factors can deter development of or even damage the fetus. In "Inside the Womb," Madeleine Nash writes about these potential threats to the unborn child along each step of uterine development.

In the next article, author Hill Walker discusses disruptive behavior. Walker observes that American children are becoming more disruptive and defiant, in other words, exhibiting difficult anti-social behaviors for parents and teachers to manage. Besides discussing what adults can do after-the-fact, Walker describes important preventative methods for anticipating those moments when a child misbehaves.

We move next to some information about adolescence. Adolescence may be a time when children concertedly search for a self-identity and head toward adulthood. This passage to adulthood can sometimes be stormy and difficult. Despite more risks and demands on them, this generation of teens is coping well with the challenges.

The final article in this series looks at the ultimate stage in development —death. Death is stigmatized in America; few people openly discuss it. The article claims that we ought to be more open and is therefore designed to stimulate dialogue on this subject. There is much information contained in the article about issues surrounding death such as hospice care, how to be with a dying person, and so forth.

The Biology of Aging

Why, after being so exquisitely assembled, do we fall apart so predictably? Why do we outlive dogs, only to be outlived by turtles? Could we catch up with them? Living to 200 is not a realistic goal for this generation, but a clearer picture of how we grow old is already within our reach.

By Geoffrey Cowley

IF ONLY GOD HAD FOUND A more reliable messenger. Back around the beginning of time, according to east African legend, he dispatched a scavenging bird known as the halawaka to give us the instructions for endless self-renewal. The secret was simple. Whenever age or infirmity started creeping up on us, we were to shed our skins like tattered shirts. We would emerge with our youth and our health intact. Unfortunately, the halawaka got hungry during his journey, and happened upon a snake who was eating a freshly killed wildebeest. In the bartering that ensued, the bird got a satisfying meal, the snake learned to molt and humankind lost its shot at immortality. People have been growing old and dying ever since.

The mystery of aging runs almost as deep as the mystery of life. During the past century, life expectancy has nearly doubled in developed countries, thanks to improvements in nutrition, sanitation and medical science. Yet the potential life span of a human being has not changed significantly since the halawaka met the snake. By the age of 50 every one of us, no matter how fit, will begin a slow decline in organ function and sensory acuity. And though some will enjoy another half century of robust health, our odds of living past 120 are virtually zero. Why, after being so exquisitely assembled, do we fall apart so predictably? Why do we outlive dogs, only to be outlived by turtles? And what are our prospects for catching up with them?

Until recently, all we could do was guess. But as the developed world's population grows grayer, scientists are bearing down on the dynamics of aging, and they're amassing crucial insights. Much of the new understanding has come from the study of worms, flies, mice and monkeys—species whose life cycles can be manipulated and observed in a laboratory. How exactly the findings apply to people is still a matter of conjecture. Could calorie restriction extend our lives by half? It would take generations to find out for sure. But the big questions of why we age—and which parts of the experience we can change—are already coming into focus.

The starkest way to see how time changes us (aside from hauling out an old photo album) is to compare death rates for people of different ages. In Europe and North America the annual rate among 15-year-olds is roughly .05 percent, or one death for every 2,000 kids. Fifty-year-olds are far less likely to ride their skateboards down banisters, yet they die at 30 times that rate (1.5 percent annually). The yearly death rate among 105-year-olds is 50 percent, 1,000 times that of the adolescents. The rise in mortality is due mainly to heart disease, cancer and stroke—diseases that anyone over 50 is right to worry about. But here's the rub. Eradicating these scourges would add only 15 years to U.S. life expectancy (half the gain we achieved during the 20th century), for unlike children spared of smallpox, octogenarians without cancer soon die of something else. As the biologist Leonard Hayflick observes, what ultimately does us in is not disease per se, but our declining ability to resist it.

Biologists once regarded senescence as nature's way of pushing one generation aside to make way for the next. But under natural conditions, virtually no creature lives long enough to experience decrepitude. Our own ancestors typically starved, froze or got eaten long before they reached old age. As a result, the genes that leave us vulnerable to chronic illness in later life rarely had adverse consequences. As long as they didn't hinder reproduction, natural selection had no occasion to weed them out. Natural selection may even *favor* a gene that causes cancer late in life if it makes young adults more fertile.

But why should "later life" mean 50 instead of 150? Try thinking of the body as a vehicle, designed by a group of genes to transport them through time. You might expect durable bodies to have an inherent advantage. But if a mouse is sure to become a cat's dinner within five years, a body that could last twice that long is a waste of resources. A 5-year-old mouse that can produce eight litters annually will leave twice the legacy of a 10-year-old mouse that delivers only four each year. Under those conditions, mice will evolve to live roughly five years. A sudden disappearance of cats may improve their odds of completing that life cycle, but it won't change their basic genetic makeup.

That is the predicament we face. Our bodies are nicely adapted to the harsh conditions our Stone Age ancestors faced, but often poorly adapted to the cushy ones we've created. There is no question that we can age better by exercising, eating healthfully, avoiding cigarettes and staying socially and mentally active. But can we realistically expect to extend our maximum life spans?

The First Years of Growth

In childhood the body is wonderfully resilient, and **sound sleep** supports the growth of tissues and bones. During the teenage years, **hormonal changes** trigger the development of sexual organs. Boys add **muscle mass**. Even the muscles in their voice box lengthen, causing voices to deepen. In girls, fat is redistributed to hips and breasts.

Researchers have already accomplished that feat in lab experiments. In the species studied so far, the surest way to increase life span has been to cut back on calories—way back. In studies dating back to the 1930s, researchers have found that species as varied as rats, monkeys and baker's yeast age more slowly if they're given 30 to 60 percent fewer calories than they would normally consume. No one has attempted such a trial among humans, but some researchers have already embraced the regimen themselves. Dr. Roy Walford, a 77-year-old pathologist at the University of California, Los Angeles, has survived for years on 1,200 calories a day and expects to be doing the same when he's 120. That may be optimistic, but he looks as spry as any 60-year-old in the photo he posts on the Web, and the animal studies suggest at least a partial explanation. Besides delaying death, caloric restriction seems to preserve bone mass, skin thickness, brain function and immune function, while providing superior resistance to heat, toxic chemicals and traumatic injury.

How could something so perverse be so good for you? Scientists once theorized that caloric restriction extended life by delaying development, or by reducing body fat, or by slowing metabolic rate. None of these explanations survived scrutiny, but studies have identified several likely mechanisms. The first involves oxidation. As mitochondria (the power plants in our cells) release the energy in food, they generate corrosive, unpaired electrons known as free radicals. By reacting with nearby fats, proteins and nucleic acids, these tiny terrorists foster everything from cataracts to vascular disease. It appears that caloric restriction not only slows the production of free radicals but helps the body counter them more efficiently.

Food restriction may also shield tissues from the damaging effects of glucose, the sugar that enters our bloodstreams when we eat carbohydrates. Ideally, our bodies respond to any rise in blood glucose by releasing insulin, which shuttles the sugar into fat and muscle cells for storage. But age or obesity can make our

cells resistant to insulin. And when glucose molecules linger in the bloodstream, they link up with collagen and other proteins to wreak havoc on nerves, organs and blood vessels. When rats or monkeys are allowed to eat at will, their cells become less sensitive to insulin over time, just as ours do. But according to Dr. Mark Lane of the National Institute on Aging, older animals on calorie-restricted diets exhibit the high insulin sensitivity, low blood glucose and robust health of youngsters. No one knows whether people's bodies will respond the same way. But the finding suggests that life extension could prove as simple, or rather as complicated, as preserving the insulin response.

Another possible approach is to manipulate hormones. No one has shown conclusively that any of these substances can alter life span, but there are plenty of tantalizing hints. Consider human growth hormone, a pituitary protein that helps drive our physical development. Enthusiasts tout the prescription-only synthetic version as an antidote to all aspects of aging, but mounting evidence suggests that it could make the clock tick faster. The first indication came in the mid-1980s, when physiologist Andrzej Bartke outfitted lab mice with human or bovine genes for growth hormone. These mighty mice grew to twice the size of normal ones, but they aged early and died young. Bartke, now based at Southern Illinois University, witnessed something very different in 1996, when he began studying a strain of rodents called Ames dwarf mice. Due to a congenital lack of growth hormone, these creatures reach only a third the size of normal mice. But they live 50 to 60 percent longer.

As it happens, the mini-mice aren't the only ones carrying this auspicious gene. The island of Krk, a Croatian outpost in the eastern Adriatic, is home to a group of people who harbor essentially the same mutation. The "little people of Krk" reach an adult height of just 4 feet 5 inches. But like the mini-mice, they're exceptionally long-lived. Bartke's mouse studies suggest that besides stifling growth hormone, the gene that causes this stunting may also improve sensitivity to—you guessed it—insulin. If so, the mini-mice, the Croatian dwarfs and the half-starved rats and monkeys have more than their longevity in common. No one is suggesting that we stunt people's growth in the hope of extending their lives. But if you've been pestering your doctor for a vial of growth hormone, you may want to reconsider.

The Early Years of Adulthood

In many ways, the 20s are the prime of life. We're blessed with an efficient metabolism, **strong bones** and **good flexibility**. As early as the 30s, however, metabolism begins to slow and women's **hormone levels** start to dip. Bones may start to lose density in people who don't exercise or who don't get the vitamin D required for calcium absorption.

Growth hormone is just one of several that decline as we age. The sex hormones estrogen and testosterone follow the same pattern, and replacing them can rejuvenate skin, bone and muscle. But like growth hormone, these tonics can have costs as well as benefits. They evolved not to make us more durable but to make us more fertile. As the British biologist Roger Gosden observed in his 1996 book, "Cheating Time," "sex hormones are required for fertility and for making biological gender distinctions, but they do not prolong life. On the contrary, a price may have to be paid for living as a sexual being." Anyone suffering from breast or prostate cancer would surely agree.

The Joys of Middle Age

Around 40, people often start noticing gray hairs, mild **memory lapses** and difficulty focusing their eyes on small type. Around 51, most women will experience **menopause**. Estrogen levels plummet, making the skin thinner and bones less dense. Men suffer more **heart disease** than women at this age. Metabolism slows down in both sexes.

In most of the species biologists have studied, fertility and longevity have a seesaw relationship, each rising as the other declines. Bodies designed for maximum fertility have fewer resources for self-repair, some perishing as soon as they reproduce (think of spawning salmon). By contrast, those with extraordinary life spans are typically slow to bear offspring. Do these rules apply to people? The evidence is sketchy but provocative. In a 1998 study, researchers at the University of Manchester analyzed genealogical records of 32,000 British aristocrats born during the 1,135-year period between 740 and 1875 (long before modern contraceptives). Among men and women who made it to 60, the least fertile were the most likely to survive beyond that age. A whopping 50 percent of the women who reached 81 were childless.

Eunuchs seem to enjoy (if that's the word) a similar advantage in longevity. During the 1940s and '50s, anatomist James Hamilton studied a group of mentally handicapped men who had been castrated at a state institution in Kansas. Life expectancy was just 56 in this institution, but the neutered men lived to an average age of 69—a 23 percent advantage—and not one of them went bald. No one knows exactly how testosterone speeds aging, but athletes who abuse it are prone to ailments ranging from hypertension to kidney failure.

All of this research holds a fairly obvious lesson. Life itself is lethal, and the things that make it sweet make it *more* lethal. Chances are that by starving and castrating ourselves, we really could secure some extra years. But most of us would gladly trade a lonely decade of stubborn survival for a richer middle age. Our bodies are designed to last only so long. But with care and maintenance, they'll live out their warranties in style.

With RACHEL DAVIS

Inside The Womb

What scientists have learned about those amazing first nine months—
and what it means for mothers

By J. Madeleine Nash

As the crystal probe slides across her belly, Hilda Manzo, 33, stares wide-eyed at the video monitor mounted on the wall. She can make out a head with a mouth and two eyes. She can see pairs of arms and legs that end in tiny hands and feet. She can see the curve of a backbone, the bridge of a nose. And best of all, she can see movement. The mouth of her child-to-be yawns. Its feet kick. Its hands wave.

Dr. Jacques Abramowicz, director of the University of Chicago's ultrasound unit, turns up the audio so Manzo can hear the gush of blood through the umbilical cord and the fast thump, thump, thump of a miniature heart. "Oh, my!" she exclaims as he adjusts the sonic scanner to peer under her fetus' skin. "The heart is on the left side, as it should be," he says, "and it has four chambers. Look—one, two, three, four!"

Such images of life stirring in the womb—in this case, of a 17-week-old fetus no bigger than a newborn kitten—are at the forefront of a biomedical revolution that is rapidly transforming the way we think about the prenatal world. For although it takes nine months to make a baby, we now know that the most important developmental steps—including laying the foundation for such major organs as the heart, lungs and brain—occur before the end of the first three. We also know that long before a child is born its genes engage the environment of the womb in an elaborate conversation, a two-way dialogue that involves not only the air its mother breathes and the water she drinks but also what drugs she takes, what diseases she contracts and what hardships she suffers.

One reason we know this is a series of remarkable advances in MRIs, sonograms and other imaging technologies that allow us to peer into the developmental process at virtually every stage—from the fusion of sperm and egg to the emergence, some 40 weeks later, of a miniature human being. The extraordinary pictures on these pages come from a new book that captures some of the color and excitement of this research: *From Conception to Birth: A Life Unfolds* (Doubleday), by photographer Alexander Tsiaras and writer Barry Werth. Their computer-enhanced images are reminiscent of the remarkable fetal portraits taken by medical photographer Lennart Nilsson, which appeared in Life magazine in 1965. Like Nilsson's work, these images will probably spark controversy. Antiabortion activists may interpret them as evidence that a fetus is a viable human being earlier than generally believed, while pro-choice advocates may argue that the new technology allows doctors to detect serious fetal defects at a stage when abortion is a reasonable option.

The other reason we know so much about what goes on inside the womb is the remarkable progress researchers have made in teasing apart the sequence of chemical signals and switches that drive fetal development. Scientists can now describe at the level of individual genes and molecules many of the steps involved in building a human, from the establishment of a head-to-tail growth axis and the budding of limbs to the sculpting of a four-chambered heart and the weaving together of trillions of neural connections. Scientists are beginning to unroll the genetic blueprint of life and identify the precise molecular tools required for assembly. Human development no longer seems impossibly complex, says Stanford University biologist Matthew Scott. "It just seems marvelous."

How is it, we are invited to wonder, that a fertilized egg—a mere speck of protoplasm and DNA encased in a spherical shell—can generate such complexity? The answers, while elusive and incomplete, are beginning to come into focus.

Only 20 years ago, most developmental biologists thought that different organisms grew according to different sets of rules, so that understanding how a fly or a worm develops—or even a vertebrate like a chicken or a fish—would do little to illuminate the process in humans. Then, in the 1980s, researchers found remarkable similarities in the molecular tool kit used by organisms that span the breadth of the animal kingdom, and those similarities have proved serendipitous beyond imagining. No matter what the species, nature uses virtually the same nails

How They Did It

With just a few keystrokes, Alexander Tsiaras does the impossible. He takes the image of a 56-day-old human embryo and peers through its skin, revealing liver, lungs, a bulblike brain and the tiny, exquisite vertebrae of a developing spine.

These are no ordinary baby pictures. What Tsiaras and his colleagues are manipulating are layers of data gathered by CT scans, micro magnetic resonance imaging (MRI) and other visualization techniques. When Lennart Nilsson took his groundbreaking photographs in the 1960s, he was limited to what he could innovatively capture with a flash camera. Since then, says Tsiaras, "there's been a revolution in imaging."

What's changed is that development can now be viewed through a wide variety of prisms, using different forms of energy to illuminate different aspects of the fetus. CT scans, for example, are especially good at showing bone, and MRI is excellent for soft tissue. These two-dimensional layers of information are assembled, using sophisticated computer software, into a three-dimensional whole.

The results are painstakingly accurate and aesthetically stunning. Tsiaras, who trained as a painter and sculptor, used medical specimens from the Carnegie Human Embryology Collection at the National Museum of Health and Medicine in Washington as models for all but a few images. The specimens came from a variety of sources, according to museum director Adrianne Noe, including miscarriages and medically necessary procedures. None were acquired from elective abortions.

—*By David Bjerklie*

sory committee recommended that embryos be considered the same as human subjects in clinical trials.)

To be sure, the marvel of an embryo transcends the collection of genes and cells that compose it. For unlike strands of DNA floating in a test tube or stem cells dividing in a Petri dish, an embryo is capable of building not just a protein or a patch of tissue but a living entity in which every cell functions as an integrated part of the whole. "Imagine yourself as the world's tallest skyscraper, built in nine months and germinating from a single brick," suggest Tsiaras and Werth in the opening of their book. "As that brick divides, it gives rise to every other type of material needed to construct and operate the finished tower—a million tons of steel, concrete, mortar, insulation, tile, wood, granite, solvents, carpet, cable, pipe and glass as well as all furniture, phone systems, heating and cooling units, plumbing, electrical wiring, artwork and computer networks, including software."

Given the number of steps in the process, it will perhaps forever seem miraculous that life ever comes into being without a major hitch. "Whenever you look from one embryo to another," observes Columbia University developmental neurobiologist Thomas Jessell, "what strikes you is the fidelity of the process."

Sometimes, though, that fidelity is compromised, and the reasons why this happens are coming under intense scrutiny. In laboratory organisms, birth defects occur for purely genetic reasons when scientists purposely mutate or knock out specific sequences of DNA to establish their function. But when development goes off track in real life, the cause can often be traced to a lengthening list of external factors that disrupt some aspect of the genetic program. For an embryo does not develop in a vacuum but depends on the environment that surrounds it. When a human embryo is deprived of essential nutrients or exposed to a toxin, such as alcohol, tobacco or crack cocaine, the consequences can range from readily apparent abnormalities—spina bifida, fetal alcohol syndrome—to subtler metabolic defects that may not become apparent until much later.

and screws, the same hammers and power tools to put an embryo together.

Among the by-products of the torrent of information pouring out of the laboratory are new prospects for treating a broad range of late-in-life diseases. Just last month, for example, three biologists won the Nobel Prize for Medicine for their work on the nematode *Caenorhabditis elegans*, which has a few more than 1,000 cells, compared with a human's 50 trillion. The three winners helped establish that a fundamental mechanism that *C. elegans* embryos employ to get rid of redundant or abnormal cells also exists in humans and may play a role in AIDS, heart disease and cancer. Even more exciting, if considerably more controversial, is the understanding that embryonic cells harbor untapped therapeutic potential. These cells, of course, are stem cells, and they are the progenitors of more specialized cells that make up organs and tissues. By harnessing their generative powers, medical researchers believe, it may one day be possible to repair the damage wrought by injury and disease. (That prospect suffered a political setback last week when a federal advi-

IRONICALLY, EVEN AS SOCIETY AT LARGE CONTINUES TO WORRY almost obsessively about the genetic origins of disease, the biologists and medical researchers who study development are mounting an impressive case for the role played by the prenatal environment. A growing body of evidence suggests that a number of serious maladies—among them, atherosclerosis, hypertension and diabetes—trace their origins to detrimental prenatal conditions. As New York University Medical School's Dr. Peter Nathanielsz puts it, "What goes on in the womb before you are born is just as important to who you are as your genes."

Most adults, not to mention most teenagers, are by now thoroughly familiar with the mechanics of how the sperm in a man's semen and the egg in a woman's oviduct connect, and it is at this point that the story of development begins. For the sperm and the egg each contain only 23 chromosomes, half the amount of DNA needed to make a human. Only when the sperm and the egg fuse their chromosomes does the tiny zygote, as a fertilized egg is called, receive its instructions to grow. And grow it does, replicating its DNA each time it divides—into two cells, then four, then eight and so on.

If cell division continued in this fashion, then nine months later the hapless mother would give birth to a tumorous ball of literally astronomical proportions. But instead of endlessly dividing, the zygote's cells progressively take form. The first striking change is apparent four days after conception, when a 32-cell clump called the morula (which means "mulberry" in Latin) gives rise to two distinct layers wrapped around a fluid-filled core. Now known as a blastocyst, this spherical mass will proceed to burrow into the wall of the uterus. A short time later, the outer layer of cells will begin turning into the placenta and amniotic sac, while the inner layer will become the embryo.

The formation of the blastocyst signals the start of a sequence of changes that are as precisely choreographed as a ballet. At the end of Week One, the inner cell layer of the blastocyst balloons into two more layers. From the first layer, known as the endoderm, will come the cells that line the gastrointestinal tract. From the second, the ectoderm, will arise the neurons that make up the brain and spinal cord along with the epithelial cells that make up the skin. At the end of Week Two, the ectoderm spins off a thin line of cells known as the primitive streak, which forms a new cell layer called the mesoderm. From it will come the cells destined to make the heart, the lungs and all the other internal organs.

At this point, the embryo resembles a stack of Lilliputian pancakes—circular, flat and horizontal. But as the mesoderm forms, it interacts with cells in the ectoderm to trigger yet another transformation. Very soon these cells will roll up to become the neural tube, a rudimentary precursor of the spinal cord and brain. Already the embryo has a distinct cluster of cells at each end, one destined to become the mouth and the other the anus. The embryo, no larger at this point than a grain of rice, has determined the head-to-tail axis along which all its body parts will be arrayed.

How on earth does this little, barely animate cluster of cells "know" what to do? The answer is as simple as it is startling. A human embryo knows how to lay out its body axis in the same way that fruit-fly embryos know and *C. elegans* embryos and the embryos of myriad other creatures large and small know. In all cases, scientists have found, in charge of establishing this axis is a special set of genes, especially the so-called homeotic homeobox, or HOX, genes.

HOX genes were first discovered in fruit flies in the early 1980s when scientists noticed that their absence caused striking mutations. Heads, for example, grew feet instead of antennae, and thoraxes grew an extra pair of wings. HOX genes have been found in virtually every type of animal, and while their number varies—fruit flies have nine, humans have 39—they are invariably arrayed along chromosomes in the order along the body in which they are supposed to turn on.

Many other genes interact with the HOX system, including the aptly named Hedgehog and Tinman genes, without which fruit flies grow a dense covering of bristles or fail to make a heart. And scientists are learning in exquisite detail what each does at various stages of the developmental process. Thus one of the three Hedgehog genes—Sonic Hedgehog, named in honor of the cartoon and video-game character—has been shown to play a role in making at least half a dozen types of spinal-cord neurons. As it happens, cells in different places in the neural tube are exposed to different levels of the protein encoded by this gene; cells drenched in significant quantities of protein mature into one type of neuron, and those that receive the barest sprinkling mature into another. Indeed, it was by using a particular concentration of Sonic Hedgehog that neurobiologist Jessell and his research team at Columbia recently coaxed stem cells from a mouse embryo to mature into seemingly functional motor neurons.

At the University of California, San Francisco, a team led by biologist Didier Stainier is working on genes important in cardiovascular formation. Removing one of them, called Miles Apart, from zebra-fish embryos results in a mutant with two nonviable hearts. Why? In all vertebrate embryos, including humans, the heart forms as twin buds. In order to function, these buds must join. The way the Miles Apart gene appears to work, says Stainier, is by detecting a chemical attractant that, like the smell of dinner cooking in the kitchen, entices the pieces to move toward each other.

The crafting of a human from a single fertilized egg is a vastly complicated affair, and at any step, something can go wrong. When the heart fails to develop properly, a baby can be born with a hole in the heart or even missing valves and chambers. When the neural tube fails to develop properly, a baby can be born with a brain not fully developed (anencephaly) or with an incompletely formed spine (spina bifida). Neural-tube defects, it has been firmly established, are often due to insufficient levels of the water-soluble B vitamin folic acid. Reason: folic acid is essential to a dividing cell's ability to replicate its DNA.

Vitamin A, which a developing embryo turns into retinoids, is another nutrient that is critical to the nervous system. But watch out, because too much vitamin A can be toxic. In another newly released book, *Before Your Pregnancy* (Ballantine Books), nutritionist Amy Ogle and obstetrician Dr. Lisa Mazzullo caution would-be mothers to limit foods that are overly rich in vitamin A, especially liver and food products that contain lots of it, like foie gras and cod-liver oil. An excess of vitamin A, they note, can cause damage to the skull, eyes, brain and spinal cord of a developing fetus, probably because retinoids directly interact with DNA, affecting the activity of critical genes.

Folic acid, vitamin A and other nutrients reach developing embryos and fetuses by crossing the placenta, the remarkable temporary organ produced by the blastocyst that develops from the fertilized egg. The outer ring of cells that compose the placenta are extremely aggressive, behaving very much like tumor cells as they invade the uterine wall and tap into the pregnant woman's blood vessels. In fact, these cells actually go in and replace the maternal cells that form the lining of the uterine arteries, says Susan Fisher, a developmental biologist at the University of California, San Francisco. They trick the pregnant woman's immune system into tolerating the embryo's presence rather than rejecting it like the lump of foreign tissue it is.

In essence, says Fisher, "the placenta is a traffic cop," and its main job is to let good things in and keep bad things out. To this end, the placenta marshals platoons of natural killer cells to patrol its perimeters and engages millions of tiny molecular pumps that expel poisons before they can damage the vulnerable embryo.

ALAS, THE PLACENTA'S DEFENSES ARE SOMETIMES BREACHED— by microbes like rubella and cytomegalovirus, by drugs like thalidomide and alcohol, by heavy metals like lead and mercury, and by organic pollutants like dioxin and PCBs. Pathogens and poisons contained in certain foods are also able to cross the placenta, which may explain why placental tissues secrete a nausea-inducing hormone that has been tentatively linked to morning sickness. One provocative if unproved hypothesis says morning sickness may simply be nature's crude way of making sure that potentially harmful substances do not reach the womb, particularly during the critical first trimester of development.

Timing is decisive where toxins are concerned. Air pollutants like carbon monoxide and ozone, for example, have been linked to heart defects when exposure coincided with the second month of pregnancy, the window of time during which the heart forms. Similarly, the nervous system is particularly vulnerable to damage while neurons are migrating from the part of the brain where they are made to the area where they will ultimately reside. "A tiny, tiny exposure at a key moment when a certain process is beginning to unfold can have an effect that is not only quantitatively larger but qualitatively different than it would be on an adult whose body has finished forming," observes Sandra Steingraber, an ecologist at Cornell University.

Among the substances Steingraber is most worried about are environmentally persistent neurotoxins like mercury and lead (which directly interfere with the migration of neurons formed during the first trimester) and PCBs (which, some evidence suggests, block the activity of thyroid hormone). "Thyroid hormone plays a noble role in the fetus," says Steingraber. "It actually goes into the fetal brain and serves as kind of a conductor of the orchestra."

PCBs are no longer manufactured in the U.S., but other chemicals potentially harmful to developing embryos and fetuses are. Theo Colborn, director of the World Wildlife Fund's contaminants program, says at least 150 chemicals pose possible risks for fetal development, and some of them can interfere with the naturally occurring sex hormones critical to the development of a fetus. Antiandrogens, for example, are widely found in fungicides and plastics. One in particular—DDE, a breakdown product of DDT—has been shown to cause hypospadias in laboratory mice, a birth defect in which the urethra fails to extend to the end of the penis. In humans, however, notes Dr. Allen Wilcox, editor of the journal *Epidemiology*, the link between hormone-like chemicals and birth defects remains elusive.

THE LIST OF POTENTIAL THREATS TO EMBRYONIC LIFE IS LONG. It includes not only what the mother eats, drinks or inhales, explains N.Y.U.'s Nathanielsz, but also the hormones that surge through her body. Pregnant rats with high blood-glucose levels (chemically induced by wiping out their insulin) give birth to female offspring that are unusually susceptible to developing gestational diabetes. These daughter rats are able to produce enough insulin to keep their blood glucose in check, says Nathanielsz, but only until they become pregnant. At that point, their glucose level soars, because their pancreases were damaged by prenatal exposure to their mother's sugar-spiked blood. The next generation of daughters is, in turn, more susceptible to gestational diabetes, and the transgenerational chain goes on.

In similar fashion, atherosclerosis may sometimes develop because of prenatal exposure to chronically high cholesterol levels. According to Dr. Wulf Palinski, an endocrinologist at the University of California at San Diego, there appears to be a kind of metabolic memory of prenatal life that is permanently retained. In genetically similar groups of rabbits and kittens, at least, those born to mothers on fatty diets were far more likely to develop arterial plaques than those whose mothers ate lean.

But of all the long-term health threats, maternal undernourishment—which stunts growth even when babies are born full term—may top the list. "People who are small at birth have, for life, fewer kidney cells, and so they are more likely to go into renal failure when they get sick," observes Dr. David Barker, director of the environmental epidemiology unit at England's University of Southampton. The same is true of insulin-producing cells in the pancreas, so that low-birth-weight babies stand a higher chance of developing diabetes later in life because their pancreases—where insulin is produced—have to work that much harder. Barker, whose research has linked low birth weight to heart disease, points out that undernourishment can trigger lifelong metabolic changes. In adulthood, for example, obesity may become a problem because food scarcity in prenatal life causes the body to shift the rate at which calories are turned into glucose for immediate use or stored as reservoirs of fat.

But just how does undernourishment reprogram metabolism? Does it perhaps prevent certain genes from turning on, or does it turn on those that should stay silent? Scientists are racing to answer those questions, along with a host of others. If they succeed, many more infants will find safe passage through the critical first months of prenatal development. Indeed, our expanding knowledge about the interplay between genes and the prenatal environment is cause for both concern and hope. Concern because maternal and prenatal health care often ranks last on the political agenda. Hope because by changing our priorities, we might be able to reduce the incidence of both birth defects and serious adult diseases.

—***With reporting by David Bjerklie and Alice Park/New York and Dan Cray/Los Angeles***

Heading Off
Disruptive Behavior

*How Early Intervention Can Reduce Defiant Behavior—
and Win Back Teaching Time*

By Hill M. Walker, Elizabeth Ramsey, and Frank M. Gresham

More and more children from troubled, chaotic homes are bringing well-developed patterns of antisocial behavior to school. Especially as these students get older, they wreak havoc on schools. Their aggressive, disruptive, and defiant behavior wastes teaching time, disrupts the learning of all students, threatens safety, overwhelms teachers—and ruins their own chances for successful schooling and a successful life.

In a poll of AFT teachers, 17 percent said they lost four or more hours of teaching time per week thanks to disruptive student behavior; another 19 percent said they lost two or three hours. In urban areas, fully 21 percent said they lost four or more hours per week. And in urban secondary schools, the percentage is 24. It's hard to see how academic achievement can rise significantly in the face of so much lost teaching time, not to mention the anxiety that is produced by the constant disruption (and by the implied safety threat), which must also take a toll on learning.

But it need not be this way in the future. Most of the disruption is caused by no more than a few students per class*—students who are, clinically speaking, "antisocial." Provided intervention begins when these children are young, preferably before they reach age 8, the knowledge, tools, and programs exist that would enable schools to head off most of this bad behavior—or at least greatly reduce its frequency. Schools are not the source of children's

behavior problems, and they can't completely solve them on their own. But the research is becoming clear: Schools can do a lot to minimize bad behavior—and in so doing, they help not only the antisocial children, they greatly advance their central goal of educating children.

In recent decades, antisocial behavior has been the subject of intense study by researchers in various disciplines including biology, sociology, social work, psychiatry, corrections, education, and psychology. Great progress has been made in understanding and developing solutions for defiant, disruptive, and aggressive behavior (see Burns, 2002). The field of psychology, in particular, with its increasingly robust theories of "social learning" and "cognition," has developed a powerful empirical literature that can assist school personnel in coping with, and ultimately preventing, a good deal of problematic behavior. Longitudinal and retrospective studies conducted in the United States, Australia, New Zealand, Canada, and various western European countries have yielded knowledge on the long-term outcomes of children who adopt antisocial behavior, especially those who arrive at school with it well developed (see Reid et al., 2002). Most importantly, a strong knowledge base has been assembled on interventions that can head off this behavior or prevent it from hardening (Loeber and Farrington, 2001).

To date, however, this invaluable knowledge base has been infused into educational practice in an extremely limited fashion. A major goal of this article (and of our much larger book) is to communicate and adapt this knowledge base for effective use by educators in coping with the rising tide of antisocial students populating today's schools. In our book, you'll find fuller explanations

---

*In the AFT's poll, of the 43 percent of teachers who said they had students in their classes with discipline problems, more than half said the problems were caused by one to three students. Poll conducted by Peter D. Hart Research Associates, October 1995.

of the causes of antisocial behavior, of particular forms of antisocial behavior like bullying, and of effective—and ineffective—interventions for schools. And all of this draws on a combination of the latest research and the classic research studies that have stood the test of time.

In this article, we look first at the source of antisocial behavior itself and ask: Why is it so toxic when it arrives in school? Second, we look at the evidence suggesting that early intervention is rare in schools. Third, we look at a range of practices that research indicates should be incorporated into school and classroom practice. Fourth, in the accompanying sidebars we give examples of how these practices have been combined in different ways to create effective programs.

I. Where Does Antisocial Behavior Come from and What Does That Mean for Schools?

Much to the dismay of many classroom teachers who deal with antisocial students, behavior-management practices that work so well with typical students do not work in managing antisocial behavior. In fact, teachers find that their tried and true behavior-management practices often make the behavior of antisocial students much worse. As a general rule, educators do not have a thorough understanding of the origins and developmental course of such behavior and are not well trained to deal with moderate to severe levels of antisocial behavior. The older these students become and the further along the educational track they progress, the more serious their problems become and the more difficult they are to manage.

How can it be that behavior-management practices somehow work differently for students with antisocial behavior patterns? Why do they react differently? Do they learn differently? Do they require interventions based on a completely different set of learning principles? As we shall see, the principles by which they acquire and exercise their behavioral pattern are quite typical and predictable.

Frequent and excessive noncompliance in school (or home) is an important first indicator of future antisocial behavior.

One of the most powerful principles used to explain how behavior is learned is known as the Matching Law (Herrnstein, 1974). In his original formulation, Herrnstein (1961) stated that the rate of any given behavior matches the rate of reinforcement for that behavior. For example, if aggressive behavior is reinforced once every three times it occurs (e.g., by a parent giving in to a temper tantrum) and prosocial behavior is reinforced once every 15 times it occurs (e.g., by a parent praising a polite request), then the Matching Law would predict that,

on average, aggressive behavior will be chosen five times more frequently than prosocial behavior. Research has consistently shown that behavior does, in fact, closely follow the Matching Law (Snyder, 2002). Therefore, how parents (and later, teachers) react to aggressive, defiant, and other bad behavior is extremely important. The Matching Law applies to all children; it indicates that antisocial behavior is learned—and, at least at a young enough age, can be unlearned. (As we will see in the section that reviews effective intervention techniques, many interventions—like maintaining at least a 4 to 1 ratio of praising versus reprimanding—have grown out of the Matching Law.)

First Comes the Family...

Antisocial behavior is widely believed to result from a mix of constitutional (i.e., genetic and neurobiological) and environmental (i.e., family and community) factors (Reid et al., 2002). In the vast majority of cases, the environmental factors are the primary causes—but in a small percentage of cases, there is an underlying, primarily constitutional, cause (for example, autism, a difficult temperament, attention deficit/hyperactivity disorder [ADHD], or a learning disorder). Not surprisingly, constitutional and environmental causes often overlap and even exacerbate each other, such as when parents are pushed to their limits by a child with a difficult temperament or when a child with ADHD lives in a chaotic environment.

Patterson and his colleagues (Patterson et al., 1992) have described in detail the main environmental causes of antisocial behavior. Their model starts by noting the social and personal factors that put great stress on family life (e.g., poverty, divorce, drug and alcohol problems, and physical abuse). These stressors disrupt normal parenting practices, making family life chaotic, unpredictable, and hostile. These disrupted parenting practices, in turn, lead family members to interact with each other in negative, aggressive ways and to attempt to control each others' behavior through coercive means such as excessive yelling, threats, intimidation, and physical force. In this environment, children learn that the way to get what they want is through what psychologists term "coercive" behavior: For parents, coercion means threatening, yelling, intimidating, and even hitting to force children to behave. (Patterson [1982] conducted a sequential analysis showing that parental use of such coercive strategies to suppress hostile and aggressive behavior actually increased the likelihood of such behavior in the future by 50 percent.)

For children, coercive tactics include disobeying, whining, yelling, throwing tantrums, threatening parents, and even hitting—all in order to avoid doing what the parents want. In homes where such coercive behavior is common, children become well-acquainted with how hostile behavior escalates—and with which of their behaviors ultimately secure adult surrender. This is the fertile ground in which antisocial behavior is bred. The negative effects tend to flow across generations much like inherited traits.*

By the time they are old enough for school, children who have developed an antisocial profile (due to either constitutional or environmental factors) have a limited repertoire of cooperative behavior skills, a predilection to use coercive tactics to control and manipulate others, and a well-developed capacity for emotional outbursts and confrontation.

...Then Comes School

For many young children, making the transition from home to school is fraught with difficulty. Upon school entry, children must learn to share, negotiate disagreements, deal with conflicts, and participate in competitive activities. And, they must do so in a manner that builds friendships with some peers and, at a minimum, social acceptance from others (Snyder, 2002). Children with antisocial behavior patterns have enormous difficulty accomplishing these social tasks. In fact, antisocial children are more than twice as likely as regular children to initiate unprovoked verbal or physical aggression toward peers, to reciprocate peer aggression toward them, and to continue aggressive behavior once it has been initiated (Snyder, 2002).**

From preschool to mid-elementary school, antisocial students' behavior changes in form and increases in intensity. During the preschool years, these children often display aversive behaviors such as frequent whining and noncompliance. Later, during the elementary school years, these behaviors take the form of less frequent but higher intensity acts such as hitting, fighting, bullying, and stealing. And during adolescence, bullying and hit-

---

*It is important to note that the kind of coercive interaction described is very different from parents' need to establish authority in order to appropriately discipline their children. This is accomplished through the clear communication of behavioral expectations, setting limits, monitoring and supervising children's behavior carefully, and providing positive attention and rewards or privileges for conforming to those expectations. It also means using such strategies as ignoring, mildly reprimanding, redirecting, and/or removing privileges when they do not. These strategies allow parents to maintain authority without relying on the coercion described above and without becoming extremely hostile or giving in to children's attempts to use coercion.

**This unfortunate behavior pattern soon leads to peer rejection (Reid, Patterson and Snyder, 2002). When behaviorally at-risk youth are rejected and forsaken by normal, well-behaved peers, they often begin to form friendships amongst themselves. If, over several years (and particularly in adolescence), these friendships solidify in such a way that these youth identify with and feel like members of a deviant peer group, they have a 70 percent chance of a felony arrest within two years (Patterson et al., 1992).

ting may escalate into robbery, assault, lying, stealing, fraud, and burglary (Snyder and Stoolmiller, 2002).

Although the specific form of the behavior changes (e.g., from noncompliance to bullying to assault), its function remains the same: Coercion remains at the heart of the antisocial behavior. As children grow older, they learn that the more noxious and painful they can make their behavior to others, the more likely they are to accomplish their goals—whether that goal is to avoid taking out the trash or escape a set of difficult mathematics problems. An important key to preventing this escalation (and therefore avoiding years of difficult behavior) is for adults to limit the use of coercive tactics with children—and for these adults to avoid surrendering in the face of coercive tactics used by the child. This has clear implications for school and teacher practices (and, of course, for parent training, which is not the subject of this article).

Frequent and excessive noncompliance in school (or home) is an important first indicator of future antisocial behavior. A young child's noncompliance is often a "gate key" behavior that triggers a vicious cycle involving parents, peers, and teachers. Further, it serves as a port of entry into much more serious forms of antisocial behavior. By treating noncompliance effectively at the early elementary age (or preferably even earlier), it is possible to prevent the development of more destructive behavior.

II. Early Intervention Is Rare

How many children are antisocial? How many are getting help early? To study the national incidence of antisocial behavior among children, researchers focus on two psychiatric diagnoses: oppositional defiant disorder and conduct disorder. Oppositional defiant disorder, the less serious of the two, consists of an ongoing pattern of uncooperative, angry behavior including things like deliberately trying to bother others and refusing to accept responsibility for mistakes. Conduct disorder is characterized by severe verbal and physical aggression, property destruction, and deceitful behavior that persist over time (usually one or more years). Formal surveys have generally indicated that between two and six percent of the general population of U.S. children and youth has some form of conduct disorder (Kazdin, 1993). Without someone intervening early to teach these children how to behave better, half of them will maintain the disorder into adulthood and the other half will suffer significant adjustment problems (e.g., disproportionate levels of marital discord and difficulty keeping a job) during their adult lives (Kazdin, 1993). (It is worth noting that on the way to these unpleasant outcomes, most will disrupt many classrooms and overwhelm many teachers.) When we add in oppositional defiant disorder (which often precedes and co-occurs with conduct disorder), estimates have been as

Students with Emotional Disturbance Served by Age, Selected School Years

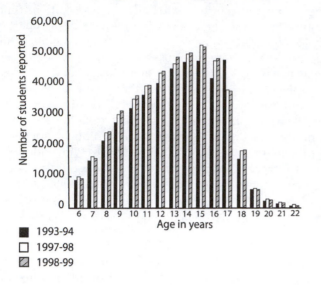

high as 16 percent of the U.S. youth population (Eddy, Reid, and Curry, 2002).

In contrast, school systems typically identify (through the Individuals with Disabilities Education Act [IDEA]) slightly less than one percent of the public school population as having emotional and behavioral problems. Further, the great tendency of schools is to identify these behavioral problems quite late in a child's school career.

The figure above provides a stark example of this practice, which is more typical than not in today's public school systems. Walker, Nikiosha, Zeller, Severson, and Feil (2000) examined the number of K-12 students in the 1993-94, 1997-98, and 1998-99 school years who were certified as emotionally disturbed (the IDEA category that captures antisocial students). As the figure shows, the number of students certified as emotionally disturbed peaks around age 15 (approximately 50,000 cases) during the 1997-98 and 1998-99 school years. Similarly, the older data, from the 1993-94 school year, show the peak in referrals spread over the ages 14, 15, and 17. These results suggest that a large number of students, who were no doubt in need of supports and services for emotional disturbance in their elementary and middle school years, were not referred, evaluated, or served under special education.* Only in adolescence, when their behavior problems had become so intractable and difficult to accommodate, were many of these students finally identified and served. This practice

of delayed referral is the polar opposite of what research clearly shows is necessary.

Our society's social, cultural, and economic problems are spilling over into our schools. They are greatly complicating schools' central task of educating students safely and effectively. But the research is clear and growing: Even though many children and youth come from and return to chaotic, coercive home environments on a daily basis, they can still acquire sufficient behavioral control to succeed in school—and to allow classmates to learn in an orderly environment.

We have substantial knowledge about how to divert at-risk children, youth, and families from destructive outcomes.** We believe the problem is not one of knowing what to do, but of convincing schools to effectively use research-based intervention programs over the long term.

The remainder of this article is devoted to providing educators with guidelines and programs for early intervention that greatly reduce antisocial behavior. There are no magic bullets in the material presented herein. Dealing with the antisocial student population is difficult, frustrating, and, because schools tend to intervene too late, often without identifiable rewards. However, of all those who suffer from conditions and disorders that impair school performance, these students are among those with the greatest capacity for change—particularly when they first start school.

III. What Can Schools Do?

Schools are not the source of children's antisocial behavior, and they cannot completely eliminate it. But schools do have substantial power to prevent it in some children and greatly reduce it in others.

First, and in some ways most importantly, schools can help by being academically effective. The fact is, academic achievement and good behavior reinforce each other: Experiencing some success academically is related to decreases in acting out; conversely, learning positive behaviors is related to doing better academically. Kellam and his colleagues (1994), for example, showed experimentally that gains in first-grade academic achievement, as measured by standardized achievement tests, resulted in substantially reduced levels of aggression, according to behavior ratings by their teachers. And, confirming what common sense tells us, Caprara, Barbaranelli, Pastorelli, Bandura, and Zimbardo (2000) found that positive behaviors (like cooperating, sharing, and consoling) among very young children contributed to their later academic achievement.

---

*Kauffman (1999) suggests that the field of education actually "prevents prevention" of behavioral disorders through well-meaning efforts to "protect" difficult children from being labeled and stigmatized by the screening and identification process.

**Successful model programs have been reviewed and described extensively by Catalano, Loeber, and McKinney (1999), by Loeber and Farrington (2001), and by Reid and his colleagues (2002).

Second, schools can, to a large and surprising extent, affect the level of aggression in young boys just by the orderliness of their classrooms. An intriguing longitudinal study dramatically illustrates the role of this variable in the development or prevention of aggressive behavior from first grade to middle school (Kellam, Rebok, Ialongo, and Mayer, 1994). After randomly assigning students to first-grade classrooms, researchers found that nearly half of the classrooms were chaotic and the remainder were reasonably well-managed. Of the boys in the study who began schooling in the top quartile of aggressive behavior (as rated by their teachers), those assigned to orderly classrooms had odds of 3:1 in favor of being highly aggressive in middle school. However, those boys assigned to chaotic classrooms had odds of 59:1 for being highly aggressive in middle school. This seminal finding suggests that poor classroom management by teachers in grade one is a huge, but preventable, factor in the development of antisocial behavior—and, conversely, that effective classroom management can have an enormous long-term positive effect on behavior. Thus, working closely with first-grade teachers (and, presumably, other early-grade teachers) on their behavior management can yield substantial future benefits for students and their schools by offsetting destructive outcomes.

Aggressive first-grade boys assigned to orderly classrooms had odds of 3:1 in favor of being highly aggressive in middle school. Those assigned to chaotic classrooms had odds of 59:1 for being highly aggressive in middle school.

But to some extent, this just begs the larger question: How can schools and their teachers create and sustain orderly classrooms? We summarize here the key findings and conclusions from 40 years of research. First, we present a three-tiered intervention model that matches the extent of children's behavioral problems to the power (and, therefore, cost) of the programs implemented. Second, we offer tools that can accurately and effectively identify students as young as kindergarten (and, in daycare or preschool settings, even at-risk three-year-olds can be identified) who are likely to become school behavior problems (and, later in life, delinquents and even adult criminals). Third, we review five techniques that, in combination, are at the heart of preventing antisocial behavior. Fourth, we describe specific programs with substantial and growing records of effectiveness that successfully incorporate all of the above into entirely doable, economical, and feasible school interventions. These programs can be purchased by schools from a variety of for-profit publishers and non-profit child and family services organizations. Some are inexpensive; the more expensive interventions tend to be individualized to meet the needs of highly aggressive children. All of the programs described in this article can be funded with either IDEA resources or school improvement funds. Programs for antisocial children, such as those described here, can also be funded in partnership with mental health agencies and/or through grants available through the Safe and Drug Free Schools division of the U.S. Department of Education. (See box, Funding Early Interventions.)

A. Three Levels of Intervention

Research has shown that the best way to prevent antisocial behavior is actually to start with an inexpensive school-wide intervention and then add on more intensive interventions for the most troubled kids. Building on work done by the U.S. Public Health Service, Hill Walker and his colleagues developed a model with three progressively more intensive levels of intervention to address challenging behavior within schools (Walker, Horner, Sugai, Bullis, Sprague, Bricker, and Kaufman, 1996). This model has proved to be very popular among educational researchers and has been broadly adopted by practitioners as a way to select and coordinate interventions. It is sometimes referred to in educational forums as "the Oregon Model." However, this approach is clearly a matter of public domain and is not owned by anyone. The three levels of intervention are known as "universal," "selected," and "indicated." Each is briefly described below.

"Universal" interventions are school or classroom practices that affect all students. Examples of universal interventions relevant to behavior are classwide social skills training and well-enforced school discipline codes. (Outside of education, the polio vaccination is an example of a "universal intervention.") It may seem odd to implement a program for all students when most teachers can easily identify children who have, or are developing, antisocial behavior. But schoolwide programs accomplish three things. First, they improve almost all students' behavior—and most students, even if they don't qualify as troublemakers, still need some practice being well-behaved. Second, universal interventions have their greatest impact among students who "are on the margins"—those students who are just beginning to be aggressive or defiant. Sometimes, systematic exposure to a universal intervention will be sufficient to tip them in the right direction. Third, the universal intervention offers a foundation that supports the antisocial students throughout the day by reinforcing what they are learning in their more intensive selected and indicated interventions; these latter interventions are more efficient and have a greater impact when they are applied in the context of a prior, well-implemented, universal intervention.

Approximately 80 to 90 percent of all students will respond successfully to a well-implemented universal intervention (Sugai et al., 2002). Once the school environment is orderly, the antisocial students pop up like corks in water. These students have "selected" themselves out as needing more powerful "selected" interventions that employ much more expensive and labor-intensive techniques. The goal with these students is to decrease the frequency of their problem behaviors, instill appropriate behaviors, and make the children more responsive to universal interventions (Sugai et al., 2002). While selected interventions typically are based in the school, to be their most effective they often require parental involvement. Nevertheless, even when parents refuse to participate, selected interventions still have positive effects and are well worth the effort.

The vast majority of antisocial students will start behaving better after being involved in universal and selected interventions, but schools can expect that a very small percentage of antisocial students (about one to five percent of the total youth population) will not. These are the most severe cases—the most troubled children from the most chaotic homes—and they require extremely intensive, individualized, and expensive interventions. These interventions, called "indicated," are typically family focused, with participation and support from mental health, juvenile justice, and social service agencies, as well as schools. Most non-specialized schools will find that running such an intervention is beyond their capacity. It's for such students that alternative education settings are necessary.

This three-tiered intervention model offers a structure that educators can use when they are reviewing and trying to coordinate programs. It ensures that all students' needs will be met efficiently—each child is exposed to the level of intervention that his behavior shows he needs. This is a very cost-effective model for schools because interventions become much more expensive as they become more specialized.

But it all begins with effective early screening.

B. Early Screening and Identification of Potentially Antisocial Students

Many fields have well-established practices to identify problems early and allow for more effective treatments. For instance, in medicine, routine screening procedures such as prostate-specific antigen (PSA) tests to detect prostate cancer, mammograms to detect breast cancer, and Papanicolaou (Pap) tests to detect the early states of cervical cancer have been routine for years. Unfortunately, similar proactive, early identification approaches are not commonly used to identify children with, or at risk of developing, antisocial behavior.

But research shows that early identification is absolutely critical: Children who have not learned appropriate, non-coercive ways to interact socially by around 8 years of age (the end of third grade) will likely continue displaying some degree of antisocial behavior throughout their lives (Loeber and Farrington, 1998). We also know that the longer such children go without access to effective and early intervention services (particularly after the age of 8), the more resistant to change their behavior problems will be (Gresham, 1991) and the more expensive it will be to induce the change.

Yet, as discussed previously, schools offer special education services to just one percent of students, though two to 16 percent manifest some form of antisocial behavior—and virtually no special education services are provided before students become adolescents. The technology (usually simple normed checklists and observation instruments, as described below) for identifying such children is gradually becoming more accurate for children at younger and younger ages (Severson and Walker, 2002).

A particularly valuable approach to screening is known as "multiple gating" (Loeber, Dishion, and Patterson, 1984). Multiple gating is a process in which a series of progressively more precise (and expensive) assessments or "gates" are used to identify children who need help with their behavior. One such screening procedure is the Systematic Screening for Behavior Disorders (SSBD) (Walker and Severson, 1990).

This screening procedure offers a cost-effective, mass screening of all students in grades one to six in regular education classrooms. The SSBD is made up of a combination of teacher nominations (Gate 1), teacher rating scales (Gate 2), and observations of classroom and playground problem behavior (Gate 3). It was nationally standardized on 4,500 students for the Gate 2 measures and approximately 1,300 students for the Gate 3 measures. It represents a significant advance in enabling the systematic and comprehensive screening of behavioral problems among general education students (Gresham, Lane, and Lambros, 2002). The major advantage of the SSBD is first, its ease of use, and second, its common set of standards for teachers to use in evaluating students' behavior; these standards remove most of the subjectivity that is endemic to the referral process commonly used in schools (Severson and Walker, 2002). If all schools employed universal screening (and backed it up with effective early interventions), an enormous amount of defiant and destructive behavior could be prevented—and innumerable teaching hours could be preserved.

Researchers have found that teachers do tend to praise their regular students for good behavior, but they tend not to seize oportunities to praise antisocial students when they are behaving well.

C. Key Features of Effective Interventions
When dealing with well-established antisocial behavior, a combination of the following techniques is usually re-

quired in order to successfully bring about behavior change: (1) a consistently enforced schoolwide behavior code, (2) social-skills training, (3) appropriately-delivered adult praise for positive behavior, (4) reinforcement contingencies and response costs, and (5) time-out (see Wolf, 1978). Each of these techniques is briefly explained below.

Over the past three decades, an extensive body of research has developed on the effectiveness of these techniques for preventing and remediating problem behavior within the context of schools. Studies of the use of these techniques show that positive strategies (appropriate praise, social-skills training, providing free-time privileges or activities) are generally sufficient for developing and maintaining the appropriate behavior of most students. However, students with challenging behavior often also require sanctions of some type (e.g. time-out or loss of privileges) in order to successfully address their problems. Extensive research clearly shows that, to be most effective, intervention programs or regimens incorporating these techniques should be applied across multiple settings (classrooms, hallways, playgrounds, etc.), operate for a sufficient time period for them to work, and should involve teachers and parents in school-home partnerships whenever possible.

No single technique applied in isolation will have an enduring impact. Used together, however, they are effective—especially for antisocial students age 8 or younger. Assembling these techniques into feasible and effective daily routines can be done by individual teachers in well-run schools. But it is difficult, time-consuming, and fraught with trial and error. Among the fruits of the past several decades of research on this topic is a group of carefully developed and tested programs that integrate these techniques into entirely doable programs that don't overly distract teachers from their main job: teaching. Several are briefly described in this and the following section.

1. A Well-Enforced Schoolwide Behavior Code

A schoolwide behavior code creates a positive school climate by clearly communicating and enforcing a set of behavioral standards. The code should consist of 5 to 7 rules—and it's essential to carefully define and provide examples of each rule. Ideally, school administrators, teachers, related services staff, students, and parents should all be involved in the development of the code. But writing the code is just the first step. Too often, teachers and others complain, a behavior code is established—and left to wither. To be effective, students must be instructed in what it means, have opportunities to practice following the rules, have incentives for adhering to it (as described in the third and fourth techniques below), and know that violating it brings consequences.

One excellent, inexpensive program for teaching the schoolwide behavior expectations reflected in a code is called Effective Behavior Support (EBS). The principal features of EBS are that all staff (administrative, classroom, lunchroom, playground, school bus, custodial, etc.) recognize and abide by the same set of behavioral expectations for all students. The behavior expectations are explicitly taught to students and they are taught in each relevant venue. In groups of 30 to 45, students are taken to various parts of the school (e.g., the bus loading zone, cafeteria, main hallway, gym, and classrooms) to discuss specific examples of behaviors that would, and would not, meet the behavior expectations. Once they have learned the expectations, they are motivated to meet them by earning rewards and praise for their good behavior.

2. Social Skills Training

As discussed earlier, many antisocial students enter school without adequate knowledge of—or experience with—appropriate social skills. These skills must be taught, practiced, and reinforced. This is the purpose of social skills training. Skills taught include empathy, anger management, and problem solving. They are taught using standard instructional techniques and practiced so that students not only learn new skills, but also begin using them throughout the school day and at home. While the training is vital for antisocial students, all students benefit from improving their social skills—especially students "on the margin" of antisocial behavior. Social skills curricula are typically taught in one or two periods a week over the course of several months and in multiple grades.

3. Adult Praise

Adult praise (from teachers, parents, or others) is a form of focused attention that communicates approval and positive regard. It is an abundantly available, natural resource that is greatly underutilized. Researchers have found that teachers do tend to praise their regular students for good behavior, but they tend not to seize opportunities to praise antisocial students when they are behaving well (Mayer & Sulzer-Azaroff, 2002). This is indeed unfortunate because praise that is behavior specific and delivered in a positive and genuine fashion is one of our most effective tools for motivating all students and teaching them important skills. Reavis et al. (1996) note that praise should be immediate, frequent, enthusiastic, descriptive, varied, and involve eye contact. We would also suggest that the ratio of praise to criticism and reprimands be at least 4:1—and higher if possible. Although antisocial students may not immediately respond to praise because of their long history of negative interactions with the adults in their lives, when paired with other incentives (such as the type of reward system described below), the positive impact of praise will eventually increase.

Funding Early Interventions

With the research reviewed here, building support for the idea of early interventions should not be difficult—but finding funds could be if you don't know where to look. One source is Title I. Schools in which at least 40 percent of the students are poor should look into using the schoolwide provision of Title I to fund universal interventions. Under Title I schoolwide, you can combine several federal, state, and local funding streams to support school improvement programs. Insofar as students are identified as emotionally disturbed, their interventions can be funded by IDEA. The federal government also provides funding to reduce behavior problems through the Safe and Drug Free Schools and Communities Act. In this case, state education agencies receive funds to make grants to local education agencies and governors receive funds to make complementary grants to community-based organizations. Schools can also partner with mental health agencies, enabling services to be covered by insurance such as Medicaid and the State Children's Health Insurance Program. Plus, most states have funding streams that could support the programs described in this article. (For more information on funding, see chapter two of *Safe, Supportive, and Successful Schools: Step by Step*, available from Sopris West for $49; order online at

www.sopriswest.com/swstore/product.asp?sku=872)

4. Reinforcement Contingencies and Response Costs

Rewards and penalties of different sorts are a common feature of many classroom management strategies. Research shows that there are specific "best" ways to arrange these reinforcements to effectively motivate students to behave appropriately. These strategies are called individual reinforcement contingencies, group reinforcement contingencies, and response costs. Individual contingencies are private, one-to-one arrangements between a teacher or parent and a student in which specified, positive consequences are made available dependent ("contingent") upon the student's performance. Earning a minute of free time for every 10 or 15 math problems correctly solved, or attempted, is an example of an individual contingency.

Group contingencies are arrangements in which an entire group of individuals (e.g., a class) is treated as a single unit and the group's performance, as a whole, is evaluated to determine whether a reward is earned, such as an extra five minutes of recess. (Note: A group can fail to earn a reward, such as an extra five minutes of recess, but should not be penalized, such as by losing five minutes of the normal recess.) This strategy gets peers involved in encouraging the antisocial student to behave better. For example, if the antisocial student disrupts the class, instead of laughing at his antics, other students will encourage him to quiet down so that they can all earn the reward. To make it easier to keep track of students' behavior, reinforcement contingencies are often set up as point systems in which students must earn a certain number of points within a certain time period in order to earn a reward.

"Response costs" are a form of penalty that is added to the package of contingencies when working toward a reward is not quite enough to change students' behavior. Teachers can increase the effectiveness of contingencies by adding a response cost so that good behavior earns points and bad behavior subtracts points—making it much harder to earn a reward. (Response costs are the basis for late fees, traffic tickets, penalties in football, foul shots in basketball, and other sanctions in public life.)

5. Time-Out

Time-out is a technique of last resort in which students are removed for just five to 15 minutes from situations in which they have trouble controlling their behavior and/or their peers' attention is drawn to their inappropriate behavior. We recommend both in-classroom time-out for minor infractions and out-of-classroom time-out (the principal's office or a desginated time-out room) for more serious infractions. Students should be given the option of volunteering for brief periods of time-out when they temporarily cannot control their own behavior, but teachers should *never* physically try to force students into time-out. Finally, *in-class* time-out should be used sparingly and should *not* be used with older students. Older students who need to be removed from a situation can be sent to the principal's office or another "cool-down" room instead of having an in-class time-out.

The research foundation for these techniques is quite strong and the empirical evidence of their effectiveness is both persuasive and growing. For the past 40 years, researchers in applied behavior analysis have worked closely with school staff and others in testing and demonstrating the effectiveness of these techniques within real world settings like classrooms and playgrounds. Literally hundreds of credible studies have documented the effectiveness of each of these techniques—as well as combinations of them—in remediating the problems that antisocial children and youth bring to schooling. The research has also surfaced guidelines for the effective application of the techniques in school contexts (Walker, 1995).

IV. Effective Programs for Preventing Antisocial Behavior

In spite of huge advances in our knowledge of how to prevent and treat antisocial behavior in the past decade, the Surgeon General's Report on Youth Violence indicates that less than 10 percent of services delivered in schools and communities targeting antisocial behavior patterns are evidence-based (see Satcher, 2001). As these children move through schools without effective intervention services and supports, their problems are likely to become more intractable and ever more resistant to change. This is simply not necessary. Effective, manageable programs exist.

Effective programs require an upfront investment of time and energy, but they more than "pay for themselves" in terms of teaching time won back.

We highlight three promising interventions—Second Step, First Step to Success, and Multisystemic Therapy—as examples of, respectively, universal, selected, and indicated interventions. The coordinated implementation of these or similar programs can make a remarkable difference in the orderliness of schools and classrooms and in the lives of antisocial youth (not to mention the victims of their aggression).

Second Step, a social skills training program for K-9 students, is described in detail. It was recently rated as the number one program for ensuring school safety by a blue ribbon panel of the U.S. Department of Education. Evaluations of Second Step have found results ranging from decreases in aggression and disruption among 109 preschool and kindergarten children from low-income, urban homes (McMahon, 2000) to less hostility and need for adult supervision among over 1,000 second- to fifth-grade students (Frey, Nolen, Van Schoiack-Edstrom, and Hirschstein, 2001).

First Step, is an intensive intervention for highly aggressive K-3 students. Experimental studies with kindergartners have found great improvments in their overall classroom behavior and academic engagement, and substantial reductions in their aggression during implementation and over many years following the end of intervention (see Walker, Kavanagh, Stiller, Golly, Severson, and Feil, 1998; Epstein and Walker, 2002). Similarly, studies involving two sets of identical twins enrolled in regular kindergarten programs found that exposure to the program produced powerful behavior changes upon introduction of the intervention that were maintained throughout the program's implementation (Golly, Sprague, Walker, Beard, and Gorham, 2000). These types of positive effects have also been replicated by other investigators. The First Step program has been included in six national reviews of effective early interventions for addressing oppositional and/or aggressive behavior in school.

Multisystemic Therapy (MST) is a family-focused intervention conducted by a trained therapist. It is aimed at the most severely at-risk youth, those who have been or are about to be incarcerated, often for violent offenses. Very often, the student has already been assigned to an alternative education setting. The therapist teaches parents the skills they need to assist their antisocial child to function more effectively across a range of social contexts. Daily contact between the student and therapist is common in the early stages of MST and reduces to several times per week as the intervention progresses. Therapists periodically talk to teachers to find out about the children's behavior, attendance, and work habits. Most importantly, teachers need to let therapists know when they perceive incremental improvements in the children's behavior—the therapists use this information to guide their work with the families. According to the Blueprints for Violence Prevention Project, MST has been found to reduce long-term rates of being rearrested by 25 to 70 percent, to greatly improve family functioning, and to lessen mental health problems (Blueprints, 2003). (To find out if MST is available in your area, visit) **www.mstservices.com**

As the research clearly shows, these three programs have the potential to prevent countless acts of aggression and positively influence both school and family functioning.

Disruptive student behavior will decrease and teaching time will increase, allowing all children to learn more. Office discipline referrals will decrease, freeing up school staff to address other school needs like supporting instruction. Effective programs do require an upfront investment of time and energy, but over the school year, and certainly over the school career, they more than "pay for themselves" in terms of teaching time won back.

An obvious subtext in the article has been that elementary schools—and especially K-3 teachers—must bear the burden of preventing antisocial behavior. This may come as a surprise since behavior problems seem so much more severe as children age. But if there's one uncontestable finding from the past 40 years of research on antisocial children, it's this: The longer students are allowed to be aggressive, defiant, and destructive, the more difficult it is to turn them around. While high schools can, and should, do what they can to help antisocial students control themselves, elementary schools can, and should, actually help antisocial children to become socially competent.

Hill M. Walker is founder and co-director of the Institute on Violence and Destructive Behavior at the University of Oregon, where he has been a professor since 1967. Walker has published hundreds of articles; in 1993 he received the Outstanding Research Award from the Council for Exceptional Children and in 2000 he became the only faculty member to receive the University of Oregon's Presidential Medal. Elizabeth Ramsey is a school counselor at Kopachuck Middle School in Gig Harbor, Wash., and a co-author of the Second Step program. Frank M. Gresham is distinguished professor and director of the School Psychology Program at the University of California-Riverside. He is co-author of the Social Skills Rating System and co-principal investigator for Project REACH. The Division of School Psychology in the American Psychological Association selected him for the Senior Scientist Award. Together, Walker, Ramsey, and Gresham wrote Antisocial Behavior in School: Evidence-Based Practices, on which this article is based.

References

Blueprints for Violence Prevention (2003). Multisystemic Therapy online at **www.colorado.edu/cspv/blueprints/model/programs/MST.html**

Burns, B. (2002). Reasons for hope for children and families: A perspective and overview. In B. Murns & K.K. Hoagwood (Eds.), *Community treatment for youth: Evidence-based interventions for severe emotional and behavioral disorders* (pp. 1–15). New York: Oxford University Press.

Caprara, G., Barbaranelli, C., Pastorelli, C., Brandura, A., & Zimbardo, P. (2000). Prosocial foundations of children's academic achievement. *Psychological Science, 11*(4), 302–306.

Catalano, R., Loeber, R., & McKinney, K. (1999). School and community interventions to prevent serious and violent offending. *Juvenile Justice Bulletin.* U.S. Department of Justice, Office of Juvenile Justice and Delinquency Prevention, Washington, D.C.

Eddy, J.M., Reid, J.B., & Curry, V. (2002). The etiology of youth antisocial behavior, delinquency and violence and a public health approach to prevention. In M.R. Shinn, H.M. Walker, & G. Stoner (Eds.), *Interventions for academic and behavior problems II: Preventive and remedial approaches,* (pp. 27–51). Bethesda, Md.: National Association for School Psychologists.

Epstein, M. & Walker, H. (2002). Special education: Best practices and First Step to Success. In B. Burns & K. Hoagwood (Eds.), *Community treatment for youth: Evidence-based intervention for severe emotional and behavioral disorders* (pp. 177–197). New York: Oxford University Press.

Frey, K.S., Nolan, S.B., Van Schoiack-Edstrom, L., and Hirschstein, M. (2001, June). "Second Step: Effects on Social Goals and Behavior." Paper presented at the annual meeting of the Society for Prevention Research, Washington, D.C.

Golly, A., Sprague, J., Walker, H.M., Beard, K., & Gorham, G. (2000). The First Step to Success program: An analysis of outcomes with identical twins across multiple baselines. *Behavioral Disorders, 25*(3), 170–182.

Gresham, F.M. (1991). Conceptualizing behavior disorders in terms of resistance to intervention. *School Psychology Review, 20,* 23–36.

Gresham, F.M., Lane, K., & Lambros, K. (2002). Children with conduct and hyperactivity attention problems: Identification, assessment and intervention. In K. Lane, F.M. Gresham, & T. O'Shaughnessy (Eds.), *Children with or at risk for emotional and behavioral disorders* (pp. 210–222). Boston: Allyn & Bacon.

Grossman, D., Neckerman, M., Koepsell, T., Ping-Yu Liu, Asher, K., Beland, K., Frey, K., & Rivara, F. (1997). Effectiveness of a violence prevention curriculum among children in elementary school: A randomized, control trial. *Journal of the American Medical Association, 277*(20), pp. 1605–1611.

Herrnstein, R. (1961). Relative and absolute strength of response as a function of frequency of reinforcement. *Journal of the Experimental Analysis of Behavior, 4,* 267–272.

Herrnstein, R. (1974). Formal properties of the matching law. *Journal of the Experimental Analysis of Behavior, 21,* 486–495.

Kauffman, J. (1999). How we prevent emotional and behavioral disorders. *Exceptional Children, 65,* 448–468.

Kazdin, A. (1993). Adolescent mental health: Prevention and treatment programs. *American Psychologist, 48,* 127–141.

Kellam, S., Rebok, G., Ialongo, N., & Mayer, L. (1994). The course and malleability of aggressive behavior from early first grade into middle school: Results of a developmental epidemiologically-based prevention trial. *Journal of Child Psychology and Psychiatry, 35*(2), 259–281.

Loeber, D. & Farrington, D. (2001). *Child delinquents: Development, intervention and service needs.* Thousand Oaks, Calif.: Sage.

Loeber, R., Dishion, T., & Patterson, G. (1984). Multiple-gating: A multistage assessment procedure for identifying youths at risk for delinquency. *Journal of Research in Crime and Delinquency, 21,* 7–32.

Loeber, R. & Farrington, D. (Eds.). (1998). *Serious and violent juvenile offenders: Risk factors and successful interventions.* Thousand Oaks, Calif.: Sage.

Loeber, R. & Farrington, D.P. (2001) *Serious and violent juvenile offenders: Risk factors and successful interventions.* Thousand Oaks, Calif.: Sage.

Mayer, G.R. & Sulzer-Azanoff, B. (2002). Interventions for vandalism and aggression. In M. Shinn, H. Walker, & G. Stoner (Eds.), *Interventions for academic and behavior problems II: Preventive and remedial approaches* (pp. 853–884). Bethesda, Md.: National Association of School Psychologists.

McMahon, S.D., et al. (2000). "Violence Prevention: Program Effects on Urban Preschool and Kindergarten Children." *Applied and Preventive Psychology, 9,* 271–281.

Patterson, G. (1982). *A social learning approach, Volume 3: Coercive family process.* Eugene, Ore.: Castalia.

Patterson, G.R., Reid, J.B., & Dishion, T.J. (1992). *Antisocial boys.* Eugene, Ore.: Castalia.

Reavis, H.K., Taylor, M., Jenson, W., Morgan, D., Andrews, D., & Fisher, S. (1996). *Best practices: Behavioral and educational strategies for teachers.* Longmont, Colo.: Sopris West.

Reid, J.B., Patterson, G.R., & Snyder, J.J. (Eds.). (2002). *Antisocial behavior in children and adolescents: A developmental analysis and the Oregon Model for Intervention.* Washington, D.C.: American Psychological Association.

Satcher, D. (2001). *Youth violence: A report of the Surgeon General.* Washington, D.C.: U.S. Public Health Service, U.S. Department of Health and Human Services.

Severson, H. & Walker, H. (2002). Proactive approaches for identifying children at risk for sociobehavioral problems. In K. Lane, F.M. Gresham, & T. O'Shaughnessy (Eds.), *Interventions for children with or at-risk for emotional and behavioral disorders,* pp. 33–53. Boston: Allyn & Bacon.

Snyder, J. (2002). Reinforcement and coercion mechanisms in the development of antisocial behavior: Peer relationships. In J. Reid, G. Patterson, & L. Snyder (Eds.), *Antisocial behavior in children and adolescents: A developmental analysis and model for intervention,* pp. 101–122. Washington, D.C.: American Psychological Association.

Snyder, J. & Stoolmiller, M. (2002). Reinforcement and coercive mechanisms in the development of antisocial behavior. The family. In J. Reid, G. Patterson, & J. Snyder (Eds.), *Antisocial behavior in children and adolescents: A developmental analysis and model for intervention* (pp. 65–100). Washington, D.C.: American Psychological Association.

Sugai, G. & Horner, R., & Gresham, F. (2002) Behaviorally effective school environments. In M. Shinn, H. Walker, & G. Stoner (Eds.). *Interventions for academic and behavior problems II: Preventive and remedial approaches* (pp. 315–350). Bethesda, Md.: National Association of School Psychologists.

Walker, H.M. (1995). *The acting-out child: Coping with classroom disruption.* Langmont, Colo.: Sopris West.

Walker, H.M., Horner, R.H., Sugai, G., Bullis M., Spraque, J.R., Bricker, D. & Kaufman, M.J. (1996). Integrated approaches to preventing antisocial behavior patterns among school-age children and youth. *Journal of Emotional and Behavioral Disorders, 4,* 193–256.

Walker, H., Kavanagh, K., Stiller, B., Golly, A., Severson, H., & Feil, E. (1997). *First Step to Success: An early intervention program for antisocial kindergartners,* Longmont, Colo.: Sopris West.

Walker, H., Kavanagh, K., Stiller, B., Golly, A., Severson, H., & Feil, E. (1998). First Step: An early intervention approach for preventing school antisocial behavior. *Journal of Emotional and Behavioral Disorders, 6*(2), 66–80.

Walker, H. & Severson, H. (1990). *Systematic screening for behavioral disorders.* Longmont, Colo.: Sopris West.

Walker, H.M., Nishioka, V., Zeller, R., Severson, H., & Feil, E. (2000). Causal factors and potential solutions for the persistent under-identification of students having emotional or behavioral disorders in the context of schooling. *Assessment for Effective Intervention, 26*(1) 29–40.

Wolf, M.M. (1978). Social validity: The case for subjective measurement, or how applied behavior analysis is finding its heart. *Journal of Applied Behavior Analysis, 11,* 203–214.

The Future of Adolescence:
Lengthening Ladders to Adulthood

BY REED LARSON

Navigating the social and economic complexities of adult life requires more savvy and education than ever.

The life stage of adolescence is a crucial link in the future of society. It is a period when young people either become prepared for and enthusiastic about taking over adult roles, or they rebel against the expectations and responsibilities of adulthood. When things go right, adolescents enter adulthood with new energy and ideas that revitalize society and its institutions.

As we move into the twenty-first century, this life stage is changing rapidly across the world due to globalization, shifting job markets, and transformations in the family, among other things. It is crucial to learn how these changes affect young people's preparedness for the social and economic complexities of the adult world. The Study Group on Adolescence in the 21st Century, composed of a consortium of international scholars, examined the various contours of adolescents' preparation for the years ahead. The Group found that, although the demands on adolescents and the hazards they face in reaching adulthood are increasing, many young people are rising to the challenge.

A Raised Bar for Adulthood

What we expect of young people is extraordinary. First, we expect them to attend school for 12 to 18 years or longer without any guarantee that this education will match what they will need for career success. We ask them to make a leap of trust based on the assumption that the skills they are learning will be relevant when they eventually enter adulthood. Furthermore, we expect them to study without financial remuneration, accept a generic identity defined by their student role, and delay starting a family while in school. These circumstances put young people in a kind of limbo status for years.

As society evolves, this period of limbo continues to lengthen. Young people around the world are being expected to delay entry into adulthood ever longer. This is happening, in large part, because the platform one needs to reach for suc-

cessful adulthood is getting higher. An information society requires that young people learn more to become full members.

In postindustrial societies, we expect people to attend school until they're at least 22 years old—with no guarantee that their studies will lead to future employment, says author Reed Larson.

Education tops the list of new demands for adulthood, as more and more jobs, including manufacturing and service jobs, require literacy, numeracy, and computer skills. Brains are increasingly valued over brawn: In the United States, entry-level wages for people with only a high-school education have fallen by more than 20% since the 1970s. Job prospects are bleaker than ever for youths who do not continue their education after high school, and while there are exceptions—like the teenager who starts a basement computer business and becomes a multi-millionaire—working a string of low-paying service jobs with no medical insurance is a much more common scenario for those with limited education.

The growing need for literacy skills in adult life extends beyond the workplace. Literacy is required to navigate complex insurance papers, retirement packages, legal regulations, and countless other complicated bureaucracies that are part of everyday life. Adults must be literate just to keep up with their own health care. Whereas 40 years ago patients were simply told what to do by their doctors, today patients are expected to be partners in their health management and to keep up with ever-changing research on diet, exercise, and disease prevention and treatment.

In addition to literacy, adolescents need to develop more versatile interpersonal skills to navigate the different worlds of home, work, and school—worlds of increasing complexity and diversity. Adult relationships are becoming less scripted and more transient, and teens need to develop skills for negotiating more *ad hoc* associations. Adults also must be able to operate in more-diverse social worlds. On the job, around the neighborhood, even within families, there is an increased likelihood that young people will need to know how to relate with people from different cultural and religious backgrounds. In developing the knowledge and vernaculars to move smoothly and communicate effectively across various social worlds, adolescents will need to acquire skills to change language, posture, tone, and negotiation strategies to adapt to multiple milieus. The adolescent who is able to function in only one world is increasingly ill-prepared for adult life.

Obstacles to Adulthood

As the platform of adulthood rises, the ladders required to get there lengthen. These boosted demands and longer ladders can increase the precariousness of adolescence, since a longer climb to adulthood creates new disadvantages for those who lack the financial means, emotional support, or mental capacity to keep climbing.

At work, at home, and at play, the human landscape increasingly features the co-mingling of individuals from different cultural, religious, and economic backgrounds. It is crucial for teens to develop social skills that will enable them to be comfortable and effective communicating with a variety of people in multiple milieus, suggests the author.

Acquiring advanced education and opportunities for learning diverse life skills often requires family wealth. In the United States, for example, annual college tuition generally ranges from $16,000 to $36,000—a full year's salary for many parents. Even when tuition is covered by grants and scholarships, families must have sufficient wealth to be able to forgo the income their college-bound children would otherwise provide; many poor families, especially in developing countries, cannot afford this sacrifice. By contrast, middle- and upper-class youths throughout the world are gaining access to new resources, such as after-school programs, camps, tutors, travel opportunities,

computers and new technologies, which will prepare them for both the literacy and life skills of modern adulthood.

Education and Earnings in the United States

High School	$1.2 million
Bachelor's	$2.1 million
Master's	$2.5 million
Ph.D.	$3.4 million
Professional	$4.4 million

Average lifetime work earnings by educational degree, based on 1999 earnings projected over a typical adult work life from age 25 to 64.

Source: U.S. Census Bureau

Girls are at a particular disadvantage in many nations, facing sex discrimination as an obstacle to obtaining even basic education and social skills. In the Middle East and South Asia, girls are more likely to be pulled from school at an early age and are thus less likely to develop critical literacy skills. Across most of the world, girls face more demands for work in the home and restrictions on movement that constrain their opportunities to gain direct experience with diverse social worlds. As rates of divorce and abandonment rise worldwide, so do the risks for young women who fail to obtain skills to function independently. As they reach adulthood, uneducated women are increasingly vulnerable to poverty and exploitation.

Even academically skilled youths from middle-class families are subject to new perils on the climb to adulthood. The rapidly changing job market makes it difficult to predict what opportunities will be available when these adolescents finally seek employment. Entire sectors can disappear on short notice when industries move their operations abroad or close shop altogether.

High school and college curricula in the United States, many critics argue, provide a poor fit to the job market. Schools in many developing countries in South Asia and Africa are using curricula that have changed little since they were colonies of Western nations, focusing on memorization rather than critical thinking and on areas such as classics rather than marketable skills in computer technology or business. The result is growing numbers of youths who are educated but unemployed.

Backlash against Limbo

It is also the case that a longer climb to adulthood, resulting in a longer period of limbo, can increase the stress experienced by adolescents. Even worse, it can lead to behaviors that arrest their process of preparation. In the United States, the experience of stress among young people has been steadily increasing. In 1999, 30% of college freshmen reported being "frequently overwhelmed," up from 16% in 1985.

The lengthening of ladders, then, increases the risk that more youths will "fall off." Adolescents who, for whatever reason, do not continue in education increasingly find themselves stuck in a low-paying and unstable labor pool.

Young people tend to live in the present moment and find immediate attractions much more appealing than long-term goals—especially when the achievement of those goals is abstract and being pushed further and further away. There is increasing possibility that adolescents will respond to the high-pressure, competitive worlds they are being asked to take on by turning off or turning away.

Societies must be concerned with a major unknown: whether young people, as a group, might rebel against the increasing demands placed upon them and the longer period of limbo they must endure. This result is increasingly probable as adolescents are spending more time with peers than they did in the past, which is creating distinct youth cultures in many societies. These youth cultures might become vehicles of mass resistance to adult society, like the hippie culture of the 1960s.

In New Zealand, Maori adolescents have drawn on American rap and hip-hop culture to resist assimilation into the mainstream. The attraction of radical Islam to many youths reflects a reaction against the competition and materialism of the new global world. In some cases these adolescents' resistance may lead to their joining militant groups, while in others it may simply mean that they enter adulthood unprepared to hold a job and raise a family.

However, we should not be too alarmist. Resistance is most likely when the ladders to adulthood are uninviting, poorly marked, and when the outcomes are uncertain—all things we can do something about. There is also a strong likelihood that the new youth cultures in the twenty-first century will lead society in positive directions. Often youth movements are inspired by pursuit of core human values: compassion, authenticity, and renewal of meaning. It is possible that generational "revolt" will pull societies away from the frantic lifestyles, shallow materialism, and divisive competitiveness that are accompanying globalization. It should be kept in mind that youths in most cases are a positive force.

Rising to the Challenge

The Study Group found that youths in most parts of the world report being optimistic about their lives and that, despite the greater demands and longer ladders, the majority of young people are rising to the challenge. Rates of illiteracy among 15-year-olds have fallen from 37% to 20% since 1970, UNESCO statistics show. Rates of high school and college graduation across most nations continue to climb. And there is little question that many young women have more versatile skills for taking care of themselves and navigating public environments today than 50 years ago. In the United States, teenage rates of pregnancy and violence have fallen substantially across the last decade, indicating that fewer teens are getting off track.

The most convincing scientific evidence of the increasing abilities of youth comes from IQ test scores. New Zealand political scientist James Flynn gathered intelligence test scores of young people over the last 70 years. Because new norms for the tests are established every few years, the publicly reported scores have shown little change. Once Flynn went back to the unadjusted scores, however, he found the IQs of young people rose dramatically over this period: The average IQ of a young adult today is 20 points higher than in 1940. There is no way to pinpoint what accounts for this increase, but it seems likely that youths' abilities have grown as they have responded to the increased complexity of modern life.

Web Resources on Youth Trends

- **Search Institute**, www.search-institute.org
  Social science organization focuses on youth development in multiple community and society settings.

- **2001 Monitoring the Future Study**,
  www.nida.nih.gov/Infofax/HSYouthtrends.html
  Study on the extent of drug abuse among eighth, tenth, and twelfth graders, conducted annually by the University of Michigan's Institute for Social Research and funded by the National Institute on Drug Abuse.

- **Ewing Marion Kauffman Foundation**,
  www.emkf.org
  Researches and identifies unfulfilled needs in society, then develops, implements, and/or funds solutions to help young people achieve success in school and life.

- **Youth Values 2000**, www.youthvalues.org
  International project, initiated by the International Sport and Culture Association, exploring young people's self-image, values, and beliefs about the world around them.

- **European Youth Forum**, www.youthforum.org
  Youth platform in Europe, composed of youth councils and nongovernmental youth organizations, that works to facilitate communication between young people and decision makers.

The general decrease in family size also contributes to youths' better preparedness for adulthood. Smaller families mean that parents can devote more attention and resources to each child. Parents in many parts of the world are adopting a more responsive and communicative parenting style, which research shows facilitates development of interpersonal skills and enhances mental health.

Other new supports and opportunities have also brightened the outlook for adolescents. Young people receive better health care than they did 50 years ago; consequently, youths around the world are much less likely to die from disease. The Internet provides an important new vehicle for some young people (though as yet a very small percentage of the world's youth) to access a wealth of information. Via the Net, adolescents can also run businesses, participate in social movements, and develop relationships; they are less handicapped by traditional barriers of age.

As a result of these opportunities and their own initiative, the current generation of youth is smarter, more mature, and more socially versatile than any generation in human history. They are better able to function in multiple worlds, collaborate in teams, and solve unstructured problems. We must not underestimate the ways in which adolescents in all parts of the world and of all social classes may draw on their youthful reservoirs of energy and optimism to forge fresh directions and develop new skills.

However, it would be a mistake to be too sanguine. Adolescence in the twenty-first century provides many opportunities for youths to make wrong turns or just become turned off, never to realize their true potential. In order to keep adolescents on the right track, society needs to provide more diverse kinds of ladders for people with different learning styles and socioeconomic backgrounds, regardless of sex or ethnicity. Many jobs involve skills that do not correspond to those tested in school, and we need to provide avenues for them to receive non-academic opportunities to grow and shine—internships, job skills workshops, even art classes, to name a few.

There should also be way stations along the climb that allow young people to rest, gather themselves, and consider alternatives. The success of government, business, the arts, and private life in 2050 and beyond depends on how well we nurture and inspire the next generation to take over and give their best.

About the Author

Reed Larson leads the Study Group on Adolescence in the 21st Century, which was sponsored by the Society for Research on Adolescence and the International Society for Behavioral Development. He is a professor in the Department of Human and Community Development at the University of Illinois, 1105 West Nevada Street, Urbana, Illinois 61801. E-mail larsonR@uiuc.edu.

For more information on the Study Group, visit its Web site, www.s-r-a.org/studygroup.html.

The Methuselah Report

Living to be 120 might be attainable, but is it desirable?

By Wayne Curtis

"I believe extraordinary longevity is absolutely inevitable," says Donald Louria, a professor at the New Jersey Medical School. "It's not a matter of if we'll have extraordinary longevity, but when."

How old is old? The average life span of an American born today is 77.2 years. It has stretched by about three months every year since the mid-19th century, says Louria, who organized a recent conference on longevity and its implications. Just by maintaining that pace the average American would expect to live more than 100 years by the end of this century. And that doesn't take into account revolutionary advances in health and medicine, which, Louria says, could very well boost the average life span to 110 or 120.

But will the future "buy us more life, or just more days alive?" wonders Vincent Mor, chair of the Department of Community Health at Brown University School of Medicine. Mor is optimistic that we'll be living not only longer but more fully as we age. Recent studies suggest older people are remaining more independent later in life, demonstrating an increase in what he calls "active life expectancy."

The larger unknown is what exactly this society of centenarians will look like and how well it will function in an era when some Americans may expect to spend nearly half their lives in retirement.

Advances in longevity come in two forms. The first is the prevention of diseases—including heart disease, cancer, stroke and diabetes—that tend to affect older people. Eliminating deaths from these causes would increase the average life span by 10 to 20 years, Louria predicts. "The first to fall will be heart disease and stroke," he says. "It's not going to happen tomorrow, but it is going to happen in this century."

The oldest documented human lived to be 122. To make that age commonplace, however, will require more than curing disease. "It's only going to occur by preventing aging and modifying the aging process itself," Louria says.

SECRETS OF AGING

When Ponce de Leon thrashed around the swamps of Florida in search of the Fountain of Youth, it turns out, he was in the wrong place. The secrets of aging are actually kept in a sort of complex biologic bank vault outfitted with multiple doors. Safecrackers from various branches of medicine and science have been striving to get in, and the faint sound you hear is that of tumblers clicking into place.

> Will the future 'buy us more life, or just more days alive?' wonders Vincent Mor, a gerontologist at Brown University.

Geneticists are fiddling with one door. Richard Miller, associate director of the University of Michigan's Geriatrics Center, says that genetic variations in mice can add as many as 173 days to their lives. That's not trivial. Producing a map of the genetic variations that lead to longer life would allow researchers to devise drugs that can manipulate the aging process, Miller says. We're closer to achieving this, he adds, than "we are to eliminating cancer or heart attacks."

At work on another vault door are nanotechnologists. Nanotechnology involves engineering matter at the molecular level, building miniature machines atom by atom. While regarded as among the most speculative of current sciences, it may well usher in a sweeping technological change.

"Living things are composed of molecular machines, and the tools for diagnosis are huge and imprecise," says Christopher Wiley of the Dartmouth-Hitchcock Medical Center. Nanobiotics would eliminate that disparity of scale, allowing the creation of biological robots that not only permit observation of the human body at the most refined level possible, but that can serve as sentinels to identify and prevent disease before symptoms even appear. In time, more sophisticated nanobots could be manufactured to enhance tissue or strengthen frail bones within the body, reversing more debilitating aspects of aging.

Nanobots might even be programmed to maintain homeostasis, that is, to keep our cells in a state of perfect equilibrium. "In theory, science could preserve a body at its peak physical state," Wiley says. "It's not that complicated," he insists. While this may sound like a futurist's fevered dream for the year 2500, Wiley points out that some nanotechnology companies are already on the brink of building tools to construct nanobots. Wiley predicts we'll see major advances in the nanotechnology of health care within the next decade or two.

RADICAL CALORIE CUTS

Only slightly less bewildering is the study of caloric restriction—or the radical curbing of calorie intake to extend life. This may be the most immediately promising door to altering the aging process. The approach is based on a simple if curious fact: Cutting the intake of calories by 30 to 40 percent has consistently resulted in significantly lengthening the maximum life span of laboratory animals. It has proved more effective than exercise.

> As the tools for longer living evolve, so must our patterns of housing, work, family relations and transportation.

Why? It's believed that a sharp drop in calories triggers a metabolic change that strengthens the immune system and increases our cells' capacity to produce new and healthy cells. Aging slows. One theory is that this mechanism evolved to help animals survive the lean winter months and thus ensure they pass on their genes by producing offspring in the more bountiful days of summer.

Even if similar effects are eventually proved in humans—and tests are just getting under way—few would choose to live a life of permanent hunger, admits George Roth, a senior scientist at the National Institute on Aging. But already in the works, Roth reports, is research to create drugs that would mimic the effects of a very low-calorie diet, providing the benefits of restricted calories without the hardships.

"We call it having your cake and eating it, too," he says.

WHAT IF IT WORKS?

That your grandchildren will have children who could reasonably expect to live a century or more is the good news. And the bad news? Some experts fear we may also be engineering a world that might not be such a grand place to live.

The U.S. Census Bureau projects the population over the age of 85 to reach 21 million in the year 2050. Other demographers predict a number in the neighborhood of 53 million within a half century. With such a range of projections, it's hard to know where to start the planning. "Imagine the policy implications," says Kevin Kinsella of the Census Bureau.

"Quality of life is the big issue," says Louria, whose specialties are preventive medicine and community health. "Are we going to have large numbers of very old people who are vigorous, reasonably healthy, involved and productive? Or are we going to have a large percentage of people who are lonely, bored, not very healthy and depressed?"

Making procedures like hip replacement and cataract surgery routine are notable steps toward longer, fuller lives. Simple objects can bring welcome freedom for a great many older people, too. "The microwave oven is probably one of the most important things that has actually contributed to a reduction in dependence," Mor says, as have well-designed walkers that reduce the need for in-home assistance. "It's a very low-tech device but has a fairly substantial effect."

As the tools for longer living evolve, so too must the nation's patterns of housing, work, family relations and transportation. Having "lots of single-family homes and getting among them by SUV" may work well for people in their 40s and 50s, but it's "calamitous" for older people, says Bruce Vladeck, professor of health policies and geriatrics at the Mount Sinai School of Medicine in New York. "We have built a set of communities over the past few years to maximize social isolation."

Vladeck notes that informal care—that is, families tending elderly relatives at home—now accounts for between 66 and 85 percent of all care for those requiring assistance. But with the rise of what some call "the super senior," he wonders if 80-year-olds will be able to care for their 105-year-old parents, or if 50-year-old grandchildren will be willing to accept responsibility for the care of family elders. "No one has seen this phenomenon before," he says.

Work patterns will also alter sharply, with more people working longer. Retirement at 65 became institutionalized decades ago when younger workers flooded the job market. With labor shortages now forecast, Vladeck predicts that corporate and government policies will likewise change to discourage retirement, so more older Americans will find incentives to remain in the work force.

Then there's that elephant in the room: How will society pay for expanded health care, retirement benefits and the building of new communities to serve the very old? "When 30 to 40 percent of the population is over age 65, and 40 to 50 percent of adult life is spent in retirement," Louria points out, "Social Security and company pensions are not likely to be viable." Knight Steel, chief of the division of geriatrics at Hackensack University Medical

Center, poses another question with no easy answer: "Who will pay for the heart transplant of a 100-year-old?"

The debate over these issues is just beginning. But before hand-wringing becomes too prevalent, maybe we should step back and take a longer view of the looming breakthrough in longevity. "In some basic ways, this is what society has sought since its inception," Vladeck says. "Rather than focus on the gloom and doom, maybe we ought to start out with the celebratory aspect of these changes."

Champagne, anyone?

Wayne Curtis, *who has written for the* Atlantic Monthly, Preservation *and other magazines, lives on Peaks Island, Maine.*

Start the Conversation

The MODERN MATURITY guide to end-of-life care

The Body Speaks

Physically, dying means that "the body's various physiological systems, such as the circulatory, respiratory, and digestive systems, are no longer able to support the demands required to stay alive," says Barney Spivack, M.D., director of Geriatric Medicine for the Stamford (Connecticut) Health System. "When there is no meaningful chance for recovery, the physician should discuss realistic goals of care with the patient and family, which may include letting nature take its course. Lacking that direction," he says, "physicians differ in their perception of when enough is enough. We use our best judgment, taking into account the situation, the information available at the time, consultation with another doctor, or guidance from an ethics committee."

Without instructions from the patient or family, a doctor's obligation to a terminally ill person is to provide life-sustaining treatment. When a decision to "let nature take its course" has been made, the doctor will remove the treatment, based on the patient's needs. Early on, the patient or surrogate may choose to stop interventions such as antibiotics, dialysis, resuscitation, and defibrillation. Caregivers may want to offer food and fluids, but those can cause choking and the pooling of dangerous fluids in the lungs. A dying patient does not desire or need nourishment; without it he or she goes into a deep sleep and dies in days to weeks. A breathing machine would be the last support: It is uncomfortable for the patient, and may be disconnected when the patient or family finds that it is merely prolonging the dying process.

The Best Defense Against Pain

Pain-management activists are fervently trying to reeducate physicians about the importance and safety of making patients comfortable. "In medical school 30 years ago, we worried a lot about creating addicts," says Philadelphia internist Nicholas Scharff. "Now we know that addiction is not a problem: People who are in pain take

pain medication as long as they need it, and then they stop." Spivack says, "We have new formulations and delivery systems, so a dying patient should never have unmet pain needs."

In Search of a Good Death

If we think about death at all, we say that we want to go quickly, in our sleep, or, perhaps, while fly-fishing. But in fact only 10 percent of us die suddenly. The more common process is a slow decline with episodes of organ or system failure. Most of us want to die at home; most of us won't. All of us hope to die without pain; many of us will be kept alive, in pain, beyond a time when we would choose to call a halt. Yet very few of us take steps ahead of time to spell out what kind of physical and emotional care we will want at the end.

The new movement to improve the end of life is pioneering ways to make available to each of us a good death—as we each define it. One goal of the movement is to bring death through the cultural process that childbirth has achieved; from an unconscious, solitary act in a cold hospital room to a situation in which one is buffered by pillows, pictures, music, loved ones, and the solaces of home. But as in the childbirth movement, the real goal is choice—here, to have the death you want. Much of death's sting can be averted by planning in advance, knowing the facts, and knowing what options we all have. Here, we have gathered new and relevant information to help us all make a difference for the people we are taking care of, and ultimately, for ourselves.

In 1999, the Joint Commission on Accreditation of Healthcare Organizations issued stern new guidelines about easing pain in both terminal and nonterminal patients. The movement intends to take pain seriously:

...ure and treat it as the fifth vital sign in hospitals, ...g with blood pressure, pulse, temperature, and respi-...on.

The best defense against pain, says Spivack, is a combination of education and assertiveness. "Don't be afraid to speak up," he says. "If your doctor isn't listening, talk to the nurses. They see more and usually have a good sense of what's happening." Hospice workers, too, are experts on physical comfort, and a good doctor will respond to a hospice worker's recommendations. "The best situation for pain management," says Scharff, "is at home with a family caregiver being guided by a hospice program."

The downsides to pain medication are, first, that narcotics given to a fragile body may have a double effect: The drug may ease the pain, but it may cause respiratory depression and possibly death. Second, pain medication may induce grogginess or unconsciousness when a patient wants to be alert. "Most people seem to be much more willing to tolerate pain than mental confusion," says senior research scientist M. Powell Lawton, Ph.D., of the Philadelphia Geriatric Center. Dying patients may choose to be alert one day for visitors, and asleep the next to cope with pain. Studies show that when patients control their own pain medication, they use less.

Final Symptoms

Depression This condition is not an inevitable part of dying but can and should be treated. In fact, untreated depression can prevent pain medications from working effectively, and antidepressant medication can help relieve pain. A dying patient should be kept in the best possible emotional state for the final stage of life. A combination of medications and psychotherapy works best to treat depression.

Anorexia In the last few days of life, anorexia—an unwillingness or inability to eat—often sets in. "It has a protective effect, releasing endorphins in the system and contributing to a greater feeling of well-being," says Spivack. "Force-feeding a dying patient could make him uncomfortable and cause choking."

Dehydration Most people want to drink little or nothing in their last days. Again, this is a protective mechanism, triggering a release of helpful endorphins.

Drowsiness and Unarousable Sleep In spite of a coma-like state, says Spivack, "presume that the patient hears everything that is being said in the room."

Agitation and Restlessness, Moaning and Groaning The features of "terminal delirium" occur when the patient's level of consciousness is markedly decreased; there is no significant likelihood that any pain sensation can reach consciousness. Family members and other caregivers may interpret what they see as "the patient is in pain" but as these signs arise at a point very close to death, terminal delirium should be suspected.

Hospice: The Comfort Team

Hospice is really a bundle of services. It organizes a team of people to help patients and their families, most often in the patient's home but also in hospice residences, nursing homes, and hospitals:

• Registered nurses who check medication and the patient's condition, communicate with the patient's doctor, and educate caregivers.
• Medical services by the patient's physician and a hospice's medical director, limited to pain medication and other comfort care.
• Medical supplies and equipment.
• Drugs for pain relief and symptom control.
• Home-care aides for personal care, homemakers for light housekeeping.
• Continuous care in the home as needed on a short-term basis.
• Trained volunteers for support services.
• Physical, occupational, and speech therapists to help patients adapt to new disabilities.
• Temporary hospitalization during a crisis.
• Counselors and social workers who provide emotional and spiritual support to the patient and family.
• Respite care—brief noncrisis hospitalization to provide relief for family caregivers for up to five days.
• Bereavement support for the family, including counseling, referral to support groups, and periodic check-ins during the first year after the death.

Hospice Residences Still rare, but a growing phenomenon. They provide all these services on-site. They're for patients without family caregivers; with frail, elderly spouses; and for families who cannot provide at-home care because of other commitments. At the moment, Medicare covers only hospice services; the patient must pay for room and board. In many states Medicaid also covers hospice services (see How Much Will It Cost?). Keep in mind that not all residences are certified, bonded, or licensed; and not all are covered by Medicare.

Getting In A physician can recommend hospice for a patient who is terminally ill and probably has less than six months to live. The aim of hospice is to help people cope with an illness, not to cure it. All patients entering hospice waive their rights to curative treatments, though only for conditions relating to their terminal illness. "If you break a leg, of course you'll be treated for that," says Karen Woods, executive director of the Hospice Association of America. No one is forced to accept a hospice referral, and patients may leave and opt for curative care at any time. Hospice programs are listed in the Yellow Pages. For more information, see Resources.

The Ultimate Emotional Challenge

A dying person is grieving the loss of control over life, of body image, of normal physical functions, mobility and strength, freedom and independence, security, and the illusion of immortality. He is also grieving the loss of an earthly future, and reorienting himself to an unknowable destiny.

At the same time, an emotionally healthy dying person will be trying to satisfy his survival drive by adapting to this new phase, making the most of life at the moment, calling in loved ones, examining and appreciating his own joys and accomplishments. Not all dying people are depressed; many embrace death easily.

Facing the Fact

Doctors are usually the ones to inform a patient that he or she is dying, and the end-of-life movement is training physicians to bring empathy to that conversation in place of medspeak and time estimates. The more sensitive doctor will first ask how the patient feels things are going. "The patient may say, 'Well, I don't think I'm getting better,' and I would say, 'I think you're right,' " says internist Nicholas Scharff.

At this point, a doctor might ask if the patient wants to hear more now or later, in broad strokes or in detail. Some people will need to first process the emotional blow with tears and anger before learning about the course of their disease in the future.

"Accept and understand whatever reaction the patient has," says Roni Lang, director of the Geriatric Assessment Program for the Stamford (Connecticut) Health System, and a social worker who is a longtime veteran of such conversations. "Don't be too quick with the tissue. That sends a message that it's not okay to be upset. It's okay for the patient to be however she is."

Getting to Acceptance

Some patients keep hoping that they will get better. Denial is one of the mind's miracles, a way to ward off painful realities until consciousness can deal with them. Denial may not be a problem for the dying person, but it can create difficulties for the family. The dying person could be leaving a lot of tough decisions, stress, and confusion behind. The classic stages of grief outlined by Elisabeth Kübler-Ross—denial, anger, bargaining, depression, and acceptance—are often used to describe post-death grieving, but were in fact delineated for the process of accepting impending loss. We now know that these states may not progress in order. "Most people oscillate between anger and sadness, embracing the prospect of death and unrealistic episodes of optimism," says Lang. Still, she says, "don't place demands on them

Survival Kit for Caregivers

A study published in the March 21, 2000, issue of **Annals of Internal Medicine** shows that caregivers of the dying are twice as likely to have depressive symptoms as the dying themselves.

No wonder. Caring for a dying parent, says social worker Roni Lang, "brings a fierce tangle of emotions. That part of us that is a child must grow up." Parallel struggles occur when caring for a spouse, a child, another relative, or a friend. Caregivers may also experience sibling rivalry, income loss, isolation, fatigue, burnout, and resentment.

To deal with these difficult stresses, Lang suggests that caregivers:

• Set limits in advance. How far am I willing to go? What level of care is needed? Who can I get to help? Resist the temptation to let the illness always take center stage, or to be drawn into guilt-inducing conversations with people who think you should be doing more.

• Join a caregiver support group, either disease-related like the Alzheimer's Association or Gilda's Club, or a more general support group like The Well Spouse Foundation. Ask the social services department at your hospital for advice. Telephone support and online chat rooms also exist (see Resources).

• Acknowledge anger and express it constructively by keeping a journal or talking to an understanding friend or family member. Anger is a normal reaction to powerlessness.

• When people offer to help, give them a specific assignment. And then, take time to do what energizes you and make a point of rewarding yourself.

• Remember that people who are critically ill are self-absorbed. If your empathy fails you and you lose patience, make amends and forgive yourself.

to accept their death. This is not a time to proselytize." It is enough for the family to accept the coming loss, and if necessary, introduce the idea of an advance directive and health-care proxy, approaching it as a "just in case" idea. When one member of the family cannot accept death, and insists that doctors do more, says Lang, "that's the worst nightmare. I would call a meeting, hear all views without interrupting, and get the conversation around to what the patient would want. You may need another person to come in, perhaps the doctor, to help 'hear' the voice of the patient."

What Are You Afraid Of?

The most important question for doctors and caregivers to ask a dying person is, What are you afraid of? "Fear aggravates pain," says Lang, "and pain aggravates fear." Fear of pain, says Spivack, is one of the most common problems, and can be dealt with rationally. Many people do not know, for example, that pain in dying is not inevitable. Other typical fears are of being separated from loved ones, from home, from work; fear of being a burden, losing control, being dependent, and leaving things undone. Voicing fear helps lessen it, and pinpointing fear helps a caregiver know how to respond.

How to Be With a Dying Person

Our usual instinct is to avoid everything about death, including the people moving most rapidly toward it. But, Spivack says, "In all my years of working with dying people, I've never heard one say 'I want to die alone.' " Dying people are greatly comforted by company; the benefit far outweighs the awkwardness of the visit. Lang offers these suggestions for visitors:

• Be close. Sit at eye level, and don't be afraid to touch. Let the dying person set the pace for the conversation. Allow for silence. Your presence alone is valuable.

• Don't contradict a patient who says he's going to die. Acceptance is okay. Allow for anger, guilt, and fear, without trying to "fix" it. Just listen and empathize.

• Give the patient as much decision-making power as possible, as long as possible. Allow for talk about unfinished business. Ask: "Who can I contact for you?"

• Encourage happy reminiscences. It's okay to laugh.

• Never pass up the chance to express love or say good-bye. But if you don't get the chance, remember that not everything is worked through. Do the best you can.

Taking Control Now

Sixty years ago, before the invention of dialysis, defibrillators, and ventilators, the failure of vital organs automatically meant death. There were few choices to be made to end suffering, and when there were—the fatal dose of morphine, for example—these decisions were made privately by family and doctors who knew each other well. Since the 1950s, medical technology has been capable of extending lives, but also of prolonging dying. In 1967, an organization called Choice in Dying (now the Partnership for Caring: America's Voices for the Dying; see Resources) designed the first advance directive—a document that allows you to designate under what conditions you would want life-sustaining treatment to be continued or terminated. But the idea did not gain popular understanding until 1976, when the parents of Karen Ann Quinlan won a long legal battle to disconnect her from respiratory support as she lay for months in a vegetative state. Some 75 percent of Americans are in favor of advance directives, although only 30–35 percent actually write them.

Designing the Care You Want

There are two kinds of advance directives, and you may use one or both. A Living Will details what kind of life-sustaining treatment you want or don't want, in the event of an illness when death is imminent. A durable power of attorney for health care appoints someone to be your decision-maker if you can't speak for yourself. This person is also called a surrogate, attorney-in-fact, or health-care proxy. An advance directive such as Five Wishes covers both.

Most experts agree that a Living Will alone is not sufficient. "You don't need to write specific instructions about different kinds of life support, as you don't yet know any of the facts of your situation, and they may change," says Charles Sabatino, assistant director of the American Bar Association's Commission on Legal Problems of the Elderly.

The proxy, Sabatino says, is far more important. "It means someone you trust will find out all the options and make a decision consistent with what you would want." In most states, you may write your own advance directive, though some states require a specific form, available at hospital admitting offices or at the state department of health.

When Should You Draw Up a Directive?

Without an advance directive, a hospital staff is legally bound to do everything to keep you alive as long as possible, until you or a family member decides otherwise. So advance directives are best written before emergency status or a terminal diagnosis. Some people write them at the same time they make a will. The process begins with discussions between you and your family and doctor. If anybody is reluctant to discuss the subject, Sabatino suggests starting the conversation with a story. "Remember what happened to Bob Jones and what his family went through? I want us to be different...." You can use existing tools—a booklet or questionnaire (see Resources)—to keep the conversation moving. Get your doctor's commitment to support your wishes. "If you're asking for something that is against your doctor's conscience" (such as prescribing a lethal dose of pain medication or removing life support at a time he considers premature), Sabatino says, "he may have an obligation to transfer you to another doctor." And make sure the person you name as surrogate agrees to act for you and understands your wishes.

Filing, Storing, Safekeeping...

An estimated 35 percent of advance directives cannot be found when needed.

• Give a copy to your surrogate, your doctor, your hospital, and other family members. Tell them where to find the original in the house—not in a safe deposit box where it might not be found until after death.

Five Wishes

Five Wishes is a questionnaire that guides people in making essential decisions about the care they want at the end of their life. About a million people have filled out the eight-page form in the past two years. This advance directive is legally valid in 34 states and the District of Columbia. (The other 16 require a specific state-mandated form.)

The document was designed by lawyer Jim Towey, founder of Aging With Dignity, a nonprofit organization that advocates for the needs of elders and their caregivers. Towey, who was legal counsel to Mother Teresa, visited her Home for the Dying in Calcutta in the 1980s. He was struck that in that haven in the Third World, "the dying people's hands were held, their pain was managed, and they weren't alone. In the First World, you see a lot of medical technology, but people die in pain, and alone." Towey talked to MODERN MATURITY about his directive and what it means.

What are the five wishes? Who do I want to make care decisions for me when I can't? What kind of medical treatment do I want toward the end? What would help me feel comfortable while I am dying? How do I want people to treat me? What do I want my loved ones to know about me and my feelings after I'm gone?

Why is it so vital to make advance decisions now? Medical technology has extended longevity, which is good, but it can prolong the dying process in ways that are almost cruel. Medical schools are still concentrating on curing, not caring for the dying. We can have a dignified season in our life, or die alone in pain with futile interventions. Most people only discover they have options when checking into the hospital, and often they no longer have the capacity to choose. This leaves the family members with a guessing game and, frequently, guilt.

What's the ideal way to use this document? First you do a little soul searching about what you want. Then discuss it with people you trust, in the livingroom instead of the waiting room—before a crisis. Just say, "I want a choice about how I spend my last days," talk about your choices, and pick someone to be your health-care surrogate.

What makes the Five Wishes directive unique? It's easy to use and understand, not written in the language of doctors or lawyers. It also allows people to discuss comfort dignity, and forgiveness, not just medical concerns. When my father filled it out, he said he wanted his favorite afghan blanket in his bed. It made a huge difference to me that, as he was dying, he had his wishes fulfilled.

For a copy of Five Wishes in English or Spanish, send a $5 check or money order to Aging With Dignity, PO Box 1661, Tallahassee, FL 32302. For more information, visit www.agingwithdignity.org.

•Some people carry a copy in their wallet or glove compartment of their car.
•Be aware that if you have more than one home and you split your time in several regions of the country, you should be registering your wishes with a hospital in each region, and consider naming more than one proxy.
•You may register your Living Will and health-care proxy online at uslivingwillregistry.com (or call 800-548-9455). The free, privately funded confidential service will instantly fax a copy to a hospital when the hospital requests one. It will also remind you to update it: You may want to choose a new surrogate, accommodate medical advances, or change your idea of when "enough is enough." M. Powell Lawton, who is doing a study on how people anticipate the terminal life stages, has discovered that "people adapt relatively well to states of poor health. The idea that life is still worth living continues to readjust itself."

Assisted Suicide: The Reality

While advance directives allow for the termination of life-sustaining treatment, assisted suicide means supplying the patient with a prescription for life-ending medication. A doctor writes the prescription for the medication; the patient takes the fatal dose him- or herself. Physician-assisted suicide is legal only in Oregon (and under consideration in Maine) but only with rigorous preconditions. Of the approximately 30,000 people who died in Oregon in 1999, only 33 received permission to have a lethal dose of medication and only 26 of those actually died of the medication. Surrogates may request an end to life support, but to assist in a suicide puts one at risk for charges of homicide.

Good Care: Can You Afford It?

The ordinary person is only one serious illness away from poverty," says Joanne Lynn, M.D., director of the Arlington, Virginia, Center to Improve Care of the Dying. An ethicist, hospice physician, and health-services researcher, she is one of the founding members of the end-of-life-care movement. "On the whole, hospitalization and the cost of suppressing symptoms is very easy to afford," says Lynn. Medicare and Medicaid will help cover that kind of acute medical care. But what is harder to afford is at-home medication, monitoring, daily help with eating and walking, and all the care that will go on for the rest of the patient's life.

"When people are dying," Lynn says, "an increasing proportion of their overall care does not need to be done by doctors. But when policymakers say the care is nonmedical, then it's second class, it's not important, and nobody will pay for it."

Bottom line, Medicare pays for about 57 percent of the cost of medical care for Medicare beneficiaries.

Another 11 percent is paid by Medicaid, 20 percent by the patient, 10 percent from private insurance, and the rest from other sources, such as charitable organizations.

Medi-what?

This public-plus-private network of funding sources for end-of-life care is complex, and who pays for how much of what is determined by diagnosis, age, site of care, and income. Besides the private health insurance that many of us have from our employers, other sources of funding may enter the picture when patients are terminally ill.

•**Medicare** A federal insurance program that covers health-care services for people 65 and over, some disabled people, and those with end-stage kidney disease. Medicare Part A covers inpatient care in hospitals, nursing homes, hospice, and some home health care. For most people, the Part A premium is free. Part B covers doctor fees, tests, and other outpatient medical services. Although Part B is optional, most people choose to enroll through their local Social Security office and pay the monthly premium ($45.50). Medicare beneficiaries share in the cost of care through deductibles and co-insurance. What Medicare does not cover at all is outpatient medication, long-term nonacute care, and support services.

•**Medicaid** A state and federally funded program that covers health-care services for people with income or assets below certain levels, which vary from state to state.

•**Medigap** Private insurance policies covering the gaps in Medicare, such as deductibles and co-payments, and in some cases additional health-care services, medical supplies, and outpatient prescription drugs.

Many of the services not paid for by Medicare can be covered by private long-term-care insurance. About 50 percent of us over the age of 65 will need long-term care at home or in a nursing home, and this insurance is an extra bit of protection for people with major assets to protect. It pays for skilled nursing care as well as non-health services, such as help with dressing, eating, and bathing. You select a dollar amount of coverage per day (for example, $100 in a nursing home, or $50 for at-home care), and a coverage period (for example, three years—the average nursing-home stay is 2.7 years). Depending on your age and the benefits you choose, the insurance can cost anywhere from around $500 to more than $8,000 a year. People with pre-existing conditions such as Alzheimer's or MS are usually not eligible.

How Much Will It Cost?

Where you get end-of-life care will affect the cost and who pays for it.

•**Hospital** Dying in a hospital costs about $1,000 a day. After a $766 deductible (per benefit period), Medicare reimburses the hospital a fixed rate per day, which varies by region and diagnosis. After the first 60 days in a hospital, a patient will pay a daily deductible ($194) that goes up (to $388) after 90 days. The patient is responsible for all costs for each day beyond 150 days. Medicaid and some private insurance, either through an employer or a Medigap plan, often help cover these costs.

•**Nursing home** About $1,000 a week. Medicare covers up to 100 days of skilled nursing care after a three-day hospitalization, and most medication costs during that time. For days 21–100, your daily co-insurance of $97 is usually covered by private insurance—if you have it. For nursing-home care not covered by Medicare, you must use your private assets, or Medicaid if your assets run out, which happens to approximately one-third of nursing-home residents. Long-term-care insurance may also cover some of the costs.

•**Hospice care** About $100 a day for in-home care. Medicare covers hospice care to patients who have a life expectancy of less than six months. (See Hospice: The Comfort Team.) Such care may be provided at home, in a hospice facility, a hospital, or a nursing-home. Patients may be asked to pay up to $5 for each prescription and a 5 percent co-pay for in-patient respite care, which is a short hospital stay to relieve caregivers. Medicaid covers hospice care in all but six states, even for those without Medicare.

About 60 percent of full-time employees of medium and large firms also have coverage for hospice services, but the benefits vary widely.

•**Home care without hospice services** Medicare Part A pays the full cost of medical home health care for up to 100 visits following a hospital stay of at least three days. Medicare Part B covers home health-care visits beyond those 100 visits or without a hospital stay. To qualify, the patient must be homebound, require skilled nursing care or physical or speech therapy, be under a physician's care, and use services from a Medicare-participating home-health agency. Note that this coverage is for medical care only; hired help for personal nonmedical services, such as that often required by Alzheimer's patients, is not covered by Medicare. It is covered by Medicaid in some states.

A major financial disadvantage of dying at home without hospice is that Medicare does not cover out-patient prescription drugs, even those for pain. Medicaid does cover these drugs, but often with restrictions on their price and quantity. Private insurance can fill the gap to some extent. Long-term-care insurance may cover payments to family caregivers who have to stop work to care for a dying patient, but this type of coverage is very rare.

Resources

MEDICAL CARE

For information about pain relief and symptom management: **Supportive Care of the Dying** (503-215-5053; careofdying.org).

For a comprehensive guide to living with the medical, emotional, and spiritual aspects of dying:
Handbook for Mortals by Joanne Lynn and Joan Harrold, Oxford University Press.

For a 24-hour hotline offering counseling, pain management, downloadable advance directives, and more:
The Partnership for Caring (800-989-9455; www.partnershipforcaring.org).

EMOTIONAL CARE

To find mental-health counselors with an emphasis on lifespan human development and spiritual discussion:
American Counseling Association (800-347-6647; counseling.org).

For disease-related support groups and general resources for caregivers:
Caregiver Survival Resources (caregiver911.com).

For AARP's online caregiver support chatroom, access **America Online** every Wednesday night, 8:30–9:30 EST (keyword: AARP).

Education and advocacy for family caregivers:
National Family Caregivers Association (800-896-3650; nfcacares.org).

For the booklet,
Understanding the Grief Process (D16832, EEO143C), e-mail order with title and numbers to member@aarp.org or send postcard to AARP Fulfillment, 601 E St NW, Washington DC 20049. Please allow two to four weeks for delivery.

To find a volunteer to help with supportive services to the frail and their caregivers:
National Federation of Interfaith Volunteer Caregivers (816-931-5442; nfivc.org).

For information on support to partners of the chronically ill and/or the disabled:
The Well Spouse Foundation (800-838-0879; www.wellspouse.org).

LEGAL HELP

AARP members are entitled to a free half-hour of legal advice with a lawyer from **AARP's Legal Services Network**. (800-424-3410; www.aarp.org/lsn).

For **Planning for Incapacity,** *a guide to advance directives in your state,* send $5 to Legal Counsel for the Elderly, Inc., PO Box 96474, Washington DC 20090-6474. Make out check to LCE Inc.

For a **Caring Conversations** *booklet on advance-directive discussion:*

Midwest Bioethics Center (816-221-1100; midbio.org).

For information on care at the end of life, online discussion groups, conferences:
Last Acts Campaign (800-844-7616; lastacts.org).

HOSPICE

To learn about end-of-life care options and grief issues through videotapes, books, newsletters, and brochures:
Hospice Foundation of America (800-854-3402; hospice-foundation.org).

For information on hospice programs, FAQs, and general facts about hospice:
National Hospice and Palliative Care Organization (800-658-8898; nhpco.org).

For **All About Hospice: A Consumer's Guide** (202-546-4759; www.hospice-america.org).

FINANCIAL HELP

For **Organizing Your Future,** *a simple guide to end-of-life financial decisions,* send $5 to Legal Counsel for the Elderly, Inc., PO Box 96474, Washington DC 20090-6474. Make out check to LCE Inc.

For **Medicare and You 2000** *and a* **2000 Guide to Health Insurance for People With Medicare** (800-MEDICARE [633-4227]; medicare.gov).

To find your State Agency on Aging: **Administration on Aging, U.S. Department of Health and Human Services** (800-677-1116; aoa.dhhs.gov).

GENERAL

For information on end-of-life planning and bereavement: (www.aarp.org/endoflife/).

For health professionals and others who want to start conversations on end-of-life issues in their community:

Discussion Guide: On Our Own Terms: Moyers on Dying, based on the PBS series, airing September 10–13. The guide provides essays, instructions, and contacts. From PBS, www.pbs.org/onourownterms Or send a postcard request to On Our Own Terms Discussion Guide, Thirteen/WNET New York, PO Box 245, Little Falls, NJ 07424-9766.

Funded with a grant from The Robert Wood Johnson Foundation, Princeton, N.J. *Editor* Amy Gross; *Writer* Louise Lague; *Designer* David Herbick

---

UNIT 8
Personality Processes

Unit Selections

27. **Psychology Discovers Happiness. I'm OK, You're OK**, Gregg Easterbrook
28. **Companies Seeking "Right" Candidates Increasingly Turn to Personality Tests**, Damon Cline
29. **Guns, Lies, and Video**, Karen Wright

Key Points to Consider

- What is positive psychology? What is optimism? Why is it important to the human condition? What other aspects of personality play a role in the theories and research endeavors of positive psychologists? How does the notion of positive psychology compare to psychoanalysis? Where should psychology head in the future according to positive psychologists?

- How can personality be tested? What does a typical personality test look like; that is, can you think of items that might appear on such a test or what traits would be important to measure? What general characteristics do personality tests assess? Why and where are personality tests utilized? What are the criticisms of the use of personality assessment?

- What are learning theories of personality? What attitudes and behaviors that shape who we are can be learned by observation? What role does the media play in influencing us in terms of our attitudes and behaviors? Why is media violence problematic? What would you recommend to reduce media violence and to whom would you make the recommendations?

- Out of all the personality theories that you studied, which do you think is best and why? Was your answer based on science, on anecdote, or something else?

 **Links: www.dushkin.com/online/**
These sites are annotated in the World Wide Web pages.

The Personality Project
http://personality-project.org/personality.html

Sabrina and Sadie are identical twins. When the girls were young children, their parents tried very hard to treat them equally. Whenever Sabrina received a present, Sadie received one. Both girls attended dance school and completed early classes in ballet and tap dance. In elementary school, the twins were both placed in the same class with the same teacher. The teacher also tried to treat them the same.

In junior high school, Sadie became a tomboy. She loved to play rough and tumble sports with the neighborhood boys. On the other hand, Sabrina remained indoors and practiced her piano. Sabrina was keenly interested in the domestic arts such as sewing, needlepoint, and crochet. Sadie was more interested in reading novels, especially science fiction, and in watching adventure programs on television.

As the twins matured, they decided it would be best to attend different colleges. Sabrina went to a small, quiet college in a rural setting, and Sadie matriculated at a large public university. Sabrina majored in English, with a specialty in poetry; Sadie switched majors several times and finally decided on a communications major.

Why, when these twins were exposed to the same early childhood environment, did their interests and paths diverge later? What makes people, even identical twins, at times so unique, and at other times so different from one another?

The study of individual differences is the domain of personality. The psychological study of personality has included two major thrusts. The first has focused on the search for the commonalties of human life and development. Its major question is: How are humans, especially their personalities, affected by specific events or activities? Personality theories are based on the assumption that a given event, if it is important, will affect almost all people in a similar way, or that the personality processes which affect people are common across events and people. Most psychological research into personality variables has made this assumption. Failure to replicate a research project are often the first clues that differences in individual responses require further investigation.

While some psychologists have focused on personality-related effects that are presumed to be universal among humans, others have devoted their efforts to discovering the bases on which individuals differ in their responses to events. In the beginning, this specialty was called genetic psychology, because most people assumed that individual differences resulted from differences in genetic inheritance. By the 1950's the term genetic psychology had given way to the more current term: the psychology of individual differences.

Does this mean that genetic variables are no longer the key to understanding individual differences? Not at all. For a time, psychologists took up the philosophical debate over whether genetic or environmental factors were more important in determining behaviors. Even today, behavior geneticists compute the heritability coefficients for a number of personality and behavior traits, including intelligence. This is an expression of the degree to which differences in a given trait can be attributed to differences in inherited capacity or ability. Most psychologists, however, accept the principle that both genetic and environmental determinants are important in any area of behavior. These researchers devote more of their efforts to discovering how the two sources of influence interact to produce the unique individual. Given the above, the focus of this unit is on personality characteristics and the differences and similarities among individuals.

What is personality? Most researchers in the area define personality as patterns of thoughts, feelings, and behaviors that persist over time and over situations, are characteristic or typical of the individual, and usually distinguish one person from another.

We will examine several theories of personality in this unit. First we look at an idea or theme in personality: positive psychology. While Freud often focused on the negative aspects of human nature, the humanists focus on the positive aspects of humanity. Psychologists are becoming more and more interested in positive psychology that examines human contentment, optimism, and well-being.

We next look at a second idea or theme in personality—personality testing. It is perhaps in this domain that personality theorists and researchers have made their greatest contributions to the field of psychology. Personality tests are found everywhere—in schools, in places of employment, in research laboratories, and even in popular magazines. The second article in this unit discloses the pros and cons of the use of personality tests, especially in the world of work.

The final selection in this unit pertains to learning theories. Social learning theory suggests that we learn by observation. Thus, watching television or engaging in violent video games teaches us many new attitudes and behaviors—namely aggressiveness and violence. Some researchers emphatically proclaim that media violence teaches violent behavior to Americans and so should be eliminated within our culture. The final article critiques this notion with an eye toward the research on media violence.

Psychology discovers happiness.
I'm OK, You're OK

By Gregg Easterbrook

"Life is divided up into the horrible and the miserable," Woody Allen tells Diane Keaton in *Annie Hall*. "The horrible would be like terminal cases, blind people, cripples—I don't know how they get through life. It's amazing to me. And the miserable is everyone else. So, when you go through life, you should be thankful that you're miserable."

That's a fairly apt summary of the last century's consensus regarding the psyche. Psychiatry now recognizes some 14 "major" mental disorders, in addition to countless lesser maladies. Unipolar depression—unremitting blue feelings—has risen tenfold since World War II and now afflicts an estimated 18 million Americans. Increasingly, even children are prescribed psychotropic drugs, while frustrated drivers are described as not merely discourteous but enraged. In the past 100 years, academic journals have published 8,166 articles on "anger," compared with 416 on "forgiveness"; in its latest edition, the presumably encyclopedic *Encyclopedia of Human Emotions*, a reference for clinicians, lists page after page of detrimental mental states but has no entry for "gratitude." Sigmund Freud declared mental torment the normal human condition and suggested that most people's best possible outcome would be to rise from neurosis into "ordinary unhappiness." It's a wonder we don't all lose our minds.

And yet, somehow, most people turn out OK. Only a tiny fraction of the populace commit antisocial acts or lose their ability to function in society. Roughly 80 percent of Americans describe themselves as basically satisfied with their lives. Not only have we not all lost our minds, but, considering modern stress, most of our minds seem in surprisingly good condition.

This observation is leading to a revolutionary development in the theory of the psyche—positive psychology, which seeks to change the focus of inquiry from what causes psychosis to what causes sanity. Researchers "tend to study the things that can go wrong in people's minds but not the things that can go right," says Robert Emmons, a psychologist at the University of California at Davis. Yet what can go right is at least as important, not just for individuals but for society. And, in contrast to much modern scholarship, positive psychology may produce knowledge that actually improves lives and makes the world a better place.

The initial ideas of positive psychology came to Martin Seligman 35 years ago when he and a colleague were giving electric shocks to dogs. Seligman, who has since become a professor of psychology at the University of Pennsylvania and is a past president of the American Psychological Association, found that by zapping dogs unless they jumped a barrier, he could reduce the animals to a state of cowering helplessness in which they would not attempt any other tasks. It may seem obvious that creatures exposed to regular pain would enter a state of wretchedness, but the psychology establishment of the time, dominated by behaviorists, rejected Seligman's result. Behaviorism claimed that dogs (or people) do that for which they are rewarded and avoid that for which they are punished: A dog shocked when performing one task should just move on to another. But the subjects of Seligman's experiment simply sat down and whimpered pitifully. Seligman took this as evidence that psychological states are in some sense *learned*, not merely involuntary reflexes to stimuli. And if negative mental states can be learned, he eventually realized, why not altruism or equanimity?

When Seligman proposed such rethinking to some older professors, it made them furious. After all, a fundamentally positive approach to psychology conflicted with the profession's modern history. Roughly since the Enlightenment, study of the mind had been flavored by the Cartesian notion that abstract thought is the brain's calling, while emotional states are handicaps. That view was briefly challenged by Charles Darwin, who, after publishing *The Origin of Species*, hypothesized that if physical traits had evolved, mental states must have, too. Darwin's final work, *The Expression of the Emotions in Man and Animals*, published in 1872, speculated that psychological qualities must be mainly beneficial or evolution would not have preserved them—loyalty, for instance, could have enhanced early humans' survival by causing them to care for one another.

But while Darwin's views on biology spread throughout the intellectual world, his views on the mind were quietly dismissed. Freud's much more negative interpretation—that the consciousness is steeped in self-delusion and emotions are repellent by-products of infantile sexual compulsions—fit the new century's zeitgeist of existential despair. When evidence for Freud's claims eventually turned out to be shaky, the equally uninviting model of behaviorism arose. Behaviorism held that we're all lab rats in a meaningless maze, and it viewed human feeling with open contempt. The dogma's low point came when the behaviorist guru John Watson pronounced that parents should "never hug and kiss" children, because this would only condition them to want affection.

At about the time behaviorism was reaching its zenith, the U.S. government established the National Institute of Mental Health and greatly expanded the Veterans Administration. The NIMH gave grants almost exclusively to researchers studying mental illness, while the VA (now the Department of Veterans Affairs) paid to train a generation of clinicians to treat World War II combat trauma. Between Freudianism, behaviorism, and a government that funded the study and treatment of the negative, psychology in the early postwar era became a truly dismal science.

Of course, this view had opponents. Humanistic psychology, founded by Abraham Maslow in the 1950s, argued both that life was well worth living and that people could find fulfillment by understanding that human needs come in a sequence, from physical to spiritual. (Seligman has been accused of borrowing ideas from humanistic psychology.) Around the same time, physicians accidentally discovered that some new tuberculosis drugs palliated depression. The discovery proved a hammer blow against Freudianism. As psychologists Fari Amini, Richard Lannon, and Thomas Lewis note in their book, *A General Theory of Love*, if a few molecules can alleviate psychological pain, "[h]ow does one square *that* with the supposed preeminence of repressed sexual urges as the cause of all matters emotional?"

The discovery that emotions have a biological component provided an opening for new views of the psyche. It meant mental states were not childhood curses (Freud) or involuntary twitches (behaviorism) but an integral element of the living world, evolving with life just as Darwin had guessed. Barbara Frederickson, a positive psychologist at the University of Michigan, has since expanded on Darwin's view, noting that while some negative emotions confer obvious survival advantages—fear causes you to run—natural selection may favor positive emotions in more subtle ways. A person who is joyful or outgoing, Frederickson supposes, is more likely

to make friends; the friends would then come to the person's aid in times of crisis, increasing the odds that friendliness would be passed to offspring. Further, as Amini, Lannon, and Lewis put it, if emotional states have a biological basis, they must be "part of the physical universe" and therefore "lawful," subject to understanding.

By the early '90s, researchers had fashioned this cluster of insights into a new movement Seligman originally called "good life" studies—the effort to determine what psychological forces caused people such as Eleanor Roosevelt (one of his heroes) to live life admirably. But because "good life" can connote champagne and dancing girls, in the late '90s advocates renamed the framework "positive psychology." Since then, the concept has gained ground with researchers.

Positive psychology's first empirical focus was figuring out who exactly is happy. Edward Diener, a psychologist at the University of Illinois, has come to the following conclusions. First, poverty causes unhappiness but wealth does not cause happiness. Second, the old as a group have more "life satisfaction" than the young. (Diener notes, "The minds of the young are full of the things they want to achieve and have not, whereas most of the elderly have either achieved what they wanted or made their peace with the fact that they never will.") And, third, according to a well-being test designed by Diener, the norm is positive; most Americans' scores on his test indicate they are "slightly satisfied" with life.

Diener's discovery that the impoverished are unhappy is hardly surprising: In a classic confirm-the-obvious exercise, he went to Calcutta and produced irrefutable data that the poor there experience "a very low level of life satisfaction." Studies by Diener and others show that as a person's income rises toward the middle-class level, his or her sense of well-being rises as well. But once basic material needs are met, income decouples from happiness. Since the 1957 publication of John Kenneth Galbraith's *The Affluent Society*, real income for the average American has trebled. But during that same period the fraction of Americans who describe themselves as "very happy" in the University of Chicago's long-running National Opinion Research Center polls has not budged: It was one-third in 1957, and it is one-third today.

Researchers surmise that once people become middle-class, additional income ceases to correlate with happiness because people begin to perceive money primarily in relation to those around them. Most do not think, *Does my house meet my needs?* but rather, *How nice is my house compared with the neighbors'?* Upon reaching upper income brackets, people may grow obsessed with what they still don't have, activating some kind of "nature's revenge" law that denies extra contentment to the wealthy. When Diener gave his tests to a group of multimillionaires from the *Forbes 400*, he found that, on average, they were only a tiny bit happier than the typical suburbanite.

Through its studies of the relationship between income and happiness, positive psychology supports the philosophical-theological conclusion that longing for material things ultimately harms the person doing the longing. Materialism also causes people to spend rather than save, which embeds anxiety in daily life—a point championed by Harvard University economist Juliet Schor. Cross-cultural studies of happiness buttress these findings. Sociologist Ronald Inglehart has found that life satisfaction is highest in the Scandinavian countries (where income is fairly evenly distributed, mitigating neighbors'-house angst) and lowest in poor nations. Life satisfaction is also unusually high in Ireland, which boasts a "count your blessings" culture. Life satisfaction is distressingly low in affluent Japan—much lower than in Argentina or Hungary—perhaps because Japanese culture emphasizes money even more relentlessly than American culture.

Exactly how "happy" a person might be is ephemeral, of course. Psychologist Daniel Kahneman of Princeton University has been attempting for years to create a wholly objective measure of well-being, without much success. Kahneman found, for instance, that if he asked college students whether they were happy, most said yes. But if he first asked how many dates they had had in the last month and then asked if they were happy, most said no. Kahneman says he stopped asking subjects if they considered themselves unhappy because the question caused some to burst into tears.

Positive psychology further finds that happiness is hard. Laura King of Southern Methodist University, writing in the current issue of the *Journal of Humanistic Psychology*, shows that a positive attitude toward life requires considerable effort; people may slip into melancholy simply because it's the path of least resistance. Freud anticipated this when he noted that "unhappiness is much less difficult to experience" than elevated feelings. As a result, positive psychologists tend to view happiness as a condition that must be actively sought. Kahneman marvels at one study that found that quadriplegics have high emotional satisfaction relative to lottery winners. The lottery winners, we can guess, got swept up in and betrayed by materialism, while the quadriplegics worked hard to adjust to their condition and in so doing learned how to appreciate life better.

Finally, positive psychology suggests individual happiness is not self-indulgent but in the interest of society, since studies show happy people are more likely to do volunteer work, give to charity, and contribute to their communities in other ways. Robert Browning wrote, "[M]ake us happy and you make us good." A wonderful, quirky 1998 book by Dennis Prager, *Happiness Is a Serious Problem*, proposes that people actually have a civic duty to become happy because this will make them altruistic.

This isn't to say that positive psychology advocates an unrealistically rosy view of life. Psychologist Lisa Aspinwall of the University of Utah has found that one reason optimists generally have better "life outcomes" than pessimists is they pay more attention to safety and health warnings: Being optimistic doesn't make them blind to threats but rather makes them want to be around for the long haul.

Reversing the logic of dogs shocked into helplessness, Seligman advocates "learned optimism"—the idea that, by learning to expect tribulations and occasional unhappiness, people can avoid pessimism. Seligman thinks primary schools should teach children to expect difficulties, so that when problems start, as inevitably they will, children will not be traumatized but will view occasional setbacks as part of the natural course of events. An idealized anticipation of life, Seligman says, only creates disillusionment, whereas expecting to have some really bad days fosters a sustainable positive outlook. Managing one's expectations in this way, of course, requires self-control. And in fact Roy Baumeister, a researcher at Case Western Reserve University, has found that self-control is a better predictor of "life outcomes"—career and marriage success, overall happiness—than IQ.

Gratitude and forgiveness also turn out to promote happiness. Recent studies have shown that people who describe themselves as grateful—to others and to God or nature for the gift of life—tend to enjoy better health, more successful careers, and less depression than the population as a whole. These results hold even when researchers factor out age and income, equalizing for the fact that the affluent or good-looking might have more to be grateful for. And just as positive psychology doesn't recommend Pollyannaish optimism, it doesn't call for Panglossian gratitude. "To say we feel grateful is not to say that everything in our lives is necessarily great," says Emmons, the University of California psychologist. "It just means… if you only think about your disappointments and unsatisfied wants, you may be prone to unhappiness. If you're fully aware of your disappointments but at the same time thankful for the good that has happened and for your chance to live, you may show higher indices of well-being."

In this regard, the power of self-suggestion is considerable: Studies show that those who dwell on negative experiences become negative, while those who keep "gratitude journals," in which they write down what they're thankful for, experience improved well-being. Counting your blessings may sound corny, but if it helps you do better in life or simply have a good day, it's perfectly rational. Adam Smith anticipated this in his 1759 *Theory of Moral Sentiments*, one premise of which is that people who do not feel grateful cheat themselves out of their experience of life. Lack of gratitude leads to bitterness, Smith wrote, and bitterness only harms the person who feels it.

Likewise, positive psychology advises forgiveness because it benefits the person who forgives. If you bear a grudge or want retribution, your own well-being declines. Even in cases when someone has done you a severe wrong, such as a crime, forgiving the person is in your self-interest, because it prevents your own life from being subsumed in bitterness.

Depression is the malady of greatest concern to positive psychology, and here the figures are haunting. Incidence of bipolar depression—exaggerated mood swings—has not changed during the postwar era; the disorder is now believed to be primarily biological and is treated with medication. But the tenfold postwar increase in incidence of unipolar depression appears to have no biological explanation, and the rate holds in all developed nations. Steadily rising Western standards of living have been accompanied by a huge upswing in the percentage of the population that constantly feels bad. What's going on?

Seligman thinks most unipolar depression is a learned condition, and he offers four causes. First, too much individualism: "Unipolar depression is a disorder of the thwarting of the I, and we are increasingly taught to view all through the I." Past emphases on patriotism, family, and faith may sometimes have been suffocating but also let individuals view their private disappointments as minor within the larger context. Today, Seligman supposes, "rampant individualism causes us to think that our setbacks are of vast importance, and thus something to become depressed about."

Next, Seligman blames the self-esteem trend. "Self-esteem emphasis has made everybody think there's something fundamentally *wrong* if you don't feel good, as opposed to 'We just don't feel good right now but will later,'" he says. If something is fundamentally wrong with your life, that's pretty depressing. Self-esteem types maintain that people should feel good about themselves all the time, an idea positive psychology proponents deem totally unrealistic. The preaching of self-esteem in schools, Seligman thinks, has backfired by increasing melancholy.

Third, Seligman thinks depression is rising because of "the promiscuity of postwar teaching of victimology and helplessness." Intellectuals and the media have spent the last couple of decades discovering victims; surveys find that ever-higher percentages of incoming college freshmen describe themselves as having been victimized or possessing little control over their fates—though, objectively, personal freedom has never been higher. The "We're all victims" view discourages people from asserting control over their psyches.

Seligman finds particularly counterproductive the fad of adults claiming they were victimized by their parents. Only in extreme cases—such as sexual abuse—is there a clear link between parenting and adult personality: "You are entitled to blame your parents for the genes they gave you, but you are not entitled, by any research I know of, to blame them for the way they treated you," Seligman says. Depressed patients often attribute their condition to their parents, but once recovered they rarely say their parents were to blame for their disorder.

Fourth on Seligman's list of depression's causes is runaway consumerism. "Shopping, sports cars, expensive chocolates—these things are shortcuts to well-being," he says. While overall happiness has not increased as national income has trebled in the postwar period, surveys show that what Americans expect materially has grown in lockstep with the earnings curve. Like a street drug, materialism requires more and more to produce the same brief high. As David Myers, a social scientist at Hope College in Holland, Michigan, has noted of this predicament, "[T]he victor belongs to the spoils."

Whatever the causes of unipolar depression, there are two main treatments. One is Prozac and an expanding variety of related medications. The other is cognitive therapy, a psychological approach based on the premise that your mind can fix its own problems. Both pharmacology and cognitive therapy show similar effectiveness—about two-thirds of patients get better, and one-third do not respond. Proponents of positive psychology generally prefer the cognitive route.

The cognitive strategy against depression includes learning to recognize the "automatic" negative thoughts that flit through the mind as the blues are coming on and to counter such thoughts. To some extent this is simply common sense and echoes what is found in "power of positive thinking" books. But previous theories of the mind have distinctly lacked common sense and, therefore, have done little good. The University of Illinois's Diener says, "Freudian theory offered little of value to society, wanting to convince us we were all screwed up and there was nothing we could do beyond getting our misery under control. Positive psychology offers patients a realistic way to treat conditions and offers society as a whole a way to build virtues and human strengths."

Seligman is trying to convey this message on a broader scale with a pilot program in Philadelphia middle schools to teach students "learned optimism." Positive psychology is also integral to the "character education" movement blooming in schools and universities, which teaches both that virtue is a duty and that it improves individual lives. These efforts may soon gain a powerful new rationale, as growing research suggests that a positive psychological outlook not only improves "life outcomes" but enhances health directly. In her new book *The Balance Within*, Esther Sternberg, chief of neuroendo-crine immunology and behavior at the National Institutes of Health, presents evidence that emotions play a role in regulating the immune system—the more positive your sense of well-being, the better your white blood cells function.

By focusing on improvement rather than dysfunction, the positive-psychology movement also hopes to destigmatize mental therapy. Today most insurers will not reimburse patients for therapy unless their diagnosis includes one of the standard codes for mental illness. The result is that many pay for treatment out of their own pockets to avoid having such an entry on medical records, while many others receive no care. Seligman and University of Michigan psychologist Christopher Peterson are trying to change this by working on a manual for classification of "the sanities," a handbook that would be the reverse of the *Diagnostic and Statistical Manual* that clinicians use to code mental illnesses. Such a volume, they believe, not only might solve the insurance records problem but could encourage the many who experience mild psychological pain to get help—just as physicians once thought patients should simply live with mild ailments, such as aching knees, but now believe people should seek every possible cure.

As positive psychology moves from the margins to the mainstream, millions may embrace the remarkable idea that it is not only in society's interest to be altruistic, optimistic, and forgiving but in your own. For roughly a century, academic theory has assumed that when people lose their minds, the awful truth about life is revealed. Now comes a theory that says the truth is revealed when people acquire happiness and virtue. Which model sounds better to you?

GREGG EASTERBROOK is a senior editor of TNR.

Companies Seeking 'Right' Candidates Increasingly Turn to Personality Tests

Give June Barksdale 30 minutes, and she can tell if you're management material or better off following orders.

All this based on a couple of questionnaires.

Ms. Barksdale is the human resources director for Augusta medical billing company Medac Inc., one of a growing number of businesses using personality tests to help make hiring and promotion decisions.

Personality tests have been around for decades but have come into vogue in recent years as increasingly tight corporate budgets make it more crucial than ever to fill positions with the "right" people.

The goal is not only to improve productivity, but reduce costly employee turnover.

"Why would I want to hire someone to be a data entry clerk who is dominant and assertive," Ms. Barksdale said. "You can't put somebody like that in a reserved role without them feeling some frustration at exhibiting behavior that is opposite of their natural tendencies. They're not going to want to sit at their desk all day long and enter data."

The trend is not widely followed, but a national survey by the Alexandria, Va.-based Society for Human Resource Management in 2000 showed 22 percent of employers have administered some type of personality test. Augusta companies using personality tests, include Blanchard and Calhoun Real Estate, Augusta Ear Nose and Throat, Morris Communications Co. and MAU Inc., the latter of which has used the tests since the early 1970s.

"These days, companies really can't afford to make mistakes in their placement, whether it's a new hire or a promotion," said Gary Holley, human resources director for Club Car Inc., whose corporate training program relies on more than a half-dozen personality tests.

The use of such tools, known as "psychometrics," were once limited to top-level positions in Fortune 500 corporations. Today, the multi-billion dollar industry has become so prevalent that even entry-level employees are being assessed.

Danny Avery, head of the staffing division of Columbus, Miss.-based CPI Group, provides personality assessment services nationwide for businesses ranging from Sara Lee Corp. to "mom and pop" companies.

"Eighty percent of all people terminated are let go not because they're technically incompetent, but because they can't get along with other folks," he said. "Using an assessment on the front end is one way of helping avoid some of those issues."

Though personality tests vary in length and format, all are crafted to give employers a behavioral sketch of an individual, such as how they prefer to interact with others and how they process information. The individual is categorized based on their tendencies: assertive or passive, introverted or extraverted, formal or informal.

Test questions tend to be multiple choice and are highly standardized, meaning that any individual can provide answers regardless of their age, race, sex or place of birth.

The assessments pass legal muster because they do not elicit information considered to be "medical." Federal law prohibits employers discriminating against people with medical disabilities or impairments.

"Generally, a personality trait isn't impairment related," said Laurel Landon, an Augusta labor attorney and partner in the Kilpatrick Stockton law firm. "I would still advise companies to check with their attorney before giving these tests."

Common workplace assessments, with names such as the Predictive Index System and the Myers-Briggs Type Indicator, are also not true psychological profiles, which can probe events that shape one's behavior.

"These tests are not necessarily predictors of behavior, they're more of a descriptor of who you are now," said Bill Beauchamp, an Augusta consultant who uses personality assessments to help companies build and improve management teams.

Because creative solutions often come from behaviorally diverse work teams, companies are increasingly using personality assessments to help "left-brained" employees communicate effectively with their "right-brained" counterparts.

Kimberly Douglas, president of Atlanta's FireFly Facilitation, uses the results of the Herrmann Brain Dominance Instrument test to get management teams to understand their differences and figure out more effective ways to communicate.

"Companies are looking for ways to make teams work better because everybody has been stressed to the max from all the cost-cutting," she said. "They realize they've got all these employees that are now doing three different jobs. If they don't make some changes, when the job market turns around, these employees are going to start jumping ship."

While some people may not like the idea of their overall demeanor being boiled down to a line on a graph or a four-letter personality "type," the tests have been validated though years of use.

"I can't believe how accurate it seems, it describes me a lot," said Pam Cowart, a Medac employee who took the Predictive Index test before her promotion to account executive, which made her a supervisor of 16 clerks.

Ms. Cowart's profile revealed she has a passive demeanor—usually a liability for managers—but also a very sociable personality with strong attention to detail and a sense of urgency.

The combination allows Ms. Cowart to be an effective manager because she is able to motivate her employees in a "non-aggressive" way, Ms. Barksdale said.

Personality assessments can benefit employees as much as employers, said Angela Woodruff-Swarts, owner of Augusta's Spherion staffing franchise, which handles job placement services for white-collar office workers.

If an employee wants to be happy at work, they need to be aware of their personality and how it would fit in with a prospective employer's corporate culture.

"Corporate culture is critical," said Ms. Woodruff-Swarts, whose company uses a proprietary personality assessment based on the Predictive Index test. "Your definition of a an administrative assistant is different from what ABC company expects from an administrative assistant."

Followers of workplace trends expect employment-based personality testing will only proliferate in the coming years.

The career center at Augusta State University encourages students to take the Myers-Briggs test so that they may familiarize themselves with the concept of a personality assessment.

"We tell them that this is something you're probably going to see in your interview process," said Julie Goley, the center's director.

COMMON TESTS

There are hundreds of personality assessments in use. Below are some of the most common:

- DISC: This test is named for the four main traits it measures - dominance, influence, steadiness and compliance. It groups people into various behavioral categories using a 24-item questionnaire and was developed in the 1920s by the inventor of the lie detector.

- Henmann Brain Dominance Instrument: The "HBDI," as it is called, hones in on an individual's preferred thinking style that influences their communication, decision-making, problem solving and management style.

- Manchester Personality Questionnaire: This test focuses on traits relevant to creative and innovative behavior. It is designed to help an employer understand an individual's strengths, weaknesses and areas of competence.

- Myers-Briggs Type Indicator: This test groups individuals into 16 personality types (identified by four-letter acronyms) based on the way they communicate and gather, process and act upon information. It is named for the mother and daughter who created it in the 1920s based on the theories of psychologist Carl Jung.

- Predictive Index System: Developed in the 1950s, the "PI" is a multiple-choice test designed to indicate an individual's general workplace behavior, such as whether they are informal or formal, reserved or extroverted, a leader or a follower.

- Watson Glaser Critical Thinking Appraisal: This test is designed to identify management candidates by measuring five areas: critical reasoning, inference, recognition of assumptions, deduction, interpretation and evaluation of arguments.

- Wonderlic Personnel Test: This 12-minute general aptitude and cognitive ability test measures a candidate's ability to learn and apply knowledge. This test, in use since 1937, is given by nearly all temporary employment and personnel services firms.

- Work Personality Index Select: Known as the "WPI," this 30-minute test assesses 17 personality traits, characteristics and tendencies that influence an individual's job performance. It also aims to predict the type of position and work environment in which a person will best function.

- Work Profile Questionnaire: The "WPQ" is used mainly for employee self-improvement and development. Individuals are asked to rate 100 adjectives and phrases describing their typical work behavior and attitudes on a five-point scale ranging from "very accurately" to "not at all."

TEST YOURSELF

Personality assessments in the workplace are administered by trained professional and follow strict guidelines to ensure their validity, but if you want to take tests just for fun, you can try these sites:

- Tickle by Emode (`web.tickle.com`) features a variety of tests and quizzes ranging from IQ tests to relationship evaluations.

- Queendom (`www.queendom.com`) has dozens of professional tests and 113 "just for fun" online tests.

- 2H Helenelund HB (`www.2h.com`) has several personality tests as well as IQ tests, entrepreneurial tests and puzzles.

- ABCs of Self Help (`www.selfhelp.com`) features an online personality test and the "E-IQ Test" for emotional intelligence.

- Personality Online (`www.personalityonline.com`) lists a variety of personality tests and a comprehensive database of personal development related resources.

Guns, Lies, and Video

Does violent TV breed violence? Do video games breed more of it?

By Karen Wright

IN A SURVEY PUBLISHED EARLIER this year, seven of 10 parents said they would never let their children play with toy guns. Yet the average seventh grader spends at least four hours a week playing video games, and about half of those games have violent themes, like Nuclear Strike. Clearly, parents make a distinction between violence on a screen and that acted out with plastic M-16s. Should they?

Psychologists point to decades of research and more than a thousand studies that demonstrate a link between media violence and real aggression. Six formidable public-health organizations, including the American Academy of Pediatrics and the American Medical Association (AMA), issued a joint statement of concern in 2000. According to one expert's estimate, aggressive acts provoked by entertainment media such as TV, movies, and music could account for 10 percent of the juvenile violence in society. And scientists say they have reason to believe that video games are the most provocative medium yet.

"With video games, you're not only passively receiving attitudes and behaviors, you're rehearsing them," says pediatrician Michael Rich, a former filmmaker and the current head of the Center on Media and Child Health at Harvard University.

But the case isn't quite closed. Last year, psychologist Jonathan Freedman of the University of Toronto published an outspoken indictment of some of the field's most influential studies. The "bulk of the research does not show that televi-

sion or movie violence has any negative effects," he argues in *Media Violence and Its Effect on Aggression.* In a 1999 editorial titled "Guns, Lies, and Videotape," the redoubtable British medical journal *The Lancet* admitted that "experts are divided on the subject," and that "both groups can support their views with a sizable amount of published work."

A 1992 study found that the average American child graduating from elementary school has seen more than 8,000 murders and more than 100,000 assaults, rapes, and other acts of violence on network television alone. Most U.S. children log about 28 hours of television viewing a week.

Those who grew up with the Three Stooges or Super Mario Brothers may have trouble seeing their youthful pastimes in a sinister light. But televised violence has been a topic of national consternation almost from the first broadcast. Congressional hearings on the subject date back to 1952; the first surgeon general's report addressing it was published in 1972. "We've been studying it at least since then, but the studies haven't given us definite answers," says Kimberly Thompson, director of the Kids Risk Project at the School of Public Health at Harvard. Thompson and others believe that the rise of TV viewing in American

households may be at least partly responsible for the eightfold increase in violent crime in this country between 1960 and 1990. Today a typical kid spends two hours a day watching television, and children's programs average between 20 and 25 violent acts per hour—four times as many as adult programs. "The message that's going out to children is that violence is OK or it's funny or it's somehow heroic," says Jeffrey G. Johnson, a psychiatric epidemiologist at the College of Physicians and Surgeons at Columbia University in New York.

Common sense argues that such exposure must have *some* effect. Designing studies to measure it is another story. So far, for example, there aren't any universal standards defining or quantifying violent content. Many early investigations simply proved that aggressive kids like to watch aggressive TV, without illuminating which tendency leads to which. And it's obvious that poverty, abuse, and ready access to weapons can put a child on the wrong path too.

One way to distinguish among the potential causes of juvenile violence is by studying large numbers of people over long periods of time. Last year, Johnson and his colleagues published results of a 17-year study following more than 700 kids from an average age of 6 to adulthood. They tallied the hours each subject spent in front of the tube and compared those numbers with subsequent acts of aggression, ranging from threats to criminal assault. The trends are clear, says Johnson: Kids who spent more than three hours a day watching television at age 14 were more than four times as likely to have acted aggressively by age 22 than kids who watched TV for less than an hour. The connection held up even after researchers accounted for other possible culprits, including poverty, neglect, and bad neighborhoods—and even among tube-addled females, who, like the rest of the subjects, were predominantly white and Catholic.

"It's not just that TV just triggers aggression in aggressive people," Johnson says. "We saw this in 'nice' girls too."

Some laboratory studies hint that violent programming may lead to a malevolent state of mind. In one classic example, 5- to 9-year-olds were told they could press buttons that would either further or foil their playmates' attempts to win a game. Children who watched segments of the 1970s crime drama *The Untouchables* beforehand showed more willingness to hinder their peers' efforts than did those who watched a track race.

A recent analysis asserts that the correlation between virtual and actual aggression is stronger than those linking passive smoke and lung cancer, calcium intake and bone density, and exposure to lead and IQ. "The correlation between media violence and aggression is stronger than many of these things that we accept as fact—such as that if you eat lead paint chips, you'll become mentally retarded," says Rich.

Rich and others think video games could have an even greater effect than TV because they're interactive. The genre term "first-person shooter" says it all. "Often the interface that the child has with the game is a gun," says Rich. "A very realistic gun."

Yet only a handful of video-game studies have been published so far. At Iowa State University in Ames, social psychologist Craig Anderson tested col-

DEATHS PER MINUTE IN SELECTED ACTION VIDEO GAMES	
Donkey Kong (1999)	.78
Q'bert (1999)	1.31
The Smurfs (1999)	.59
Super Mario Brothers (1985)	4.8
Super Mario 64 (1996)	.23

Source: *JAMA*, Vol. 286, No. 5

lege students' willingness to provide help to others after playing 20 minutes of benign games like Glider Pro or malignant ones like the pedestrian-plowing Carmageddon. Anderson timed how long his subjects waited before responding to a person left whimpering in the hallway after a staged attack. "The people who played a violent video game took about four times as long to come to the aid of the victim than people who played a nonviolent game," says Anderson.

Skeptics like Freedman say such correlations don't amount to causation and that other, well-established risk factors such as poverty and neglect are important to consider. All true, Rich concedes. "But it's only correlations that suggest we should all wear seat belts," he says. "And [exposure to media violence] is one of the few risk factors that is easily controllable."

Laboratory studies have also been criticized for attributing to violent content behavior that could be a result of general physiological arousal. Any exciting program will cause an increase in heart rate, for example, and it's known that a racing heart can make an individual more bellicose. So Anderson took care to compare only video games that elevated his subject's heart rates to the same degree. And child psychologist John Murray of Kansas State University in Manhattan has used real-time MRI scans to observe whether violent content triggers unique patterns of brain activity. One group of Murray's kids watched

fight scenes from *Rocky IV*; the other, an action-packed mystery called *Ghostwriter*. Only the boxing bouts activated an area in the right hemisphere called the right posterior cingulate, which may store long-term memories of trauma.

"We were surprised to find this, and worried," says Murray. He fears that violent programs may pack the same emotional punch as actual violence. "It's not 'just' entertainment," he says. "It becomes a story about how life is."

The advertising industry is built on the faith that media content and consumption can change human behavior, Rich points out. So why does society question the influence of dramatized violence? The obvious answer is that, despite the reams of paper devoted to its pernicious influence, violent entertainment remains entertaining. Americans appear to regard its consequences, whatever they may be, as an acceptable risk. Even hard-liners like Anderson, Rich, and the AMA don't recommend banning violent content. Instead, they lobby for greater parental awareness and control.

But maybe parents themselves should beware. The effect of violent media on adults is still unexplored territory. And television news, a staple of grown-up media consumption, carries some of the nastiest carnage on the airwaves.

"There is some evidence that violent media has a bigger effect on children," Anderson says. "But there's no age group that's immune."

A 1992 study found that the average American child graduating from elementary school has seen more than 8,000 murders and more than 100,000 assaults, rapes, and other acts of violence on network television alone. Most U.S. children log about 28 hours of television viewing a week.

UNIT 9
Social Processes

Unit Selections

30. **Are You Looking at Me? Eye Gaze and Person Perception**, C. Neil Macrae et al.
31. **Got Time for Friends?**, Andy Steiner

Key Points to Consider

- How do we perceive another person; that is, what processes do we depend on? When you assess another individual, how can you be sure that your judgment is accurate? What role does gaze play in our person perception? Why is it important to study eye gaze?

- What is friendship? Why are friends important? How do adulthood and childhood friendships differ? Why should adults maintain their friendships, especially today when life already seems so full?

 **Links: www.dushkin.com/online/**
These sites are annotated in the World Wide Web pages.

National Clearinghouse for Alcohol and Drug Information
http://www.health.org
Nonverbal Behavior and Nonverbal Communication
http://www3.usal.es/~nonverbal/

Everywhere we look there are groups of people. Your introductory psychology class is a group. It is what social psychologists would call a secondary group, a group that comes together for a particular, somewhat contractual reason and then disbands after its goals have been met. Other secondary groups include athletic teams, church associations, juries, committees, and so forth.

There are other types of groups, too. One other type is a primary group. A primary group has much face-to-face contact, and there is often a sense of "we-ness" in the group (cohesiveness as social psychologists would call it.) Examples of primary groups include families, suite mates, sororities, and teenage cliques.

Collectives or very large groups are loosely knit, massive groups of people. A bleacher full of football fans would be a collective. A long line of people waiting to get into a rock concert would also be a collective. A mob in a riot would be construed as a collective, too. As you might guess, collectives behave differently from primary and secondary groups.

Mainstream American society and any other large group that shares common rules and norms is also a group, albeit an extremely large group. While we might not always think about our society and how it shapes our behavior and our attitudes, society and culture nonetheless have a measureless influence on us. Psychologists, anthropologists, and sociologists alike are all interested in studying the effects of a culture on its members.

In this unit we will look at both positive and negative forms of social interaction. We will move from focused forms of social interaction to broader forms of social interaction. In other words, we will move from interpersonal to group to societal processes.

In this unit's two articles, we concentrate on interpersonal phenomena such as person perception and friendship. In the first essay about eye gaze, the authors explore the important role gaze plays in shaping interpersonal interactions and perceptions of others. Gazing at another person appears to do more than simply bring us visual information about another person.

ARE YOU LOOKING AT ME?
Eye Gaze and Person Perception

Abstract—*Previous research has highlighted the pivotal role played by gaze detection and interpretation in the development of social cognition. Extending work of this kind, the present research investigated the effects of eye gaze on basic aspects of the person-perception process, namely, person construal and the extraction of category-related knowledge from semantic memory. It was anticipated that gaze direction would moderate the efficiency of the mental operations through which these social-cognitive products are generated. Specifically, eye gaze was expected to influence both the speed with which targets could be categorized as men and women and the rate at which associated stereotypic material could be accessed from semantic memory. The results of two experiments supported these predictions: Targets with nondeviated (i.e., direct) eye gaze elicited facilitated categorical responses. The implications of these findings for recent treatments of person perception are considered.*

C. Neil Macrae, Bruce M. Hood, Alan B. Milne, Angela C. Rowe, and Malia F. Mason

Humans and many other species tend to look at things in their environment that are of immediate interest to them. You might be the recipient of another's gaze, for instance, because you are a potential meal, a mate or simply because you are someone with whom they would like to interact. (Langton, Watt, & Bruce, 2000, pp. 51–52)

Direction of eye gaze is a crucial medium through which humans and other animals can transmit socially relevant information. In some contexts, the mere establishment of eye contact can be interpreted as a sign of hostility or anger (Argyle & Cook, 1976). Indeed, in many primate societies, staring is deemed to be an unambiguously threatening gesture (Hinde & Rowell, 1962). Yet mutual eye contact can also convey positive messages. For example, staring can be taken to be a sign of friendliness, romantic attraction, or general interest (Argyle & Cook, 1976; Kellerman, Lewis, & Laird, 1989; Kleinke, 1986). As von Grünau and Anston (1995) have noted, "whether maintained stare is a sign of dislike or like, it is certainly an indication for a potential social interaction" (p. 1297).

Given the acknowledged informational value of eye gaze, it makes sound evolutionary sense that people should be sensitized to eye gaze in others. As gaze direction signals the appearance and relative importance of objects in the environment (e.g., friends, predators, food), considerable adaptive advantages can be gained from an information processing system that is finely tuned to gaze detection and interpretation (see Baron-Cohen, 1994, 1995; Perrett & Emery, 1994). Luckily for the smooth running of everyday life, the available evidence confirms that people are indeed highly sensitive to gaze direction, an ability that emerges in the very early stages of childhood. Young infants prefer to look at the eyes more than at other regions of the face (Morton & Johnson, 1991) and by the age of 4 months can discriminate staring from averted eyes (Vecera & Johnson, 1995). This fascination with gaze continues into adulthood, particularly with respect to mutual eye contact (Baron-Cohen, 1994, 1995). Although this sensitivity to eye gaze undoubtedly serves a variety of useful functions (e.g., reflexive visual orienting; see Driver et al., 1999; Friesen & Kingstone, 1998; Hood, Willen, & Driver, 1998), one function in particular is of considerable social importance. Understanding the nonverbal language of the eyes facilitates the development of social cognition, notably the cognitive and affective construal processes that guide people's daily interactions with others (see Baron-Cohen, 1994, 1995; Perrett & Emery, 1994).

EYE GAZE AND SOCIAL COGNITION

An intriguing account of the role that eye gaze may play in social cognition has been offered by Baron-Cohen (1995) in his writings on mind reading (i.e., theory of mind). According to Baron-Cohen (1994, 1995), the mind contains a series of specialized modules that have evolved to enable humans to attribute mental states to others (see also Brothers, 1990). One of these modules, the *eye-direction detector* (EDD), deals explicitly with gaze detection and interpretation and plays a critical role in the development of social cognition. In summary, the EDD has three basic functions: It (a) detects the presence of eyes or eyelike stimuli in the environment, (b) computes the direction of gaze (e.g., direct or averted), and (c) attributes the mental state of "seeing" to the gazer. As Baron-Cohen (1995) put it, the "EDD is a mindreading mechanism specific to the visual system; it computes whether there are eyes out there and, if so, whether those eyes are looking at me or looking at not-me" (p. 43). Such a system is believed to occupy a pivotal role in everyday social interaction. Indeed, without the ability to read the language of the eyes, perceivers would find it difficult to adopt the "intentional stance" (Dennett, 1987) when interpreting the actions of others (Baron-Cohen, 1994, 1995).

Whether or not one endorses the view that the mind contains an EDD or some functionally equivalent module (e.g., *direction of attention detector,* DAD; see Perrett & Emery, 1994), it is apparent that a specialized processing system deals with the problem of gaze detection and interpretation. Electrophysiological research has suggested that such a system may be localized in the superior temporal sulcus (STS; see Allison, Puce, & McCarthy, 2000; Haxby, Hoffman, & Gobbini, 2000; Hoffman & Haxby, 2000). A number of early studies identified cells in areas of temporal cortex that were highly receptive to facial stimuli (Bruce, Desimone, & Gross, 1981; Perrett, Rolls, & Cann, 1982). In subsequent research, Perrett and his colleagues located specific cells in the STS that responded selectively to the direction of gaze (Perrett et al., 1985). In particular, whereas some cells were tuned to eye contact, others were tuned to detect averted gaze. As it turns out, however, these cells appear to be only part of a broader system that is dedicated to the detection of social attention (Perrett & Emery, 1994). In recent research, individual cells in the STS region of the macaque brain have been shown to be responsive to particular conjunctions of eye, head, and body position (Perrett & Emery, 1994), suggesting that the direction of social attention can be signaled by a variety of stimulus cues.

Given, then, the fundamental role that gaze detection and interpretation plays in the development of social cognition (Baron-Cohen, 1994, 1995; Perrett & Emery, 1994), it is surprising that no empirical studies have yet investigated the effects of eye gaze on basic aspects of social-cognitive functioning, such as the pivotal process of person construal (i.e., person categorization). This oversight is puzzling as the categorical inferences that people draw about others are widely acknowledged to be the building blocks of social cognition (Allport, 1954; Brewer, 1988; Bodenhausen & Macrae, 1998; Fiske & Neuberg, 1990; Macrae & Bodenhausen, 2000). Rather than construing people in terms of their unique collections of attributes and proclivities, perceivers typically characterize them instead on the basis of the social groups to which they belong (Allport, 1954; Bargh, 1999). They do so for good reason, however. Not only does categorical thinking simplify the complexities of person perception, but also the products of this process shape the direction and nature of people's social interactions. Specifically, once targets have been categorized in a particular way, associated knowledge structures (e.g., stereotypes) guide people's impressions, evaluations, and recollec-

tions of others (Bodenhausen & Macrae, 1998; Brewer, 1988; Fiske & Neuberg, 1990; Macrae & Bodenhausen, 2000). Given this state of affairs, one might expect the efficiency of the person-construal process to be moderated by factors that have obvious biological significance to perceivers, such as the eye gaze of others (Baron-Cohen, 1994, 1995; Perrett & Emery, 1994). That is, in making sense of the persons who populate their social worlds, perceivers may use eye gaze as a cue for computing the relative importance or relevance of the individuals they encounter (e.g., looking at me vs. not looking at me). In turn, this cuing process may moderate the efficiency of the mental operations that furnish perceivers with category-related knowledge about others (Macrae & Bodenhausen, 2000).

EYE GAZE AND PERSON CONSTRUAL

There is good reason to suspect that the efficiency of the person-construal process may be influenced by a target's direction of gaze. Given that eye gaze can signal the potential intentions of friend and foe alike, it is useful to have an information processing system that can deal with this perceptual input in a rapid and effective manner (Baron-Cohen, 1994, 1995; Perrett & Emery, 1994). As Baron-Cohen (1995) has argued, "it makes…sense that we should be hypersensitive to when another organism is watching us, since this is about the best early warning system that another organism may be about to attack us, or may be interested in us for some other reason" (p. 98). Of course, in such a situation it is not simply enough to detect the presence of eyes or eyelike stimuli in the environment. To discern the potential intentions or motives of another organism (e.g., friend, enemy, predator, potential mate), it is also necessary to establish the identity of the organism in question and then to access any relevant information that may be stored in memory. After all, it is only after this knowledge has been accessed that appropriate action plans can be generated and implemented. For this reason, we suspect that the efficiency of the person-construal process may be moderated by the direction of eye gaze. As the most relevant stimulus targets are usually those with whom mutual eye contact has been established, we hypothesized that individuals would be categorized most rapidly when they display nondeviated (i.e., direct) eye gaze. Moreover, as a result of this categorization advantage, we expected that generic category-related knowledge (i.e., stereotypic information) would be highly accessible for these persons. We investigated these predictions in the following two experiments.

EXPERIMENT 1: EYE GAZE AND PERSON CATEGORIZATION

Method

Participants and design

Thirty-two undergraduates (14 men, 18 women) participated in the experiment for course credit. The experiment had a single-factor (eye gaze: full face, direct vs. 3/4 face, direct vs. averted vs. closed) repeated measures design.

Table 1. *Gender categorization times and knowledge accessibility as a function of eye gaze*

Measure	Eye Gaze			
	3/4 face, direct	Full face, direct	Laterally averted	Closed
	Experiment 1			
Gender categorization (ms)	534	525	630	611
	Experiment 2			
Knowledge accessibility (ms)				
Stereotypic items	—	587	626	621
Counterstereotypic items	—	647	645	650
Nonwords	—	692	690	684

Procedure and stimulus materials

Upon arrival in the laboratory, each participant was greeted by a female experimenter and seated facing the monitor of an Apple Macintosh iMac microcomputer. The experimenter explained that the study involved a classification task in which participants had to judge the gender of persons depicted in a series of photographs. Each photograph appeared in the center of the screen, and the participant responded by pressing, as quickly and accurately as possible, one of two appropriately labeled keys ("male" or "female"). Throughout the experiment, the participant was instructed to fixate on a small black cross that was located in the center of the screen. It was explained that the photographs would always be located on the fixation cross. On each trial, the fixation cross was blanked out 30 ms before the onset of the stimulus. Each photograph remained on the screen until the participant made a response, and the intertrial interval was 2,000 ms.

In total, 48 black-and-white photographs were presented (i.e., 24 men and 24 women). Across the stimulus set, 12 targets (6 men and 6 women) displayed full-face, direct gaze; 12 targets (6 men and 6 women) displayed 3/4-face, direct gaze; 12 targets (6 men and 6 women) displayed laterally averted gaze (i.e., 6 laterally averted to the right and 6 laterally averted to the left); and 12 targets (6 men and 6 women) had their eyes closed. The 3/4-face, direct condition was included to confirm that any effects observed were not driven by low-level properties of the images (e.g., symmetry, which holds only for direct gaze in full-face views; see George, Driver, & Dolan, 2001). The eyes-closed targets were included as an additional control condition because it is possible that laterally averted gaze may cue covert shifts in visual attention, which in turn may impair categorization performance (Driver et al., 1999; Hood et al., 1998). Presentation of the stimuli was randomized for each participant by computer software. On completion of the task, participants were debriefed, thanked for their participation, and dismissed.

Results and Discussion

The dependent measure of interest in this experiment was the mean time taken by participants to categorize the photo-graphs by gender. Given the presence of outlying responses in the data set, categorization times that were slower than 3 *SD*s from the mean were excluded from the analysis, as were trials in which participants categorized the targets incorrectly. This resulted in 3.2% of the data being excluded from the statistical analysis. Prior to the statistical analysis, a log transformation was performed on the data. For ease of interpretation, however, the nontransformed treatment means are reported in Table 1. Participants' mean gender-categorization times were submitted to a single-factor (eye gaze: full face, direct vs. 3/4 face, direct vs. averted vs. closed) repeated measures analysis of variance (ANOVA). This revealed an effect of eye gaze on categorization times, $F(3, 93) = 11.47, p < .0001$ (see Table 1 for treatment means). Post hoc Tukey tests confirmed that gender-categorization times were faster for targets with direct gaze (both 3/4 face and full face) than for either targets with laterally averted gaze or targets with their eyes closed (all $ps < .01$). No other differences were significant.

As expected, therefore, basic aspects of the person-construal process were moderated by the direction of eye gaze of to-be-categorized targets. Confirming the importance and informational value of mutual eye contact (Baron-Cohen, 1994, 1995; Perrett & Emery, 1994), gender-categorization times were fastest when targets were looking straight ahead. This effect was independent of the orientation of the face (i.e., 3/4 face or full face), thereby confirming that gaze direction was driving the observed effect (see also George et al., 2001).

Of course, identifying social objects is only one aspect of the person-construal process. Equally important is the task of accessing information about the social objects of interest (e.g., what do I know about the person?). After all, once this material has been generated, social interaction can be guided in an appropriate (e.g., purposive) manner (Bargh, 1999; Bodenhausen & Macrae, 1998; Macrae & Bodenhausen, 2000). The results of Experiment 1 suggest a possible route through which perceivers may gain enhanced access to category-related material in memory. Specifically, given the observed differences in gender-categorization times, it is possible that categorical knowledge may also be moderated by a person's direction of gaze. That is, just as category identification is facilitated for targets displaying direct eye gaze, so too associated categorical knowledge may be highly accessible for such targets. If this is indeed the case, then it should be possible to detect such an effect in a semantic priming task (Blair & Banaji, 1996; Macrae, Bodenhausen, & Milne, 1995; Macrae, Bodenhausen, Milne, Thorn, & Castelli, 1997). That is, priming effects should be most pronounced when category-related items follow the presentation of targets who are displaying nondeviated (i.e., direct) eye gaze. We investigated this prediction in our second experiment.

EXPERIMENT 2: EYE GAZE AND KNOWLEDGE ACCESSIBILITY

Method

Participants and design

Eighteen undergraduates (9 men, 9 women) participated in the experiment. The experiment had a 3 (eye gaze: direct vs. averted vs. closed) × 2 (item type: stereotypic vs. counterstereotypic) repeated measures design.

Procedure and stimulus materials

Participants arrived at the laboratory individually, were greeted by a female experimenter, and were seated facing the monitor of an Apple Macintosh G3 microcomputer. Written instructions explained that the experiment involved an investigation of the speed with which people could categorize letter strings as words. Participants were informed that, on the computer screen, they would see a series of letter strings (e.g., *jeep, dlab*). Their task was simply to decide, as quickly and accurately as possible, whether each letter string was a word or a nonword. Responses were made by pressing one of two appropriately labeled keys ("word" or "nonword"). In total, 72 letter strings (36 words and 36 nonwords) were used in the experiment. The target words were selected from those normed by Blair and Banaji (1996) and comprised 18 masculine (e.g., *jeep, cigars, rebellious*) and 18 feminine (e.g., *flowers, lingerie, passive*) items. The nonwords were rearranged (but pronounceable) versions of the target items. Participants were told that, prior to the presentation of each letter string, they would briefly see another item appear on the screen. It was emphasized, however, that these items were irrelevant to the task and should be ignored (in reality, of course, these items were the critical priming photographs).

Thirty-six photographs were used as priming stimuli in the experiment: 18 male faces and 18 female faces. Of these priming stimuli, 12 depicted targets (6 men and 6 women) displaying full-face, direct gaze; 12 depicted targets (6 men and 6 women) displaying laterally averted gaze (6 laterally averted to the left and 6 laterally averted to the right); and 12 depicted targets (6 men and 6 women) with their eyes closed. As the two direct-gaze conditions produced comparable effects in Experiment 1, only the full-face, direct targets were used in the second experiment. Each priming stimulus was followed by a stereotypic item, a counterstereotypic item, and a nonword, giving a total of 108 experimental trials. For all trials, the priming stimulus appeared for 150 ms, a blank screen was presented for 100 ms, and then the letter string appeared and remained on the screen until participants made a response (i.e., stimulus onset asynchrony = 250 ms). The intertrial interval was 2,000 ms. The computer recorded the accuracy and latency of each response. On completion of the task, participants were debriefed, thanked for their participation, and dismissed.

Results and Discussion

The dependent measure of interest in this experiment was the mean time taken by participants to classify the category-related letter strings as words. These data were trimmed and normalized using the procedures outlined in Experiment 1. In total, 2.6% of the trials were excluded from the statistical analysis. Prior to the statistical analysis, a log transformation was performed on the data. For ease of interpretation, however, the nontransformed treatment means are reported in Table 1.

Participants' mean lexical decision times were submitted to a 3 (eye gaze: direct vs. averted vs. closed) × 2 (item type: stereotypic vs. counterstereotypic) repeated measures ANOVA. This analysis revealed main effects of eye gaze, $F(2, 34) = 3.26$, $p < .05$, and item type, $F(1, 17) = 7.33$, $p < .02$, on participants' responses. As expected, however, these effects were qualified by an Eye Gaze × Item Type interaction, $F(2, 34) = 3.50$, $p < .04$ (see Table 1 for treatment means). Simple effects analysis confirmed an effect of eye gaze on participants' responses to the stereotypic items, $F(2, 34) = 4.90$, $p < .02$. Lexical decisions were faster when stereotypic items were preceded by targets with direct gaze than when they were preceded by either targets with laterally averted gaze or targets with their eyes closed (both ps < .05). In addition, responses were faster to stereotypic than counterstereotypic items when the priming stimuli were targets with direct gaze, $F(1, 17) = 11.40$, $p < .004$. Interestingly, this priming effect (i.e., faster responses to stereotypic than counterstereotypic items) was only marginally significant for targets with laterally averted gaze or targets with their eyes closed.

The time taken by participants to classify letter strings as nonwords was not affected by gaze direction, $F(2, 34) < 1$, n.s. (see Table 1), thereby confirming that direct eye gaze does not prompt a general enhancement in task performance. Instead, the effects of gaze direction were confined to the accessibility of categorical knowledge. This study extends the results of Experiment 1, showing that stereotypic knowledge as most accessible when targets were looking directly ahead. This finding is important as it demonstrates that the task of understanding other persons (i.e., accessing relevant material in semantic memory) is facilitated when mutual eye contact is established between the perceiver and target of interest.

GENERAL DISCUSSION

According to recent writings, the detection and interpretation of eye gaze plays a prominent role in both the development of social cognition and the smooth running of everyday social interaction (Baron-Cohen, 1994, 1995; Perrett & Emery, 1994). Understanding the language of eyes enables perceivers to attribute mental states to others, and hence describe their behavior using a rich variety of mentalistic terms (e.g., intentions, desires, hopes, plans; see Baron-Cohen 1995; Dennett, 1978). This turns out to be an important ability. As Dennett (1987) has argued, "we use folk psychology all the time, to explain and predict each other's behavior; we attribute beliefs and desires to each other with confidence—and quite unselfconsciously—and spend a substantial portion of our waking lives formulating the world—not excluding ourselves—in these terms" (p. 48). We suspected that people's sensitivity to eye gaze would also prompt the emergence of some important social-cognitive effects pertaining to the efficiency of the person-construal process. Our results corroborated this prediction. The speed with which targets were categorized according to their gender and the rate at which associated knowledge was extracted from semantic memory were shown to be contingent upon the target's direction of gaze. Specifically, person construal was facilitated when targets displayed direct eye gaze. This finding not only is of theoretical significance (Baron-Cohen, 1994, 1995; Perrett & Emery, 1994), but also has important practical implications for the dynamics of everyday social interaction. It is obviously beneficial if perceivers can respond to significant (i.e., relevant, salient) others as quickly and effectively as possible. Through enhancements in the efficiency of the person-construal process when mutual eye contact has been established between perceiver and target, this objective can clearly be attained.

Interestingly, recent neuroimaging research has investigated the neural mechanisms that underlie the detection of eye gaze (Kawashima et al., 1999). It has long been known that the amygdala plays an important role in the processing of emotional stimuli (Adolphs, Tranel, Damasio, & Damasio, 1994). For example, studies have demonstrated activation within the amygdala in response to overt (Adolphs et al., 1994) or masked (Morris, Öhman, & Dolan, 1998) emotionally expressive (i.e., angry) faces and in response to threatening or fear-provoking stimuli (LaBar, Gatenby, Gore, LeDoux, & Phelps, 1998). Similar effects have also been obtained when eye gaze is directed toward a person (Kawashima et al., 1999), suggesting that mutual eye contact induces a strong emotional response. This is perhaps to be expected if shared gaze signals the relevance or importance of another person in the environment (Baron-Cohen, 1995). It is possible, therefore, that the social-cognitive effects demonstrated in the present study may be mediated by differential amygdala activation as perceivers strive to understand the people who populate their social worlds. One task for future research will be to investigate this intriguing possibility.

By emphasizing the functional nature of categorical thinking, researchers have unraveled some of the more perplexing mysteries of the person-perception process (Macrae & Bodenhausen, 2000). As economizing mental devices (Macrae, Milne, & Bodenhausen, 1994), categorical knowledge structures confer order, meaning, and predictability to an otherwise chaotic social world. Notwithstanding the acknowledged benefits that accrue from a category-based conception of others, however, some unresolved issues remain. Notable among these is the question of when exactly perceivers activate categorical knowledge structures in their dealings with others. Is categorical thinking an inevitable aspect of the person-perception process, or is its occurrence regulated by a variety of cognitive and mo-

tivational factors (see Bargh, 1999; Macrae & Bodenhausen, 2000)? Rather than attempting to resolve this thorny debate, we considered a closely related issue in the present study: Are there factors that moderate the relative efficiency of person construal, such that targets are processed more rapidly (and effectively) under some circumstances than others? Our results confirmed that this is indeed the case, with eye gaze moderating the efficiency of the construal processes that furnish perceivers with categorical knowledge about others. This finding is theoretically noteworthy as it provides an initial demonstration of the important role that biological factors play in the regulation of social cognition. To gain a complete understanding of the dynamics of person construal, it may therefore be useful to consider the wider evolutionary context in which this process emerged.

Acknowledgments— The authors would like to thank Giff Weary, Bill von Hippel, Norman Freeman, Dave Turk, and an anonymous reviewer for their helpful comments on this work.

REFERENCES

Adolphs, R., Tranel, D., Damasio, H., & Damasio, A. (1994). Impaired recognition of emotion in facial expressions following bilateral damage to the human amygdala. *Nature, 372*, 669–672.

Allison, T., Puce, A., & McCarthy, G. (2000). Social perception from visual cues: Role of the STS region. *Trends in Cognitive Sciences, 4*, 267–278.

Allport, G. W. (1954). *The nature of prejudice.* Reading, MA: Addison-Wesley.

Argyle, M., & Cook, M. (1976). *Gaze and mutual gaze.* Cambridge, England: Cambridge University Press.

Bargh, J. A. (1999). The cognitive monster: The case against the controllability of automatic stereotype effects. In S. Chaiken & Y. Trope (Eds.), *Dual process theories in social psychology* (pp. 361–382). New York: Guilford.

Baron-Cohen, S. (1994). How to build a baby that reads minds: Cognitive mechanisms in mindreading. *Cahiers de Psychologie Cognitive, 13*, 513–552.

Baron-Cohen, S. (1995). *Mindblindness: An essay on autism and theory of mind.* Cambridge, MA: MIT Press.

Blair, I. V., & Banaji, M. R. (1996). Automatic and controlled processes in stereotype priming. *Journal of Personality and Social Psychology, 70*, 1142–1163.

Bodenhausen, G. V., & Macrae, C. N. (1998). Stereotype activation and inhibition. In R. S. Wyer, Jr. (Ed.), *Stereotype activation and inhibition: Advances in social cognition* (Vol. 11, pp. 1–52). Hillsdale, NJ: Erlbaum.

Brewer, M. B. (1988). A dual process model of impression formation. In R. S. Wyer, Jr., & T. K. Srull (Eds.), *Advances in social cognition* (Vol. 1, pp. 1–36). Hillsdale, NJ: Erlbaum.

Brothers, L. (1990). The social brain: A project for integrating primate behavior and neurophysiology in a new domain. *Concepts in Neuroscience, 1*, 27–51.

Bruce, C., Desimone, R., & Gross, C. (1981). Visual properties of neurones in a polysensory area in superior temporal sulcus of the macaque. *Journal of Neurophysiology, 46*, 369–384.

Dennett, D. (1978). *Brainstorms: Philosophical essays on mind and psychology.* London: Harvester.

Dennett, D. (1987). *The intentional stance.* Cambridge, MA: MIT Press.

Driver, J., Davis, G., Ricciardelli, P., Kidd, P., Maxwell, E., & Baron-Cohen, S. (1999). Gaze perception triggers visuospatial orienting. *Visual Cognition, 6*, 509–540.

Fiske, S. T., & Neuberg, S. L. (1990). A continuum model of impression formation from category based to individuating processes: Influences of information and motivation on attention and interpretation. In M. P. Zanna (Ed.), *Advances in experimental social psychology* (Vol. 3, pp. 1–74). San Diego, CA: Academic Press.

Friesen, C. K., & Kingstone, A. (1998). The eyes have it!: Reflexive orienting is triggered by nonpredictive gaze. *Psychonomic Bulletin & Review, 5,* 490–495.

George, N., Driver, J., & Dolan, R. J. (2001). Seen gaze-direction modulates fusiform activity and its coupling with other brain areas during face processing. *NeuroImage, 13,* 1102–1112.

Haxby, J. V., Hoffman, E. A., & Gobbini, M. I. (2000). The distributed human neural system for face perception. *Trends in Cognitive Sciences, 4,* 223–233.

Hinde, R. A., & Rowell, T. E. (1962). Communication by posture and facial expression in the rhesus monkey. *Proceedings of the Zoological Society of London, 138,* 1–21.

Hoffman, E. A., & Haxby, J. V. (2000). Distinct representations of eye gaze and identity in the distributed human neural system for face processing. *Nature Neuroscience, 3,* 80–84.

Hood, B. M., Willen, J. D., & Driver, J. (1998). Gaze perception triggers corresponding shifts of visual attention in young infants. *Psychological Science, 9,* 131–134.

Kawashima, R., Sugiura, M., Kato, T., Nakamura, A., Hatano, K., Ito, K., Fukuda, H., Kojima, S., & Nakamura, K. (1999). The human amygdala plays an important role in gaze monitoring: A PET study. *Brain, 122,* 779–783.

Kellerman, J., Lewis, J., & Laird, J. D. (1989). Looking and loving: The effects of mutual gaze on feelings of romantic love. *Journal of Research in Personality, 23,* 145–161.

Kleinke, C. L. (1986). Gaze and eye contact: A research review. *Psychological Review, 100,* 78–100.

LaBar, K. S., Gatenby, J. C., Gore, J. C., LeDoux, J. E., & Phelps, E. A. (1998). Human amygdala activation during conditioned fear acquisition and extinction: A mixed-trial fMRI study. *Neuron, 20,* 937–945.

Langton, S. R. H., Watt, R. J., & Bruce, V. (2000). Do the eyes have it? Cues to the direction of social attention. *Trends in Cognitive Sciences, 4,* 50–59.

Macrae, C. N., & Bodenhausen, G. V. (2000). Social cognition: Thinking categorically about others. *Annual Review of Psychology, 51,* 93–120.

Macrae, C. N., Bodenhausen, G. V., & Milne, A. B. (1995). The dissection of selection in person perception: Inhibitory processes in social stereotyping. *Journal of Personality and Social Psychology, 69.* 397–407.

Macrae, C. N., Bodenhausen, G. V., Milne, A. B., Thorn, T. M. J., & Castelli, L. (1997). On the activation of social stereotypes: The moderating role of processing objectives. *Journal of Experimental Social Psychology, 33,* 471–489.

Macrae, C. N., Milne, A. B., & Bodenhausen, G. V. (1994). Stereotypes as energy-saving devices: A peek inside the cognitive toolbox. *Journal of Personality and Social Psychology, 66,* 37–47.

Morris, J. S., Öhman, A., & Dolan, R. J. (1998). Conscious and unconscious emotional learning in the human amygdala. *Nature, 393,* 417–418.

Morton, J., & Johnson, M. (1991). CONSPEC and CONLEARN: A two-process theory of infant face recognition. *Psychological Review, 98,* 164–181.

Perrett, D., & Emery, N. J. (1994). Understanding the intentions of others from visual signals: Neuropsychological evidence. *Cahiers de Psychologie Cognitive, 13,* 683–694.

Perrett, D., Rolls, E., & Cann, W. (1982). Visual neurones responsive to faces in the monkey temporal cortex. *Experimental Brain Research, 47,* 329–342.

Perrett, D., Smith, P., Potter, D., Mistlin, A., Head, A., Milner, A., & Jeeves, M. (1985). Visual cells in the temporal cortex sensitive to face view and gaze direction. *Proceedings of the Royal Society of London B, 223,* 293–317.

Vecera, S., & Johnson, M. (1995). Gaze detection and the cortical processing of faces: Evidence from infants and adults. *Visual Cognition, 2,* 59–87.

von Grünau, M., & Anston, C. (1995). The detection of gaze direction: A stare-in-the-crowd effect. *Perception, 24,* 1297–1313.

(Received 5/23/01; Revision accepted 12/01)

C. Neil Macrae, *Dartmouth College*

Bruce M. Hood, *University of Bristol, Bristol, England*

Alan B. Milne, *University of Aberdeen, Aberdeen, Scotland*

Angela C. Rowe, *University of Bristol, Bristol, England*

Malia F. Mason, *Dartmouth College*

Address correspondence to Neil Macrae, Department of Psychological and Brain Sciences, Dartmouth College, Moore Hall, Hanover, NH 03755; e-mail: c.n.macrae@dartmouth.edu

Got time for Friends?

Sure, you're busy. But are you paying attention to what's really important?
Why finding—and keeping—friends is the key to a happy life.

BY ANDY STEINER

It's not the last time my daughter will make me look foolish, but it was one of the first. Maybe it was silly to take a toddler to an art opening, but there we were, the effervescent Astrid and her uptight mama. As I hovered near her, hoping to intercept toppling *objets d'art*, Astrid spotted Claire across the room.

Maybe their attraction was predestined, since Claire and Astrid, 18 and 16 months respectively, were the only under-three-footers in what to them must have looked like a sea of kneecaps. Still, Astrid's eyes lit up when she saw young Claire, and she turned on the charm, hopping and squealing and running in some strange kiddie ritual. Claire squealed back, Astrid flashed her tummy, and that was it: They were fast friends.

The culture-at-large tells us that once school is over or we hit 30, friendship ought to take a back-seat to more pressing concerns.

It wasn't so easy for Claire's mother and me. When our kids started making nice, we smiled politely, and as the junior friendship heated up, we attempted shy (on my part at least) and distracted attempts at conversation. "How old is she?" I asked. "What's her name?" she countered. I'd like to say that today Claire's mommy is a good friend, but that's not the case. We continued to exchange pleasantries while our daughters pranced around together, but when our partners appeared, we picked up our squirmy squirts and said good-bye. We haven't seen each other since. Too bad, because I could have used a new friend. Who couldn't?

In college, and for several years after, I was immersed in a warm circle of friends, the kind of exciting and exotic people I'd spent my small-town youth dreaming about. These friends came to my college from around the world, and after graduation, many of them stayed. We had a great time. We went to movies—and for a bit created our own monthly film group. We gathered at each other's apartments to cook big dinners and stay up late, sharing our opinions on music, sex, and dreams. We even took a few trips together—to a friend's wedding in the mountains of Colorado and to a cabin on the edge of a loon-covered lake. But time passes, and as these friends moved on, got married, or found great jobs, my gang of compatriots began to dwindle.

"We cannot tell the precise moment when friendship is formed. As in filling a vessel drop by drop, there is at last a drop which makes it run over; so in a series of kindnesses there is at last one which makes the heart run over."

Samuel Johnson

Now many of them have moved to other states—other countries, even. Though a precious core group still lives within shouting distance, I worry that grown-up life will soon scatter them all and I'll be left, lonely and missing them.

So it goes for many of us as we leave our youth behind and face "real" life. While generations of young adults have probably felt the same way, the yearning for close friends takes on a greater sense of urgency now as modern life makes our lives busier and more fragmented. "It's not that it's so hard to make friends when you're older," says sociologist Jan Yager, author of *Friendshifts*, "but making friends—and finding time to maintain and nurture old friendships as well as new ones—is just one of the many concerns that occupy your time."

155

Astrid's encounter with Claire (and my parallel one with her mother) cast a spotlight on one reality: Kids see potential friends everywhere. Adults, on the other hand, have a harder time of it, especially as we (and our potential friends) enter the realm of romantic commitments, full-time jobs, motherhood and fatherhood. While we may wish to add to our collection of friends, we feel too busy, too consumed by other obligations, too caught up in everyday bustle to make time to help a friendship blossom and grow.

"Be a friend to thyself, and others will befriend thee."

English proverb

And we may be following subtle clues from the culture-at-large telling us that, once school is over or we near 30, friendship ought to take a back seat to more pressing concerns. Despite the central role that idealized gangs of pals play on sitcoms, our primary sources of information—self-help books, magazines, and personal interest TV shows—rarely talk about how to get—or keep—friends. Instead they barrage us with detailed advice on how to attract a lover, get ahead in a career, rekindle a marriage, or keep peace in the family. Friendships, unlike these other kinds of relationships, are supposed to just happen, with little effort on your part. But what if they don't?

"Friends can get relegated to secondary status," says Aurora Sherman, assistant professor of psychology at Brandeis University. "Even if you don't have children or a partner or aging parents, the pressures of adult responsibility can force people to place friendship in the background."

"All I can do is to urge you to put friendship ahead of all other human concerns, for there is nothing so suited to man's nature, nothing that can mean so much to him, whether in good times or in bad... I am inclined to think that with the exception of wisdom, the gods have given nothing finer to men than this."

Marcus Tullius Cicero

Children's full-scale focus on friendship may have to do with more than just their carefree attitude about life. Sherman cites the research theorizing that kids' interest in making friends serves a larger developmental purpose.

"A young person's primary motivation for social interaction is to get information and to learn about the world," Sherman explains. "When you're a kid, practically everybody that you meet has the potential to help you learn about something that you didn't know." Grown-ups already know most things (or at least they think they do), so as you get older, you may feel less of a drive to make new friends.

So, if you're someone who embraces the goal of lifelong learning, it's important not to write off friendship as a thing of the past. Meeting new people is a lot less work than going back to college for another degree, and more fun, too. Want to learn yoga or steep yourself in South American culture? How about sharpening your skills as an entrepreneur or activist? Think outside the classroom by finding someone eager to show what they know. An added benefit is that you, too, can share your passion about knitting or bocce ball or radical history. If the people you currently hang out with don't know much about the things you want to know, maybe it's time to break into some new circles.

"The proper office of a friend is to side with you when you are in the wrong. Nearly anybody will side with you when you are in the right."

Mark Twain

The tangible rewards of friendship go far beyond exchanges of information. In 1970 Lenny Dee left New York and moved across the country to Portland, Oregon, where he knew barely a soul. "The first week I was there I met probably half the people who became my lifelong friends," says Dee. "It was like I walked through this magic door and a whole world opened up for me." Within a day of his arrival, he had moved into a house that was an epicenter of the city's alternative culture. He could barely step out of the house without running into one of his new friends.

"At one point in my life all of the people I knew were footloose and fancy free," Dee says, "but over the years that changed. A certain segment of my friends in Portland became more settled while I remained less settled. People got families and jobs, and they started disappearing. Now you have to make an appointment to get together."

Still, Dee has been vigilant in nurturing old friendships; people all across the country can count on a birthday phone call from Portland. "I have always thought you could invest your energies in making money or making friends," Dee says, "and they achieve much the same ends—security, new experiences, personal options, travel, and so forth. I have always found it more fulfilling to make friends."

And Dee's life has been shaped in many ways by the enduring connections he's maintained, including a key position at the start-up of a now successful educational software company and a recent vacation in Corsica at the summer home of an old Portland friend who now lives in Paris.

A slew of recent research supports Dee's example that friends make life complete.

"As hard as it is with everyone so busy and consumed with the day-to-day workings of their lives, it's important to understand that making and maintaining friendships is really pivotal to social, emotional, and physical well-being," says Yager. She ticks off research that touts the value of building strong nonfamilial bonds, including: an in-depth study of thousands of Northern California residents that revealed that having ties to at least one close friend extends a person's life, and another study of 257 human resource managers that discovered adults who have friends at work report not only higher productivity but also higher workplace satisfaction.

When you know who his friend is, you know who he is.
Senegal proverb

For New York psychotherapist Kathlyn Conway, a three-time cancer survivor and author of the memoir *An Ordinary Life*, friends provided an anchor during times when she felt her life was drifting off course.

"I had friends I could talk to at any time," Conway says of her 1993 battle with breast cancer. "If I was upset, it was easy for me to call someone and expect them to listen—no matter what."

And when the busy mother of two needed physical help, friends came to her aid. "One friend went to the hospital after my mastectomy and helped me wash my hair," Conway recalled in an article she wrote for the women's cancer magazine *Mamm*. "Another, who herself had had breast cancer, visited and stealthily, humorously, kindly opened her blouse to show me her implanted breast in order to reassure me. Yet another left her very busy job in the middle of the week to go shopping with me for a wig."

One time when adults tend to make new friends is during major life changes, like a move, a new job, or the birth of a child. Ellen Goodman and Patricia O'Brien, authors of *I Know Just What You Mean*, a book chronicling their quarter-century friendship, met in 1973 when both were completing Neiman fellowships at Harvard. At the time, Goodman, now a nationally syndicated newspaper columnist, and O'Brien, a novelist and former editorial writer for the *Chicago Sun-Times*, were both newly divorced mothers in their 30s.

"We were both broke and busy and we were not at all alike—at least on the surface," Goodman recalls, "but we bonded, maybe out of some sense of great urgency, and during that year we spent an enormous amount of time in Harvard Square, drinking coffee and talking. We missed a lot of classes, but those times together were some of the best seminars either of us ever attended."

"Life shifts—like a divorce or an illness or another unexpected change—can occur at any time, and when that happens, there's always this powerful draw to another person who's going through the same thing," O'Brien says. "For Ellen and me there was this wonderful opportunity to talk to another woman who was hitting the same bumps in the road as we were. We could talk for hours and always understand what the other person was saying." After the short spell at Harvard, they never again lived in the same place but kept the friendship going with letters, phone calls, and frequent visits.

Three is the magic number

When it comes to making friends, there's much we can learn from kids about flashing a wide grin and harboring a playful spirit. But Stanford University psychology professor Laura Carstensen emphasizes that an important lesson also comes from the over-65 set. In studying senior citizens' social networks, she has found that "it is the *quality* of their relationships that matters—not the *quantity*. In our work we find that three is the critical friend number. If you have three people in your life that you can really count on, then you are doing as well as someone who has 10 friends. Or 20, for that matter. If you have fewer than three friends, then you could be a little precarious."

So sit down, get out a piece of paper, and start listing your friends. Got three folks you're always excited about seeing and feel certain you can trust? Then put down the pencil. Who says you can't put a number on success?

—Andy Steiner

A while back—inspired by my daughter's happy, open face and ready giggle—I resolved that making new friends might be just the cure for the post-baby blahs I was experiencing.

So I set my sights on one particular woman. Even though I have wonderful old friends, people I wouldn't trade for a billion dollars, this particular woman caught my eye. She seemed smart and funny. We were both writers. I'd heard that she lived in my neighborhood. Then, the kicker: Someone we both knew suggested that we would hit it off. So I called her—out of the blue—and invited her to coffee. Sure, she said. So we met.

Just the other day, this woman told me that at the time she wondered about my motivation, this strange, nervously enthusiastic young woman who peppered her with questions about writing and reading and her impressions of the university we'd both attended, she as an undergraduate, I as a master's student. Still, a few weeks later she took me up on my invitation to go for a walk, and our conversation soon became natural and fun. Suddenly, she became my new friend.

Astrid, riding in her stroller, witnessed it all. Besides babbling and napping, she was watching closely as my new friend and I laughed and told the stories of our lives. Taking a risk and extending yourself is one way to form a bond with someone. We weren't squealing or flashing our tummies, but it was close.

Andy Steiner, mother of gregarious Astrid, is a senior editor of Utne Reader.

UNIT 10
Psychological Disorders

Unit Selections

32. **How We Get Labeled**, John Cloud
33. **The Power of Mood**, Michael D. Lemonick
34. **The Science of Anxiety**, Christine Gorman
35. **Post-Traumatic Stress Disorder**, Harvard Health Letter
36. **Deconstructing Schizophrenia**, Constance Holden

Key Points to Consider

- Do you know anyone with a mental illness? If yes, can you describe the symptoms experienced by the individual? How did this individual get diagnosed? Is the individual on medication or in therapy? Is the treatment working?

- Do you believe everyone has the potential for developing a mental disorder? Just how widespread is mental illness in the U.S.? What circumstances lead an individual to emotional problems? In general, what can be done to reduce the number of cases of mental disorder or to promote better mental health in the U.S.?

- Do you think that mental disorders are biologically or psychologically caused or both? If we discover that mental disorders are instigated by something physiological, do you think mental disorders will remain the purview of psychology? Why? What other professionals will need to be involved in diagnosis, treatment, and research?

- If mental disorders are biological, do you think they might be "contagious" (caused by disease and passed from person to person? Do you think that most mental disorders are brain disorders? Why did you answer this way? What do brain imaging studies show? How do you think treatments might differ depending on the origin of a mental disorder?

- What do you think of the way mental health professionals diagnose mental disorder? Do you really believe that each disorder has a distinct symptoms pattern? How could we diagnose someone who shows symptoms of multiple disorders? Do you think it is possible for someone to have more than one disorder at a time?

- What is depression? How widespread are depressive episodes? What causes depression? How are ordinary episodes of depression different from clinical depression? What biological causes are implicated in depression? Are there psychological causes for depression? What are some promising treatments for this disorder?

- What are anxiety disorders? What are specific anxiety disorders and their symptoms? What causes anxiety disorders? What role does the nervous system play in anxiety and anxiety disorders?

- What is schizophrenia? What are its symptoms? Can a person with schizophrenia appear "normal" at times? Does the schizophrenic brain look different from a normal brain? How so? What are the suspected causes of schizophrenia? What are the currently available treatments for schizophrenia?

- If you had to pick a disorder to "suffer" from, which one would you pick and why? Have you ever recognized in yourself some of the symptoms discussed in the book? Do you think you have any mental disorders? If you think you do, what will you do about it? If a friend came to you for advice about a common disorder, what advice would you offer?

 **Links: www.dushkin.com/online/**
These sites are annotated in the World Wide Web pages.

Jay and Harry were two brothers who owned a service station. They were the middle children of four. The other two children were sisters, the oldest of who had married and moved out of the family home. Their father who once owned the service station retired and turned it over to his sons.

Harry and Jay had a good working relationship. Harry was the "up-front" man, taking customer orders, accepting payments, and working with parts distributors. Harry dealt most directly with the public, delivery personnel, and other people accessing the station. Jay worked behind the scenes. While Harry made the mechanical diagnoses, Jay did the corrective work. Some of his friends thought Jay was a mechanical genius.

Preferring to spend time by himself, Jay had always been a little odd and a bit of a loner. Jay's friends thought his emotions had been more inappropriate and intense than other people's emotional states, but they passed it off as part of his eccentric genius. On the other hand, Harry was the stalwart in the family—the acknowledged leader and decision-maker when it came to family finances.

One day Jay did not show up for work on time. When he did, he was dressed in the most garish outfit and was laughing hysterically and talking to himself. Harry at first suspected that his brother had taken some illegal drugs. However, Jay's condition persisted and, in fact, worsened. Out of concern, his family took him to their physician who immediately sent Jay and his family to a psychiatrist. After several visits, the diagnosis was schizophrenia. Jay's maternal uncle had also been schizophrenic. The family grimly left the psychiatrist's office and traveled to the local pharmacy to fill a prescription for anti-psychotic medications. They knew that Jay would probably take this medicine the rest of his life.

What caused Jay's drastic and rather sudden change in mental health? Was Jay destined to be schizophrenic because of his family tree? Did competitiveness with his brother and the feeling that he was less revered than Harry cause Jay's decent into mental disorder? How can psychiatrists and clinical psychologists make accurate diagnoses? Once a diagnosis of mental disorder is made, can the individual ever completely recover?

These and other questions are the emphasis in this unit. Mental disorder has fascinated and, on the other hand, haunted us for centuries. At various times in our history those who suffered from these disorders were persecuted as witches, tortured to drive out demons, punished as sinners, jailed as a danger to society, confined to insane asylums, or at best hospitalized for simply being too ill to care for themselves.

Today, psychologists propose that the notion of mental disorders as "illnesses" has outlived its usefulness. We should think of mental disorders as either biochemical disturbances or disorders of learning in which the person develops a maladaptive pattern of behavior that is then maintained by the environment. At the same time, we need to recognize that these reactions to stressors in the environment or to the inappropriate learning situations may be genetically preordained; some people may be more susceptible to disorders than others. Serious disorders are serious problems and not just for the individual who is the patient or client. The impact of mental disorder on the family (just as for Jay's family) and friends also deserves our full attention. Diagnosis, symptoms, and the implications of the disorders are covered in some of the articles in this section. The following unit, will explore further the concept of treatment of mental disorders.

The first article in this unit offers a general introduction to the concept of mental disorder. In it, the strategies by which we get labeled or diagnosed with a mental disorder is explicated. The standard procedure, the commentary claims, is for doctors, psychiatrists, and psychologists to use *The Diagnostic and Statistical Manual* (DSM) to match a person's cluster of symptoms to the symptoms of a disorder so described in the DSM. There are many problems swirling around the use of this technique, and the author, John Cloud details some of them.

We turn next to some specific disorders. Depression is one of the most common forms of mental disorder. No scientist or diagnostician knows for sure from where depression comes—biochemistry, genes, or environment. Depression in its severe form can lead to suicide. In "The Power of Mood," the author looks at the causes, symptoms, and treatments for clinical depression.

Another common mental affliction is anxiety and fear. Anxiety disorders take several forms—such as panic attacks—that are addressed in the next article. The role of the nervous system in anxiety disorders is also revealed.

An increasingly common disorder is post-traumatic stress disorder. Some individuals are able to recover from terrorist attacks and traumatic automobile accidents; others are not. An article in the *Harvard Health Letter* explains why this is the case. It also helps the reader differentiate post-traumatic stress disorder from normal stress reactions. The article would be incomplete if it did not also include advice about how to cope with either type of stress—everyday or traumatic.

The final disorder covered in this unit is the one from which Jay suffered—schizophrenia. Constance Holden, in her article "Deconstructing Schizophrenia" examines the causes and treatments for this baffling and debilitating disorder.

How We Get Labeled

The first thing doctors do is open a curious book called the *DSM*. Here's what it says

By JOHN CLOUD

PARDON THE PERSONAL QUESTION, BUT HAVE YOU ever had a sexual fantasy involving the use of a nonliving object—Anna Kournikova's tennis outfit, say, or Tom Cruise's *Risky Business* skivvies? Actually, don't answer that—we really don't want to know—and you should probably think twice before telling your therapist. She might diagnose you with fetishism, which is listed along with schizophrenia and bipolar disorder in a curious but extremely influential book called the *Diagnostic and Statistical Manual of Mental Disorders*, or *DSM* for short.

The *DSM* lists the criteria used by mental-health professionals to make their various diagnoses, from "mild mental retardation" (the first listing) to "personality disorder not otherwise specified" (the last); there are more than 350 in all. Hence this 943-page doorstop is one of the most important books you've never heard of. And the inscrutable process of writing it is starting up again. The American Psychiatric Association (A.P.A.), the manual's publisher, recently began planning a giant review of the book. The new edition, the fifth—called *DSM V*—will appear around 2010. Evidently, it takes a long time to figure out all the ways America is nuts.

The first official attempt to measure the prevalence of mental illness in the U.S. came in 1840, when the Census included a question on "idiocy/insanity." From that single category flowered many more disorders, but each asylum classified them differently. The *DSM* was first published in 1952 so that "stress reaction" would mean the same in an Arkansas hospital as it does in a Vermont one.

The *DSM* works like this: imagine you are Tony Soprano in the first season of *The Sopranos*. You have, in *DSM*-ese, "recurrent, unexpected panic attacks." You also have "persistent concern about having additional attacks," and you fear you're "losing control, having a heart attack, 'going crazy.'" You aren't on drugs (other than all those bottles of Vesuvio's wine), so—presto—Dr. Melfi gives you a diagnosis of panic disorder, *DSM* No. 300.01. By the way, if you truly think you are Tony Soprano, see No. 295, schizophrenia.

Of course, in the real world, psychiatric diagnosis doesn't—or at least shouldn't—work like a checklist at a sushi counter.

Many of the items that appear as diagnostic criteria in the *DSM* are sometimes symptoms of a disorder and sometimes signs of perfectly normal behavior. An adolescent who "often argues with adults" may have an unusual condition called "oppositional defiant disorder" or a more common condition called "being 14 years old." The *DSM* includes a cautionary statement saying it takes clinical training to tell the difference. But many nonspecialists use the book too: insurers open the *DSM* when disputes arise over the proper course of treatment for particular conditions. (If your treatment doesn't jibe with the *DSM*, you may not get reimbursed.) *DSM* diagnoses can be used by courts to lock you in a mental hospital or by schools to place your child in special-education classes. A *DSM* label can become a stigma.

All of which raises a pressing question: What actually goes into defining a disorder? A.P.A. officials take this question seriously, and they understand the high stakes of a *DSM* diagnosis. That's one reason they so often revise the book to keep it current with the latest research. (Three editions have been published since 1986.) According to Dr. Darrel Regier, chief of A.P.A. research, roughly 1,000 mental-health professionals will help produce *DSM V*. The A.P.A. will host at least a dozen conferences, review unending piles of literature and conduct new studies to see whether proposed changes would work in clinical settings.

But like the conditions it helps diagnose, the *DSM* is more than the sum of its symptoms. As the American storehouse of insanity—the dictionary of everything we consider mentally unbalanced—it's a window into the national psyche. And so it bears close reading, and close questioning, by those outside the psychiatric establishment. Why is caffeine intoxication included as a disorder when sex addiction isn't? Why is pathological gambling apparently crazy when compulsive shopping isn't?

More important, can even a thousand Ph.D.s gathered at a dozen conferences ever really know the significance of such vague symptoms as "fatigue," "low self-esteem" and "feelings of hopelessness"? (You need only two of those, along with a couple of friends telling the doctor you seem depressed, to be a good candidate for something called dysthymic disorder.) Though it's fashionable these days to think of psychiatry as just

CHANGING DIAGNOSES

WHAT'S IN
Post-Traumatic Stress Disorder
Vietnam veterans helped persuade the A.P.A. to add it to the third edition, published in 1980

WHAT'S OUT
Homosexuality
Under pressure from gay activists, A.P.A. leaders decided to remove it. Rank-and-file members affirmed its ouster in a 1974 vote

WHAT'S IN
Attention-Deficit/Hyperactivity Disorder
Appeared in 1987 after some questioned ther validity of a previous diagnosis, Attention-Deficit Disorder

WHAT'S OUT
Identity Disorder
Once used to describe teens' questioning of goals and friendships; the A.P.A. decided in 1994 that these questions are normal

another arm of medicine, there is no biological test for any of these disorders. While imaging techniques have shown abnormalities in the brain of some people with schizophrenia, no scan can diagnose even that severe condition, let alone something opaque like "histrionic personality disorder." (For which the *DSM* lists the following as a sign: "consistently uses physical appearance to draw attention to self." So I'm sick if I exchange my Aunt Thelma's drab sweaters for flashier ones every Christmas?)

If the *DSM* is all we've got, why is it inherently flawed? Because many forces besides science shape it, including politics, fashion and tradition. The A.P.A. actually once held a vote among its members to see whether an alleged disorder—homosexuality—existed. (In 1974, being gay was deemed sane by a vote of 5,854 to 3,810.) Women's groups helped excise "self-defeating personality disorder" from the book. The revised third edition, in 1987, said the typical sufferer "chooses people and situations that lead to disappointment, failure, or mistreatment even when better options are clearly available." But feminists successfully argued that battered women could unfairly fit this category.

Other questionable diagnoses stay in the book because no one fights hard enough to remove them. Thus heterosexual men can be diagnosed with a supposed disorder called "transvestic fetishism" if they meet only two criteria: they have sexual fantasies about cross-dressing, and those fantasies cause "impairment in social, occupational, or other important areas." In other words, someone is sick not if he has the fantasies but if he *gets caught* having them—for instance, if his boss reads a kinky e-mail he sent at work, which then leads to a pink slip ("occupational impairment").

"For some of these, there is an issue of grandfathering," admits Dr. Michael First, editor of *DSM IV*. "The onus is on the person who wants to change it to prove that we should do so." First also acknowledges that the A.P.A. does not subject every criterion to rigorous scientific testing, "for practical reasons of continuity." Which may be another way of saying some old-timers still bill sessions for "transvestic fetishists," and they don't want to lose the *DSM* stamp of approval needed for insurance reimbursement.

To be sure, a few disorders are dropped from each edition. First notes that a supposed childhood condition called identity disorder was excluded from *DSM IV* even though many child psychologists wanted to keep it. Kids could qualify for that disorder if they were "uncertain" about long-term goals, career choice and friendship patterns. We said, "Wait a minute. This looks like normal adolescence," says First, "and so we eliminated it."

The *DSM*'s critics say this sit-around-the-table-and-jawbone method isn't really science. Jerome Wakefield, a Rutgers professor of social work, says that while the *DSM*'s authors do try to eliminate errors so that normal emotional reactions aren't diagnosed as disorders, "there's no systematic process here. Changes are made on a very ad hoc basis, where people say, 'Oh, my god, we forgot X.'" Others have even harsher criticism. Dr. Paul McHugh, who chairs the department of psychiatry and behavioral sciences at Johns Hopkins University School of Medicine, says the DSM has lost its usefulness partly because it has "permitted groups of "experts' with a bias to propose the existence of conditions without anything more than a definition and a checklist of symptoms. This is just how witches used to be identified." He cites multiple-personality disorder as an example of an "imagined diagnosis"; while much of the evidence supporting its existence has been debunked, multiple-personality disorder is still listed in the DSM, though today it's called "dissociative identity disorder."

New controversies have already erupted over what to put in *DSM V*. For instance, the A.P.A. is considering adding "relational disorders"—severe problems between spouses or siblings—to the fifth edition. Relational-disorder sufferers are completely sane except when they are around, say, their spouse. Skeptics contend that marital spats shouldn't be considered mental illnesses. A group of Stanford researchers wants to put "compulsive shopping disorder" into *DSM V*, but First doesn't seem to like the idea. While a number of studies have shown that pathological gambling exists and can be measured, he says, compulsive shopping "has received virtually no research attention to date." (The same goes for sex addiction, according to other psychiatrists: it's just Clinton-era pop psychology thus far, not a documentable illness.)

How could the *DSM* be improved? Critics say the A.P.A. should start by holding every diagnosis to tough scientific standards. Antiquated notions about deviant sexuality should be brought up to date or scrapped altogether. McHugh of Johns Hopkins suggests that the *DSM* become more than a laundry list of symptoms—some of which are always going to be ambiguous—by organizing psychiatric conditions around what he calls their "fundamental natures." Accordingly, he would use four categories of disorders: those arising from brain disease, those arising from problems controlling one's drive, those arising from problematic personal dispositions and those arising from life circumstances. While such groupings are imperfect— is alcoholism caused by a brain disease or a problem in controlling one's drive, or a little of both?—they at least get clinicians focused not only on the symptoms of an illness but on its possible causes as well.

In the end, though, the *DSM* can't achieve certainty because psychiatry can't. Unless brain researchers discover exactly how neurological mechanisms become abnormal, the *DSM* will always include more hypotheses than answers. Which means all those guys fantasizing about tennis outfits are probably just weird, not certifiable.

The Power of Mood

Lifting your spirits can be potent medicine. How to make it work for you

By Michael D. Lemonick

BILL VALVO COULD SENSE THAT SOMETHING WAS GOING VERY wrong with his health. He had worked for a software-development company in Fairfax, Va., for 10 years following a 22-year hitch with the Air Force, and the pressure was finally too much. "I left to start my own business," says Valvo, now 55, "but I could feel that all the stress was having physiological effects." Sure enough, he was diagnosed with coronary-artery disease and underwent bypass surgery in 1999. But after the operation, he spiraled into a severe depression, which would recede and then return with renewed force. Finally, Valvo's physician put him on an antidepressant—which not only relieved the depression but also made him a convert to a new way of thinking about illness and health. "Did my heart operation cause the depression I'm experiencing?" he wrote recently in an article for a newsletter for a chapter of Mended Hearts, a support group for heart patients and their families. "Does depression cause heart disease? The answer to both those questions is probably yes."

A few years ago, doctors would have dismissed Valvo as a New Age crank. But these days he is solidly in the medical mainstream.

More and more doctors—and patients—recognize that mental states and physical well-being are intimately connected. An unhealthy body can lead to an unhealthy mind, and an illness of the mind can trigger or worsen diseases in the body. Fixing a problem in one place, moreover, can often help the other.

The brain, after all, is only another organ, and it operates on the same biochemical principles as the thyroid or the spleen. What we experience as feelings, good or bad, are at the cellular level no more than a complex interaction of chemicals and electrical activity. Depression represents an imbalance in that interaction, one that can kill just as directly as more obviously physical ailments. Each year in the U.S., an estimated 30,000 people commit suicide, with the vast majority of cases attributable to depression. But depression's physical toll goes far beyond the number of people who take their own life and even beyond the impact on depressed people's relationships and productivity (which costs the U.S. economy some $50 billion a year).

The pathology of depression shows with especial clarity that mind and body aren't separate at all; they are part of a single system. In the case of depression, this interconnectedness takes the insidious form of making other serious diseases dramatically worse. Once you have had a heart attack,

---

CLINICAL DEPRESSION

Symptoms
Sadness, sleep problems, suicidal feelings, inability to feel pleasure

Treatment
Antidepressant medications, electroshock, psychotherapy, stress reduction

Prognosis
Tends to come and go in cycles. Properly treated, can be controlled

May affect

20

million in U.S.

---

for example, your risk of dying from cardiovascular disease is four to six times greater if you also suffer from depression.

It's not just that people tend to be depressed because they have a life-threatening illness or that depressed people smoke, are too lethargic to take their medicine or aren't motivated to eat right or exercise. "Even when we take those factors into consideration," says Dr. Dwight Evans, a professor of psychiatry, medicine and neuroscience at the University of Pennsylvania, "depression jumps out as an independent risk factor for heart disease. It may be as bad as cholesterol."

Heart disease is one of a long list of illnesses that worsen with depression. People with such afflictions as cancer, diabetes, epilepsy and osteoporosis all appear to run a higher risk of disability or premature death when they are clinically depressed. The effect is potentially so significant that the medical profession has begun to focus serious attention and resources on trying to understand what's going on. At a national conference in Washington in November, Evans served as co-chairman of a meeting, sponsored by the nonprofit Depression and Bipolar Support Alliance (DBSA), to get a better handle on how widespread the problem is. For two days, experts in cancer, aids, heart disease, diabetes and other diseases, along with patient advocates, listened to the evidence linking depression with one illness after another.

WHAT YOU CAN DO

We've come a long way from Freud's couch. The big breakthrough arrived in the late 1980s with the advent of safer and more widely effective drugs, like Prozax. According to Dr. Bruce Cohen of Harvard's McLean Hospital, we're on the cusp of a new era in treatment as the search for a single magic pill for depression gives way to a broad spectrum of therapies.

DRUGS

TODAY'S TREATMENTS

- Most antidepressants work by tweaking levels of various neurotransmitters, the chemicals that carry signals, from one neuron to another. Prozax, Paxil, Zoloft and the other SSRIs slow the absorption of serotonin. Effective antidepressants that act on both serotonin and norepinephrine include Effexor and Remeron. Drugs like Wellbutrin work in similar way but probably on the neurotransmitters norepinephrine and dopmaine. The tricyclic antidepressants (such as Elavil and Tofranil) also blocked the absorption of neurotransmitters, especially norepinephrine, but the drugs had significant side effects. Another class of first-generation drugs, the monoamine oxidase inhibitors (MAOIs) such as Nardil and Marplan, can be effective but can also produce dangerous side effects. A transdermal patch just approved by the Food and Drug Administration will give new life to MAOIs by reducing the side effects they sometimes caused when taken orally.

ON THE HORIZON

- Researchers are exploring two related molecules, gaba and glutamate, that are responsible for 90% of chemical signaling in the brain. Because they control so much of the brain's activity, the trick is to fine-tune their levels in ways that relieve depression but don't effect other brain functions. Other targets of drug development: the sex hormone testosterone (a transdermal patch proved effective in recent clinical trial for men); the stress horome cortisol, which researchers are trying to regulate with the abortion drug RU 486 and compounds called CRF antagonists; the dynorphins (the evil twins of feel-good endorphins); and a chemical called substance P, involved in pain pathways closely related to depression.

ELECTRICAL AND MAGNETIC

TODAY'S TREATMENTS

- Electroshock therapy, despite its unsavory reputation, is actually quite effective, especially for patients who don't respond to drugs and seniors for whom drug interactions pose problems. The treatment today uses a small current to trigger a mild seizure—a rhythmic firing of neurons—that can push a depressed brain out of its rut.

ON THE HORIZON

- Researchers are exploring a similar technique that sends an electrical current through the vagus nerve—a major conduit wiring the heart and intestines—which then delivers it to the brain. Another approach, called regional transcranial magnetic stimulation, uses an electric coil shaped like a figure eight to create a magnetic field inside the prefrontal cortex, which plays a key role in mood regulation.

TALKING CURES

TODAY'S TREATMENTS

- Most research today is focused on the physiology of depression, yet clinicians find that approaches combining medical and psychological treatments are still the most effective. Freud's techniques have been adapted and streamlined, but analysts still try to get patients to probe the unconscious roots of their problems.
- Newer techniques like cognitive therapy, by contrast, teach patients to recognize destructive patterns in their lives and develop practical steps for changing bad mental habits.

ON THE HORIZON

- Meditation, mindfulness training and biofeedback have long been championed as proven stress relievers. Now proponents believe these techniques may also provide relief to people with depression by lowering levels of cortisol.

ALTERNATIVE THERAPIES

TODAY'S TREATMENTS

- More patients today help themselves to over-the-counter aids, from St. John's wort to ginkgo biloba and biloba and soybean extracts. But herbs, like prescription drugs, can have side effects, and researchers are investigating their efficacy. The popular supplement DHEA, for example, has been linked to an increased risk of cancer.

THE HORIZON

- Omega-3 fatty acids (in fish oils) are good for the heart and also may be good for the brain by promoting the health of nerve-cell membranes. Studies are under way.

—*By David Bjerklie*

Fortunately, scientists have made great strides in sorting out the underlying causes of depression: it is almost certainly a defect in some combination of key genes, plus the right triggering environment. And researchers are well along in developing some promising therapies, pharmacological and otherwise, to supplement what is already available. But while the disease-depression connection is becoming more and more clear, how to uncouple them is an uncharted process. "You would think that treatment would alter the negative relationship between depression and other illness," says Dr. Dennis Charney, head of mood- and anxiety-disorders research at the National Institute of Mental Health (NIMH). But, he adds with proper scientific caution, "we don't have proof of that yet."

The idea that treating depression might lessen the severity of other diseases, though, makes basic biochemical sense. Everyday experience makes it clear that brain chemistry governs more than just the emotions. When your mind

HOW STRESS TAKES ITS TOLL

Like its more severe cousin depression, ordinary stress is harmful to the body as well as the mind. Stress comes in two forms, each with its own biochemistry

ACUTE

A response to imminent danger, it turbocharges the system with powerful hormones that can damage the cardiovascular system

CHRONIC

Caused by constant emotional pressure the victim can't control, it produces hormones that can weaken the immune system and damage bones

1 A stress response starts in the brain ...

When the brain detects a threat, a number of structures, including the hypothalamus, amygdala and pituitary gland, go on alert: they exchange information with each other and then send signaling hormones and nerve impulses to the rest of the body to prepare for fight or flight

2 ... and the body unleashes a flood of hormones ...

Adrenal glands react to the alert by releasing epinephrine (adrenaline), which makes the heart pump faster and the lungs work harder to flood the body with oxygen

The Adrenal glands also release extra cortisol and other glucocorticoids, which help the body convert sugars into energy

Nerve cells release norepinephrine, which tenses the muscles and sharpens the senses to prepare for action. Digestion shuts down

3 ... that can cause significant damage

When the threat passes, epinephrine and norepinephrine levels drop, but if danger comes too often they can damage arteries. Chronic low-level stress keeps the glucocorticoids in circulation, leading to a weakened immune system, loss of bone mass, suppression of the reproductive system and memory problems

—Text by Michael Lemonick

---

feels terror, the resulting surge of adrenaline makes your stomach churn. When your mind is sexually aroused, the body responds in unmistakable fashion. The effect is even more direct with the 60 or so chemicals known as neurotransmitters, which signal one cell that its neighbor has just sparked and that it should pass along the message. Brain chemicals such as serotonin circulate everywhere, not only in the brain. "Depression really is a systemic disorder," says Evans, "and many of the neurotransmitters that we believe are involved in the pathophysiology of depression have effects throughout the body."

Precisely how these powerful chemicals affect the course of heart disease, cancer and other illnesses isn't well understood yet, but preliminary research has yielded some tantalizing clues. When serotonin circulates in the bloodstream, for example, it appears to make platelets less sticky and thus less likely to clump together in artery-blocking blood clots. For years, heart-attack survivors have been advised to take a children's aspirin daily for clot prevention;

such drugs as Prozac, which keep serotonin in circulation, seem to have a similar effect.

Another mechanism may also be at work. It turns out that the heartbeat of a person with depression is unusually steady. That's not necessarily a good thing, says Charney, who co-chaired the DBSA conference. "Ideally, your heart rate should be variable—it means your heart can respond appropriately to the different tasks it's called upon to respond to." Yet another possible link between heart disease and depression is a chemical called C-reactive protein (CRP). The liver normally produces CRP in response to an immune-system alarm when the body is infected or injured, and CRP is associated with the inflammation that results. For reasons still unknown, though, a recent study of depressed individuals found elevated levels of CRP. And in patients whose arteries have been damaged by the buildup of cholesterol plaques, heightened inflammation may increase the chance that a bit of plaque will break off and shut down an artery.

Diabetes is another illness that doesn't go well with depression. It's well known that 10% of diabetic men and 20% of diabetic women also have depression—about twice the rate in the general population. It's natural to be depressed about having a chronic, potentially fatal illness, but that doesn't entirely explain the discrepancy. Moreover, depressed diabetics are much more likely than those without depression to suffer complications including heart disease, nerve damage and blindness. Somehow depression makes the body less responsive to insulin, the hormone that processes blood sugar—plausibly through the action of cortisol, a hormone that can interfere with insulin sensitivity and that is often elevated in depressed patients.

Cortisol may also make depressed patients more prone to osteoporosis. Studies by Dr. Philip Gold and Dr. Giovanni Cizza at the NIMH have shown that premenopausal women who are depressed have a much higher rate of bone loss than their nondepressed counterparts—and this disparity increases as women pass through menopause. Indeed, Cizza estimates that some 350,000 women get osteoporosis each year because of depression. Cortisol appears to interfere with the ability of the bones to absorb calcium and offset the natural calcium loss that comes with menopause and aging. Another class of chemicals, the pro-inflammatory cytokines, have also been implicated in osteoporosis and diabetes, but their role is less clear.

Studies have established links between the incidence of depression and several other diseases, including cancer, Parkinson's disease, epilepsy, stroke and Alzheimer's. In some cases at least, researchers have clues, if not definitive evidence, as to which molecules might be involved. In Parkinson's, the problem is the death of cells in the brain that produce the neurotransmitter dopamine. While dopamine is crucial to the control of movement, it's probably a major factor in mood as well. "Depression almost certainly has multiple causes that produce similar symptoms," observes Dr. Bruce Cohen, president of McLean Hospital in Belmont, Mass.

That could explain why drugs that improve serotonin chemistry don't always work on depression—and why Parkinson's and depression can feed on each another. Epilepsy, stroke and Alzheimer's, which, like Parkinson's, involve physical alteration of the brain, probably also affect

EVOLUTION'S ROLE

A Frazzled Mind, a Weakened Body

A major mental illness like clinical depression will send biochemical shock waves through the body. But the intimate relationship of body to mind isn't limited to serious disease. Researchers have come to understand that what lies below the neck can also be harmed by less acute kinds of brain disturbances. The chronic stress that millions of people feel from simply trying to deal with the pressures of modern life can unleash a flood of hormones that are useful in the short term but subtly toxic if they persist. Thus it shouldn't come as a surprise that stress-reduction strategies that take pressure off the mind—meditation, yoga, relaxation exercises and such—can take the heat off the body as well.

Humanity's physical reaction to stress, known as the "fight-or-flight" response, probably evolved to help our primitive ancestors deal with a treacherous world. When confronted with imminent danger—a sabertoothed tiger, say, or a club-wielding enemy Homoerectus—the body had to be instantly ready either to defend itself or to run like hell.

So the terrified brain would signal the adrenal glands, located on top of the kidneys, to release hormones, including adrenaline (its more technical name: epinephrine) and glucocorticoids, and the nerve cells to release norepinephrine. These powerful chemicals made the senses sharper, the muscles tighter, the heart pound faster, the bloodstream fill with sugars for ready energy. Then, when the danger passed, the response would turn off.

In the modern world, stress usually takes other forms. But the fight-or-flight response hasn't changed. Sometimes it's still useful: a demanding job can lead to a sense of pride; a bout of precurtain jitters can motivate a spectacular performance. But many modern stresses are continuing, not acute, and arise in situations we can neither fight nor flee: an unreasonable boss, a harrowing commute, a stormy relationship, a plummeting stock market, a general sense that life is out of control.

While some stress hormones can't stay elevated indefinitely, glucocorticoids can and do. Cortisol in particular can weaken the immune system, potentially making cancer and infectious diseases worse. Measuring the influence of stress, though, is tough. Some studies have shown no effect at all. Others offer intriguing clues. Dr. David Spiegel, director of Stanford's Psychosocial Treatment Laboratory, cites a study of psoriasis patients in which half practiced meditation and half didn't; the first group healed faster. Other studies show that patients who are part of a rich social network have lower cortisol levels than loners, that people who pray regularly tend to live longer and that breast-cancer patients who have an optimistic attitude or an ability to express anger about their disease tend to live somewhat longer than those who don't.

Such positive results are encouraging, but they carry risks. Patients might blame themselves for not meditating hard enough, say, if they don't improve. And in the face of serious illness, stress reduction is likely to produce only minor effects compared with conventional medical treatment. But if meditation, prayer, exercise or relaxation techniques take even a little pressure off the immune system, that could add up over decades to a significantly healthier life.

—By Michael D. Lemonick

that organ's ability to make or process neurotransmitters—not only serotonin and dopamine but also glutamate and norepinephrine, all of which may be involved in different forms of depression.

Most treatments for depression aim to restore the electrochemical imbalance that leads a depressed brain into warped thinking. The so-called tricyclic antidepressant drugs popular in the 1960s, for example, boosted the activity of the neurotransmitters serotonin and norepinephrine, and two other neurotransmitters, active throughout the body. That often relieved depression but caused side effects, including overwhelming sleepiness, blurred vision and dizziness. The drugs also proved potentially lethal when taken in overdose.

Then in the 1970s, neuropharmacologists realized that they could minimize side effects by focusing just on serotonin. Antidepressant drugs like Prozac, Paxil and Zoloft, known as selective serotonin reuptake inhibitors, or SSRIs, were developed to keep serotonin from being reabsorbed quickly into nerve cells when it is produced.

Meanwhile, electroconvulsive therapy (ECT), better known as shock treatment, resets the electrical state of the brain by inducing a seizure. (Despite ECT's lurid reputation, it involves mild doses of current and can be almost miraculously successful in patients whose depression will not yield to drugs.) Even old-fashioned, low-tech talk therapy can help adjust a patient's brain chemistry and lessen the severity of depression, especially in conjunction with other treatments.

Unfortunately, the research that may unravel the interplay between depression and other diseases has barely begun. Even though there is a strong statistical link between depression and epilepsy, for example, we know very little about how to treat depression in epileptics. And as Charney has noted, it hasn't been proved, in a rigorous, scientific sense, that treating depression will reduce the excess risks of complication or death from a coexisting illness.

But if depression treatments rebalance the biochemistry that worsens disease, there is every reason to expect that they will reduce its deadly impact. So Charney, Evans and other experts want to make physicians more aware of the intimate connection between depression and other illnesses. "When you only have roughly eight minutes with your primary doctor," says Lydia Lewis, president of the Depression and Bipolar Support Alliance, "it's kind of hard to get into the realm of depression. And when you go to see a specialist, the cardiologist is thinking just about your heart."

So while researchers hold conferences, do studies and write scholarly papers, Lewis has some more immediate advice for patients. "We need to get people to go in and ask these questions of their physicians. Bill Valvo could not agree more. "I think people are totally unaware of what's going on," he says, "and I'm convinced that education is a key part of what we need to be doing." The essence of that education: cure the mind, and you might just help save the body.

THE SCIENCE OF ANXIETY

WHY DO WE WORRY OURSELVES SICK? BECAUSE THE BRAIN IS HARDWIRED FOR FEAR, AND SOMETIMES IT SHORT-CIRCUITS

By CHRISTINE GORMAN

IT'S 4 A.M., AND YOU'RE WIDE AWAKE—PALMS SWEATY, HEART racing. You're worried about your kids. Your aging parents. Your 401(k). Your health. Your sex life. Breathing evenly beside you, your spouse is oblivious. Doesn't he—or she—see the dangers that lurk in every shadow? He must not. Otherwise, how could he, with all that's going on in the world, have talked so calmly at dinner last night about flying to Florida for a vacation?

How is it that two people facing the same circumstances can react so differently? Why are some folks buffeted by the vicissitudes of life while others glide through them with grace and calm? Are some of us just born more nervous than others? And if you're one of them, is there anything you can do about it?

The key to these questions is the emotional response we call anxiety. Unlike hunger or thirst, which build and dissipate in the immediate present, anxiety is the sort of feeling that sneaks up on you from the day after tomorrow. It's supposed to keep you from feeling too safe. Without it, few of us would survive.

All animals, especially the small, scurrying kind, appear to feel anxiety. Humans have felt it since the days they shared the planet with saber-toothed tigers. (Notice which species is still around to tell the tale.) But we live in a particularly anxious age. The initial shock of Sept. 11 has worn off, and the fear has lifted, but millions of Americans continue to share a kind of generalized mass anxiety. A recent TIME/CNN poll found that eight months after the event, nearly two-thirds of Americans think about the terror attacks at least several times a week. And it doesn't take much for all the old fears to come rushing back. What was surprising about the recent drumbeat of terror warnings was how quickly it triggered the anxiety so many of us thought we had put behind us.

This is one of the mysteries of anxiety. While it is a normal response to physical danger—and can be a useful tool for focusing the mind when there's a deadline looming—anxiety becomes a problem when it persists too long beyond the immediate threat. Sometimes there's an obvious cause, as with the shell-shocked soldiers of World War I or the terror-scarred civilians of the World Trade Center collapse. Other times, we don't know why we can't stop worrying.

GLOSSARY

STRESS Any external stimulus, from threatening words to the sound of a gunshot, that the brain interprets as dangerous

FEAR The short-term physiological response produced by both the brain and the body in response to stress

ANXIETY A sense of apprehension that shares many of the same symptoms as fear but builds more slowly and lingers longer

DEPRESSION Prolonged sadness that results in a blunting of emotions and a sense of futility; often more serious when accompanied by anxiety disorder

There is certainly a lot of anxiety going around. Anxiety disorder—which is what health experts call any anxiety that persists to the point that it interferes with one's life—is the most common mental illness in the U.S. In its various forms, ranging from very specific phobias to generalized anxiety disorder, it afflicts 19 million Americans (*see* "Are You Too Anxious?").

And yet, according to a survey published last January by researchers from UCLA, less than 25% of Americans with anxiety disorders receive any kind of treatment for their condition. "If mental health is the stepchild of the health-care system," says Jerilyn Ross, president of the Anxiety Disorders Association of America, "then anxiety is the stepchild of the stepchild."

Sigmund Freud was fascinated with anxiety and recognized early on that there is more than one kind. He identified two major forms of anxiety: one more biological in nature and the other more dependent on psychological factors. Unfortunately, his followers were so obsessed with his ideas about sex drives and unresolved conflicts that studies of the physical basis of anxiety languished.

In recent years, however, researchers have made significant progress in nailing down the underlying science of anxiety. In just the past decade, they have come to appreciate that whatever the factors that trigger anxiety, it grows out of a response that is hardwired in our brains. They have learned, among other things:

ARE YOU TOO ANXIOUS?

Everybody feels a bit of anxiety from time to time, but a clinical anxiety disorder is a different matter. If you suspect you may be suffering from one, you should consult a professional for a diagnosis. The psychological diagnostic manual lists 12 anxiety conditions. Here are the signs of five of the most common ones:

PANIC DISORDER

WHAT IT IS: Recurrent, unexpected attacks of acute anxiety, peaking within 10 minutes. Such panic may occur in a familiar situation, such as a crowded elevator

WHAT IT ISN'T: Occasional episodes of extreme anxiety in response to a real threat

WHAT TO LOOK FOR: Palpitations; chest pains, sweating, chills or hot flushes; trembling; shortness of breath or choking; nausea; light-headedness or feeling of unreality; fear of losing control or dying

BOTTOM LINE: Four or more of these symptoms in at least two discrete episodes could spell trouble

SPECIFIC PHOBIA

WHAT IT IS: Consuming fear of a specific object or situation, often accompanied by extreme anxiety symptoms

WHAT IT ISN'T: Powerful aversion to certain places or things

WHAT TO LOOK FOR:
- Do you come up with elaborate ways to avoid the object or situation?
- Do you dread the next possible encounter?
- Are you aware that the fear is excessive but you are unable to control it?
- Does merely thinking about the thing you fear make you anxious?

BOTTOM LINE: Don't worry if you just plain hate, say, snakes or crowds or heights. The key is how powerful your feelings are—and how you handle them

OBSESSIVE-COMPULSIVE DISORDER

WHAT IT IS: A preoccupation with specific thoughts, images or impulses, accompanied by elaborate and sometimes bizarre rituals

WHAT IT ISN'T: Fastidious—even idiosyncratic—behavior that does not significantly interfere with your quality of life

WHAT TO LOOK FOR: Are the obsessive thoughts persistent and intrusive?
- Do you expend a lot of energy suppressing the thoughts, usually unsuccessfully?
- Are you generally aware that the thoughts are irrational?
- Is the anxiety temporarily eased by a repetitive ritual such as hand washing or a thought ritual such as praying?
- Are the rituals time consuming?

BOTTOM LINE: Some researchers question whether OCD is a genuine anxiety disorder. Whatever it is, it does respond to treatment—provided you seek help

POST-TRAUMATIC STRESS DISORDER

WHAT IT IS: Repeated, anxious reliving of a horrifying event over an extended period of time

WHAT IT ISN'T: Anxiety following a trauma that fades steadily over the course of a month or so

WHAT TO LOOK FOR: After witnessing, experiencing or hearing about an event that caused or threatened to cause serious injury, do you:
- Have recurrent recollections or dreams about the experience?
- Feel emotionally or physically as if the event were still occurring?
- Experience intense anxiety when something reminds you of the event?
- Try to avoid thoughts, feelings, activities or places associated with the event?
- Have difficulty recalling details of the event?
- Experience anxiety symptoms such as irritability, jumpiness, difficulty sleeping, feelings of detachment from others, diminished interest in things, feelings that your future is in some way limited?

BOTTOM LINE: Sometimes, PTSD will not appear until six months after the event. Seek help whenever symptoms occur

GENERALIZED ANXIETY DISORDER

WHAT IT IS: Excessive anxiety or worry, occurring more days than not for six months

WHAT IT ISN'T: Occasional serious worry that doesn't markedly diminish quality of life

WHAT TO LOOK FOR: Restlessness; difficulty concentrating or sleeping; irritability; fatigue; muscle tension

BOTTOM LINE: If you have three or more symptoms for the required six months, the diagnosis may fit

—By Jeffrey Kluger

- There is a genetic component to anxiety; some people seem to be born worriers.
- Brain scans can reveal differences in the way patients who suffer from anxiety disorders respond to danger signals.
- Due to a shortcut in our brain's information-processing system, we can respond to threats before we become aware of them.
- The root of an anxiety disorder may not be the threat that triggers it but a breakdown in the mechanism that keeps the anxiety response from careening out of control.

Before we delve into the latest research, let's define a few terms. Though we all have our own intuitive sense of what the words stress and fear mean, scientists use these words in very specific ways. For them, stress is an external stimulus that signals danger, often by causing pain. Fear is the short-term response such stresses produce in men, women or lab rats. Anxiety has a lot of the same symptoms as fear, but it's a feeling that lingers long after the stress has lifted and the threat has passed.

In general, science has a hard time pinning down emotions because they are by nature so slippery and subjective. You can't

THE ANATOMY OF ANXIETY

WHAT TRIGGERS IT...
When the senses pick up a threat—a loud noise, a scary sight, a creepy feeling—the information takes two different routes through the brain

.... AND HOW THE BODY RESPONDS
By putting the brain on alert, the amygdala triggers a series of changes in brain chemicals and hormones that puts the entire body in anxiety mode

A THE SHORTCUT
When startled, the brain automatically engages an emergecy hot line to its fear center, the amygdala. Once activated, the amygdala sends the equivalent of an all-points bulletin that alerts other brain structures. The result is the classic fear response: sweaty palms, rapid heartbeat, increased blood pressure and a burst of adrenaline. All this happens before the mind is conscious of having smelled or touched anything. Before you know why you're afraid, you are

B THE HIGH ROAD
Only after the fear response is activated does the conscious mind kick into gear. Some sensory information, rather than traveling directly to the amygdala, takes a more circuitous route, stopping first at the thalamus—the processing hub for sensory cues—and then the cortex—the outer layer of brain cells. The cortex analyzes the raw data streaming in through the senses and decides whether they require a fear response. If they do, the cortex signals the amygdala, and the body stays on alert

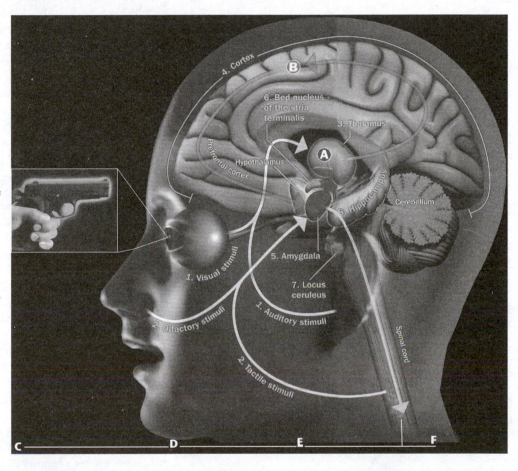

4. Cortex
B
6. Bed nucleus of the stria terminalis
3. Thalamus
Prefrontal cortex
Hypothalamus
A
8. Hippocampus
Cerebellum
5. Amygdala
1. Visual stimuli
7. Locus ceruleus
2. Olfactory stimuli
1. Auditory stimuli
Spinal cord
2. Tactile stimuli

C   D   E   F

C Stress-Hormone Boost
Responding to signals from the hypothalamus and pituitary gland, the adrenal glands pump out high levels of the stress hormone cortisol. Too much cortisol shortcircuits the cells in the hippocampus, making it difficult to organize the memory of a trauma or stressful experience. Memories lose their context and become fragmented

D Racing Heartbeat
The body's sympathetic nervous system, responsible for heart rate and breathing, shifts into overdrive. The heart beats faster, blood pressure rises and the lungs hyperventilate. sweat increases, and even the nerve endings on the skin tingle into action, creating goose bumps

E Fight, Flight or Fright
The senses become hyperalert, drinking in every detail of the surroundings and looking for potential new threats. Adrenaline shoots to the muscles, preparing the body to fight or flee

F Digestion shutdown
The brain stops thinking about things that bring pleasure, shifting its focus instead to identifying potential dangers. To ensure that no energy is wasted on digestion, the body will sometimes respond by emptying the digestive tract through involuntary vomiting, urination or defecation

(Continued on following page)

Source: Dennis S. Charney, M.D., National Institute of Mental Health.   TIME Diagram by Joe Lertola.   Text by Alice Park

THE ANATOMY OF ANXIETY

continued

1. Auditory and visual stimuli

Sights and sounds are processed first by the thalamus, which filters the incoming cues and shunts them either directly to the amygdala or to the appropriate parts of the cortex

2. Olfactory and tactile stimuli

Smells and touch sensations bypass the thalamus altogether, taking a shortcut directly to the amygdala. Smells, therefore, often evoke stronger memories or feelings than do sights or sounds

3. Thalamus

The hub for sights and sounds, the thalamus breaks down incoming visual cues by size, shape and color, and auditory cues by volume and dissonance, and then signals the appropriate parts of the cortex

4. Cortex

It gives raw sights and sounds meaning, enabling the brain to become conscious of what it is seeing or hearing. One region, the prefrontal cortex, may be vital to turning off the anxiety response once a threat has passed

5. Amygdala

The emotional core of the brain, the amygdala has the primary role of triggering the fear response. Information that passes through the amygdala is tagged with emotional significance

6. Bed nucleus of the stria terminalis

Unlike the amygdala, which sets off an immediate burst of fear, the BNST perpetuates the fear response, causing the longer-term unease typical of anxiety

7. Locus ceruleus

It receives signals from the amygdala and is responsible for initiating many of the classic anxiety responses: rapid heartbeat, increased blood pressure, sweating and pupil dilation

8. Hippocampus

This is the memory center, vital to storing the raw information coming in from the senses, along with the emotional baggage attached to the data during their trip through the amygdala

ask a rat if it's anxious or depressed. Even most people are as clueless about why they have certain feelings as they are about how their lungs work. But fear is the one aspect of anxiety that's easy to recognize. Rats freeze in place. Humans break out in a cold sweat. Heartbeats race, and blood pressure rises. That gives scientists something they can control and measure. "You can bring on a sensory stimulus that makes an animal—or human—fearful and study its effects," says Dr. Wayne Drevets of the National Institute of Mental Health (NIMH). "Then you can take the stimulus away and see how the animal calms down."

Indeed, a lot of what researchers have learned about the biology of anxiety comes from scaring rats and then cutting them open. Just as the Russian physiologist Ivan Pavlov showed 100 years ago that you could condition a dog to salivate at the sound of a bell, scientists today have taught rats to fear all kinds of things—from buzzers to lights—by giving them electrical shocks when they hear the buzzer or see the light. The animals quickly learn to fear the stimulus even in the absence of a shock. Then researchers destroy small portions of the rats' brains to see what effect that has on their reactions (an experiment that would be impossible to conduct in humans). By painstakingly matching the damaged areas with changes in behavior, scientists have, bit by bit, created a road map of fear as it travels through the rat's brain.

The journey begins when a rat (we'll get to humans later) feels the stress, in this case an electric shock. The rat's senses immediately send a message to the central portion of its brain, where the stimulus activates two neural pathways. One of these pathways is a relatively long, circuitous route through the cortex, where the brain does its most elaborate and accurate processing of information. The other route is a kind of emergency shortcut that quickly reaches an almond-shaped cluster of cells called the amygdala.

What's special about the amygdala is that it can quickly activate just about every system in the body to fight like the devil or run like crazy. It's not designed to be accurate, just fast. If you have ever gone hiking and been startled by a snake that turned out to be a stick, you can thank your amygdala. Joseph LeDoux, a neuroscientist at New York University, calls it "the hub in a wheel of fear."

But while the amygdala is busy telling the body what to do, it also fires up a nearby curved cluster of neurons called the hippocampus. (A 16th century anatomist named it after the Greek word for seahorse.) The job of the hippocampus is to help the brain learn and form new memories. And not just any memories. The hippocampus allows a rat to remember where it was when it got shocked and what was going on around it at the time. Such contextual learning helps the poor rodent avoid dangerous places in the future. It probably also helps it recognize what situations are likely to be relatively safe.

By this point, the other half of the stress signal has reached the cortex, which confirms that there's a danger present and figures out that it's causing pain. Once the shock has warn off, a part of the brain called the prefrontal cortex sends out an all-clear message and lets the amygdala know that it's O.K. to stand down. At least it's supposed to. It seems that it's harder to turn off a stress response than to turn it on. This makes sense, in terms of survival. After all, it's better to panic unnecessarily than to be too relaxed in the face of life-threatening danger.

Discovering this basic neural circuitry turned out to be a key breakthrough in understanding anxiety. It showed that the anx-

WHAT CAN YOU DO

There are as many ways to relieve anxiety as there are things that make us anxious. The key is to find the way that works for you—and use it

BEHAVIORAL THERAPY

When the brain sets anxiety alarms ringing, our first inclination is to find the off switch. Behavioral scientists take the opposite approach. They want you to get so accustomed to the noise that you don't hear it anymore. The standard behavioral treatment for such anxiety conditions as phobias, obsessive-compulsive disorder (OCD) and panic disorder is to expose patients to a tiny bit of the very thing that causes them anxiety, ratcheting up the exposure over a number of sessions until the brain habituates to the fear. A patient suffering from a blood phobia, for example, might first be shown a picture of a scalpel or syringe, then a real syringe, then a vial of blood and so on up the anxiety ladder until there are no more rungs to climb. There is a risk that if treatment is cut short (before the patient has become inured to the anxiety triggers), the anxious feelings could be exacerbated. But done right, behavioral therapy can bring relief from specific phobias in as little as two or three sessions. Social anxiety takes somewhat longer, and OCD may take a good deal longer still.

COGNITIVE THERAPY

Rather than expect patients to embrace anxiety, cognitive therapists encourage them to use the power of the mind to reason through it. First popularized in the 1980s, cognitive therapy teaches people who are anxious or depressed to reconfigure their view of the world and develop a more realistic perspective on the risks or obstacles they face. Patients suffering from social-anxiety disorder, for example, might see a group of people whispering at a party and assume the gossip is about them. A cognitive therapist would teach them to rethink that assumption. Some behavioral therapists question cognitive techniques, arguing—not without some justification—that a brain that was so receptive to reason wouldn't be all that anxious in the first place. Cognitive therapists dispute that idea, though some have begun incorporating behavior-modification techniques into their treatment.

ANTIDEPRESSANTS

When talk therapy doesn't work—or needs a boost—drugs can help, especially the class of antidepressants called selective serotonin reuptake inhibitors. Prozac is the best known of these drugs, which work by preventing the brain from reabsorbing too much of the neurotransmitter serotonin, leaving more in nerve synapses and thus helping to improve mood. Another SSRI, Paxil, was recently approved by the Food and Drug Administration specifically for the treatment of social-anxiety disorder, though the others seem to work as well. A third, Zoloft, has been approved for OCD and panic disorder. Each formulation of SSRI is subtly different—targeting specific subclasses of serotonin. And side effects—which can include dry mouth, fatigue and sexual dysfunction—will vary from person to person. A new group of antidepressants, known as serotonin-norepinephrine reuptake inhibitors, may be even more effective in treating anxiety disorders than the SSRIs are. As the name implies, SNRIs target a second neurotransmitter called norepinephrine, which is secreted by the adrenal fight-or-flight response—thus actually increasing anxiety symptoms in many situations. However, norepinephrine also helps control emotion and stabilize mood, and, properly manipulated along with serotonin, may be able to do just that for the anxious person.

MINOR TRANQUILIZERS

If the antidepressants have a flaw, it's that they sometimes don't start working for weeks—a lifetime for the acutely anxious. For this reason, many doctors recommend judicious doses of fast-acting relaxants such as the benzodiazepines Xanax, Valium or Klonopin to serve as a temporary bridge until the SSRIs have a chance to kick in. The downside of such drugs is that they can be highly addictive and may merely mask symptoms. For this reason, doctors will prescribe them very carefully and strictly limit refills.

EXERCISE

Before turning to drugs or talk therapy, many people prefer to try to bring their anxiety under control on their own. Unlike most emotional or physical conditions, anxiety disorders respond well to such self-medication—provided you know how to administer the treatment. One of the most effective techniques is simple exercise. It's no secret that a good workout or a brisk walk can take the edge off even the most acute anxiety. Scientists once believed the effect to be due to the release of natural opiates known as endorphins, but new research has called this into question. Regardless, working out regularly—most days of the week, if possible for at least 30 minutes or so—may well help recalibrate the anxious brain.

ALTERNATIVE TREATMENTS

One of the most popular self-treatments is yoga, which is both a form of exercise and a way to quiet the mind by focusing attention on breathing. Indeed, even without yoga, breathing exercises can help quell an anxiety episode, if only by slowing a racing heart and lengthening the short, shallow breaths of a panic attack. Many anxiety sufferers have relief through meditation or massage—even just a 10-min. foot treatment. For those willing to travel a little farther from the mainstream there's aromatherapy (enthusiasts recommend rose and lavender scents), guided imager (a form of directed meditation used with some success by people recovering from cancer and open-heart surgery) and acupuncture.

LIFESTYLE CHANGES

If all else fails, go back to basics and try cleaning up your lifestyle. For starters, you can cut back or eliminate the use of sugar, caffeine, nicotine, alcohol and any recreational drugs you may be taking. Are you eating right and getting enough sleep and leisure time? Finally, if your job or the place you live is making you anxious, you might consider moving to a less stressful environment or finding a different line of work.

—By Jeffrey Kluger. With reporting by Sora Song/New York

iety response isn't necessarily caused by an external threat; rather, it may be traced to a breakdown in the mechanism that signals the brain to stop responding. Just as a car can go out of control due to either a stuck accelerator or failed brakes, it's not always clear which part of the brain is at fault. It may turn out that some anxiety disorders are caused by an overactive amygdala (the accelerator) while others are caused by an under-active prefrontal cortex (call it the brake).

It may also be that an entirely different part of the brain holds the key to understanding anxiety. Michael Davis, a behavioral neuroscientist at Emory University in Atlanta, has spent six years studying a pea-size knot of neurons located near the amygdala with an impossible name: the bed nucleus of the stria terminalis, or BNST. Rats whose BNST has been injected with stress hormones are much jumpier than those that have got a shot in their amygdala. Could the BNST be at the root of all anxiety disorders? The clues are intriguing, but as scientists are so fond of saying, more research is needed.

Of course, what you would really like to know is whether any of the work done in rats applies to humans. Clearly researchers can't go around performing brain surgery on the amygdalas of living patients to see if it affects their anxiety levels. But the fascinating case of a woman known only by her research number, SM046, suggests that when it comes to fear, rodents and hominids really aren't so different.

Owing to an unusual brain disorder, SM046 has a defective amygdala. As a result, her behavior is abnormal in a very particular way. When scientists at the University of Iowa show SM046 pictures of a series of faces, she has no trouble picking out those that are happy, sad or angry. But if the face is displaying fear, she cannot recognize the feeling. She identifies it as a face expressing some intense emotion, but that is all. Her unusual condition strongly suggests that even in *Homo sapiens*, fear takes hold in the amygdala.

But studying brain-damaged patients can teach scientists only so much. They would also like to know how anxiety works in normal, intact brains. For this, brain scans have proved invaluable.

For years, doctors have used CAT scans and MRIs to help them diagnose strokes, brain tumors and other neurological conditions. But as the technology has become more sophisticated, researchers have started to employ it to tease out some of the subtle changes associated with mental illness. "We're not yet able to use these scans in a diagnostic way," says Dr. David Silbersweig of the Weill Cornell Medical College in New York City. "But we're getting pretty specific about the areas of the brain that are implicated in a number of psychiatric disorders."

One type of brain scan helps identify structures that are the wrong size or shape. Two years ago, researchers at the University of Pittsburgh showed that the amygdalas of a group of over-anxious young children were, on average, much larger than those of their unaffected peers. Perhaps they just had more fear circuits to contend with? Neuroscientists are tempted to say yes, but they admit the conclusion is pretty speculative. Another group of researchers found that patients with post-traumatic stress disorder had a smaller hippocampus than normal. Perhaps their stressful experiences had somehow interfered with the hip-

pocampus' ability to make new memories and, just as important, forget the old ones? Again, no one knows for sure.

Another type of brain scan tells scientists which brain cells are using the most oxygen or soaking up the most nutrients. The idea, explains Dr. Scott Rauch of Massachusetts General Hospital, is that any area that seems more active than usual while someone is anxious may play an important role in making the person that way. Rauch's team has spent the past eight years scanning groups of combat veterans, some with post-traumatic stress disorder and some without, to see which areas of the brain light up when they hear tapes recounting their most troubling memories. So far, the signals in the amygdala appear to be more active in those with PTSD than in those without. In addition, signals to the prefrontal cortex of PTSD subjects seem to be weaker than in those without the disorder. Perhaps this explains why the patients still feel threatened even when they are perfectly safe.

The next step, Rauch says, is to scan groups of people who are likely to be thrust into dangerous situations—fire fighters, say, or police officers. Then it may be possible to determine if any changes in their brains are the result of traumatic situations or if the changes predate them. Either is plausible. The stress of surviving a building collapse, for example, could turn a normal amygdala into an overactive one. Or an already overactive amygdala may overwhelm the brain in the wake of a disaster.

Eventually, researchers would like to learn what role our genes, as opposed to our environment, play in the development of anxiety. "It has been known for some time that these disorders run in families," says Kenneth Kendler, a psychiatric geneticist at Virginia Commonwealth University in Richmond, Va. "So the next logical question is the nature-nurture issue." In other words, are anxious people born that way, or do they become anxious as a result of their life experiences?

Kendler and his colleagues approached the question by studying groups of identical twins, who share virtually all their genes, and fraternal twins, who, like any other siblings, share only some of them. What Kendler's group found was that both identical twins were somewhat more likely than both fraternal twins to suffer from generalized anxiety disorder, phobias or panic attacks. (The researchers have not yet studied twins with post-traumatic stress disorder or obsessive-compulsive disorder.)

The correlation isn't 100%, however. "Most of the heritability is in the range of 30% to 40%," Kendler says. That's a fairly moderate genetic impact, he notes, akin to the chances that you will have the same cholesterol count as your parents. "Your genes set your general vulnerability," he concludes. "You can be a low-vulnerable, intermediate-vulnerable or a high-vulnerable person." But your upbringing and your experiences still have a major role to play. Someone with a low genetic vulnerability, for example, could easily develop a fear of flying after surviving a horrific plane crash.

There is plenty to learn about how anxiety and fear shape the brain. One of the biggest mysteries is the relationship between anxiety and depression. Researchers know that adults who suffer from depression were often very anxious as children. (It's also true that many kids outgrow their anxiety disorders to become perfectly well-adjusted adults.) Is that just a coincidence, as many believe, or does anxiety somehow prime the brain to become depressed later in life? Brain scans show that the amygdala is very active in depressed patients, even when they are sleeping. Studies of twins suggest that many of the same genes could be involved. "There's a lot of overlap," says Dr. Dennis Charney, chief of the research program for mood and anxiety disorders at the NIMH. "Anxiety and depression have a similar underlying biology, and the genetics may be such that anxiety surfaces early in life and depression later on." Still, no one can say for sure.

Certainly antidepressants, like the serotonin reuptake inhibitors (Prozac and others) have proved very helpful in treating anxiety; some doctors think they are even more effective against anxiety than they are against depression. Although no one knows exactly why these antidepressants work, one important clue is that their effects don't show up until after a few weeks of treatment. The pathways for toning down anxiety are apparently much more resistant than those for ratcheting it up.

It's a mistake, however, to think that pills alone can soothe your neurochemistry. Remember the cortex? That's where you would expect psychotherapy to work, increasing the repertoire of calming messages that can be passed along to the amygdala. Certain desensitization techniques can also help the brain learn, through the hippocampus, to be less reactive. Of course, you have to do it right. Reliving a trauma too soon after it happened could also make the memory harder to erase.

There are no guidebooks to tell you when it's safe to venture out again. In many ways, the whole country last September was made part of an unwitting experiment in mass anxiety. Our brains are even now in the process of rewiring themselves. How successfully we navigate this delicate transition will depend a lot on our genes, our environment and any future attacks.

—Reported by Alice Park/Bethesda, Leslie Whitaker/Chicago and Dan Cray/Los Angeles

9/11/01
Post-Traumatic Stress Disorder

September 11th affected all of us, and even at this short interval it seems to mark a new, frightening turn in history. But obviously, anyone who lost a loved one or who was in direct danger that day had an emotional experience that was altogether different than the general reaction. The thousands of rescue workers who dug through the ruins afterward also shouldered special emotional burdens.

Grief, shock, and their elements of disbelief, apathy, and sometimes anger are normal—and healthy—responses to terrible events and sudden loss. Remarkably, many people recover—daunted and with a darker world view perhaps, but ready to continue on with their lives. Studies have shown this to be true of Holocaust survivors, combat veterans, and rape victims. The human psyche is resilient.

Some will have psychiatric problems

But if past experience is any indication, a significant fraction of September 11th survivors and the families of the deceased will have psychiatric problems. The symptoms vary but can include an intense irritability, jumpiness, emotional numbness, flashbacks, and nightmares. Sufferers may struggle with sleep problems. Marriages and personal relationships may fray under the strain.

All of this falls under the heading of *post-traumatic stress disorder* (PTSD), a diagnosis many Americans associate with Vietnam War veterans. Many people diagnosed with PTSD are afflicted with overlapping mental health problems, including depression. *Acute stress disorder* shares some of the same symptoms as PTSD, but is a diagnosis reserved for the first month after a traumatic experience.

It is hard to say how many will suffer from full-fledged PTSD. For Americans, the attacks two months ago have no real parallel either in kind or degree. The closest precedent is the 1995 bombing of the federal office building in Oklahoma City that killed 167 people. A study of survivors of that terrorist attack was published in the Aug. 25, 1999, *Journal of the American Medical Association*. The researchers interviewed approximately 200 people six months after the explosion. A person was eligible for the study if they were within a couple of hundred yards from the blast. Forty-five percent met the criteria for having some kind of psychiatric disorder and 34% had PTSD.

What qualifies as exposure?

By definition, PTSD is a consequence of exposure to a traumatic experience, with trauma being some kind of serious harm. In 1994, the American Psychiatry Association broadened the definition of exposure considerably. In addition to facing a threat of death or serious injury directly, it now includes "witnessing or learning about the unexpected or violent death, serious harm, or threat of death or injury experienced by a family member or close associate."

Who is vulnerable?

It stands to reason that the more direct and severe the traumatic experience, the more likely PTSD will develop. But there isn't a predictable dose-response relationship. Some people with a fairly remote connection to an event will have a strong psychiatric reaction, whereas others will go through a horrifying experience and bounce back.

Researchers have found some patterns. Studies have shown consistently, for example, that women are more susceptible to developing PTSD than men. In the Oklahoma City survivor study, women had twice the PTSD rate as men (45% vs. 23%). A traumatic experience is more likely to trigger PTSD in someone who has had a prior experience. A study done several years ago of women recovering from rape found that those who had been raped before were three times more likely to develop PTSD. Most vulnerable of all are people with prior psychiatric problems such as depression, anxiety, or a personality disorder.

Well shy of mental illness, certain personality traits seem to make PTSD more likely. *Neuroticism* is a tendency to react with strong emotion to adverse events. People with this kind of personality are more sensitive to stress: their response is faster, stronger, and slower to level off than normal. Research has connected high-test scores for neuroticism to PTSD. There may also be a link between PTSD and *impulsivity*, because it leads to recklessness that puts people in harm's way.

Researchers have looked at brain anatomy for clues. Several studies have found that an unusually small *hippocampus*, the part of the brain believed to control the narrative structure of memories, is associated with PTSD. It isn't settled, however, whether that is a cause or an effect.

Acute stress

During the traumatic event itself, some people often enter a *dissociative state,* perhaps as a defense mechanism. They imagine they are elsewhere. In their mind's eye, they see it happening to someone else. People with this kind response are more likely to develop PTSD. If they get stuck in this detached phase, it can turn into total amnesia or various identity disorders. Yet particularly during disasters, many survivors stay amazingly levelheaded and focus on saving themselves—and often others. As horrible as the collapse of the World Trade Center Towers was, it would have been much worse if so many hadn't stayed calm and gotten out of the buildings.

More on PTSD symptoms

PTSD symptoms don't stick to a decipherable time line. They can happen right away or emerge months or years later. After disasters, however, they usually begin within three months, perhaps because there isn't much stigma and people feel freer to express their emotions. In the case of the Oklahoma City bombing, 76% of the survivors said their PTSD started the same day.

The first set of PTSD symptoms includes insomnia, edginess, and irritability. People are easily startled. They have a hard time concentrating. Then, sometimes, an emotional flatness sets in as if the mind is struggling to bury or get rid of the whole experience. People feel listless. They may withdraw socially. They may start to have stomachaches, headaches, dizzy spells, and feel profoundly tired. At odds with this numbness is another set of classic PTSD symptoms that include nightmares, flashbacks, and what psychiatrists aptly term *intrusive thoughts.* The slightest reminder of the traumatic experience can set people off and cause emotional suffering.

How are family members and close friends affected?

The sudden death of a significant other can create a special kind of grief that includes *separation* and *traumatic distress.* People can't stop thinking about the deceased person. They may feel as though part of them has died. Life seems to have no purpose. Some have *facsimile illness symptoms,* which involve reliving the symptoms or pain of the person who died. Relatives of homicide victims may relive the crime, putting themselves in the place of their loved ones. Some psychiatrists believe *traumatic bereavement* should be added as a diagnosis, related to but separate from PTSD. Certainly, normal grief has some of these qualities. The difference is that normal grief tends to taper off. People adjust and find they can lead meaningful lives again.

Are rescue workers vulnerable?

Technically, the PTSD diagnosis won't apply to rescue workers who are not themselves in serious danger. Several studies have shown, however, that up to 40% of people responsible for body handling and recovery after a disaster show signs of distress and are at risk of developing PTSD.

How can it be treated?

No consensus exists about how to best treat PTSD. A wide range of antidepressants are used. Antiseizure medications like carbamazepine and valproate are sometimes prescribed on the theory that a traumatic experience may lower the arousal threshold of the brain's *limbic system,* which is where seizures originate but it also controls emotions. Beta-blockers, traditionally prescribed to lower blood pressure, may quiet the nervous system and thereby reduce anxiety and restlessness.

Several varieties of psychotherapy have been tried, too, most with some but not complete success. *Cognitive therapy* focuses on memories and breaking negative thought patterns. *Behavioral therapy* aims to cut off a conditioned response that has become automatic.

Many therapists advocate using a technique called *debriefing* right after a traumatic event. It involves getting people to talk, usually in a group, about their experiences and vent their emotions. Some experts believe this is the best way to head off PTSD. Others see it as possibly stirring up thoughts and emotions that people might not otherwise have had.

Are we all suffering from PTSD?

Edgy? The possibility of future attacks has jangled many people's nerves. Waves of bad economic news have added to the background anxiety. Numb? Many Americans say September 11th changed the way in which they look at the world. They no longer feel safe. They are looking for meaning. They pray more. Intrusive thoughts and flashbacks? We don't need to think them up ourselves. Television and other news media bring up plenty of frightening pictures.

No, we don't have PTSD. To say we do trivializes the suffering of others. Still, we're allowed a pang of self-recognition in the broad outlines and descriptions of the condition. These are, after all, disordered times we're living in.

Deconstructing Schizophrenia

Large-scale family studies and new drug probes focus on cognitive deficits that may lie at the heart of the disease

By Constance Holden

Generations of researchers have struggled to get at the core of schizophrenia, but with little success: No one knows the cause of this dread disease, many efforts to unravel the genetics behind it have ended in frustration, and no cure is in sight. But in recent years, scientists have made significant gains—not by tackling the disease head-on but by picking apart its components, especially those involved in cognition. And this has given them hope that they might finally be able to unlock some of schizophrenia's intractable secrets.

The disease's most infamous feature is psychosis, which is characterized by delusions and hallucinations. But there are many other facets to schizophrenia, including flattened emotions and disordered thinking. As drugs have successfully controlled the psychosis, they have laid bare the persisting cognitive problems, leading researchers to view them as the symptoms closest to the heart of the disease. Several large studies, one of which will begin this month, are probing these symptoms in both patients and their relatives. Schizophrenia has a strong genetic component; for example, a child of someone with the disease is 10 times as likely as the average person to develop it. The new studies might yield solid clues about the genetic causes of the disease and guide ways to treat it.

The introduction of antipsychotic drugs in the 1950s made possible the massive deinstitutionalization of schizophrenia patients, but there's been "no real change in the outcome of the illness," says Philip Harvey of Mount Sinai School of Medicine in New York City. A new generation of drugs introduced in the early 1990s lacks many of the distressing side effects of earlier antipsychotic drugs, such as extreme agitation and the Parkinson's disease-like movement disorder tardive dyskinesia. But even these treatments "don't normalize patients," says Michael Green of the University of California, Los Angeles (UCLA). "Fewer than 10% of schizophrenia pa-

tients ever get a regular job or live independently." In fact, he says, outcomes aren't much better now than in 1895, when the treatment was fresh air and water.

Research on the brains of schizophrenia patients helps explain why the disease can be so intractable. The frontal and temporal lobes are shrunken, neurons may be mispacked in some regions, and neural circuits based on the neurotransmitter dopamine go haywire, among other problems. Some of these defects arise as early as the second trimester of fetal development.

But schizophrenia is still "a disease whose mechanism is totally unknown," says Carol Tamminga of the Maryland Psychiatric Research Center in Baltimore. Dozens of genetic studies have failed to reveal more than a tiny contribution from any single gene. And despite some common brain changes, anatomical studies are ambiguous: There is "no marked signature like plaques and tangles in Alzheimer's," says Patricia Goldman-Rakic of Yale University.

In recent years, however, prospects for understanding the disease have brightened somewhat. Researchers are armed with new imaging technologies and the human genome sequence. But equally important is a shift in approach: Instead of comparing people with schizophrenia to those without, scientists are "deconstructing" the disease, says Stephen Hyman, former director of the National Institute of Mental Health (NIMH), attempting to unravel it by looking at its characteristic features in both the sick and the well.

The components that scientists are most eager to get a grasp on are the cognitive disruptions that affect short-term memory, attention, and so-called executive functions needed for planning and problem solving. "It's become increasingly clear that the driver of disability—and the reason patients never reintegrate [into the community]—is the cognitive deficits of the disease," says Ken-

White Matter's the Matter

Scientists have long known that connections somehow go awry in the brains of people with schizophrenia. Now advances in imaging and gene technology are allowing them to trace the axons that connect from neuron to neuron and make up the brain's white matter. "White matter is a very new focus," says brain researcher Monte Buchsbaum of Mount Sinai School of Medicine in New York City.

Kenneth Davis of Mount Sinai uses microarray technology to look at thousands of genes that are expressed in the brain, from schizophrenia patients and controls. His team has identified a half-dozen genes for oligodendrocytes—the cells that make up the myelin sheath covering axons—that malfunction. Buchsbaum has corroborating data from an imaging technique, called diffusion tensor technology, showing that the alignment of axons is askew in the frontal lobes of patients with schizophrenia. The new data comport with earlier observations from postmortem brains indicating that even though schizophrenia patients aren't short on brain cells, connecting fibers are sparse.

Davis says this new tack is "very interesting, because other demyelinating diseases also have cognitive abnormalities." Indeed, a genetic disease called metachromatic leukodystrophy often produces psychosis "indistinguishable from schizophrenic psychosis," and the cognitive profiles are similar, indicating that the same brain areas are being affected.

Myelin defects might help scientists understand the cortical shrinkage seen in many cases of schizophrenia. But it still doesn't get to the issue of causation, and it's just a piece of the still-endless puzzle. Says Yale University's Patricia Goldman-Rakic: "All of the things that can go wrong with a brain cell and its connections we can find evidence for in schizophrenia."

—C.H.

neth Davis of Mount Sinai School of Medicine. Researchers view psychosis as a secondary symptom; Harvard's Ming Tsuang compares it to fever: an acute response to other insults rather than a primary pathology. "If you can't think clearly, then you have delusions and hallucinations and thought disorganization," says Monte Buchsbaum of Mount Sinai. "Before, it was thought to be the other way around."

Even by focusing on cognition, however, researchers don't expect to find simple, independent risk factors. Rather, says Goldman-Rakic, there are "multiple subtle deficiencies" that can accumulate to cross the threshold into schizophrenia. People are starting to think that "it's the particular combination [of disease components] and their magnitude" that tip a person over the edge into the disease, says Irving Gottesman, a schizophrenia researcher for 40 years.

Mind modules

The keys to unlocking schizophrenia may therefore lie not in the patients but in their relatives. According to Tsuang, somewhere between 20% and 50% of first-degree relatives exhibit some of the disease's features, such as social withdrawal, or more subtle symptoms, such as difficulty in visually tracking a moving object. Instead of looking for catch-all genes, scientists now hope to develop a picture of schizophrenia by tracking genes behind these behavior modules, which they call endophenotypes.

Unlike usually transient psychotic symptoms, traits that qualify as endophenotypes are stable over time. They often predate the onset of the disease and are little affected by antipsychotic medication. Looking at unaffected family members allows researchers to see features of the disease in unfettered form—uncontaminated by drugs, psychosis, or factors such as prenatal exposure to viruses that may have triggered the full-blown disease in their schizophrenic kin. One oft-cited analogy is with colon cancer: The disease itself is not genetic, but it is secondary to an endophenotype that is: a tendency to form polyps.

Studying relatives of schizophrenia patients is not a new approach, says Steven Moldin of NIMH, but previous work has been inconclusive, marred by small sample sizes and difficulties in standardizing measurements. Now three big new studies are joining the hunt for genes that contribute to the disease. Researchers haven't entirely given up on finding individual genes that dramatically increase one's risk of developing schizophrenia. But they suspect that, as in other so-called complex diseases such as type II diabetes or heart disease, most genetic risk factors will exert subtle effects that are difficult to discern in small samples. The new studies will attempt to identify such genes, known as quantitative trait loci, by screening the entire genome sequence of each individual. "For schizophrenia now, you have weak linkage signals scattered all over the genome," says Bernard Devlin of the University of Pittsburgh. "We want to come up with much stronger ones in specific locations." The studies represent "a tremendous conceptual leap" because of their size and the number of traits and genes they're examining, says Moldin, who believes that this "may very well make all the difference between finding genes and not."

Two of the studies were launched in 2002 from the University of Pennsylvania in Philadelphia, headed by Penn's Raquel Gur in cooperation with the University of Pittsburgh. One will involve up to 150 families consisting of about 1000 people of European descent; each family has at least two affected members. The other will be by far the largest study ever undertaken of black schizophrenia patients. "African-American schizophrenia patients have been notoriously understudied," says Moldin. Small studies have hinted that some genetic linkage patterns are different in the two races. Now, the Project Among African Americans to Explore Risks for Schizophrenia, launched in November, "will be the definitive study to resolve the genetic differences between African-American and Caucasian schizophrenia patients," he predicts. This study will ultimately involve 5000 people and include a comparison of 400 pairs of siblings who both have schizophrenia.

Both studies will test participants' attention, working memory, and executive functions, including organization, problem-solving, and decision-making. They'll follow up on previous studies, such as those showing that if asked to learn a list of 16 words, most people will group the words into categories and remember them well. But people with schizophrenia and some of their relatives don't make categories, reflecting the difficulty they have in organizing information. They also have trouble retaining the memory of a target image after it has been "masked" by a second stimulus. And a test requiring the viewer to discriminate between different facial emotional expressions often stumps patients. Tsuang says the genetic components of these studies "will allow us to determine whether [different] liabilities" are caused by the same or different sets of genes.

The third major study is a seven-center affair, the Consortium on the Genetics of Schizophrenia, headed by David Braff of the University of California, SanDiego. The 5-year study, which will start this month, eventually will consist of 2200 people, all schizophrenia patients or first-degree family members. In addition to cognitive tests like those in the Penn studies, the study will include three neurophysiological tests.

The latter tests are aimed at defining the defects in neural circuitry underlying attention problems that characterize the disease. The researchers' working hypothesis is that patients' brains can't focus on a stimulus because they can't inhibit, or "gate," irrelevant material. One test measures the suppression or inhibition of an electric signal called P50 that is normally elicited by a novel stimulus. If a novel sound is quickly repeated, a nonschizophrenic brain will repress the P50 response by 80%. The brains of most schizophrenia patients, however, respond as though the second tone is as novel as the first. Braff calls this endophenotype "the genetically most advanced" of any yet studied. The problem has been tracked down to a defect in a gene for a nicotinic receptor that has been linked to attention.

In another measure of gating, a target appears on one side of a computer screen, and a person is supposed to look in the opposite direction—a task that requires suppressing the impulse to look at the flashed image. Braff is optimistic that some breakthroughs are on the horizon. "I think we're in the first phase of really being able to parse the complex genetic architecture" of the disease, he says.

Drugs for thought

The shift in focus toward cognitive dysfunction is apparent in the search for new drugs to treat the disease. "The drugs we have today are based on elaborations of drugs discovered serendipitously over 50 years ago," says Wayne Fenton of NIMH. And although some help with the problems of disordered thinking, their main job is still to fight psychosis, he says. But recent research suggests a variety of targets directly related to cognitive functioning. One top candidate is the dopamine system. Current antipsychotic drugs reduce dopamine levels where the neurotransmitter is overexpressed. But the disease reduces the amount of dopamine released in other parts of the cortex, such as the striatum. Goldman-Rakic has found that a dopamine shortage impedes primates' short-term memory ability.

Nicotinic receptors offer another tantalizing target. Nicotine transiently normalizes the P50 gating response, leading some researchers to suspect that the high incidence of smoking in schizophrenia patients is the result of unconscious efforts to self-medicate. Another candidate of interest is glutamate, the brain's main excitatory neurotransmitter. A shortage of it has been linked to both psychotic symptoms and cognitive impairments.

Some novel compounds are already being tested on patients. Researchers at NIMH, for example, are experimenting with a drug targeted at an enzyme named COMT that breaks down dopamine in the prefrontal cortex. Genetic studies have shown that certain alleles of the COMT gene run in families with a high incidence of schizophrenia. The suspect versions of COMT result in less dopamine in the prefrontal cortex, a region necessary for executive functions. Michael Egan and Daniel Weinberger of NIMH are conducting a study of COMT inhibitors in schizophrenia patients and controls with and without the high-risk combination of alleles. Although COMT may account for only a tiny fraction of cases, Egan says, "we hope to detect an effect with [functional magnetic resonance imaging] in the first 20 subjects … [and] get some preliminary results in a year." With such studies, says Braff, ultimately, "we will be able to take gene and neurological profiles of individuals and give them drugs that are more tailored, much like oncology with cancer."

To achieve this vision, new surveillance strategies are required in the world of cognitive enhancement. NIMH recently entered into a contract with UCLA to recommend regulations covering possible new drug candidates aimed at systems such as dopamine and nicotinic receptors. UCLA's Green says that at present, companies "don't want to invest too much till they know what [the U.S. Food and Drug Administration] will require, [and] FDA doesn't know what to require" because it has no definitions or standards for evaluating cognitive enhancement. A series of meetings, the first of which will be held in Washington, D.C., in April, will explore standards for assessing cognition in schizophrenia, targets for intervention, and appropriate experimental designs.

But ultimately, says Tsuang, "the future is toward prevention." Although some neural irregularities are laid down during fetal development, the disease emerges in late adolescence. Psychiatrist Larry Siever of Mount Sinai and the Bronx Veterans Administration Hospital explains that it is only in adolescence that the human brain's executive areas have matured and myelination is finally completed. "If we could intervene before this vulnerable time, we might head off the negative spiral of cognitive impairment, psychosis, and social isolation," he says. There is already evidence that endophenotypes can help predict the disease: A 30-year longitudinal study of 324 children of people with schizophrenia, conducted by Niki Erlenmeyer-Kimling of Columbia University, has shown that children with deficits in three parameters—attention, verbal memory, and a hopping test of gross motor skills—had a 50% likelihood of developing the disease.

Some evidence suggests that preventive treatment can stave off the disease, says Tsuang. He has gotten good results in a very small study: Of six "at risk" family members with mild impairments who were treated with low doses of risperidone, a second-generation antipsychotic, five showed improvements. But drugs targeting the cognitive and emotional symptoms of schizophrenia are even more important, says Braff. He says that with a combination of knowledge of endophenotypes and a sophisticated new array of drug targets—and eventually gene therapy—the prospect of protecting vulnerable people from schizophrenia might become very real. Schizophrenia prevention might still be a long way off, admits Braff. But, he says, it is finally being taken "out of the realm of the ineffable and put it into the realm of other genetically mediated complex diseases."

UNIT 11

Psychological Treatments

Unit Selections

37. **Psychotherapies: Can We Tell the Difference?**, Harvard Mental Health Letter
38. **Can Freud Get His Job Back?**, Lev Grossman
39. **Treating Anxiety**, Sarah Glazer
40. **Computer- and Internet-Based Psychotherapy Interventions**, C. Barr Taylor and Kristine H. Luce

Key Points to Consider

- Do you know what varieties of psychotherapy are commonly available? Does psychotherapy work? Why are Americans in love with psychotherapy? Or are they? Do you think that supportive lay persons can be as effective as psychotherapists? Is professional assistance for psychological problems always necessary? Can people successfully change themselves without benefit of therapy?

- Can therapists easily differentiate their brand of therapy from another? What makes therapy successful? Who do you think is more important to the therapeutic alliance, the client or the therapist? What characteristics of each person make therapy effective? Do you think one type of therapy would work better for you than another?

- Why would doing research on psychotherapy as a process be difficult? Besides the process itself and how it works (for example, the therapist displaying empathy), what other measures would be important to research?

- What is psychoanalysis? Why is it being replaced by briefer therapies today? Are these forms of brief treatment effective? What is managed care and how has it changed the way mental disorders are treated? Should managed care providers be required to offer as much or as many treatments for a mental disorder as they do, say, for cancer?

- Why are more and more people turning to cybertherapy or the internet for help with mental disorders and other psychological problems? How can we research whether this form of therapy is effective? Why is this an important research topic? Do you think, in general, that the internet is a safe place to seek advice? How would you know a reliable web site on mental disorder from an inaccurate one?

 **Links: www.dushkin.com/online/**
These sites are annotated in the World Wide Web pages.

The C.G. Jung Page
http://www.cgjungpage.org

Knowledge Exchange Network (KEN)
http://www.mentalhealth.org

NetPsychology
http://netpsych.com/index.htm

Sigmund Freud and the Freud Archives
http://plaza.interport.net/nypsan/freudarc.html

Have you ever had the nightmare that you are trapped in a dark, dismal place? No one will let you out. Your pleas for freedom go unanswered and, in fact, are suppressed or ignored by domineering authority figures around you. You keep begging for mercy but to no avail. What a nightmare! You are fortunate to awake to your normal bedroom and to the realities of your daily life. For the mentally ill, the nightmare of institutionalization, where individuals can be held against their will in what are sometimes terribly dreary, restrictive surroundings, is a reality. Have you ever wondered what would happen if we took perfectly normal individuals and institutionalized them in such a place? In one well-known and remarkable study, that is exactly what happened.

In 1973, eight people, including a pediatrician, a psychiatrist and some psychologists, presented themselves to psychiatric hospitals. Each claimed that he or she was hearing voices. The voices, they reported, seemed unclear but appeared to be saying "empty" or "thud." Each of these individuals was admitted to a mental hospital, and most were diagnosed as being schizophrenic. Upon admission, the "pseudopatients" or fake patients gave truthful information and thereafter acted like their usual, normal selves.

Their hospital stays lasted anywhere from 7 to 52 days. The nurses, doctors, psychologists, and other staff members treated them as if they were schizophrenic and never saw through their trickery. Some of the real patients in the hospital, however, did recognize that the pseudopatients were perfectly normal. Upon discharge almost all of the pseudopatients received the diagnosis of "schizophrenic in remission," meaning that they were still clearly defined as schizophrenic; they just weren't exhibiting any of the symptoms at the time of release.

What does this study demonstrate about mental illness? Is true mental illness readily detectable? If we can't always pinpoint mental disorders (the more professionally accepted term for mental illness), how can we treat them? What treatments are available and what treatments work better for various diagnoses? The treatment of mental disorders is a challenge. The array of available treatments is ever increasing and can be downright bewildering—and not just to the patient or client! In order to demystify and simplify your understanding of various treatments, we will look at them in this unit.

We commence with a general article on psychotherapy. There are as many forms of therapy as there are theories. Can all of the various practitioners discriminate one form of psychotherapy from another? Is there any such thing as a pure form of psychotherapy as practiced today?

In the second article in this unit, "Can Freud Get His Job Back?," Lev Grossman describes the ever-changing state of today's mental health system. He concludes that classic psychoanalysis is outmoded and that newer therapies seem to be in vogue, which are briefer and more problem-focused than psychoanalysis. Why? Because research and health insurance companies support these newer types of treatment.

More and more people are turning to the internet for help with mental disorders. Researchers are just now researching whether this trend bodes well for the future. As you will read in the next article of this unit, much more research is needed on the efficacy and safety of cyber-therapy.

Psychotherapies: Can we tell the difference?

If, as a patient or a therapist, you have tried one kind of psychotherapy, you may have tried more than one. Despite labels, different kinds of psychotherapy are often almost indistinguishable in practice. At least that's the conclusion some Harvard and Berkeley researchers have arrived at after examining the records of the National Institute of Mental Health (NIMH) Treatment of Depression Collaborative Research Program.

That clinical trial, one of the most carefully conducted ever, compared antidepressant medication, interpersonal psychotherapy, and cognitive behavioral therapy in the treatment of depressed patients. Cognitive behavioral therapy concentrates on changing maladaptive habits, irrational beliefs, and self-defeating attitudes. Interpersonal therapy, in principle, is concerned mainly with life changes and personal relationships, especially grief and loss. Detailed manuals lay out procedures for both forms of therapy.

The researchers asked experts to compare their own understanding of interpersonal and cognitive behavioral therapy with a process rating list—100 statements describing some typical features of psychotherapy sessions. The experts rated each item on the list from 1 to 100, depending on how accurately it described the proceedings during an ideal session of interpersonal or cognitive behavioral therapy. Then, without being told which kind of therapy they were observing, independent judges read transcripts of sessions from the NIMH trial and sorted items on the process rating list to match what they were reading.

Cognitive behavioral therapists rated five items as best representing their practice:

1. discussing specific activities and tasks for the patient to attempt outside of psychotherapy sessions;
2. discussing the patient's ideas or belief systems;
3. discussing the patient's treatment goals;
4. encouraging the patient to test new ways of behaving with others;
5. controlling the interaction between therapist and patient by introducing new topics.

For interpersonal therapists, the top five items were:

1. emphasizing the patient's personal relationships;
2. emphasizing the patient's feelings to help him or her experience them more deeply;
3. encouraging the patient to talk of feelings about being close to or needing someone;
4. discussing love or romantic relationships;
5. explaining the reasons for their approach to treatment.

The transcripts of 35 interpersonal and 29 cognitive behavioral therapy sessions did not show the expected contrast. No matter what the label, process ratings resembled the cognitive behavioral model more than the interpersonal model (although the interpersonal therapy sessions matched more features of the interpersonal ideal than cognitive behavioral therapy sessions did). Use of cognitive behavioral procedures was generally associated with a better outcome, but the interpersonal therapists, despite the label, were also using those procedures most of the time, and they were just as successful as the cognitive behavioral therapists.

According to the authors, other studies—including some of their own—show that in practice psychodynamic therapists often use cognitive behavioral methods as well. And in this study, even the ideal forms of cognitive behavioral therapy and interpersonal therapy as described by experts were not as different as they may seem. Six of the first 20 items on the process rating list were common to both. Successful therapists of all persuasions, the authors believe, adopt an authoritative and benevolent manner, offer advice and reassurance, and coach patients in ways to change their behavior.

The patient's contribution was also important. Readers of the transcripts found that if they judged by the patient's statements alone, the two forms of psychotherapy were almost indistinguishable. In an earlier study, what patients did and said during therapy sessions proved to be more important in determining the outcome than what therapists did and said.

The authors believe that most comparative tests of psychotherapy are based on the wrong assumptions. The standard description of a form of psychotherapy may be unrelated to what actually goes on in the encounters between a therapist and a patient. Better understanding of how change occurs during those encounters, they say, is the key to improving psychotherapeutic practice.

Reference

Ablon, J. et al. "Validity of Controlled Clinical Trials of Psychotherapy: Findings from the NIMH Treatment of Depression Collaborative Research Program," American Journal of Psychiatry (May 2002): Vol. 159, No. 5, pp. 775–83.

Can Freud Get His Job Back?

In the age of happy pills and quick fixes, the "talking cure" still has something to offer

By LEV GROSSMAN

How many Freudians does it take to change a light bulb? Two. One to change the bulb, and one to hold the penis ... *I mean ladder!* Although Sigmund Freud isn't exactly famous for his sense of humor, he actually liked jokes—in fact, he wrote a book about them, *Jokes and Their Relation to the Unconscious*. But he probably wouldn't have liked that one. Freudian psychoanalysis was one of the great innovations of the 20th century, and only 50 years ago, it was a mainstay of mental-health care. But since then it has gone from a medical and cultural institution to the punch line of a mildly dirty joke told by psychiatry residents. The members of the American Psychoanalytic Association today treat fewer than 5,000 patients in the U.S. How did the treatment Freud called the "talking cure" fall from grace? And now that it has fallen, can it get up again?

For almost a century, Freud's followers have treated his techniques like Holy Scripture. Now they are being forced to update his theories to compete with new drugs and new therapies, even if it means using methods that would have been unthinkable to their patriarch. At the same time, post-Freudian psychotherapists are figuring out that the old master still has something to offer the science of mental health: an understanding of the human mind and its many malfunctions that's richer, fuller and more exciting than anything invented since.

Cognitive therapy is everything psychoanalysis isn't: simple, quick, practical, goal oriented

In their time—the early decades of the 20th century—Freud's ideas radically and irrevocably changed the way we think about who we are. He both explained the human mind and made it more mysterious. One of Freud's key insights was to divide the mind into the conscious and the unconscious: he showed us that beneath the surface banality of everyday

Freudian Analysis

Types
Classic Freudian psychoanalysis is rare. Psychodynamic therapy, a quicker variant, has become more common

Symptoms
Used for symptoms like anxiety and depression, as well as for more general goals, like improving self-understanding

Duration
Long, but not endless. A recent survey puts the average length of treatment at five to six and a half years

Effectiveness
Quantitative studies of its value are surprisingly scarce, but some recent studies have shown positive results

Analysands in U.S.
5,000

thoughts and gestures lurk subterranean caverns of forbidden longings that reach all the way back to our earliest childhood memories. Freud's therapeutic technique, psychoanalysis, was an intellectual exploration of those depths, where patients could confront their deepest, darkest desires. If they recognized and overcame those repressed desires, the theory went, they could return to the surface with a calmer, healthier mind.

By the 1920s, psychoanalysis had become wildly popular in America (a country Freud visited only once and hated). Jazz age sophisticates held "Freuding" parties at which they told one another their dreams. Samuel Goldwyn, the movie-studio magnate, offered Freud $100,000 to write a love story that Goldwyn could turn into a motion picture. (He was rebuffed.) But Freud died in 1939, and the golden age of psychoanalysis lasted only until the 1950s. By then competing psychotherapeutic theories and approaches had begun to spring up, among them ego psychology, self-psychology, the object-relations school, interpersonal therapy and existential therapy. All revised Freud, and some rejected him outright.

Cognitive therapy is one of the most virulently anti-Freudian strains of post-Freudian therapy, and it has become one of the dominant approaches to therapy today. It was pioneered in the early 1960s by the psychiatrist Aaron Beck, who was trained as a Freudian but—in classic Oedipal fashion—rebelled against his master. Beck dismissed Freud's ideas about the subconscious as so much scientifically unverifiable cigar smoke. In their place he crafted a quick, pragmatic therapeutic approach that dispensed with abstract theories and focused on results. Cognitive therapy attacks such symptoms as anxiety and depression by "coaching" patients on how to think about their lives more clearly.

Not only did Beck reject Freud's idea of the unconscious self, but he also abandoned the formal reserve of the classic Freudian analyst. Freud believed the analyst should be as neutral and silent as possible. That way, Freud theorized, the patient can project personalities from his or her past onto the analyst and relive past conflicts right there on the couch. Freud called this process "transference." Beck and his followers aren't interested in transference. Instead cognitive therapists talk back to their patients, pointing out their misconceptions and advising them on how to see their lives more clearly.

Cognitive therapy is everything psychoanalysis isn't: simple, quick, practical, goal oriented. "There's this mystique about psychoanalysis," says Judith Beck, daughter of Aaron and herself a leading cognitive therapist. "Psychoanalysis is esoteric and creative and interesting, and the psychoanalyst holds himself up as the expert who interprets what the patient is saying and has all the answers. It's kind of the opposite in cognitive therapy." Cognitive therapists tend to follow the same basic script for each session, so the treatment is remarkably standardized. It's also remarkably effective; research shows that when it comes to treating depression, cognitive therapy works as well as drugs like Prozac. And though it's not quite as quick as antidepressants, the results last longer after treatment stops. One study published in the *New England Journal of Medicine* found that, used together, cognitive therapy and antidepressants can help 85% of patients suffering from chronic major depression.

How can psychoanalysis compete with that? Freud's methods may be intellectually exciting, but they're slow and largely unproven. A course of cognitive therapy can take as little as six to eight sessions to finish; a course of analysis often takes five to 10 *years*. Even its supporters admit there are few clinical studies to show that psychoanalysis actually works. After all, they argue, the ultimate goal of psychoanalysis is deeper self-understanding, and how can you demonstrate that with a study?

But try telling that to an insurance company. Another reason cognitive therapy has been so successful—Judith Beck estimates that there are 5,000 cognitive therapists nationwide—is that it's the perfect therapy for the age of managed care: quick, cheap and backed by statistics. Classical Freudian psychoanalysis demands four or five sessions a week, and a session with a qualified psychoanalyst can easily run you $125, if not twice that amount. Few insurance companies will pay for a treatment that costs $30,000 a year and has hardly any clinical outcome studies to back it up. Insurers would rather pay for a cognitive therapist—or for that matter, a psychopharmacologist, especially since the introduction of Prozac in 1987. Prozac and the other selective serotonin reuptake inhibitors are widely used to treat disorders like depression and anxiety, which were once the bread and butter of psychoanalysis. Of the 14 million patients treated for depression in the U.S. every year, around 80% take some form of antidepressant medication.

Psychoanalysts are abandoning the formal reserve that Freud insisted on. In fact, analysis as it is practiced today has changed so much, Freud would probably not recognize it

That's how Freud has gone from being the founding father of psychotherapy to a poor, eccentric cousin on the fringes of psychotherapeutic practice. "Classical analysis is a very, very small percentage of what is practiced in this country," says Dr. T. Byram Karasu, editor in chief of the *American Journal of Psychotherapy*. "It's almost a negligible fraction." Judith Beck believes psychoanalysis will die out in our lifetime. "Managed-care companies and insurance companies," she says, "are finally waking up and looking at research, and finding that it's not effective." Practically the only place patients actually lie down on couches anymore is in Woody Allen movies and *New Yorker* cartoons.

In the hope of finding a place in modern mental-health care, however, its practitioners are trying to change with the times. One way they're doing that is by dropping the austere, formal pose of the classic Freudian analyst. "The image of Sigmund Freud sitting there smoking on his pipe is nothing like the modern 21st century analyst," says Kerry Sulkowicz, chairman of the committee on public information at the American Psychoanalytic Association. In modern psychoanalysis, that formal reserve is disappearing, and the analyst's personality comes much more into play in treatment. "The process is far more transparent today," says Sulkowicz. "An analyst may say, 'I'm choosing to remain silent to allow your thoughts to bubble up.' Analysts are much more up front. That never would have happened in Freud's day." Many analysts have even given up the beloved couch in favor of face-to-face conversation. "I don't know if that's gotten out to the general public," says Dr. Elio Frattaroli, a psychoanalyst who practices in Pennsylvania. "We made a lot of mistakes by being too much in our heads."

Psychoanalysts are also learning to borrow from other disciplines. According to a survey conducted by the *Journal of the American Psychoanalytic Association,* more than 18% of pa-

If Everyone Were on Prozac ...

By SANJAY GUPTA, M.D.

When Prozac arrived in the U.S. in 1987, with its catchy, computer-generated name and massive marketing campaign, it didn't just take over the market for antidepressants; it expanded that market many times over, quickly becoming one of the world's best-selling drugs. Although originally approved only for adults with "symptoms of depressive illness," Prozac and its imitators (Zoloft, Paxil, Celexa, Luvox) are taken today by millions of patients—including more and more children—who don't necessarily meet the textbook criteria for clinical depression. Veterinarians have even made Prozac their No. 1 choice for dogs with the blues

Prozac and the other so-called SSRIs have been a breakthrough on several levels. Compared with first-generation antidepressants, they are remarkably effective and relatively free of serious side effects. They work by slowing the brain's absorption of the mood-enhancing neurotransmitter serotonin (thus the term selective serotonin reuptake inhibitor).

What makes serotonin such an important brain chemical is that it affects everybody, not only depressives. According to Dr. Jonathan Metzl, author of *Prozac on the Couch*, if you were to go on the drug today, there's a good chance that you would feel better, even if you aren't depressed. Dr. Peter Kramer, author of *Listening to Prozac*, describes the effect as feeling "better than well."

And that raises an intriguing question about the future of mood-altering pharmaceuticals: If Prozac can make you feel better even if you are not depressed, why shouldn't we all be taking it? Is that the direction we're going, as the drugs become more socially acceptable and heavily marketed? (More than 11 million Americans already take some form of antidepressant.) It's a question that arises only because SSRIs are relatively mild and subtle medications. There are plenty of drugs that can make you feel better, at least temporarily—alcohol and heroin come immediately to mind—but they tend to be addictive or toxic or both. Prozac is neither.

The drug does have its risks. According to several clinical studies, Prozac is associated with insomnia, restlessness, nausea, weakness, loss of appetite and tremors. For up to 60% of users, Prozac will interfere with their sex drive. Given indiscriminately to manic-depressives, it can trigger serious manic episodes. And there is anecdotal evidence linking Prozac with suicide and other violent behavior although whether Prozac or the underlying depression is to blame is still an open question.

But what if antidepressants like Prozac were one day made completely free of side effects and served only to elevate mood? Would there be an objection to prescribing them for the entire nation? Every psychiatrist I spoke with still answered "probably." Some see SSRIs as a kind of mental shortcut that relieves patients of the need to work through their problems. Others fear that a nation on Prozac would miss the inherent value of struggle and strife. Dr. Kramer thinks there may be an intrinsic virtue in what he calls the "unmodified personality." Although this month the FDA approved Prozac for treating children and adolescents ages 7 to 14, Dr. Jerry Rushton, a pediatrician at the University of Michigan, bemoans its use for kids, fearing that it may interfere with their emotional development.

Maybe that's something we should all worry about. It doesn't take anything away from the good that modern antidepressants have done for the clinically depressed to say that if what we are seeking is something of real and lasting value, we will probably never find it in a pill.

tients undergoing psychoanalysis in America also take some form of psychoactive medication. Some psychoanalysts even borrow techniques from cognitive therapy. "The analysts have moved more in the direction of understanding cognitive distortions," says Dr. Glen Gabbard, a psychoanalyst and professor of psychiatry at Baylor University. "If you look at good therapists on videotape, you'll find that the cognitive therapists and the analysts do many things in common." Many psychoanalysts also offer patients a treatment known as psychodynamic therapy, which requires less of a time commitment. It's like psychoanalysis lite: the same techniques are used, but the patient comes for only one or two sessions a week. "The current state of psychoanalysis is such that Freud would probably not recognize it," says Gabbard.

But old-school Freudian psychoanalysis has its true believers, and not all of them are doctors. Some are patients. "It's allowed me to figure out some pretty basic things about myself and why certain situations keep coming up," says a graduate student in her 30s in Brooklyn, N.Y., who went into analysis after a difficult breakup. "A lot of the jokes about analysis talk about blaming your parents, but being in analysis is more about learning to take responsibility for yourself and to take care of the people around you. That kind of control only comes from understanding your past." After four years of analysis, she is more productive, less moody, less angry and less depressed. "It was one of the best decisions I ever made."

Whatever else may have changed, the intellectual adventure of psychoanalysis, the delving into the depths, is still part of the Freudian tradition, and that's not going to disappear. Psychoanalysis is based on the fundamental belief that we aren't just a collection of neurotransmitters to be fixed with a pill, or a set of cognitive skills to be coached back into shape like a slumping quarterback. To Freudians, the mind is a complex and mysterious thing, and symptoms like depression and anxiety are the language in which deep inner conflicts express themselves. "Now most psychiatrists have scorn for psychoanalysis," says

Frattaroli. "In this age of the quick fix, the idea is to get rid of the symptom with a pill or some sort of therapy. But one of the problems with the current thinking is the belief that symptoms are bad. In psychoanalysis, symptoms are messages from the subconscious that something is out of balance. They have meaning. The symptom points to something deeper, and if you just get rid of the symptom, you're not solving the underlying problem."

In other words, the future of psychoanalysis depends on who, deep down, we really think we are. With or without clinical studies, the idea that the mind is a deep, mysterious place is too powerful to go away by itself. But to keep psychoanalysis alive, psychoanalysts will have to learn to innovate and evolve. A sense of humor might not be a bad place to start.

Treating Anxiety

BY SARAH GLAZER

The Issues

Last December, Arlene Gellman got stuck in a mysteriously long traffic jam in New York's Brooklyn-Battery Tunnel. Suddenly terrified that a new terrorist attack had occurred, her heart began to race, and she felt as if the tunnel walls were closing in on her. She thought she was about to die.

As a psychotherapist, Gellman recognized the symptoms immediately: She was experiencing a panic attack for the first time in her life.

Moving into survival mode, she knocked on the door of the bus stalled next to her and asked the driver to talk her down from the panic. He confessed that he was suffering the same symptoms. The last time he had been stuck in the tunnel, he said, was the day the World Trade Center collapsed.[1]

Five months after the Sept. 11 terrorist attacks on the twin towers and the Pentagon killed more than 3,000 people, New Yorkers and other Americans are suffering lingering symptoms of anxiety and trauma. Children's author Rachel Leventhal, who ran for her life from the falling debris with her 3-year-old daughter in tow, is still haunted by vivid recollections of the horrifying moments and has had trouble returning to work. Miramax films executive Jennifer Horowitz, who arrived at work in time to watch the second tower collapse, avoided subways and buses for weeks and still avoids midtown Manhattan, convinced it's the next target of terrorists. (*See box, "The Day the Sky Fell—A Mother's Story."*)

Experts say these feelings are normal in the days and weeks immediately after a traumatic event. Physical and psychosomatic symptoms common after a trauma—including heart palpitations and hypertension—help explain why New York physicians reported a rise in patients since Sept. 11 complaining of symptoms like heart trouble or head pain.

But if certain symptoms continue for more than three months following a traumatic event, they could signal more serious psychological consequences, such as depression, anxiety disorders characterized by panic attacks and post-traumatic stress disorder (PTSD).[2]

America's largest mental health emergency to date has turned the spotlight on a debate over which treatments are most effective for treating PTSD and anxiety disorders. Many experts say studies show that cognitive-behavioral therapy (CBT) is the most effective, but others put their faith in so-called talk therapy. Still, others believe drugs and group therapy show promise.

A diagnosis of PTSD, according to the American Psychiatric Association, requires that the person must have been exposed to an event that triggered a sense of "fear, helplessness or horror" and must experience three types of symptoms. The symptoms must persist at least one month past the event or in the case of long-term chronic PTSD, at least three months past the event. The three symptoms are:

- repeated re-experiencing of the event—including distressing nightmares, flashbacks or intrusive mental images;

- avoiding reminders of the event—such as places, persons or thoughts associated with the event; and

- physiological symptoms such as insomnia, irritability, impaired concentration and increased "startle" reactions.[3] (*See table, "How Men and Women Respond to Trauma".*)

Before Sept. 11, studies showed that about 6 percent of American men and 10 to 14 percent of women experienced PTSD at some time in their lives, making it the fourth most common psychiatric disorder. While women are twice as likely as men to develop PTSD, it is not clear whether women are more psychologically vulnerable or whether they suffer more PTSD because they are more likely to be sexually molested than men. (*See table, "How Men and Women Respond to Trauma".*)

In addition, personal violence is more likely to cause PTSD than events like earthquakes or car accidents. For example, PTSD developed in 55 percent of people who reported being raped, compared with 7.5 percent of those involved in accidents. The disorder also develops more often in women than men after a physical assault, such as a mugging. Some experts believe that if trauma victims feel some sense of mastery over the situation, they are more likely to come through it without developing PTSD.

A recent article in the prestigious *New England Journal of Medicine* suggested that PTSD rates among men and women touched by Sept. 11 may be similar to those experienced by men and women in accidents, natural disasters or the sudden loss of loved ones.[4]

How Men and Women Respond to Trauma

Men and women often develop post-traumatic stress disorder (PTSD) at different rates in response to similar traumatic events. In the case of physical assaults, for example, only about 2 percent of the men developed PTSD, compared with 21 percent of the women.

Overall, men experienced more traumatic events than women, but women's PTSD rates were twice as high as shown by data collected by two researchers (bottom two categories).

Traumatic Event	Prevalence of Event		Rate of PTSD in Response to Event	
	Men	Women	Men	Women
Rape	0.7%	9.2%	65.0%	45.9%
Molestation	2.8	12.3	12.2	26.5
Physical assault	11.1	6.9	1.8	21.3
Accident	25.0	13.8	6.3	8.8
Natural Disaster	18.9	15.2	3.7	5.4
Combat	6.4	0.0	38.8	-
Witnessed death or injury	40.1	18.6	9.1	2.8
Learned about traumatic event	63.1	61.8	1.4	3.2
Sudden death of loved one	61.1	59.0	12.6	16.2
Any traumatic event*	60.7	51.2	8.1	20.4
Any traumatic event**	92.2	87.1	6.2	13.0

*Data from Kessler et. al.

**Data from Breslau et. al.

Judging from the rates of PTSD that occurred after the 1995 bombing of the Oklahoma City federal building, about 35 percent of those directly exposed to the Trade Center tragedy will suffer from PTSD. Since tens of thousands of people fled the Sept. 11 attacks, and an estimated 100,000 people directly witnessed the event, the toll could be substantial. And that's not counting the tens of millions worldwide who watched it on television.[5] The risk of developing PTSD increases with the observers' proximity to the traumatic event, whether the observers lost a loved one or felt their own lives were in danger and their experience with previous traumas.

In New York, city, state and federal officials are gearing up to provide mental health services to an unprecedented number of potential patients. As many as 2 million New Yorkers may need some form of counseling, ranging from a one-time talk with a minister or a group-counseling session to more extended psychotherapy, according to the New York State Office of Mental Health.

The New York City Police Department in November ordered all of its 55,000 employees and officers to attend group-therapy sessions to relieve stress in the aftermath of the disaster.[6] "By making it mandatory, no one has to be the macho guy who doesn't show up, but who really needs it and is home beating his wife or drinking too much or who takes his gun and kills himself. Those things happen," says JoAnn Difede, director of Acute Trauma Response at New York Weill Cornell Medical Center, who is advising the department.

To help remove the stigma often associated with mental health counseling, city and state health departments in mid-January plastered advertisements on the city's subway cars urging New Yorkers still experiencing classic PTSD symptoms to seek help. Some of the ads profiled regular New Yorkers seeking counseling. One ad shows a list of things that helped relieve the stress for "William," 35, of Brooklyn. It includes such things as "talked with my co-workers about everything" and "went to three

sessions with a therapist to talk with other men about our feelings."

Chip Felton, director of mental health disaster-related services at the New York State Office of Mental Health, says the ads—some of which feature New York celebrities like Yankees manager Joe Torre—are intended to send the message, "If it's OK for them to ask for help, it's OK for me to do it too."

Some city residents call the effort overkill. "This must be unique in human history—that an entire town has been pathologized and treated like the walking wounded," says Andrew J. Vickers, a British researcher at the Sloan-Kettering Memorial Cancer Institute in New York. During German bombing raids on London in World War II, he points out, "We had the blitz. It was all about the indomitable spirit. It's a very different time psychologically."

But experts in treating PTSD say not treating the syndrome can have dangerous and costly consequences, including alcohol and drug abuse to numb unbearable feelings, wrecked family relation-

---

The Paralyzing Power of Anxiety Disorders

Most people have experienced anxiety before a big exam, a job interview or a first date. Unlike such brief bouts of intense worry, anxiety disorders are illnesses that fill people's lives with overwhelming anxiety and fear. According to the National Institute of Mental Health, anxiety disorders are "chronic" and "relentless" and potentially disabling, in some cases keeping a sufferer housebound. More than one anxiety disorder can be experienced at a time, and some people may suffer from an anxiety disorder along with other kinds of illnesses, such as depression.

Five major types of anxiety disorders are:

- *Panic disorder*—*Repeated episodes of intense fear that strike often and without warning. Physical symptoms include chest pain, heart palpitations, shortness of breath, dizziness, feelings of unreality and fear of dying.*
- *Post-traumatic stress disorder*—*Persistent symptoms, including nightmares, numbing of emotions and being easily startled, that occur for more than one month after experiencing or witnessing a traumatic event.*
- *Generalized anxiety disorder*—*Constant, exaggerated, worrisome thoughts and tension about routine life events, lasting at least six months.*
- *Obsessive-compulsive disorder*—*Repeated, unwanted thoughts or compulsive behaviors that seem impossible to stop or control.*
- *Phobias*—*Extreme disabling fear of something that poses little or no actual danger. People with social phobia, for example, have an overwhelming fear of humiliation in social situations.*

Source: National Institute of Mental Health

---

ships and suicide. Children and teenagers may also express anxiety and depression through substance abuse, premarital sex or even avoiding attending a college far from home, say experts at the New York University (NYU) Child Study Center. The center is treating children who attended school near the trade center, now known worldwide as "Ground Zero."[7]

Psychotherapist Gellman's first experience with PTSD was with Vietnam veterans while she was in training at a veterans' hospital in Philadelphia in the early 1970s. Of the survivors of the Sept. 11 tragedy she has been treating, she says, "I am seeing the same symptoms. Here some people are having nightmares and awakenings with night terrors, but I think we're yet to see what the full reaction is going to be. We're still in the grief stage."

Gellman says that one reason people who have been exposed to horrifying events like Sept. 11 have nightmares or awaken in terror is that while they are asleep, they slip into an unconscious state and their normal defenses are relaxed. Some people have vivid reimaginings during the day that are like nightmares while awake.

Survivors who were at the World Trade Center on Sept. 11 tell Gellman they keep visualizing people throwing themselves out of the buildings. "That seems to be the most recurring thought," she says. "Among people who lost loved ones, it's different," she adds. "The most prominent thought seems to be: 'What was it like for their loved ones burning to death in there?'"

As policy-makers, researchers and mental health professionals debate how best to treat PTSD and anxiety disorders, here are some of the questions being asked:

Is cognitive-behavioral therapy the most effective treatment for PTSD?

Research on treating PTSD overwhelmingly points to cognitive-behavioral therapy (CBT) as the most effective approach. Through a technique known as "exposure," the victim of a trauma retells the story of the traumatic incident repeatedly—sometimes even revisits the scene of the trauma—in order to become desensitized to the painful memories.

"The whole point of the treatment is to explain that a memory can't hurt you,"

says Rachel Yehuda, director of the Division of Traumatic Stress Studies at Mt. Sinai School of Medicine/Bronx Veterans Affairs Medical Center in New York.

For example, firefighters recovering from severe burns have reported flashbacks in which they feel the searing pain of their flesh burning and smell the odors of smoke and flames, according to Difede, who specializes in treating New York firefighters with burn injuries.

A common response among such trauma victims is to avoid anything that reminds them of the event. Avoidance can range from a firefighter feeling unable to return to work, a raped woman refusing to walk in the neighborhood where she was attacked, or—in extreme cases—experiencing difficulty leaving one's home. When a person goes to such lengths to avoid painful memories of the event, Yehuda explains, "they're not open to corrective information" such as the fact that the event is unlikely to happen again. And that information is considered crucial to helping the person get used to remembering the event without being paralyzed by it.

The process of getting used to the memory is sometimes termed "desensitization." One approach is to assign a pa-

The Day the Sky Fell—A Mother's Story

On Sept. 11, Rachel Leventhal had planned to shop for clothes for her 3-year-old daughter at the World Trade Center's underground mall, a mere six blocks from her home.

Her daughter Zoe was still in her pajamas when they both heard a plane fly directly overhead, so low that they could see a bizarre shadow cross the front window. Three seconds later, Leventhal and her daughter were startled by an unusually loud sound. Unbeknown to them, it was the first plane crashing into the famous skyscraper.

The scene from their window looking onto Broadway resembled a Superman movie. Hundreds of people were streaming down the street gasping and pointing downtown in horror. Downstairs on the street to investigate, Leventhal felt an earthquake-like boom.

"Time started to move really slowly. We looked and there was a gigantic hole in the Trade Center," Leventhal recalls. Neighbors on the street were saying it must have been a drunken pilot, but Leventhal had a terrible feeling it wasn't over yet.

She took her daughter upstairs and tried to keep her busy making crafts. Then she turned on the TV news. As the second plane was striking the second tower on live TV, she heard and felt the explosion. Her floor shook. There was another huge rumble.

"I screamed to Zoe to get away from the windows and threw her down on the floor," she remembers shielding her daughter with her body. "I thought we were being bombed and the house was about to come down on top of us. You couldn't see outside; it was blackened with smoke and debris."

Her husband called from his office and told her to get out of their Tribeca neighborhood right away. Grabbing a toothbrush and thrusting Zoe in her stroller, Leventhal fled the building. Just as they reached the street the second tower came down. "I was worried it was a nuclear bomb. Debris was snowing all over us," Leventhal recalled. "Smoke and clouds of debris enveloped us."

At first, Zoe looked up at her mother and smiled, saying, "A bad Pokemon hit the building." Her mother answered, "No, this is a real thing."

They began a long, terrible run uptown, away from the trade center, weaving their way through thousands of New Yorkers who were looking back at the towers gasping and crying.

Zoe became hysterical, crying, "Don't stop here!" each time her mother stopped.

Finally, Leventhal reached a church where parishioners were standing outside offering help. "I'm Jewish, but I thought, 'This is what churches are for.'" A group of African-American women standing on the church steps, greeted her with: "Praise the Lord, you're OK." Leventhal stayed with them until her husband, whom she reached by cell phone, arrived.

Leventhal and her family spent the next two weeks in her mother's apartment uptown. That's when she and her daughter started to experience classic signs of traumatic stress.

"I couldn't eat. I lost 15 pounds," she recalls. "If my mom was 10 minutes late getting back from her health club, I was scared. I couldn't sleep at all." The fear had gripped her so deeply, she says, that her sleep felt more like restless hallucinations than dreams. Her daughter obsessively replayed the Twin Towers' collapse in the form of Pokemon figures knocking down towers of blocks. Such repetitive re-enactments are a classic sign of trauma in children.

Gradually, Leventhal started taking her daughter to nursery school in their Lower Manhattan neighborhood even though their apartment was still off-limits. For the first three weeks, Leventhal stayed at the school for six hours a day, afraid of another terrorist or anthrax attack. "I didn't know if I would have to save Zoe," she explains.

Eventually the teachers started sending Leventhal to the local coffee shop at lunch time, pleading with her to eat something. She started volunteering, making food for Ground Zero workers at a local restaurant.

The family has finally moved back to their Tribeca apartment. "I'm doing really well now," she says. But her plans to go back to work as a children's book writer are on hold. She says she cleans house and exercises "obsessively."

And some days, if she hears a tale like the one about the Catholic priest who administered last rites to firemen entering the towers on Sept. 11, it sets her back a few days. "I feel very sad, depressed. I have vivid imagery of the firemen. I can imagine the scene as they went to their deaths. I think maybe I'll leave the city. It's hard."

---

tient "homework" of listening several times a week to a tape recording of herself recounting her rape, for example, until it loses some of its emotional impact.

The International Society for Traumatic Stress Studies (ISTSS) strongly recommends exposure therapy as the first line of treatment for PTSD. "[N]o other treatment modality has such strong evidence for its efficacy," the groups said in recently published guidelines for treating PTSD. The guidelines noted that in a dozen high-quality studies of various therapies, patients treated with exposure consistently showed more improvement in PTSD and anxiety symptoms—after as few as nine to 12 sessions.[8]

Joseph LeDoux, a neuroscientist at NYU and a leading expert in anxiety, says his brain research helps explain why cognitive-behavioral therapy works better in the short run than insight-oriented psychoanalytic therapy. His work has found that an almond-shaped structure deep inside the brain, called the amygdala, plays a role in generating the kinds of persistent memories that haunt survivors of traumatic events.

He says the part of the brain activated during cognitive-behavioral condition-

Several Treatments Target Anxiety Disorders

Alison Scherr, a 30-year-old Manhattan artist, has been plagued with panic attacks since college. They would come on suddenly, often when she felt overwhelmed by work. She would hyperventilate, shake uncontrollably, feel disconnected from her surroundings, lose a sense of time and, most of all, feel incredibly frightened.

Over the years, she has seen therapists and tried anti-depressants. Nothing really helped, she says, until she began seeing a clinical psychologist who uses cognitive-behavioral therapy (CBT).

Steven Phillipson explained to Scherr that her panic attacks tended to snowball because she was so afraid of them. "He said to let it take over," Scherr recalls. "It was really scary at first, but it was the only way that ever got through to me." Together, in weekly sessions over six months, Alison and Phillipson practiced talking back to the internal force that was causing the panic attacks as if it was another person.

Today, as soon as Scherr feels a panic attack coming on, she acknowledges the power of the attack and then takes a confrontational attitude. She addresses her panic as if it were a person: "You can make me start hallucinating," she says. "You can make me convulse. I'm just going to continue walking down the street, and then I'm going to my meeting."

Scherr says this challenging bring-it-on attitude was "very empowering in a weird way," and usually causes the attack to dissipate. And although she still has panic attacks, she says she's "not running around afraid of them, and they don't last as long."

Experts see anxiety attacks as a form of the primitive "fight or flight" response developed by humans as a response to danger. A person jumping out of the path of an oncoming truck will feel many of the same physical symptoms, such as a racing heartbeat or rapid breathing.

But panic attacks are scary because they seem to occur "out of context," explains Manhattan psychologist Ethan Gorenstein. People experiencing them often think they are dying or suffering a heart attack because their physiological responses are so overpowering. Physical symptoms similar to those accompanying panic attacks are one reason traumatic memories can be so frightening to people suffering from post-traumatic stress disorder (PTSD).

Originally developed to treat obsessive-compulsive disorder, CBT also has been found effective with other anxiety disorders. The method has been most successful in treating adult rape victims with PTSD, which is typically characterized by intrusive flashbacks of a traumatic event and avoiding reminders of the event for more than one month after the event.

Trauma patients undergoing CBT "exposure" treatment confront the traumatic event by repeatedly describing the experience or physically revisiting places and routines associated with it. The International Society for Traumatic Stress Studies (ISTSS) recommends CBT exposure as the method with the strongest research evidence for effectiveness in reducing trauma symptoms.[1]

In addition to CBT, several other treatments, some traditional and others in the "alternative" category, have been developed to treat post-traumatic stress disorder and related problems, including:

Eye Movement Desensitization and Reprocessing (EMDR) was developed by California psychologist Francine Shapiro in 1987. It shares some aspects of CBT but asks patients to remember a traumatic image while the therapist moves a finger back and forth in front of the patient's face. Some EMDR therapists tap a patient's hand rhythmically, have the patient listen to audio tones, or follow flashing lights. EMDR has been found effective in treating civilian post-traumatic stress. But no one can really explain how it works, which is a matter of hot debate. Some proponents suggest it taps into non-verbal memories or produces a form of hypnosis. But some studies suggest the treatment works equally well without the eye movements.

Group therapy, often used by Vietnam veterans to deal with traumatic memories of warfare, is considered helpful, but there is little research on it.

Antidepressant drug therapy has been found to help reduce PTSD symptoms, particularly two drugs similar to Prozac, Zoloft and Paxil. Other antidepressants may also help.

Individual psychotherapy, the "talk therapy" developed by the founder of psychoanalysis, Sigmund Freud, has been studied in only a few clinical trials, but many case studies support its efficacy. Some studies also find that short-term, trauma-focused talk therapy is also effective with PTSD.

Psychological debriefing, originally developed for emergency workers, typically involves a single group session immediately after a traumatic event, in which those involved are asked to retell their experience. There is little research supporting the method, and some research has found that it can re-traumatize those involved.

Hypnosis has been used for more than a century to treat trauma symptoms. Practitioners included Freud and his colleague Joseph Breuer. Studies suggest that hypnosis can help PTSD patients remember traumatic events and can relive nightmares and dissociation—the emotional numbing and sense of detachment felt by some trauma victims. However, experts warn that hypnosis can also lead to "false memories" among suggestible patients. More studies are needed to determine whether hypnosis enhances the benefits of CBT, psychodynamic and drug therapies.[2]

Massage, acupuncture and yoga also can reduce anxiety symptoms, according to Andrew J. Vickers, a research methodologist in the Integrative Medicine Service at Memorial Sloan-Kettering Cancer Center in New York City. It is unknown whether the techniques can also relieve more serious anxiety disorders.

1. Edna B. Foa *et al.*, *Effective Treatments for PTSD: Practice Guidelines from the International Society for Traumatic Stress Studies* (2000), p. 78.
2. *Ibid.*, pp. 352–3.

ing has a direct connection to the amygdala. By contrast, the parts of the brain involved in the kind of thinking and reasoning crucial to psychoanalytic therapy are not directly connected to the amygdala and must follow a more complex neural pathway.

"So in order for insight into your problem to gain control over the amygdala [in psychoanalysis], it has to go through the back roads and side streets; whereas the medial prefrontal cortex, [the part of the brain involved in behavioral regulation], has a superhighway to the amygdala," LeDoux says.

But only a fraction of therapists have training in CBT. Most use traditional talk therapy, also known as psychodynamic therapy, which some experts say isn't good enough.

"It's pretty clear from research that you can't do regular old counseling. You're much better off if you do this trauma-focused [CBT] therapy," says Randall D. Marshall, director of Trauma Studies and Services at the New York State Psychiatric Institute/New York State Office of Mental Health. Marshall is coordinating a four-hospital consortium to train New York City mental health professionals in CBT techniques for treating Sept. 11 mental health victims.

Talk therapy, whose historical roots lie in the case-history approach of its founder, Sigmund Freud, has been subjected to very few studies of the type of ISTSS considers the gold standard. These "gold standard" studies enroll large numbers of trauma patients and randomly assign them to different types of treatment or a placebo. The studies then compare how the patients rate on standard tests of anxiety and PTSD symptoms.

For psychodynamic therapy, the number of such studies can be counted on one hand, compared with a score of CBT trials and about a dozen trials of promising drugs like antidepressants, according to Matthew J. Friedman, executive director of the National Center for Posttraumatic Stress Disorder at the Department of Veterans Affairs (VA).[9]

"There is a rich literature on psychodynamics used with World War I veterans and by Freud, but it's a descriptive literature," Friedman says. "It does not conform to current standards for randomized clinical trials." Nevertheless, Friedman maintains, "to say, 'The only treatment worth a damn is that with effective research behind it' is to throw out work by very creative thinkers."

One randomized trial comparing 18 sessions of psychodynamic therapy to hypnosis and desensitization therapy found little difference in benefits among the 112 patients immediately after the treatment. However, when patients were followed up over a longer period, the psychodynamic treatment group showed greater improvement than the other two groups. They had fewer symptoms like nightmares or disturbing memories. Psychodynamic therapy may help patients develop coping mechanisms that continue long after the therapy ends and may have a broader impact on their lives, suggests Harold S. Kudler, assistant chief of psychiatry at the VA Medical Center in Durham, N.C.[10]

"It's harder to study the long-term effects of psychodynamic treatment, which aims more at personal growth and development than specific symptom reduction," says Kudler, who was trained in psychoanalysis and authored the ISTSS guidelines chapter on psychodynamic therapy. "Psychodynamic therapy attempts to help the survivor deal with individual responses to trauma, which may be broader than the symptoms listed in the *Diagnostic and Statistical Manual Of Mental Disorders*. I think CBT is helpful; it's a useful and effective treatment," Kudler agrees. "But it will not serve some patients as well, and other patients feel a need to take a deeper look—where they play more of a role in initiating the conversation."

Some researchers suggest that CBT's effectiveness may be limited to certain kinds of patients—those with a specific traumatic experience in adulthood and those who are willing to confront their disturbing memories. So far, most of the successful trials of CBT have been done with adult female sexual-assault victims, notes Charles R. Marmar, vice-chairman of the department of psychiatry at the University of California, San Francisco.

"There still needs to be more research on how CBT generalizes with a whole range of other kinds of trauma victims," Marmar says. "There's not a lot of convincing evidence that CBT is safe and effective for the majority of combat veterans." Marmar is affiliated with the VA clinic in San Francisco, one of the largest VA facilities treating PTSD in war veterans.

Compared with the victim of a single rape, combat veterans with PTSD have typically suffered repeated traumas in war, often have longstanding drug- and alcohol-abuse problems and may have other psychiatric illnesses complicating the picture, Marmar notes.

"They're less able to tolerate the exposure component"—where the patient is forced to confront memories of the trauma—Marmar says. "They get very flooded with overwhelming and unmanageable anxiety and get very phobic about it." Veterans also tend to have a lot of anger about their experience, and studies find that traumatized patients who are also angry tend to respond poorly to CBT.

"CBT is aimed at anxiety and fear; it's fear deconditioning; it's not anger deconditioning," Marmar points out.

In addition, specific types of trauma may produce idiosyncratic responses, such as the belief among some victims of childhood sexual abuse that they have multiple personalities.[11] Dori Laub, a psychoanalyst and trauma expert at Yale University, describes patients sexually abused in childhood who take on as many as 100 personalities in adulthood, such as the persona of an imaginary teenager who kicks her abuser. "What can CBT say to all this? Nothing in my opinion," Laub says. "CBT is a limited approach to damaging behavior; it can be effective but it tucks the [behaviors] away in some way and the traumatic experience is still there."

A study published by Marmar in 1988 found that short-term psychodynamic therapy was helpful for widows who had lost husbands in traumatic or lingering deaths and who still suffered prolonged grief years after the death. Widows don't necessarily suffer the terror and helplessness that characterizes the rape victim at the time of the event—it's more the horror of getting the news, Marmar suggests.

The death of a close relationship often activates a longstanding psychological conflict, which is tailor-made for psychodynamic therapy, Marmar notes. He cites the case of a woman patient whose husband was killed by a tour bus, a traumatic accident that she witnessed. At first, it seemed to be the core of her problem. Underlying her grief, however, was the fact that years before the husband had had a love affair. "She'd never dealt with it; she was angry [about the affair] and guilty about the anger. Those issues were successfully dealt with in dynamic psychotherapy," Marmar recalls.

The kind of short-term psychodynamic therapy Marmar has found effective for trauma is "very different" than

Chronology

1880s–1890s

Austrian psychoanalyst Sigmund Freud theorizes that mental disorders are often rooted in traumatic events and that symptoms can be alleviated when memories are put into words—forming the basis for modern psychotherapy.

1880

French neurologist Jean-Martin Charcot demonstrates that the symptoms of female "hysteria"—similar to modern-day post-traumatic stress disorder (PTSD)—are psychological, since they can be induced or relieved through hypnosis.

1895

Joseph Breuer, an Austrian physician, and Freud publish *Studies on Hysteria,* proposing that mental disorders are sometimes rooted in psychological trauma.

1896

Freud publishes *The Aetiology of Hysteria,* claiming that childhood sexual abuse is at the root of every case of hysteria, a claim he later modifies.

Early 1900s

Mental breakdowns, known as "shell shock," represent 40 percent of British battle casualties in World War I.

1919

W. H. R. Rivers, a psychiatrist in Scotland, begins to treat returning veterans by having them recall traumatic events.

1940s

During World War II, 25 percent of evacuations from the front are for psychiatric reasons. Psychiatrists pioneer talking cures to return men to battle quickly.

1941

American psychologist Abraham Kardiner publishes *The Traumatic Neuroses of War,* outlining the traumatic syndrome known as "battle fatigue." He successfully treats hundreds of combat veterans.

1960s

Studies of Holocaust and Hiroshima survivors reveal the impact of massive trauma on civilians.

1967

Robert Jay Lifton publishes *Death in Life: Survivors of Hiroshima,* demonstrating that overwhelming events can numb basic human capacities.

1970s

Psychologists begin to recognize that survivors of war and rape show many of the same symptoms.

1972

Ann Burgess and Lynda Holmstrom coin the term "rape trauma syndrome" to describe symptoms resembling those of traumatized combat veterans, such as nightmares and numbing.

1975

A center for research on rape is created within the National Institute of Mental Health.

1979

Lenore Walker publishes *The Battered Women.*

1980s

Post-traumatic stress disorder is officially recognized by the psychology profession.

1980

Post-traumatic stress disorder first appears as a diagnosis in the American Psychiatric Association's *Diagnostic and Statistical Manual of Mental Disorders.*

1990s

The definition of PTSD is expanded to include short-lived symptoms and reactions to common life events like the sudden death of a loved one.

1994

The revised *Diagnostic and Statistical Manual* includes "acute stress disorder" for post-traumatic stress symptoms that last less than three months after a traumatic event.

2000s

New York City is faced with the largest mental health emergency in recent U.S. history.

Sept. 11, 2001

The World Trade Center and the Pentagon are hit by terrorists who hijacked airliners, killing more than 3,000. Experts predict tens of thousands of civilians who witnessed the events will suffer PTSD, depression and other mental disorders.

Helping Children Deal With Fears

Sept. 11 was the first day of school at the Washington Market School, a preschool just seven blocks north of the World Trade Center. Virtually every parent and child walking to school that morning saw the first hijacked plane hit the north tower.

Many of the parents arrived dazed, shaking or hysterical, recalls school head Ronnie Moskowitz, who promptly corralled the parents off to a separate room to express their fears and tears.

"I didn't want the children to see their parents out of control, because then the children would lose it," says Moskowitz, who is also a psychotherapist. "The children would not know who would keep them safe."

Research shows that parents' responses to a violent event strongly influence their children's ability to recover.[1] A parent's anxious reaction is one of the best predictors of whether a child will develop an anxiety disorder, according to Tamar Chansky, a child psychologist and director of the Children's Center for Obsessive-Compulsive Disorder and Anxiety in Plymouth Meeting, Pa.

"Children will look to their parents' faces as a guide to how hopeless this is," Chansky says. It's reasonable for parents to express their alarm, she says. "Kids need to know it's normal to feel upset. But when a parent lays off discipline or bedtime [rules]—that's not a good message. Children need to feel they are getting back to normal."

Research after previous large-scale disasters, like the 1995 bombing of the federal building in Oklahoma City, suggests that children who still show symptoms of post-traumatic stress disorder (PTSD)—like having repeated nightmares or being too easily startled—for more than three months after the event are likely to have them a year later. Other children exhibit what experts call a "sleeper" effect: They seem fine until they have to do something that reminds them of the event, like getting on a plane or returning to the school where the disaster occurred.

While this research suggests children should be screened for PTSD soon after a traumatic event, experts note that it's important not to force children to talk about a trauma. Elissa J. Brown, a trauma expert at New York University Child Study Center, worries about approaches like "drama therapy," where schoolchildren are instructed to act out a traumatic event in a one-shot session. That approach, she cautions, can stir up feelings of anxiety related to the event without giving children skills to cope with them.

In Oklahoma City, children watched a lot of TV coverage after the bombing were more likely to demonstrate PTSD symptoms, Brown says. Throughout the New York area, child experts reported that preschoolers who watched the repetitive news footage of the towers collapsing thought they were being attacked repeatedly or that multiple buildings were being attacked.

"Let's turn off that TV," Brown told a group of teachers and mental health professionals assembled in December at NYU.

Here are some additional guidelines the NYU Child Study Center issued for parents shortly after Sept. 11:

- Parents can show children that they themselves are sad, but they should temper their own intense emotions.
- Don't be afraid to talk about the attack. Children are likely to be concerned about things of immediate importance, such as whether or not their school is safe.
- Be truthful and honest in answers. Hiding information causes children to feel confused, reluctant to turn to adults for help and mistrustful of other information.
- Allow and encourage expression in private ways, such as through journals or art.
- Maintain as much of a normal routine as possible.
- Determine your child's risk for problems. Those at most risk are children who have some personal experience with the tragedy. They may have been close to the area or have family or friends who have been hurt or killed.
- Reassure children of their safety and that you and many others are working to make sure they are safe.[2]

Chansky concedes the last recommendation can be tricky in the case of terrorists. "No one wants to lie to a child and say, 'It will never happen again,' but you can say, 'Millions of people, the president and the Army are working to make sure it will never happen again.'"

1. "Helping Children and Adolescents Cope with Violence and Disasters," National Institute of Mental Health, updated at www.nimh.nih.gov
2. *Helping Children and Teens Cope with Traumatic Events and Death; Manual for Parents and Teachers,* New York University Child Study Center, Sept. 25, 2001.

general psychodynamic psychotherapy, he stresses. "It is very tightly trauma-focused, and it deals more with the event and the meaning of the event," he says. "In that sense, it may be more like CBT than other forms of psychotherapy."

Some trauma experts argue that forcing a patient to confront a memory can be dangerous in extreme cases. Asher Aladjem, chief psychiatrist at the Program for Survivors of Torture at New York University-Bellevue Hospital, says

he frequently sees patients from foreign countries who have no memory of being tortured although their bodies bear the evidence—scars of unspeakable physical abuse. Amnesia about a traumatic event is a well-recognized symptom in

The Warning Signs of PTSD

Diagnostic experts say post-traumatic stress disorder occurs only after a person has been exposed to a traumatic event that involved either a perceived or actual threat to the person or another person. Moreover, the person's response to the event involved fear, helplessness or horror. People diagnosed with PTSD have clinically significant distress or impairment in social, occupational or other areas. Furthermore, the following three symptoms must be present together for at least one month:

I. The person persistently re-experiences the event in at least one of several ways, such as:

- Intrusive recollections of the event
- Nightmares
- Flashbacks
- Intense physiological reaction to reminders of the event, such as palpitation and other panic responses

II. The person avoids reminders of the event and has generalized numbness of feeling as evidenced by any of the following behaviors:

- Avoids pursuits, people and places that remind him or her of the event
- Unable to recall aspects of the event
- Restricted range of emotions
- Loss of interest in, or less participation in, activities

III. The person has increased physical symptoms, such as:

- Difficulty falling or staying asleep
- Irritability or outbursts of anger
- Becomes more vigilant and concerned about safety
- Exaggerated startle reactions to sounds or movements

Source: Diagnostic and Statistical Manual of Mental Disorders, *4th ed.*

the avoidance category of PTSD symptoms, he notes.

In a recent case of a refugee who could not remember his own torture and who was under pressure from the U.S. government to come up with an account to qualify for refugee status, Aladjem's hospital team decided against administering sodium amytal, a truth serum that is used to help people remember repressed memories.

"The feeling was that if the patient is defending himself so much he can't remember, once you bring up that memory, what happens? Then the patient gets stuck with the memory, and you basically strip them of their defense," Aladjem says. That defense could be standing between a patient and psychosis, some experts believe.

Challenging the view that a memory cannot hurt trauma victims, Aladjem counters, "I cannot say for sure that the memory could not kill them. They could become suicidal; the memory itself could be very dangerous." He adds, "CBT is not the panacea for PTSD. If it were, it would have helped a lot more people. It's one theory and one way that is helpful but it's not the only way to approach the problem."

In fact, concedes the New York State Psychiatric Institute's Marshall, many patients who start out with CBT drop out before completing the treatment because they find the prospect of their memories too frightening. And about 20 to 30 percent of people who stick with the therapy find it to be of only minimal benefit, he says.

Therapists from both the CBT and psychoanalytic camps generally share the view that antidepressants can be a useful adjunct to therapy, particularly as a way of calming a patient's fears sufficiently to permit them to talk about distressing memories.[12] "If someone starts therapy and can't do it, we'll suggest medication; if they do medications, we'd raise psychotherapy again and maybe it won't seem so scary to them," Marshall says.

Are children's anxieties being adequately identified and treated?

In September 1991, when a fire at a chicken-processing plant in Hamlet, N.C., killed 15 people and injured 57, virtually every child in the small, mostly poor community was affected, according to Duke University researchers who studied the impact of the fire on schoolchildren. Almost every child either knew someone who was killed or injured or witnessed bodies falling out of the doorway to the plant.

Children who had experienced previous traumas in their lives were far more likely than their classmates to develop PTSD after the fire.[13] Many had experienced prior horrifying events, including the rape of a mother or the violent death of a parent or loved one. Yet none had ever been diagnosed or treated, according to John S. March, a professor of psychiatry at Duke University and author of a study of the incident.[14]

Experts say children suffering from PTSD, anxiety and depression often go undiagnosed because they typically respond to trauma by being quiet or just withdrawing. "These are silent sufferers," says NYU Child Study Center Director Harold S. Koplewicz. "These are children who may stop attending school or have trouble concentrating but will rarely be rambunctious. In a class of 30, you can see four or five kids who don't look good: They're inattentive, they look sad. Yet, if you ask the teacher, they wouldn't have picked out those kids."

In New York City, because public schools had only been in session a few days before the terrorist attacks, many teachers did not have time to get to know the children in their classes well enough to detect changes that could signal

PTSD, such as setbacks in toilet training or increased aggression, pointed out Elyssa J. Brown, assistant director of the NYU Institute for Children at Risk.

"I encourage you to look at past records," Brown urged school and mental health professionals at a December symposium sponsored by NYU. Children who had previous psychological or behavior problems could be predisposed to PTSD, she said.

For sheer scale, Sept. 11 will be the largest exposure of U.S. children to a traumatic event in recent history. About 8,000 children were evacuated from schools near the World Trade Center on Sept. 11, according to Spencer Eth, medical director of behavior health services for St. Vincent Catholic Medical Centers and a professor of psychiatry at New York Medical College. "Many of these children saw buildings burning, saw people falling from buildings, and they were evacuated in a time of great crisis and turmoil," Eth says.

Based on what happened after the Oklahoma City bombing, Eth estimates that about a third of the children will experience such symptoms as nightmares or bad memories, although not necessarily enough symptoms to be diagnosed with full-blown PTSD. Koplewicz estimates that another 5,000 children not evacuated were traumatized by the deaths of parents, relatives or adult friends.

Because of the magnitude of the problem in New York, finding and treating children who are suffering will be an enormous undertaking. Since January, child experts from NYU's Child Study Center and from St. Vincent's have been working with teachers at schools near Ground Zero to help identify children who may need mental health services. In the process, they hope to learn more about how children respond to a trauma of such magnitude and to cognitive behavioral therapy—the primary treatment they will be offering.

Under the screening program, mental health professionals spend a class period asking children whether they are having any post-traumatic symptoms, such as anger, depression, difficulty sleeping or concentrating, recurrent nightmares or physical sensations like choking or a racing heartbeat. During preliminary screening, about 25 percent of the children reported symptoms and asked for help.

However, it wasn't only the youngsters near the Twin Towers who were affected by the attacks, according to Koplewicz. Another 50,000 of the city's children—about 5 percent of the child population—were suffering from anxiety or depression beforehand, he says, making them vulnerable to PTSD. "In New York City alone, we're talking about 70,000–80,000 kids who are at risk and are more vulnerable than the rest of the population," Koplewicz says.

Kids in neighboring towns were affected, too, says Leslie Bogan, a child psychologist in suburban Westchester County. Since Sept. 11, she has been seeing increased anxiety disorders among her child patients, including regressive behavior in toilet training, irritability, difficulty sleeping and eating. In addition, child experts say numerous schoolchildren in the area have complained of psychosomatic pains like headaches or stomach aches.

Bogan, who is affiliated with Cornell University and the Yale Child Study Center, says that since Sept. 11 she and colleagues have offered their help to suburban schools. "They don't want our help," she says. "The schools will tell you they're very well prepared and their kids are having no difficulty whatsoever."

Bogan is skeptical of that assessment. "I'm not sure school personnel are well-trained" to recognize signs of PTSD or anxiety, she says. "They tend to react to acting out. Kids who are sad go underdiagnosed."

Although schools in Lower Manhattan have been receptive to help from mental health professionals, child trauma experts say large-scale school screening for PTSD in the rest of the country would raise some delicate questions.

Screening can be potentially harmful if children are asked to describe a traumatic event and aren't given coping skills to deal with it, says John A. Fairbank, co-director of the National Center for Child Traumatic Stress, a federally funded center located at Duke University and the University of California-Berkeley. The center is planning to study better ways to identify children who suffer sexual abuse, family violence or who live in neighborhoods assaulted by violent crime.

Yet, Fairbank acknowledges that many children with problems go unnoticed unless they are brought to the attention of a school official or a physician. "There isn't any systematic screening" in most of the country, he points out. Schools and parents are often resistant to taking time from academic learning to deal with social issues like childhood trauma.

The debate over how best to treat traumatized children mirrors that for treating adults—except that for children the debate centers on whether CBT is better than play therapy, which springs from the same roots as psychoanalysis.

The mental health experts from St. Vincent's and NYU plan to treat the World Trade Center youngsters with CBT pegged to the child's developmental level. Treating a child with CBT typically involves having the child tell the story of the traumatic event—through pictures, for young children, or through writing, for older children—until they can repeat it without disabling sensations of fear. They then discuss the event in individual sessions with a therapist and/or in a group of other children in order to correct mistaken ideas, often of self-blame, which continue to haunt them.

Although CBT has more research supporting it than other methods of treating traumatized children, Fairbank notes that, in general, far fewer studies have been conducted on trauma treatment for children than for adults.

"The most common treatment children get is child-centered play therapy, which is a dinosaur... mostly worthless," says March, a strong CBT advocate. If play therapy includes such CBT components as narrating the story of the trauma and facing one's fears, it can be helpful, March says. "But [if] it involves shooting basketball outside with kids—which most therapists end up doing—or focusing on the parent-child relationship, it's not very helpful at all," he maintains. March's study of the impact of the Hamlet fire found that CBT was effective in reducing symptoms for children and teens across a variety of age and school settings.[15]

But Fairbank maintains that the verdict is still out on competing therapies, since there has been so little research to date. "I wouldn't call [play therapy] a dinosaur at all," he says. "There's art therapy; there is play therapy. They may be effective. I don't think we should toss them out without evaluating them." He also thinks Prozac-like antidepressants constitute another promising therapy, particularly for teens, that needs further testing.

A $10 million federal initiative, funded by the Department of Health and Human Services' Substance Abuse and Mental Health Services Administration, created the National Center for Child Traumatic Stress in September before the terrorist attacks. It was established to identify the most effective treatments for traumatized children and to funnel information about those techniques to mental health professionals around the nation. The initiative includes funding for 17 other institutions treating children across the country.

Notes

1. For background, see David Masci and Kenneth Jost, "War on Terrorism," *The CQ Researcher*, Oct. 12, 2001. pp. 817–848.
2. For background, see Kathy Koch, "Childhood Depression," *The CQ Researcher*, July 16, 1999, pp. 593–616, and Sarah Glazer, "Boys' Emotional Needs," *The CQ Researcher*, June 18, 1999, pp. 521–544.
3. American Psychiatric Association, *Diagnostic and Statistical Manual of Mental Disorders*, 4th edition, 1994.
4. Rachel Yehuda, "Post-Traumatic Stress Disorder," *The New England Journal of Medicine*, Jan. 10, 2001, pp. 108–114.
5. *Ibid.*
6. Richard Lezin Jones, "All in Police Dept. Face Counseling," *The New York Times*, Nov. 30, 2001, p. A1.
7. For background, see Sarah Glazer, "Preventing Teen Drug Use," *The CQ Researcher*, July 28, 1995, pp. 657–680, and Karen Lee Scrivo, "Drinking on Campus," *The CQ Researcher*, March 20, 1998, pp. 241–264.
8. Edna B. Foa, *et al.*, eds., *Effective Treatments for PTSD: Practice Guidelines from the International Society for Traumatic Stress Studies*, p. 78.
9. For background, See Mary H. Cooper, "Prozac Controversy," *The CQ Researcher*, Aug. 19, 1994, pp. 721–744.
10. Harlod S. Kudler, *et al.*, "Psychodynamic Therapy," in Foa, op. cit., pp. 186–187.
11. For background, see Kathy Koch, "Child Sexual Abuse," *The CQ Researcher*, Jan. 15, 1993, pp. 25–48.
12. Tamar Nordenberg, "Escaping the Prison of a Past Trauma: New Treatment for Post-traumatic Stress Disorder," *FDA Consumer Magazine*, May-June 2000, at www.fda.gov.
13. John S. March *et al.*, "Posttraumatic Symptomatology in Children and Adolescents After an Industrial Fire," *Journal of the American Academy of Child and Adolescent Psychiatry*, August 1997, pp. 1080–1088.
14. *Ibid.*
15. John S. March, *et al.*, "Cognitive Behavioral Psychotherapy for Children and Adolescents with Posttraumatic Stress Disorder After a Single-Incident Stressor," *Journal of the American Academy of Child and Adolescent Psychiatry*, June 1998, pp. 583–593.

Computer- and Internet-Based Psychotherapy Interventions

Abstract

Computers and Internet-based programs have great potential to make psychological assessment and treatment more cost-effective. Computer-assisted therapy appears to be as effective as face-to-face treatment for treating anxiety disorders and depression. Internet support groups also may be effective and have advantages over face-to-face therapy. However, research on this approach remains meager.

Keywords

computer applications; Internet applications; psychotherapy and technology

C. Barr Taylor[1] and Kristine H. Luce
Department of Psychiatry, Stanford University Medical Center, Stanford, California

In recent years, the increasing number of users of computer and Internet technology has greatly expanded the potential of computer- and Internet-based therapy programs. Computer- and Internet-assisted assessment methods and therapy programs have the potential to increase the cost-effectiveness of standardized psychotherapeutic treatments by reducing contact time with the therapist, increasing clients' participation in therapeutic activities outside the standard clinical hour, and streamlining input and processing of clients' data related to their participation in therapeutic activities. Unfortunately, the scientific study of these programs has seriously lagged behind their purported potential, and these interventions pose important ethical and professional questions.

COMPUTER-BASED PROGRAMS

Information

A number of studies have demonstrated that computers can provide information effectively and economically. An analysis of a large number of studies of computer-assisted instruction (CAI) found that CAI is consistently effective in improving knowledge (Fletcher-Flinn & Gravatt, 1995). Surprisingly, few studies evaluating the use of CAI for providing information related to mental health or psychotherapy have been conducted.

Assessment

Traditional paper-based self-report instruments are easily adapted to the computer format and offer a number of advantages that include ensuring data completeness and standardization. Research has found that computer-administered assessment instruments work as well as other kinds of self-report instruments and as well as therapist-administered ones. Clients may feel less embarrassed about reporting sensitive or potentially stigmatizing information (e.g., about sexual behavior or illegal drug use) during a computer-assisted assessment than during a face-to-face assessment, allowing for more accurate estimates of mental health behaviors. Studies show that more symptoms, including suicidal thoughts, are reported during computer-assisted interviews than face-to-face interviews. Overall, the evidence suggests that computers can make assessments more efficient, more accurate, and less expensive. Yet computer-based assessment interviews do not allow for clinical intuition and nuance, assessment of behavior, and nonverbal emotional expression, nor do they foster a therapeutic alliance between client and therapist as information is collected.

Recently, handheld computers or personal digital assistants (PDAs) have been used to collect real-time, naturalistic data on a variety of variables. For example, clients can record their thoughts, behaviors, mood, and other variables at the same time and when directed to do so by an alarm or through instructions from the program. The assessment of events as they occur avoids retrospective recall biases. PDAs can be programmed to beep to cue a response and also to check data to determine, for instance, if responses are in the right range. The data are easily downloaded into computer databases for further analysis. PDAs with interactive transmission capabilities further expand the potential for real-time data collection. Although PDAs have been demonstrated to be useful for research, they have not been incorporated into clinical practice.

Computer-Assisted Psychotherapy

Much research on computer-based programs has focused on anxiety disorders (Newman, Consoli, & Taylor, 1997). Researchers have developed computer programs that direct participants through exercises in relaxation and restfulness; changes in breathing frequency, regularity, and pattern; gradual and progressive exposure to aspects of the situation, sensation, or objects they are afraid of; and changes in thinking patterns. Although the majority of studies report symptom reduction, most are uncontrolled trials or case studies and have additional methodological weaknesses (e.g., small sample sizes, no follow-up to assess whether treatment gains are maintained, focus on individuals who do not have clinical diagnoses).

Computer programs have been developed to reduce symptoms of simple phobias, panic disorder, obsessive-compulsive disorder (OCD), generalized anxiety disorder, and social phobia. In a multi-center, international treatment trial (Kenardy et al., 2002), study participants who received a primary diagnosis of panic disorder were randomly assigned to one of four groups: (a) a group that received 12 sessions of therapist-delivered cognitive behavior therapy (CBT), (b) a group that received 6 sessions of therapist-delivered CBT augmented by use of a handheld computer, (c) a group that received 6 sessions of therapist-delivered CBT augmented with a manual, or (d) a control group that was assigned to a wait list. Assessments at the end of treatment and 6 months later showed that the 12-session CBT and the 6-session CBT with the computer were equally effective. The results suggested that use of a handheld computer can reduce therapist contact time without compromising outcomes and may speed the rate of improvement.

An interactive computer program was developed to help clients with OCD, which is considered one type of anxiety disorder. The computer provided three weekly 45-min sessions of therapy involving vicarious exposure to their obsessive thoughts and response prevention (a technique by which clients with OCD are taught and encouraged not to engage in their customary rituals when they have an urge to do so). Compared with a control group, the clients who received the intervention had significantly greater improvement in symptoms. In a follow-up study with clients diagnosed with OCD, computer guided telephone behavior therapy was effective; however, clinician-guided behavior therapy was even more effective. Thus, computer-guided behavior therapy can be a helpful first step in treating patients with OCD, particularly when clinician-guided behavior therapy is unavailable. Computers have also been used to help treat individuals with other anxiety disorders, including social

phobia and generalized anxiety disorder, a condition characterized by excessive worry and constant anxiety without specific fears or avoidances.

CBT also has been adapted for the computer-delivered treatment of depressive disorders. Selmi, Klein, Greist, Sorrell, and Erdman (1990) conducted the only randomized, controlled treatment trial comparing computer- and therapist-administered CBT for depression. Participants who met the study's criteria for major, minor, or intermittent depressive disorder were randomly assigned to computer-administered CBT, therapist-administered CBT, or a wait-list control. Compared with the control group, both treatment groups reported significant improvements on depression indices. The treatment groups did not differ from each other, and treatment gains were maintained at a 2-month follow-up.

Little information exists on the use of computer-assisted therapy for treating patients with complicated anxiety disorders or other mental health problems. Thus, further study is needed.

THE INTERNET

Internet-based programs have several advantages over stand-alone computer-delivered programs. The Internet makes health care information and programs accessible to individuals who may have economic, transportation, or other restrictions that limit access to face-to-face services. The Internet is constantly available and accessible from a variety of locations. Because text and other information on the Internet can be presented in a variety of formats, languages, and styles, and at various educational levels, it is possible to tailor messages to the learning preferences and strengths of the user. The Internet can facilitate the collection, coordination, dissemination, and interpretation of data. These features allow for interactivity among the various individuals (e.g., physicians, clients, family members, caregivers) who may participate in a comprehensive treatment plan. As guidelines, information, and other aspects of programs change, it is possible to rapidly update information on Web pages. The medium also allows for personalization of information. Users may select features and information most relevant to them, and, conversely, programs can automatically determine a user's needs and strengths and display content accordingly.

Information

Patients widely search the Internet for mental health information. For example, the National Institute of Mental Health (NIMH) public information Web site receives more than 7 million "hits" each month. However, the mental health information on commercial Web sites is often inaccurate, misleading, or related to commercial interests. Sites sponsored by nonprofit organizations provide better and more balanced information, but search engines often list for-profit sites before they generate nonprofit sites. Furthermore, education Web sites rarely follow solid pedagogical principles.

Screening and Assessment

Many mental health Web sites have implemented screening programs that assess individuals for signs or symptoms of various psychiatric disorders. These programs generally recommend that participants who score above a predetermined cutoff contact a mental health provider for further assessment. The NIMH and many other professional organizations provide high-quality, easily accessible information combined with screening instruments. Houston and colleagues (2001) evaluated the use of a Web site that offered a computerized version of the Center for Epidemiological Studies' depression scale (CES-D; Ogles, France, Lunnen, Bell, & Goldfarb, 1998). The scale was completed 24,479 times during the 8-month study period. Fifty-eight percent of participants screened positive for depression, and fewer than half of those had previously been treated for depression. The Internet can incorporate interactive screening, which already has been extensively developed for desktop computers. Screening can then be linked to strategies that are designed to increase the likelihood that a participant will accept a referral and initiate further assessment or treatment.

On-Line Support Groups

Because Internet-delivered group interventions can be accessed constantly from any location that has Internet access, they offer distinct advantages over their face-to-face counterparts. Face-to-face support groups often are difficult to schedule, meet at limited times and locations, and must accommodate inconsistent attendance patterns because of variations in participants' health status and schedules. On-line groups have the potential to help rural residents and individuals who are chronically ill or physically or psychiatrically disabled increase their access to psychological interventions.

A wide array of social support groups is available to consumers in synchronous (i.e., participants on-line at the same time) or asynchronous formats. The Pew Internet and American Life Project (www.pewinternet.org) estimated that 28% of Internet users have attended an on-line support group for a medical condition or personal problem on at least one occasion. After a morning television show featured Edward M. Kennedy, Jr., promoting free on-line support groups sponsored by the Wellness Community (www.wellness-community.org), the organization received more than 440,000 inquiries during the following week! The majority of published studies on Internet-based support groups suggest that the groups are beneficial; however, scientific understanding of how and when is limited. Studies that examine the patterns of discourse that occur in these groups indicate that members' communication is similar to that found in face-to-face support groups (e.g., high levels of mutual support, acceptance, positive feelings).

Only a few controlled studies have examined the effects of Internet-based support programs. One such study investigated the effects of a program named Bosom Buddies on reducing psychosocial distress in women with breast cancer (Winzelberg et al., in press). Compared with a wait-list control group, the intervention group reported significantly reduced depression, cancer-related trauma, and perceived stress.

On-Line Consultation

On-line consultation with "experts" is readily available on the Internet. There are organizations for on-line therapists (e.g., the International Society for Mental Health Online, www.ismho.org) and sites that verify the credentials of on-line providers. However, little is known about the efficacy, reach, utility, or other aspects of on-line consultation.

Advocacy

The Internet has become an important medium for advocacy and political issues. Many organizations use the Internet to facilitate communication among members and to encourage members to support public policy (e.g., the National Alliance for the Mentally Ill, www.nami.org).

Internet-Based Psychotherapy

The Internet facilitates the creation of treatment programs that combine a variety of interactive components. The basic components that can be combined include psychoeducation; social support; chat groups; monitoring of symptoms, progress, and use of the program; feedback; and interactions with providers. Although many psychotherapy programs developed for desktop computers and manuals are readily translatable to the Internet format, surprisingly few have been adapted in this way, and almost none have been evaluated. Studies show that Internet-based treatments are effective for reducing symptoms of panic disorder. Compared with patients in a wait-list control group, those who participated in an Internet-based posttraumatic stress group reported significantly greater improvements on trauma-related symptoms. During the initial 6-month period of operation, an Australian CBT program for depression, MoodGYM, had more than 800,000 hits (Christensen, Griffiths, & Korten, 2002). In an uncontrolled study of a small subsample of participants who registered on this site, program use was associated with significant decreases in anxiety and depression. Internet-based programs also have been shown to reduce symptoms of eating disorders and associated behaviors. Users consistently report high satisfaction with these programs.

Treatment programs for depression, mood swings, and other mental health disorders are being designed to blend computer-assisted psychotherapy and psychoeducation with case management (in which a therapist helps to manage a client's problems by following treatment and therapy guidelines) and telephone-based care. These programs might also include limited face-to-face interventions, medication, and support groups. The effectiveness of these programs remains to be demonstrated.

Eventually, the most important use of the Internet might be to deliver integrated, home-based, case-managed, psychoeducational programs that are combined with some face-to-face contact and support groups. Unfortunately, although a number of such programs are "under development," none have been evaluated in controlled trials.

ETHICAL AND PROFESSIONAL ISSUES

Web-based interventions present a number of ethical and professional issues (Hsiung, 2001). Privacy is perhaps the most significant concern. The Internet creates an environment where information about patients can be easily accessed and disseminated. Patients may purposely or inadvertently disclose private information about themselves and, in on-line support groups, about their peers. Although programs can be password-protected, and electronic records must follow federal privacy guidelines, participants must be clearly informed that confidentiality of records cannot be guaranteed.

Internet interventions create the potential that services will be provided to patients who have not been seen by a professional or who live in other states or countries where the professionals providing the services are not licensed to provide therapy. Professional organizations are struggling to develop guidelines to address these concerns (e.g., Hsiung, 2001; Kane & Sands, 1998).

Because of its accessibility and relative anonymity, patients may use the Internet during crises and report suicidal and homicidal thoughts. Although providers who use Internet support groups develop statements to clearly inform patients that the medium is not to be used for psychiatric emergencies, patients may ignore these instructions. Thus, providers need to identify ancillary procedures to reduce and manage potential crises.

Given the continuing advances in technology and the demonstrated effectiveness and advantages of computer- and Internet-based interventions, one might expect that providers would readily integrate these programs into their standard care practice. Yet few do, in part because programs that are easy to install and use are not available, there is no professional or market demand for the use of computer-assisted therapy, and practitioners may have ethical and professional concerns about applying this technology in their clinical practice. Thus, in the near future this technology may primarily be used for situations in which the cost-effectiveness advantages are particularly great.

CONCLUSION

Computers have the potential to make psychological assessments more efficient, more accurate, and less expensive. Computer-assisted therapy appears to be as effective as face-to-face therapy for treating anxiety disorders and depression and can be delivered at lower cost. However, applications of this technology are in the early stages.

A high priority is to clearly demonstrate the efficacy of this approach, particularly compared with standard face-to-face, "manualized" treatments that have been shown to be effective for common mental health disorders. Studies that compare two

potentially efficacious treatments require large samples for us to safely conclude that the therapies are comparable if no statistically significant differences are found. Kenardy et al. (2002) demonstrated that multi-site, international studies sampling large populations could be conducted relatively inexpensively, in part because the intervention they examined was standardized. If a treatment's efficacy is demonstrated, the next step would be to determine if the therapy, provided by a range of mental health professionals, is useful in large, diverse populations. Examination of combinations of therapies (e.g., CBT plus medication) and treatment modalities (Taylor, Cameron, Newman, & Junge, 2002) should follow. As the empirical study of this technology advances, research might examine the utility and cost-effectiveness of adapting these approaches to treating everyone in a community who wants therapy.

Continued use of the Internet to provide psychosocial support and group therapy is another promising avenue. As in the case of individual therapy, research is needed to compare the advantages and disadvantages between Internet and face-to-face groups, determine which patients benefit from which modality, compare the effectiveness of professionally moderated groups and self- or peer-directed groups, and compare the effectiveness of synchronous and asynchronous groups.

As research progresses, new and exciting applications can be explored. Because on-line text is stored, word content can be examined. This information may teach us more about the therapeutic process or may automatically alert providers to patients who are depressed, dangerous, or deteriorating.

Although research in many aspects of computer-assisted therapy is needed, and the professional and ethical concerns are substantial, computers and the Internet are likely to play a progressively important role in providing mental health assessment and interventions to clients. Thus, mental health professionals will need to decide how they will incorporate such programs into their practices.

RECOMMENDED READING

Taylor, C. B., Winzelberg, A. J., & Celio, A. A. (2001). The use of interactive media to prevent eating disorders. In R. H. Striegal-Moore & L. Smolak (Eds., *Eating disorders: Innovative directions in research and practice* (pp. 255–269). Washington, DC: American Psychological Association.

Yellowlees, P. (2001). *Your guide to e-health: Third millennium medicine on the Internet.* Brisbane, Australia: University of Queensland Press.

REFERENCES

Christensen, H., Griffiths, K. M., & Korten, A. (2002). Web-based cognitive behavior therapy: Analysis of site usage and changes in depression and anxiety scores. *Journal of Medical Internet Research, 4*(1), Article e3. Retrieved July 16, 2002, from http://www.jmir.org/2002/1/e3

Fletcher-Flinn, C. M., & Gravatt, B. (1995). The efficacy of computer assisted instruction (CAI): A meta-analysis. *Journal of Educational Computing Research, 3,* 219–241.

Houston, T. K., Cooper, L. A., Vu, H. T., Kahn, J., Toser, J., & Ford, D. E. (2001). Screening the public for depression through the Internet. *Psychiatric Services, 52,* 362–367.

Hsiung, R. C. (2001). Suggested principles of professional ethics for the online provision of mental health services. *Medinfo, 10,* 296–300.

Kane, B., & Sands, D. Z. (1998). Guidelines for the clinical use of electronic mail with patients: The AMIA Internet Working Group, Task Force on Guidelines for the Use of Clinic-Patient Electronic Mail. *Journal of the American Medical Informatics Association, 5,* 104–111.

Kenardy, J. A., Dow, M. G. T., Johnston, D. W., Newman, M. G., Thompson, A., & Taylor, C. B. (2002). *A comparison of delivery methods of cognitive behavioural therapy for panic disorder: An international multicentre trial.* Manuscript submitted for publication.

Newman, M. G., Consoli, A., & Taylor, C. B. (1997). Computers in assessment and cognitive behavioral treatment of clinical disorders: Anxiety as a case in point. *Behavior Therapy, 28,* 211–235.

Ogles, B. M., France, C. R., Lunnen, K. M., Bell, M. T., & Goldfarb, M. (1998). Computerized depression screening and awareness. *Community Mental Health Journal, 34* (1), 27–38.

Selmi, P. M., Klein, M. H., Greist, J. H., Sorrell, S. P., & Erdman, H. P. (1990). Computer-administered cognitive-behavioral therapy for depression. *American Journal of Psychiatry, 147,* 51–56.

Taylor, C. B., Cameron, R., Newman, M., & Junge, J. (2002). Issues related to combining risk factor reduction and clinical treatment for eating disorders in defined populations. *The Journal of Behavioral Health Services and Research, 29,* 81–90.

Winzelberg, A. J., Classen, C., Alpers, G., Roberts, H., Koopman, C., Adams, R., Ernst, H., Dev, P., & Taylor, C. B. (in press). An evaluation of an Internet support group for women with primary breast cancer. *Cancer.*

NOTE

1. Address correspondence to C. Barr Taylor, Department of Psychiatry, Stanford University Medical Center, Stanford, CA 94305-5722; e-mail: btaylor@stanford.edu.

From *Current Directions in Psychological Science,* February 2003, pp. 18-22. © 2003 by Blackwell Publishers Ltd. Reprinted by permission.

Test Your Knowledge Form

We encourage you to photocopy and use this page as a tool to assess how the articles in *Annual Editions* expand on the information in your textbook. By reflecting on the articles you will gain enhanced text information. You can also access this useful form on a product's book support Web site at *http://www.dushkin.com/online/*.

NAME: _____   DATE: _____

TITLE AND NUMBER OF ARTICLE: _____

BRIEFLY STATE THE MAIN IDEA OF THIS ARTICLE:

_____

LIST THREE IMPORTANT FACTS THAT THE AUTHOR USES TO SUPPORT THE MAIN IDEA:

_____

WHAT INFORMATION OR IDEAS DISCUSSED IN THIS ARTICLE ARE ALSO DISCUSSED IN YOUR TEXTBOOK OR OTHER READINGS THAT YOU HAVE DONE? LIST THE TEXTBOOK CHAPTERS AND PAGE NUMBERS:

_____

LIST ANY EXAMPLES OF BIAS OR FAULTY REASONING THAT YOU FOUND IN THE ARTICLE:

_____

LIST ANY NEW TERMS/CONCEPTS THAT WERE DISCUSSED IN THE ARTICLE, AND WRITE A SHORT DEFINITION:

We Want Your Advice

ANNUAL EDITIONS revisions depend on two major opinion sources: one is our Advisory Board, listed in the front of this volume, which works with us in scanning the thousands of articles published in the public press each year; the other is you—the person actually using the book. Please help us and the users of the next edition by completing the prepaid article rating form on this page and returning it to us. Thank you for your help!

ANNUAL EDITIONS: Psychology 05/06

ARTICLE RATING FORM

Here is an opportunity for you to have direct input into the next revision of this volume.
We would like you to rate each of the articles listed below, using the following scale:

1. **Excellent: should definitely be retained**
2. **Above average: should probably be retained**
3. **Below average: should probably be deleted**
4. **Poor: should definitely be deleted**

Your ratings will play a vital part in the next revision.
Please mail this prepaid form to us as soon as possible.
Thanks for your help!

RATING	ARTICLE
	1. Why Study Psychology?
	2. Does Psychology Make a Significant Difference in Our Lives?
	3. Causes and Correlations
	4. What Makes You Who You Are
	5. Genetic Influence on Human Psychological Traits
	6. Neuroscience: Breaking Down Scientific Barriers to the Study of Brain and Mind
	7. Vision Seekers: Giving Eyesight to the Blind Raises Questions About How People See
	8. A Matter of Taste
	9. It's a Noisy, Noisy World Out There!
	10. Pain and Its Mysteries
	11. Night Life
	12. Brains in Dreamland
	13. The Seven Sins of Memory: How the Mind Forgets and Remembers
	14. Memories of Things Unseen
	15. The Power of Babble
	16. The Mind's Self-Portrait: An Illusion of Conscious Will
	17. Fundamental Feelings
	18. The Value of Positive Emotions
	19. Can You Interview for Integrity?
	20. The Power of Goal-Setting
	21. The Biology of Aging
	22. Inside the Womb
	23. Heading Off Disruptive Behavior
	24. The Future of Adolescence: Lengthening Ladders to Adulthood
	25. The Methuselah Report
	26. Start the Conversation
	27. Psychology Discovers Happiness. I'm OK, You're OK
	28. Companies Seeking "Right" Candidates Increasingly Turn to Personality Tests
	29. Guns, Lies, and Video
	30. Are You Looking at Me? Eye Gaze and Person Perception

RATING	ARTICLE
	31. Got Time for Friends?
	32. How We Get Labeled
	33. The Power of Mood
	34. The Science of Anxiety
	35. Post-Traumatic Stress Disorder
	36. Deconstructing Schizophrenia
	37. Psychotherapies: Can We Tell the Difference?
	38. Can Freud Get His Job Back?
	39. Treating Anxiety
	40. Computer- and Internet-Based Psychotherapy Interventions

(Continued on next page)

BUSINESS REPLY MAIL
FIRST CLASS MAIL PERMIT NO. 551 DUBUQUE IA

POSTAGE WILL BE PAID BY ADDRESEE

McGraw-Hill/Dushkin
2460 KERPER BLVD
DUBUQUE, IA 52001-9902

NO POSTAGE
NECESSARY
IF MAILED
IN THE
UNITED STATES

ABOUT YOU

Name   Date

Are you a teacher? ❏   A student? ❏
Your school's name

Department

Address   City   State   Zip

School telephone #

YOUR COMMENTS ARE IMPORTANT TO US!

Please fill in the following information:
For which course did you use this book?

Did you use a text with this ANNUAL EDITION?   ❏ yes ❏   no
What was the title of the text?

What are your general reactions to the *Annual Editions* concept?

Have you read any pertinent articles recently that you think should be included in the next edition? Explain.

Are there any articles that you feel should be replaced in the next edition? Why?

Are there any World Wide Web sites that you feel should be included in the next edition? Please annotate.

May we contact you for editorial input?   ❏ yes ❏   no
May we quote your comments? ❏ yes ❏   no